BOICHI

I stress about a lot of things while drawing and one of them is lids. Senku stores a bunch of science stuff in bottles and pots, but I often don't know what to do about the lids...

I also altered the way Senku's rocket operated by matching it to his age and technical capabilities.

Wood and stone tools and the way the characters use them are drawn differently depending on their time periods. The same is true of the village's details.

I always think hard about this stuff so I don't ruin Inagaki Sensei's amazing story, but there are plenty of times where I end up feeling disappointed because I don't have the time or talent.

I've drawn sci-fi manga, studied physics and read about a thousand books on science, yet I'm always blown away by *Dr. Stone*'s faithful portrayal of science. It fills me with a sense of wonder and reminds me of my own inadequacy.

RIICHIRO INAGAKI

I went to a glass workshop to try crafting some glassware! Basically, it's like super soft clay and really fun!

It filled me with this feeling, like I could make anything and everything, once I got the hang of it.

I have no doubt that if a genuine artisan saw glass for the first time, he or she would love to get their hands on some.

Therefore, Kaseki's reaction felt really natural to me.

Boichi is a Korean-born artist currently living and working in Japan. His previous works include *Sun-Ken Rock* and *Terra Formars Asimov*.

Riichiro Inagaki is a Japanese manga writer from Tokyo. He is the writer for the sports manga series *Eyeshield 21*, which was serialized in *Weekly Shonen Jump*.

Dr.STONE

4

SHONEN JUMP Manga Edition

Story **RIICHIRO INAGAKI**
Art **BOICHI**

Translation/**CALEB COOK**
Touch-Up Art & Lettering/**STEPHEN DUTRO**
Design/**JULIAN [JR] ROBINSON**
Editor/**JOHN BAE**
Science Consultant/**KURARE**

Consulted Works:
• Asari, Yoshito, *Uchu e Ikitakute Ekitainenryo Rocket wo DIY Shite Mita (Gakken Rigaku Sensho)*, Gakken Plus, 2013
• Dartnell, Lewis, *The Knowledge: How to Rebuild Civilization in the Aftermath of a Cataclysm*, translated by Erika Togo, Kawade Shobo Shinsha, 2015
• Davies, Barry, *The Complete SAS Survival Manual*, translated by Yoshito Takigawa, Toyo Shorin, 2001
• Kazama, Rinpei, *Shinboken Techo (Definitive Edition)*, Shufu to Seikatsu Sha, 2016
• McNab, Chris, *Special Forces Survival Guide*, translated by Atsuko Sumi, Hara Shobo, 2016
• Olsen, Larry Dean, *Outdoor Survival Skills*, translated by Katsuji Tani, A&F, 2014
• Weisman, Alan, *The World Without Us*, translated by Shinobu Onizawa, Hayakawa Publishing, 2009
• Wiseman, John, *SAS Survival Handbook, Revised Edition*, translated by Kazuhiro Takahashi and Hitoshi Tomokiyo, Namiki Shobo, 2009

First published in Japan in 2017 by SHUEISHA Inc., Tokyo.
English translation rights arranged by SHUEISHA Inc.

Printed in the U.S.A.

Published by VIZ Media, LLC
P.O. Box 77010
San Francisco, CA 94107

10 9 8 7 6 5 4 3 2 1
First printing, March 2019

VIZ MEDIA
viz.com

SHONEN JUMP
shonenjump.com

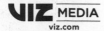

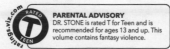

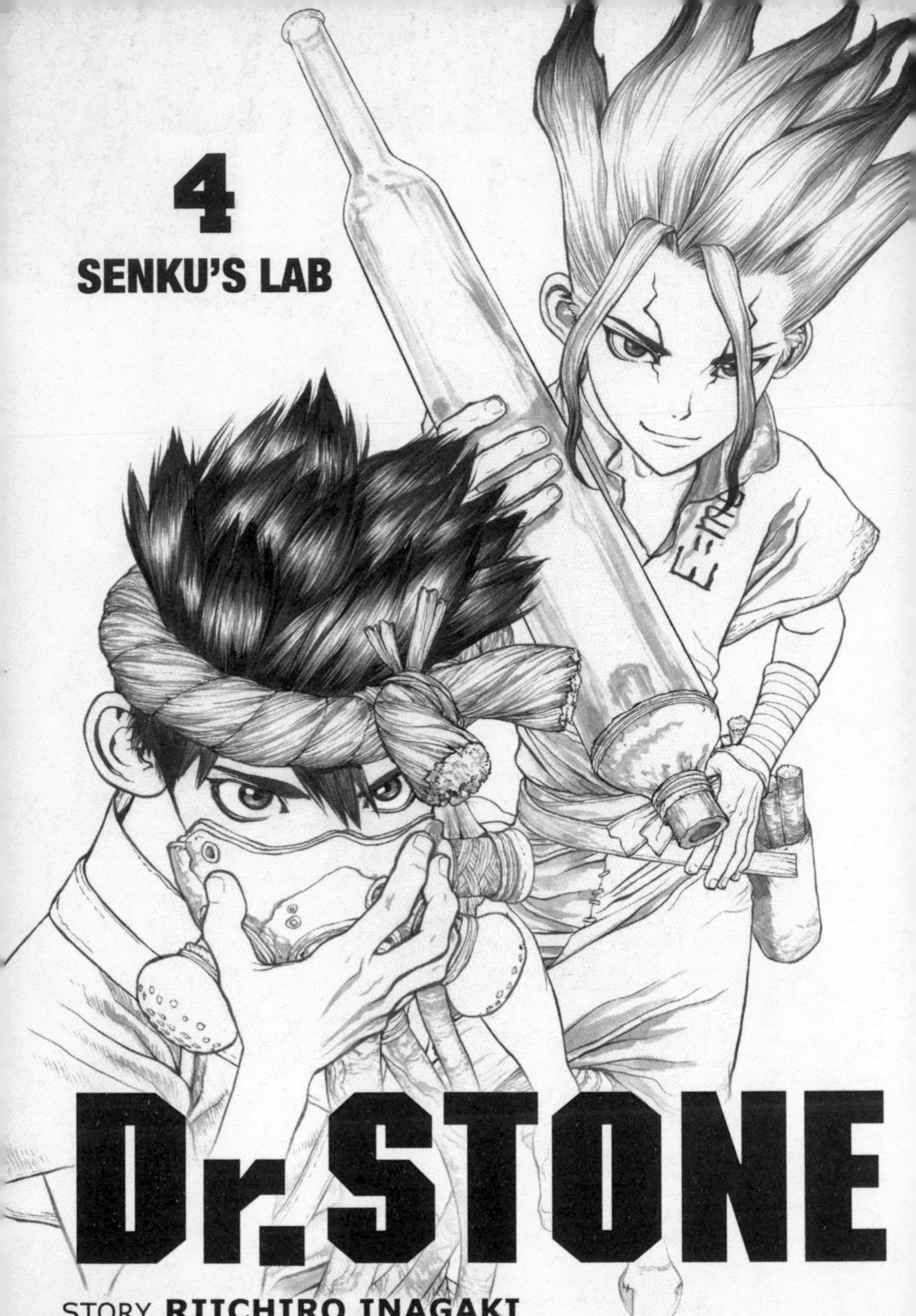

4

SENKU'S LAB

Dr.STONE

STORY **RIICHIRO INAGAKI**
ART **BOICHI**

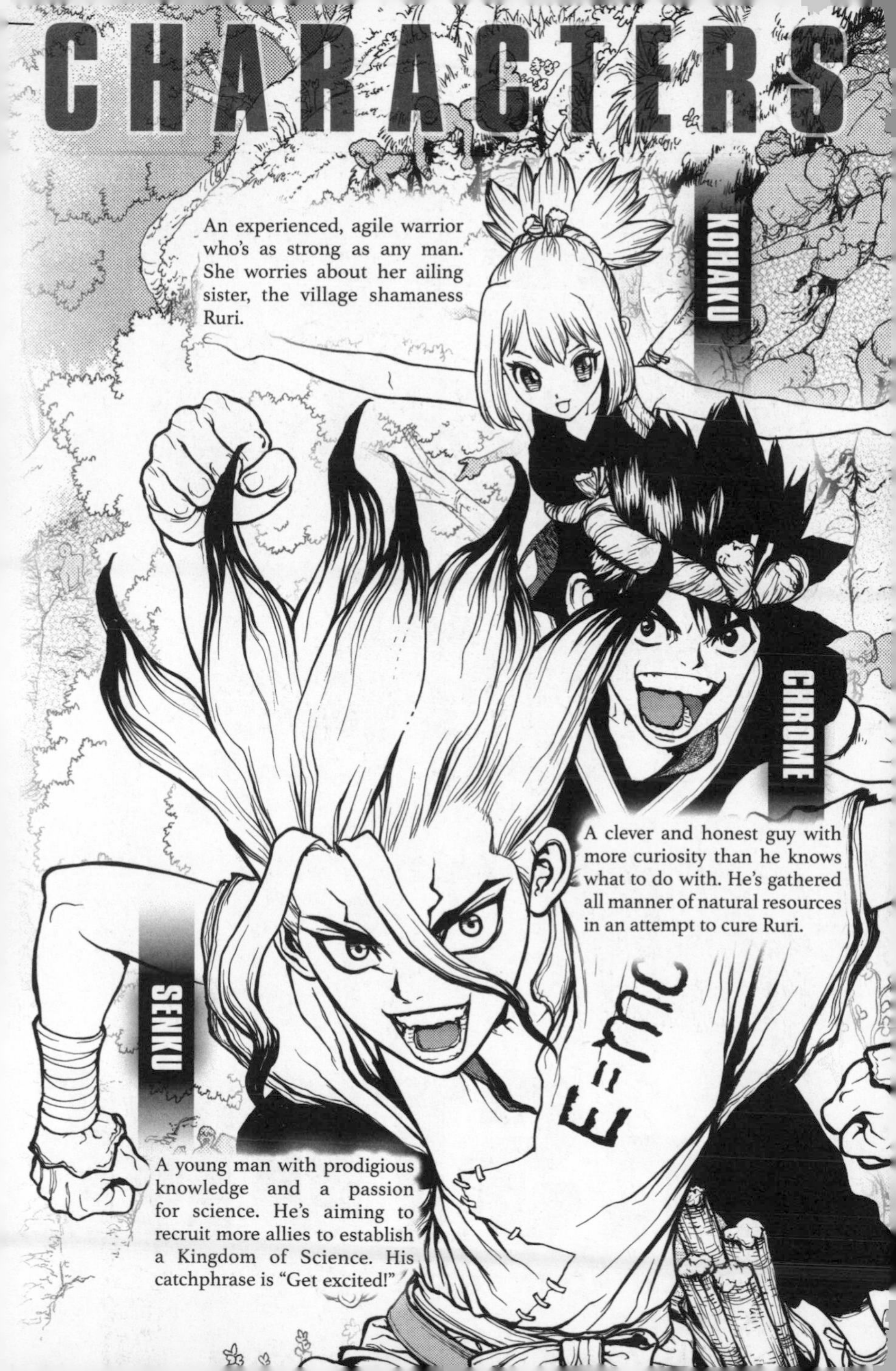
CHARACTERS
KOHAKU
An experienced, agile warrior who's as strong as any man. She worries about her ailing sister, the village shamaness Ruri.
CHROME
A clever and honest guy with more curiosity than he knows what to do with. He's gathered all manner of natural resources in an attempt to cure Ruri.
SENKU
A young man with prodigious knowledge and a passion for science. He's aiming to recruit more allies to establish a Kingdom of Science. His catchphrase is "Get excited!"

Dr.STONE

STORY

Every human on Earth is turned to stone by a mysterious phenomenon, including high school student Taiju. Nearly 3,700 years later, Taiju awakens and finds his friend Senku, who revived a bit earlier. Together, they vow to restore civilization, but Tsukasa, once considered the strongest high schooler alive, nearly kills Senku in order to put a stop to his scientific plans. Forced to act decisively, Taiju and Senku decide to split up to fight.

After they separate , Senku runs into another human—Kohaku! But Kohaku isn't from Senku's time period. She lives in a remote village that is somehow thriving despite the petrification. When Senku learns that Kohaku's older sister and the village shamaness, Ruri, is sick, he decides to concoct a cure.

After much trial and tribulation, Senku gets his hands on the first two items they need—iron and electricity. It's on to the next step, but he'll have to keep an eye on Gen Asagiri, who might very well be a spy sent by Tsukasa!

GINRO

KINRO

SUIKA

KASEKI

GEN ASAGIRI

CONTENTS

4

SENKU'S LAB

Z=26: A Shallow Alliance

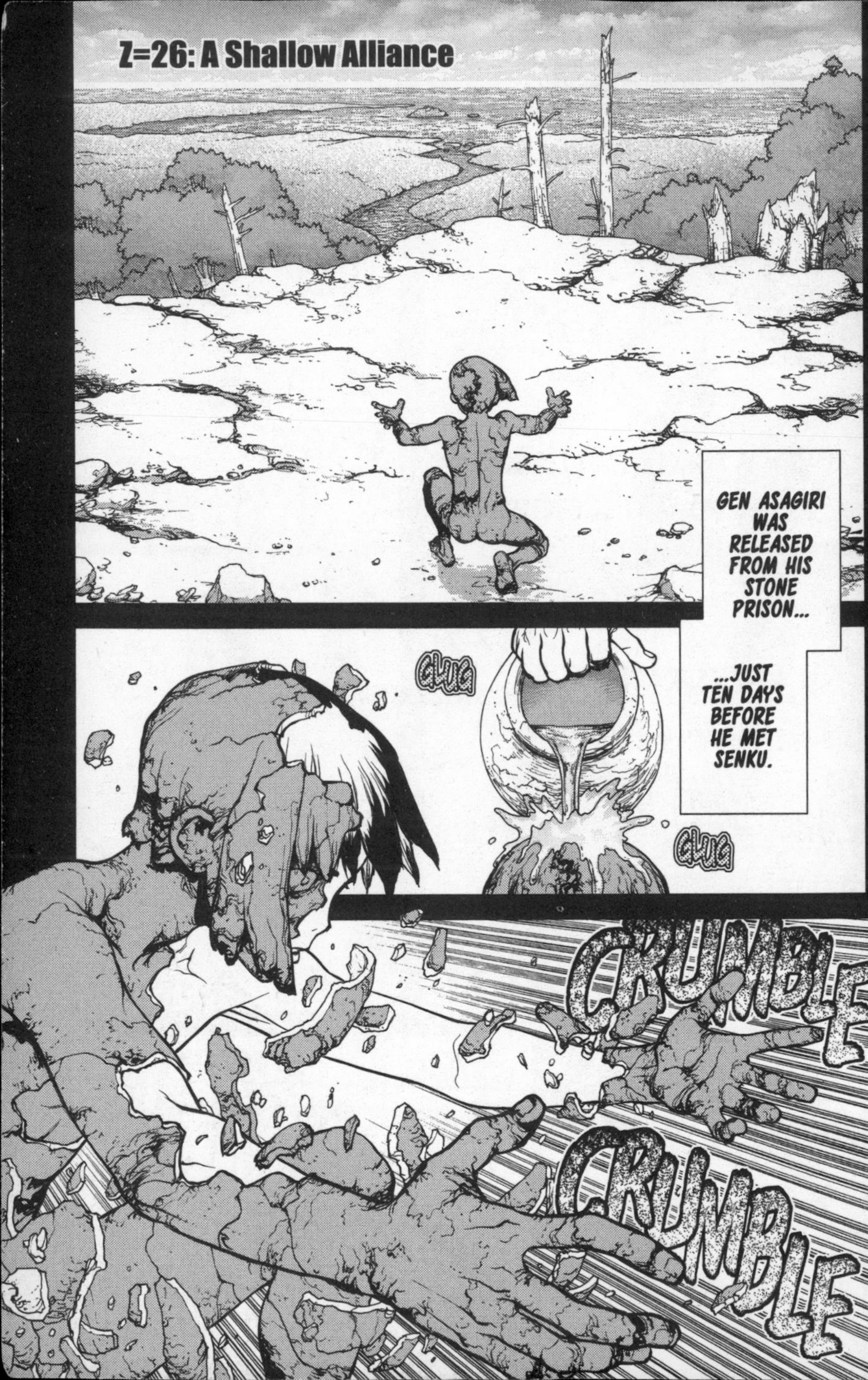

GEN ASAGIRI WAS RELEASED FROM HIS STONE PRISON...
...JUST TEN DAYS BEFORE HE MET SENKU.
GLUG
GLUG
CRUMBLE
CRUMBLE

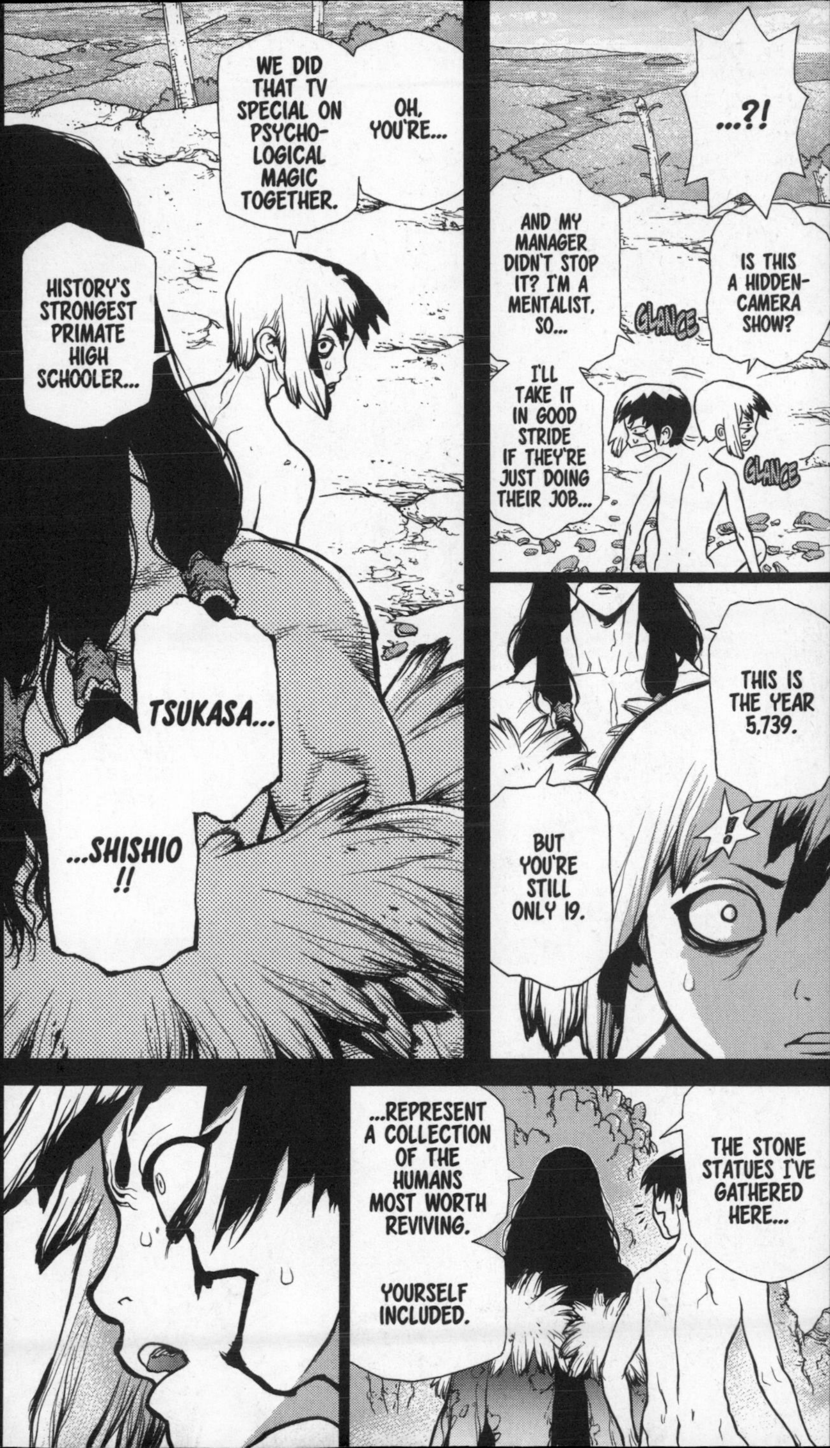
...?!
IS THIS A HIDDEN-CAMERA SHOW?
GLANCE
AND MY MANAGER DIDN'T STOP IT? I'M A MENTALIST, SO...
I'LL TAKE IT IN GOOD STRIDE IF THEY'RE JUST DOING THEIR JOB...
GLANCE
THIS IS THE YEAR 5,739.
!
BUT YOU'RE STILL ONLY 19.
OH, YOU'RE...
WE DID THAT TV SPECIAL ON PSYCHO-LOGICAL MAGIC TOGETHER.
HISTORY'S STRONGEST PRIMATE HIGH SCHOOLER...
TSUKASA...
...SHISHIO!!
THE STONE STATUES I'VE GATHERED HERE...
...REPRESENT A COLLECTION OF THE HUMANS MOST WORTH REVIVING.
YOURSELF INCLUDED.

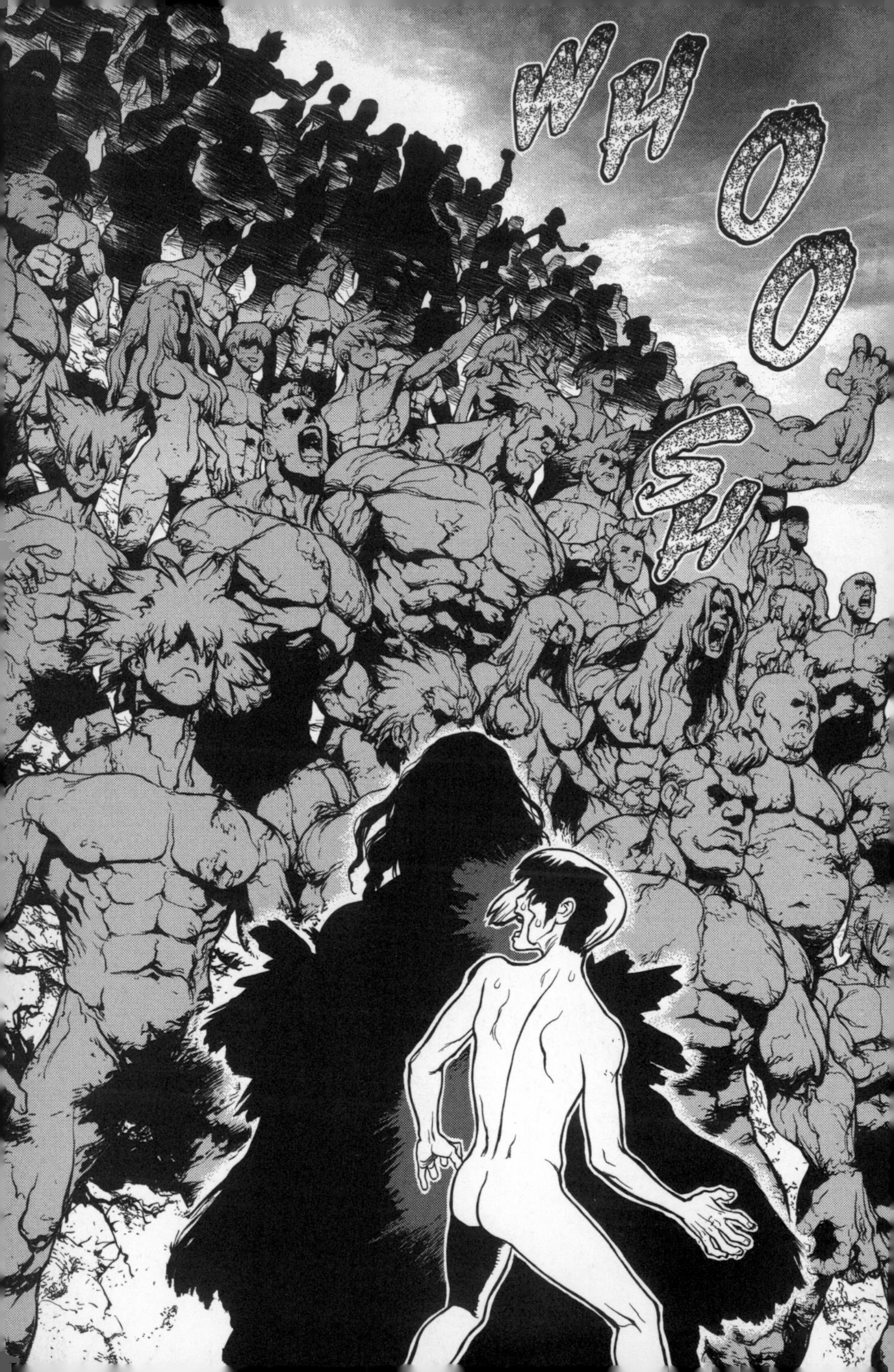
WHOOOSH

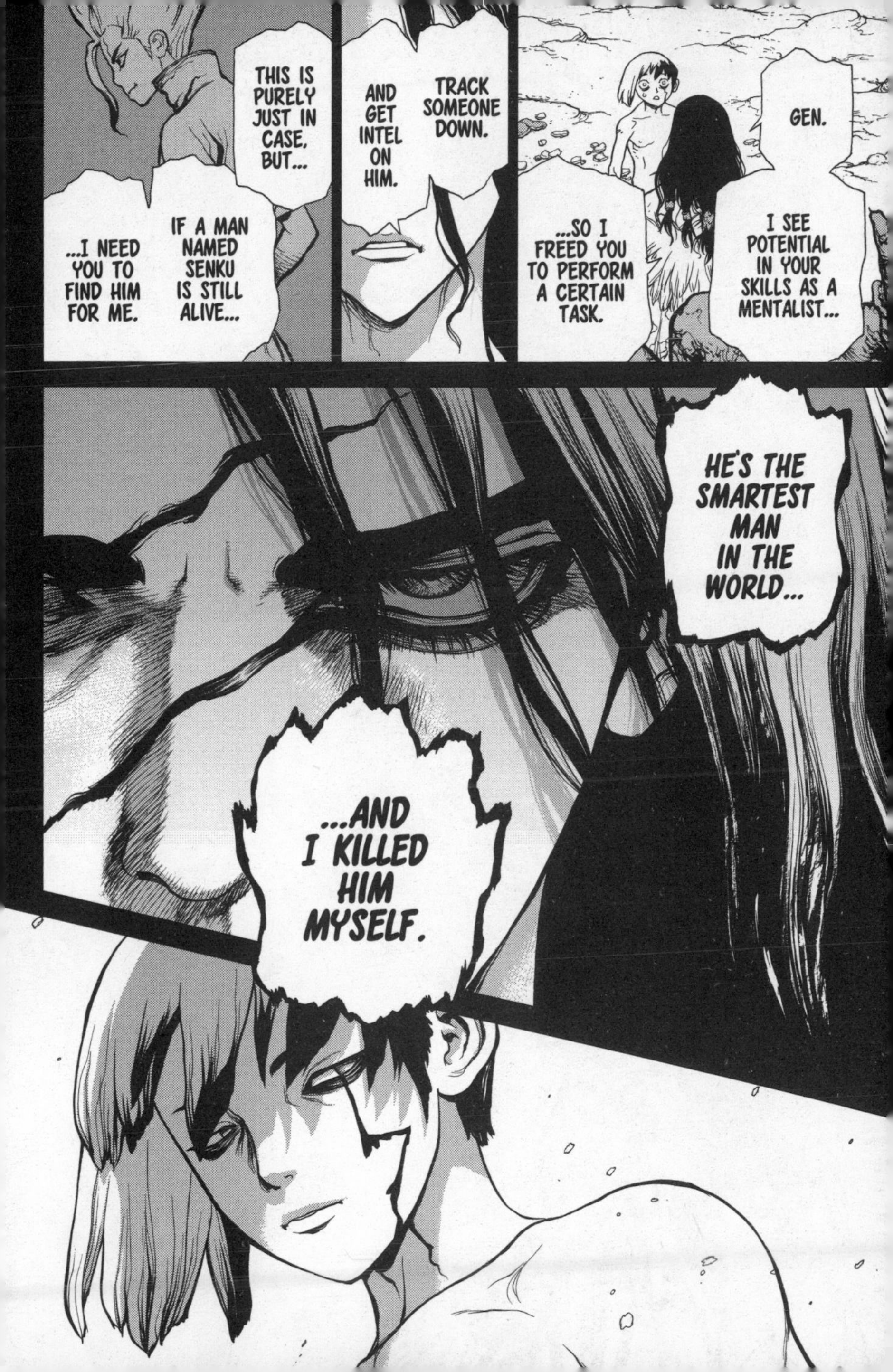
GEN.
I SEE POTENTIAL IN YOUR SKILLS AS A MENTALIST...
...SO I FREED YOU TO PERFORM A CERTAIN TASK.
TRACK SOMEONE DOWN.
AND GET INTEL ON HIM.
THIS IS PURELY JUST IN CASE, BUT...
IF A MAN NAMED SENKU IS STILL ALIVE...
...I NEED YOU TO FIND HIM FOR ME.
HE'S THE SMARTEST MAN IN THE WORLD...
...AND I KILLED HIM MYSELF.

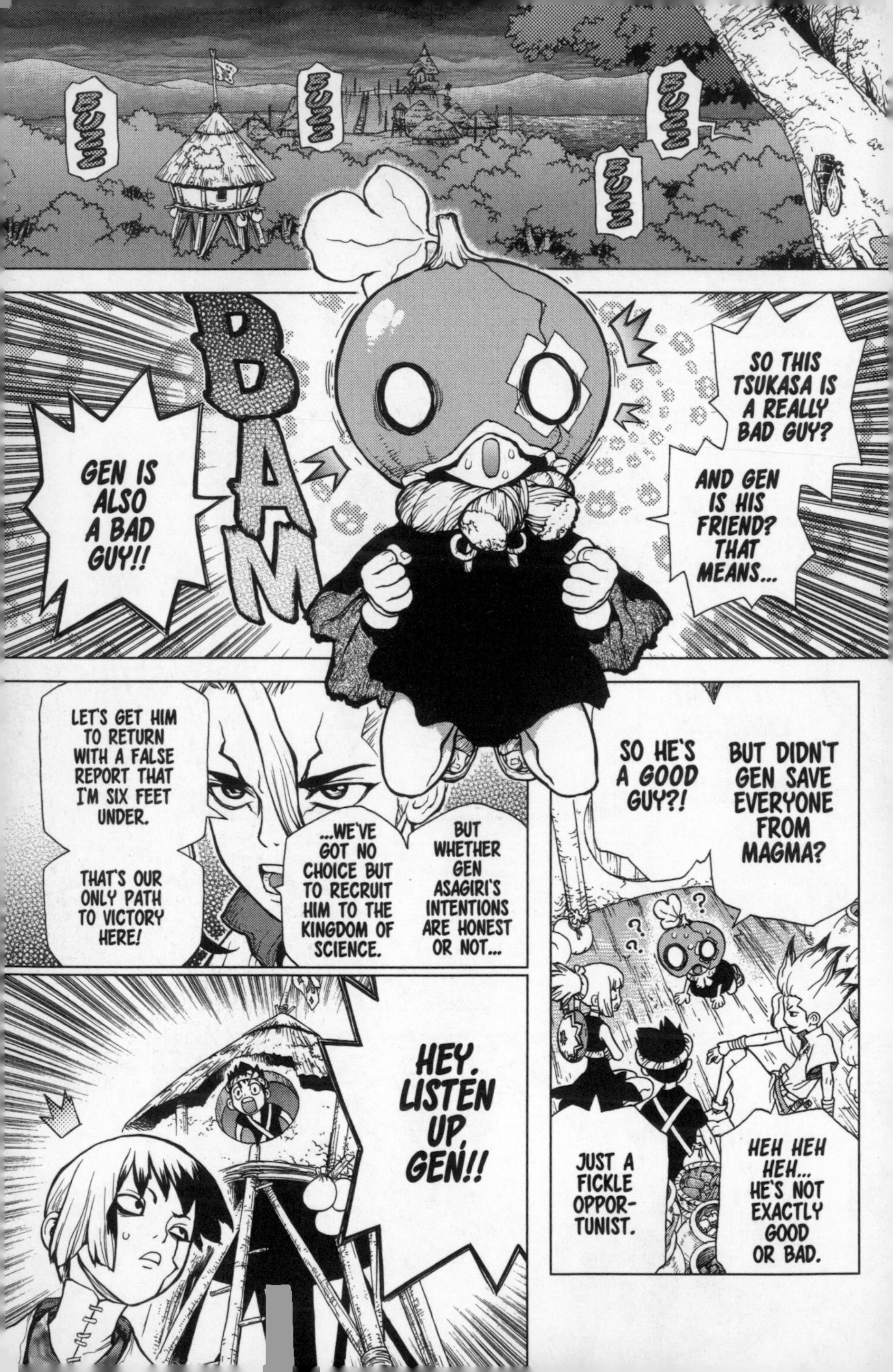
SO THIS TSUKASA IS A REALLY BAD GUY?
AND GEN IS HIS FRIEND? THAT MEANS...
BAM
GEN IS ALSO A BAD GUY!!
BUT DIDN'T GEN SAVE EVERYONE FROM MAGMA?
SO HE'S A GOOD GUY?!
HEH HEH HEH... HE'S NOT EXACTLY GOOD OR BAD.
JUST A FICKLE OPPOR-TUNIST.
BUT WHETHER GEN ASAGIRI'S INTENTIONS ARE HONEST OR NOT...
...WE'VE GOT NO CHOICE BUT TO RECRUIT HIM TO THE KINGDOM OF SCIENCE.
LET'S GET HIM TO RETURN WITH A FALSE REPORT THAT I'M SIX FEET UNDER.
THAT'S OUR ONLY PATH TO VICTORY HERE!
HEY. LISTEN UP, GEN!!

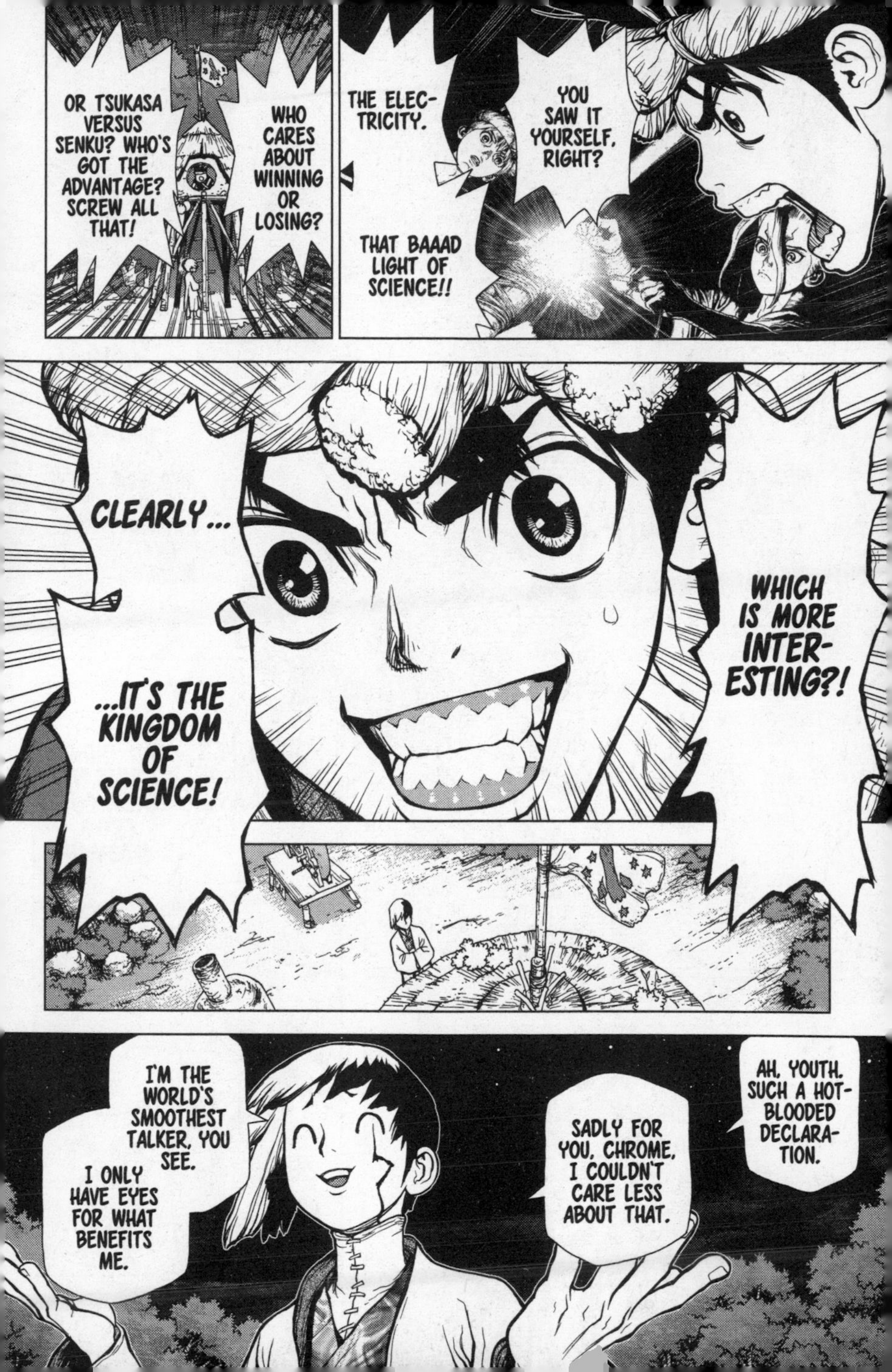
YOU SAW IT YOURSELF, RIGHT?
THE ELEC-TRICITY.
THAT BAAAD LIGHT OF SCIENCE!!
WHO CARES ABOUT WINNING OR LOSING?
OR TSUKASA VERSUS SENKU? WHO'S GOT THE ADVANTAGE? SCREW ALL THAT!
WHICH IS MORE INTER-ESTING?!
CLEARLY...
...IT'S THE KINGDOM OF SCIENCE!
AH, YOUTH. SUCH A HOT-BLOODED DECLARA-TION.
SADLY FOR YOU, CHROME, I COULDN'T CARE LESS ABOUT THAT.
I'M THE WORLD'S SMOOTHEST TALKER, YOU SEE.
I ONLY HAVE EYES FOR WHAT BENEFITS ME.

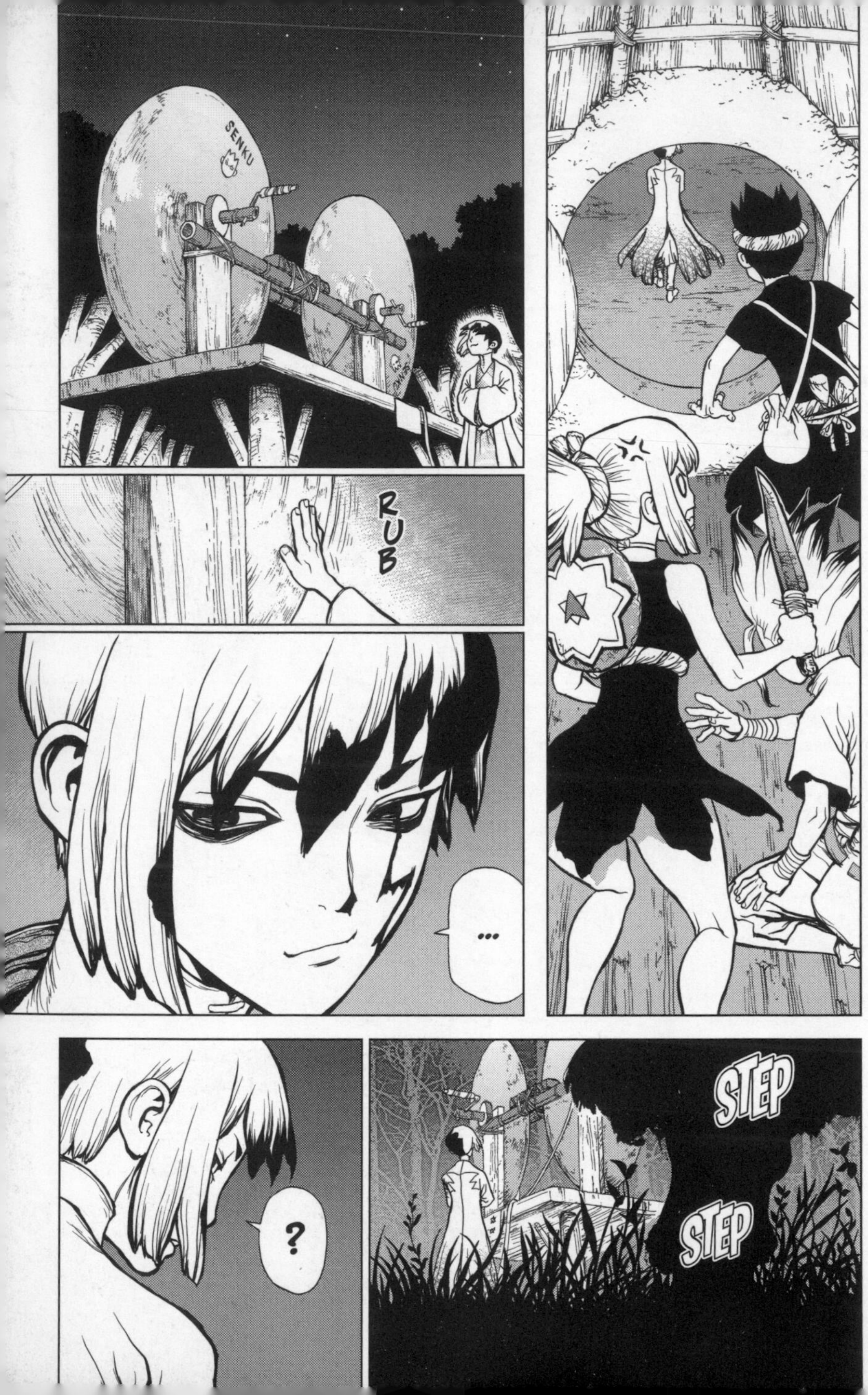
SENKU
RUB
...
STEP
STEP
?

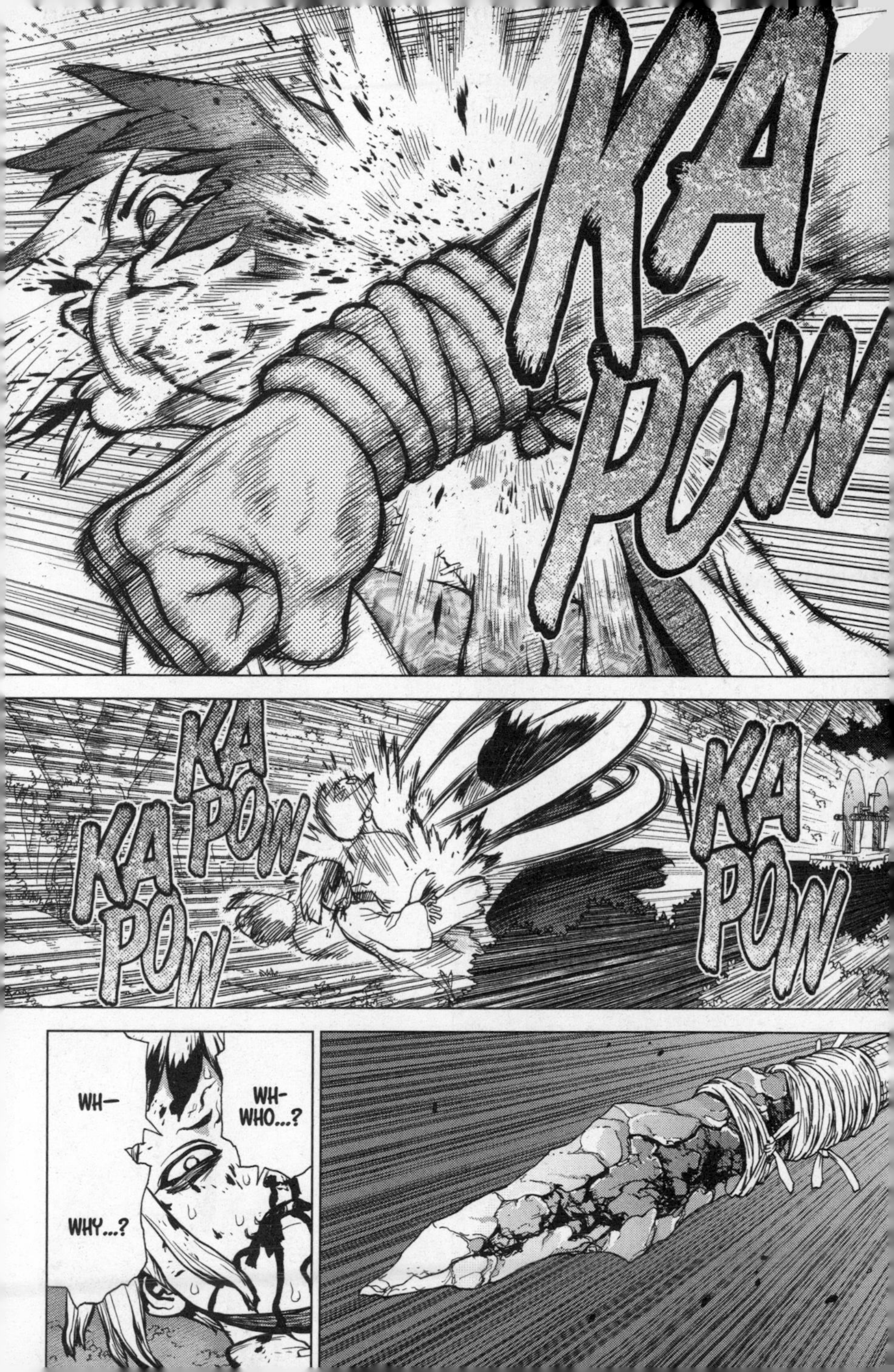
KA POW
KA POW
KA POW
KA POW
WH-WHO...?
WH-
WHY...?

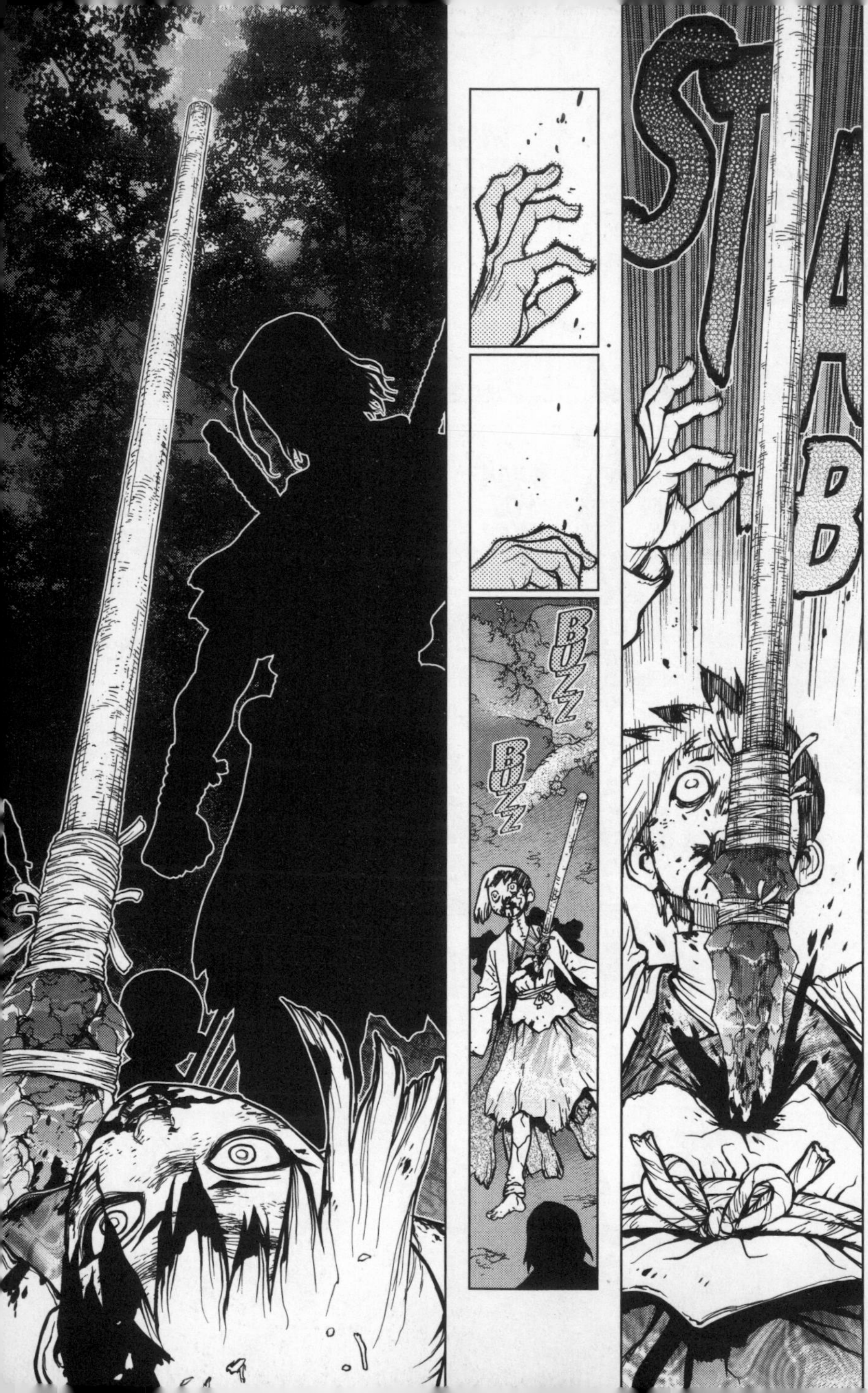
STAB
BUZZ
BUZZ

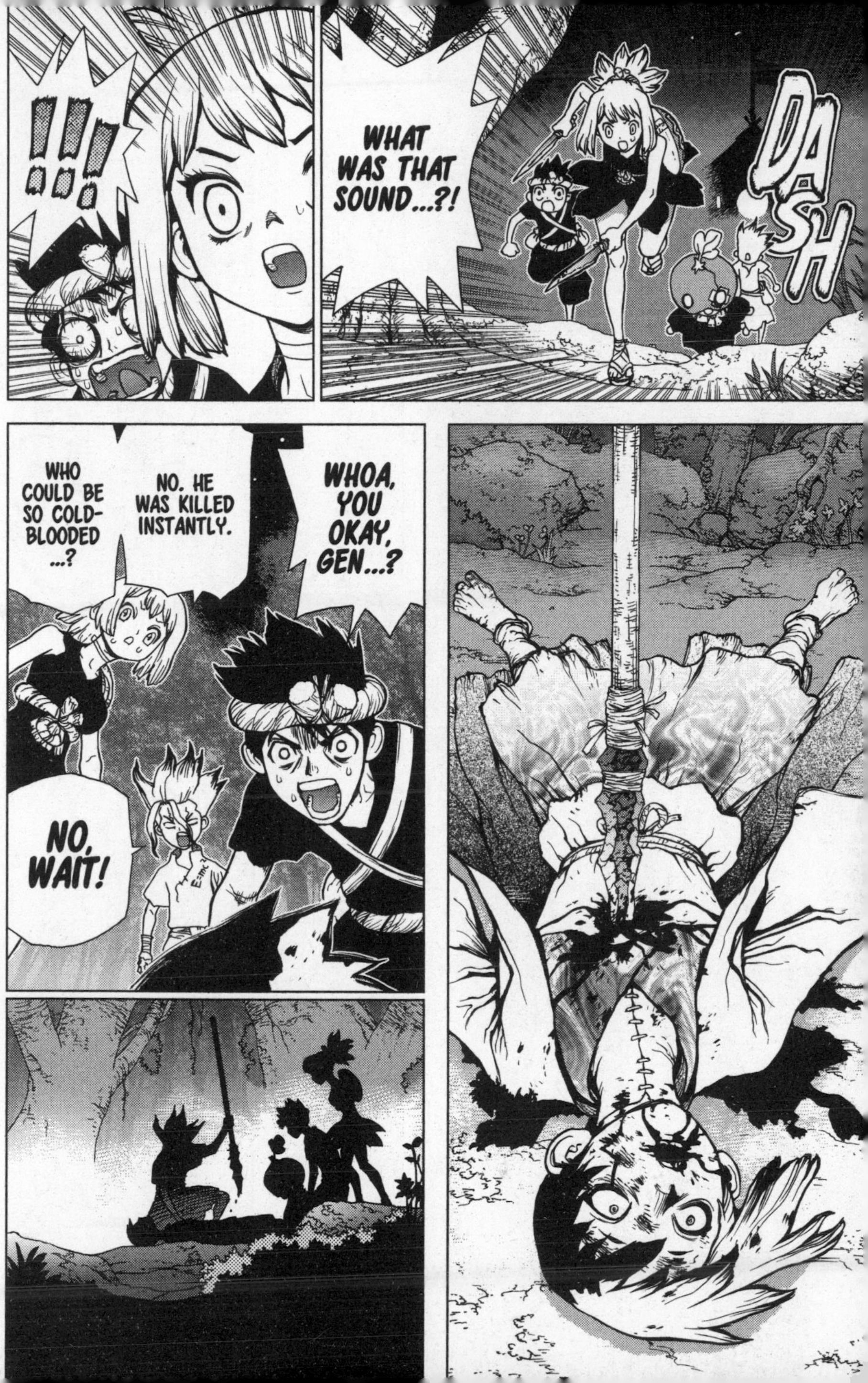
DASH
WHAT WAS THAT SOUND...?!
!!!!
WHOA, YOU OKAY, GEN...?
NO. HE WAS KILLED INSTANTLY.
WHO COULD BE SO COLD-BLOODED ...?
NO, WAIT!

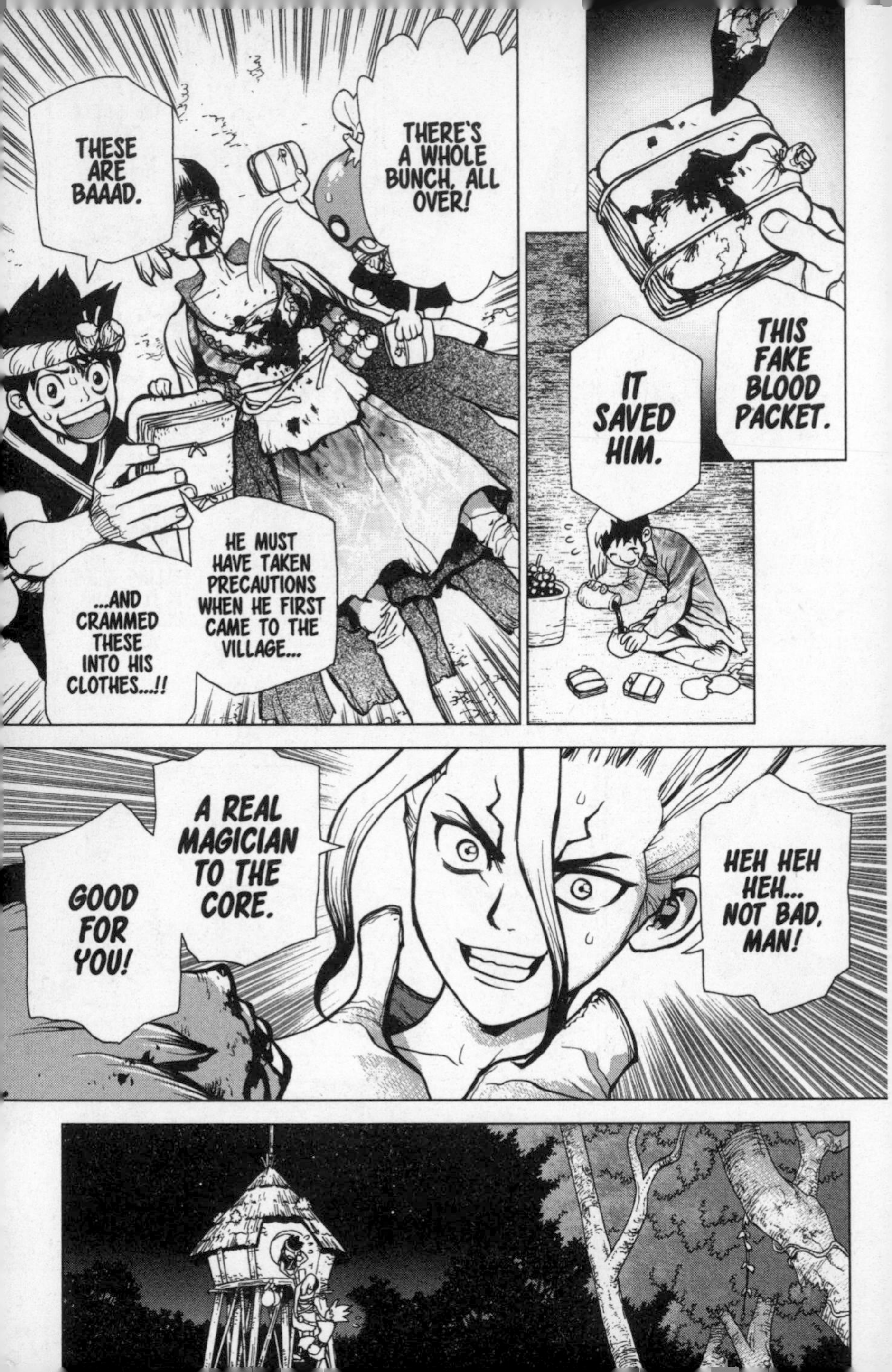
THIS FAKE BLOOD PACKET.
IT SAVED HIM.
THERE'S A WHOLE BUNCH, ALL OVER!
THESE ARE BAAAD.
HE MUST HAVE TAKEN PRECAUTIONS WHEN HE FIRST CAME TO THE VILLAGE...
...AND CRAMMED THESE INTO HIS CLOTHES...!!
HEH HEH HEH... NOT BAD, MAN!
A REAL MAGICIAN TO THE CORE.
GOOD FOR YOU!

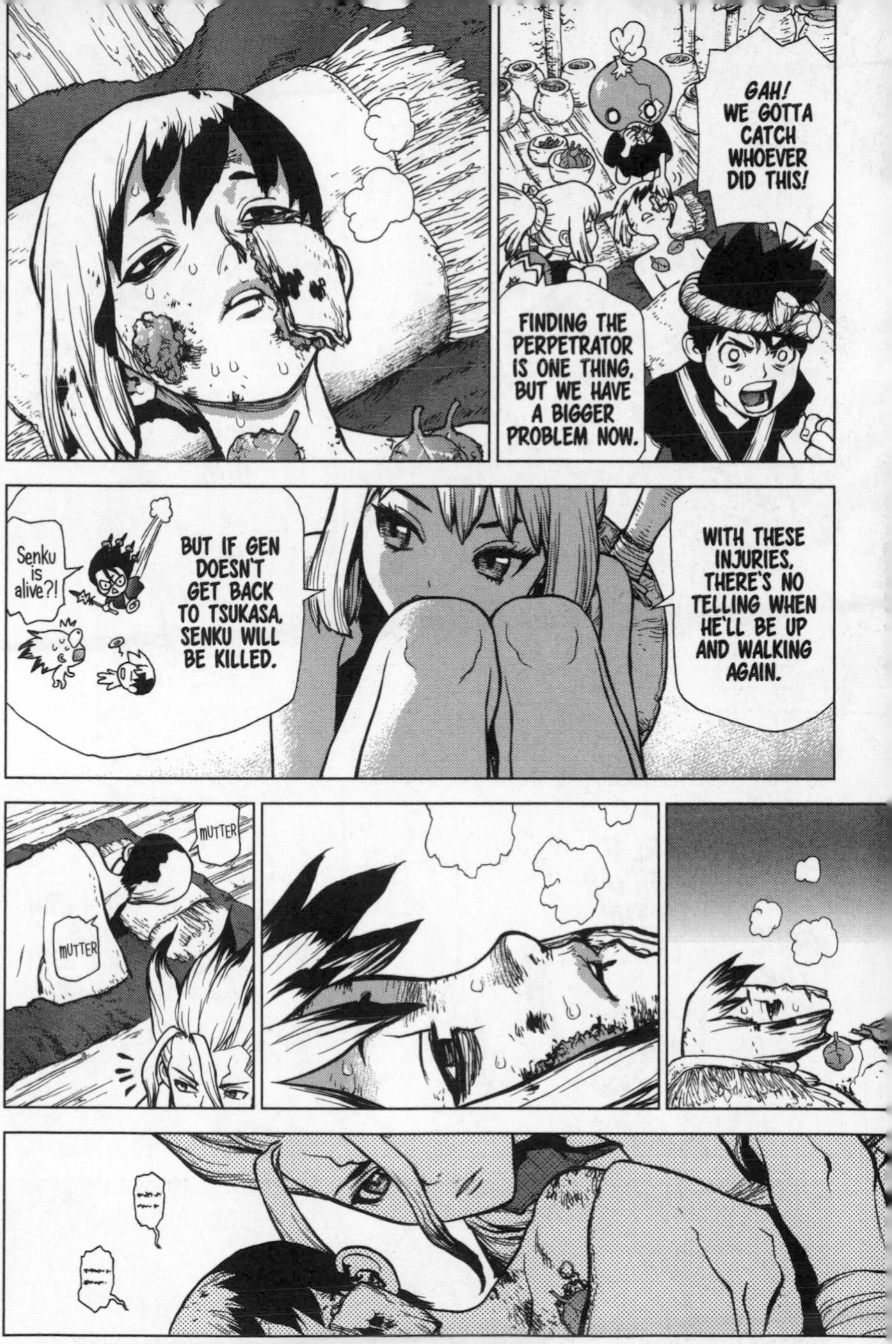
GAH! WE GOTTA CATCH WHOEVER DID THIS!
FINDING THE PERPETRATOR IS ONE THING, BUT WE HAVE A BIGGER PROBLEM NOW.
WITH THESE INJURIES, THERE'S NO TELLING WHEN HE'LL BE UP AND WALKING AGAIN.
BUT IF GEN DOESN'T GET BACK TO TSUKASA, SENKU WILL BE KILLED.
Senku is alive?!
MUTTER
MUTTER

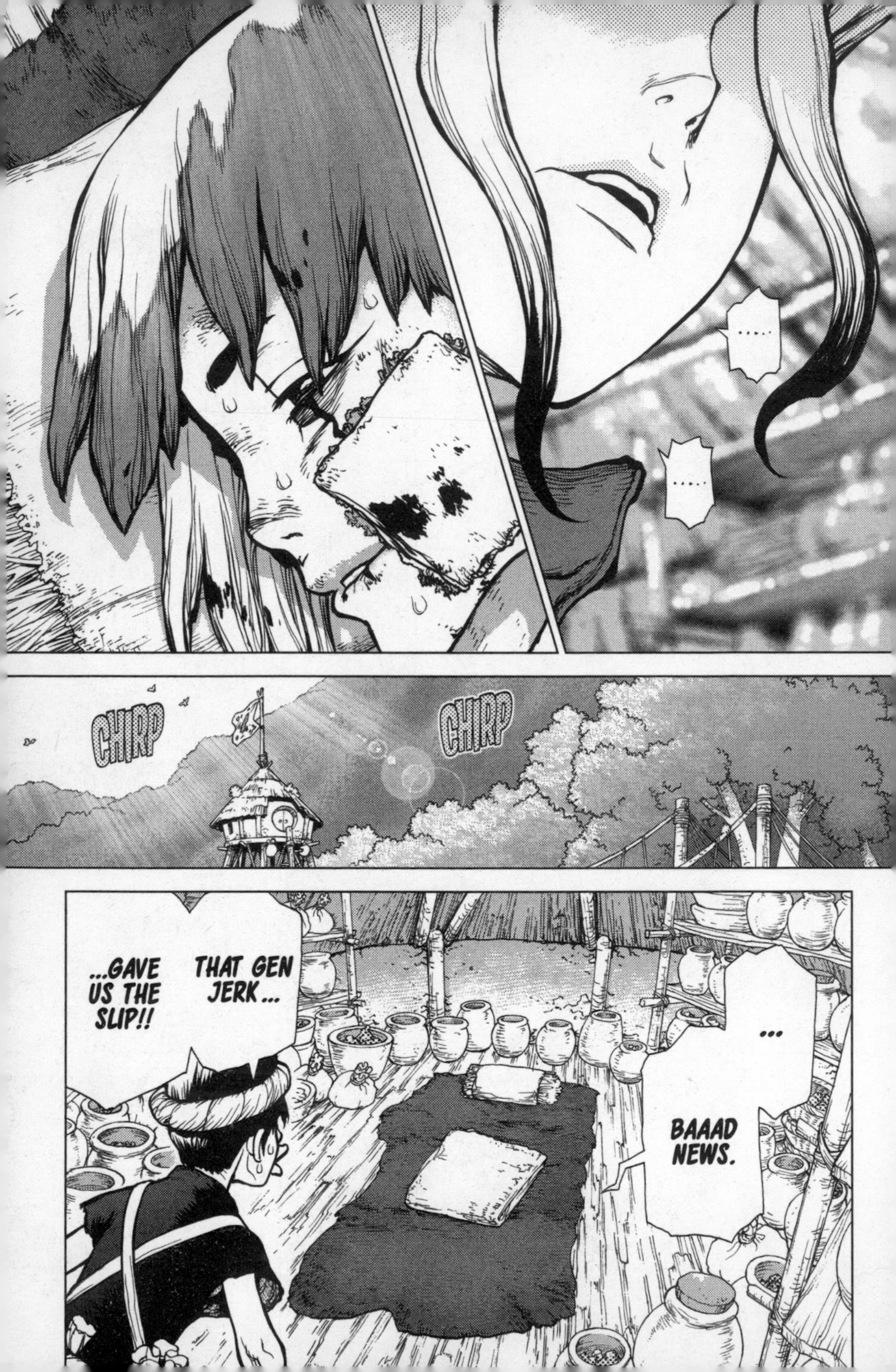
......
......
CHIRP
CHIRP
... BAAAD NEWS.
THAT GEN JERK...
...GAVE US THE SLIP!!

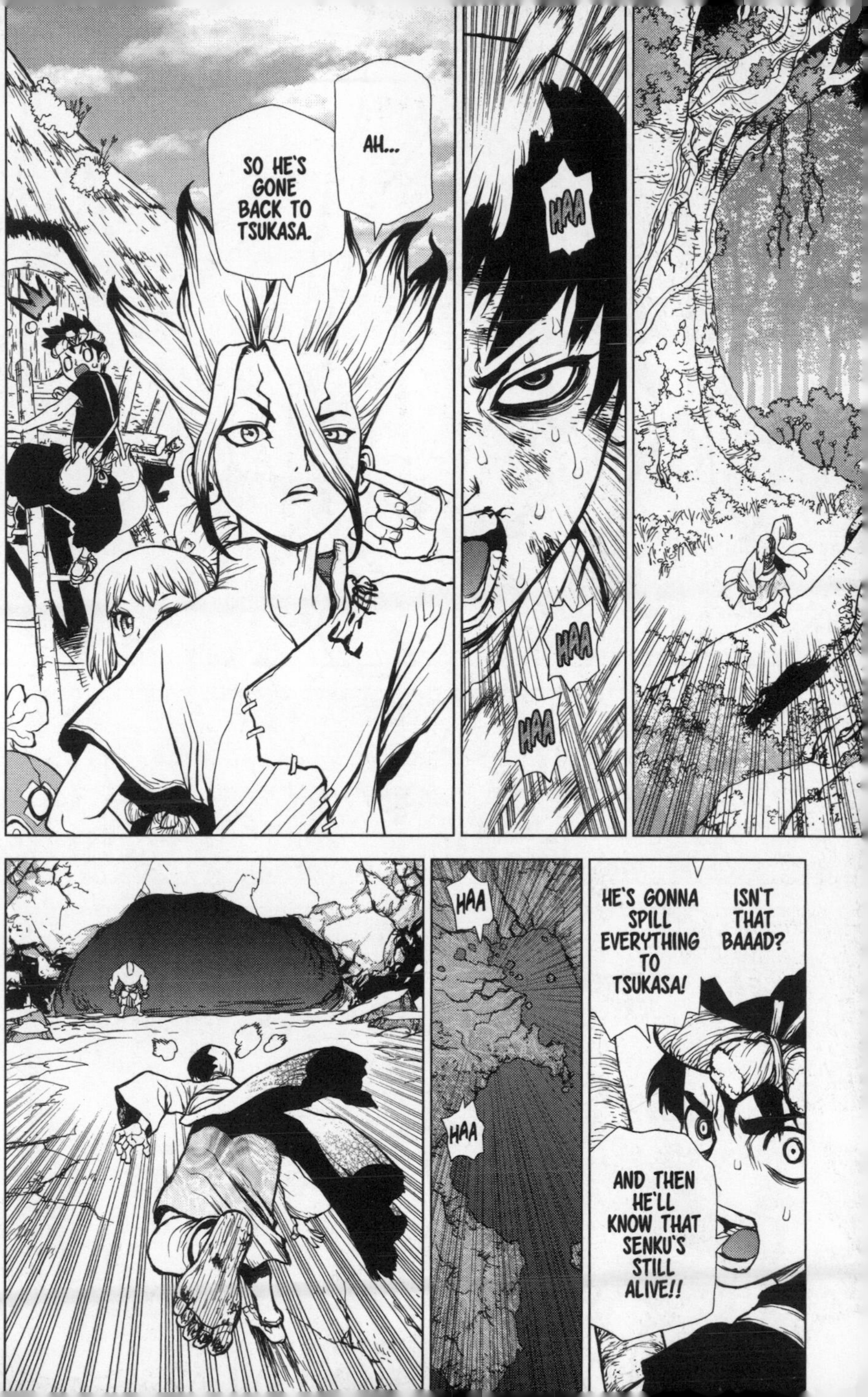
HAA
HAA
HAA
AH...
SO HE'S GONE BACK TO TSUKASA.
ISN'T THAT BAAAD?
HE'S GONNA SPILL EVERYTHING TO TSUKASA!
AND THEN HE'LL KNOW THAT SENKU'S STILL ALIVE!!
HAA
HAA

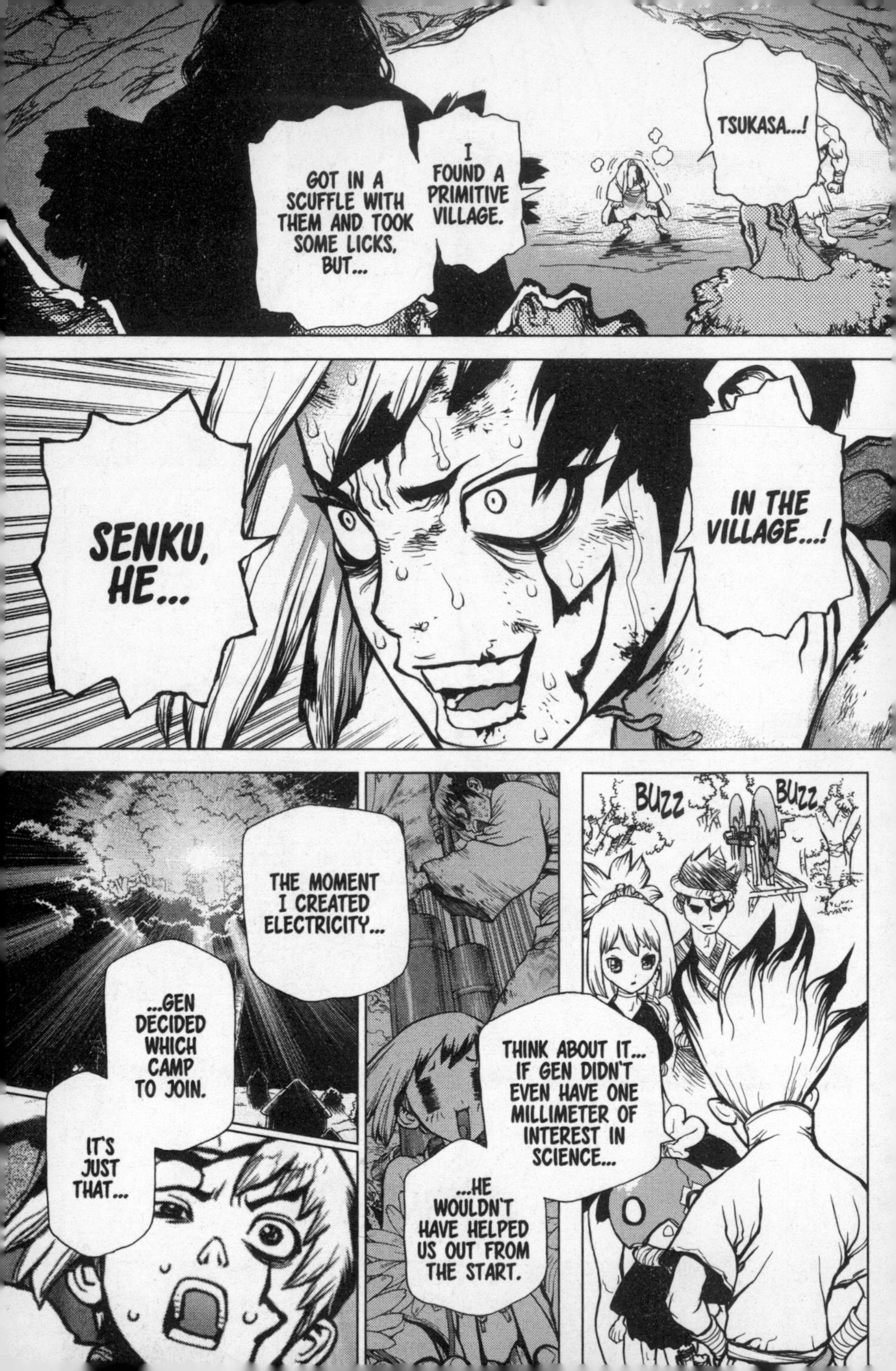
TSUKASA...!
I FOUND A PRIMITIVE VILLAGE.
GOT IN A SCUFFLE WITH THEM AND TOOK SOME LICKS, BUT...
IN THE VILLAGE...!
SENKU, HE...
BUZZ
BUZZ
THINK ABOUT IT... IF GEN DIDN'T EVEN HAVE ONE MILLIMETER OF INTEREST IN SCIENCE...
...HE WOULDN'T HAVE HELPED US OUT FROM THE START.
THE MOMENT I CREATED ELECTRICITY...
...GEN DECIDED WHICH CAMP TO JOIN.
IT'S JUST THAT...

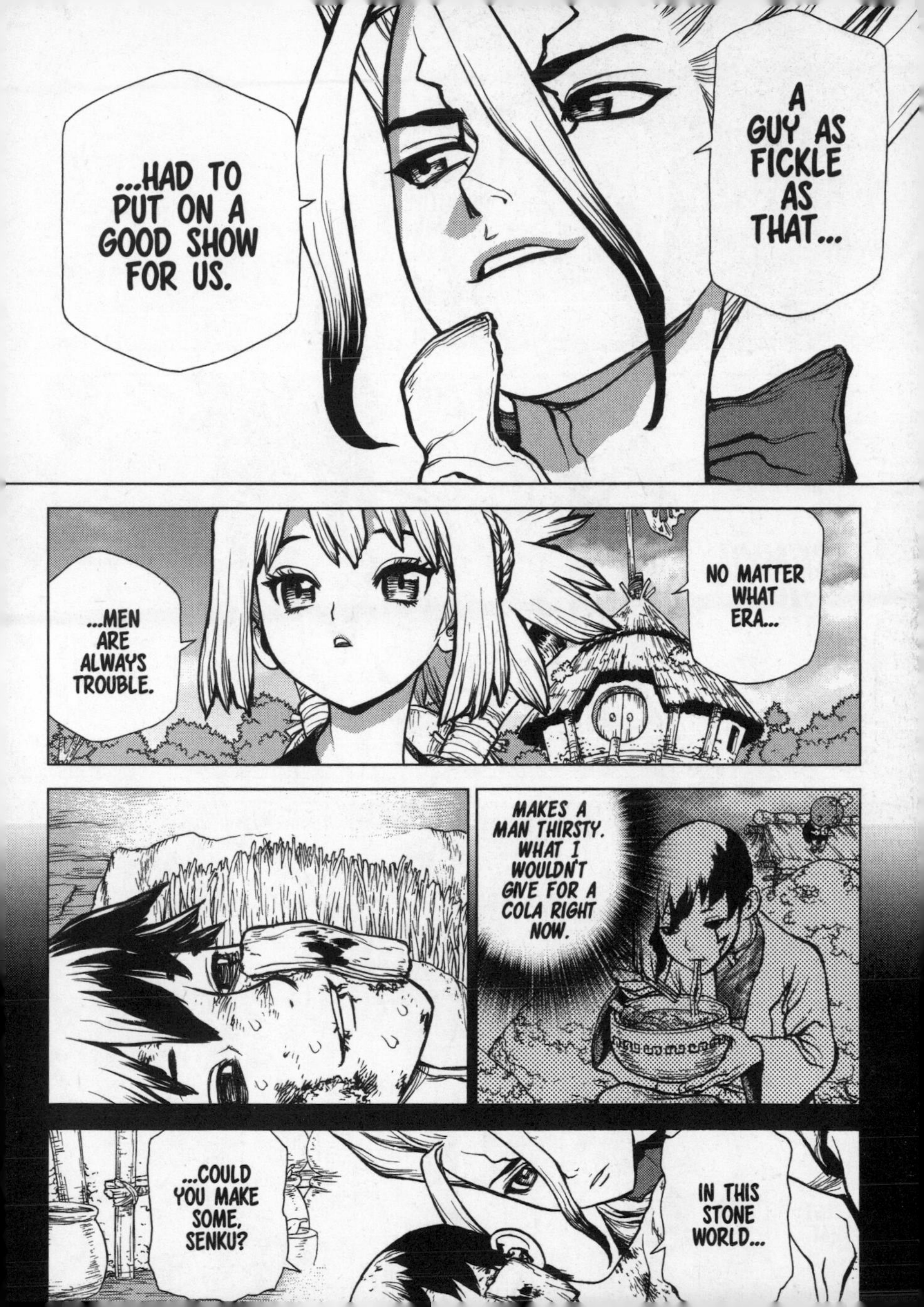
A GUY AS FICKLE AS THAT...
...HAD TO PUT ON A GOOD SHOW FOR US.
NO MATTER WHAT ERA...
...MEN ARE ALWAYS TROUBLE.
MAKES A MAN THIRSTY. WHAT I WOULDN'T GIVE FOR A COLA RIGHT NOW.
IN THIS STONE WORLD...
...COULD YOU MAKE SOME, SENKU?

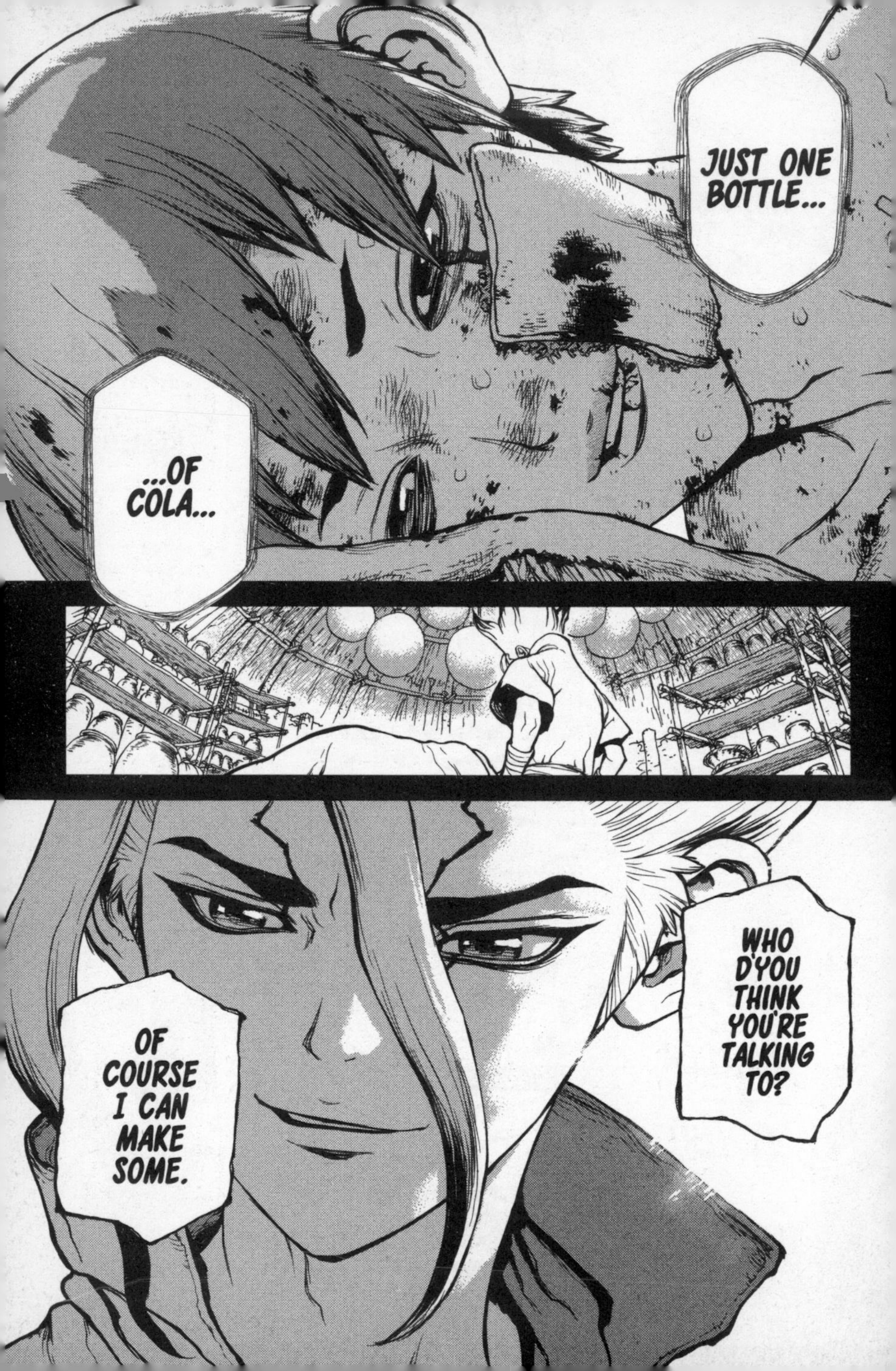
JUST ONE BOTTLE...
...OF COLA...
WHO D'YOU THINK YOU'RE TALKING TO?
OF COURSE I CAN MAKE SOME.

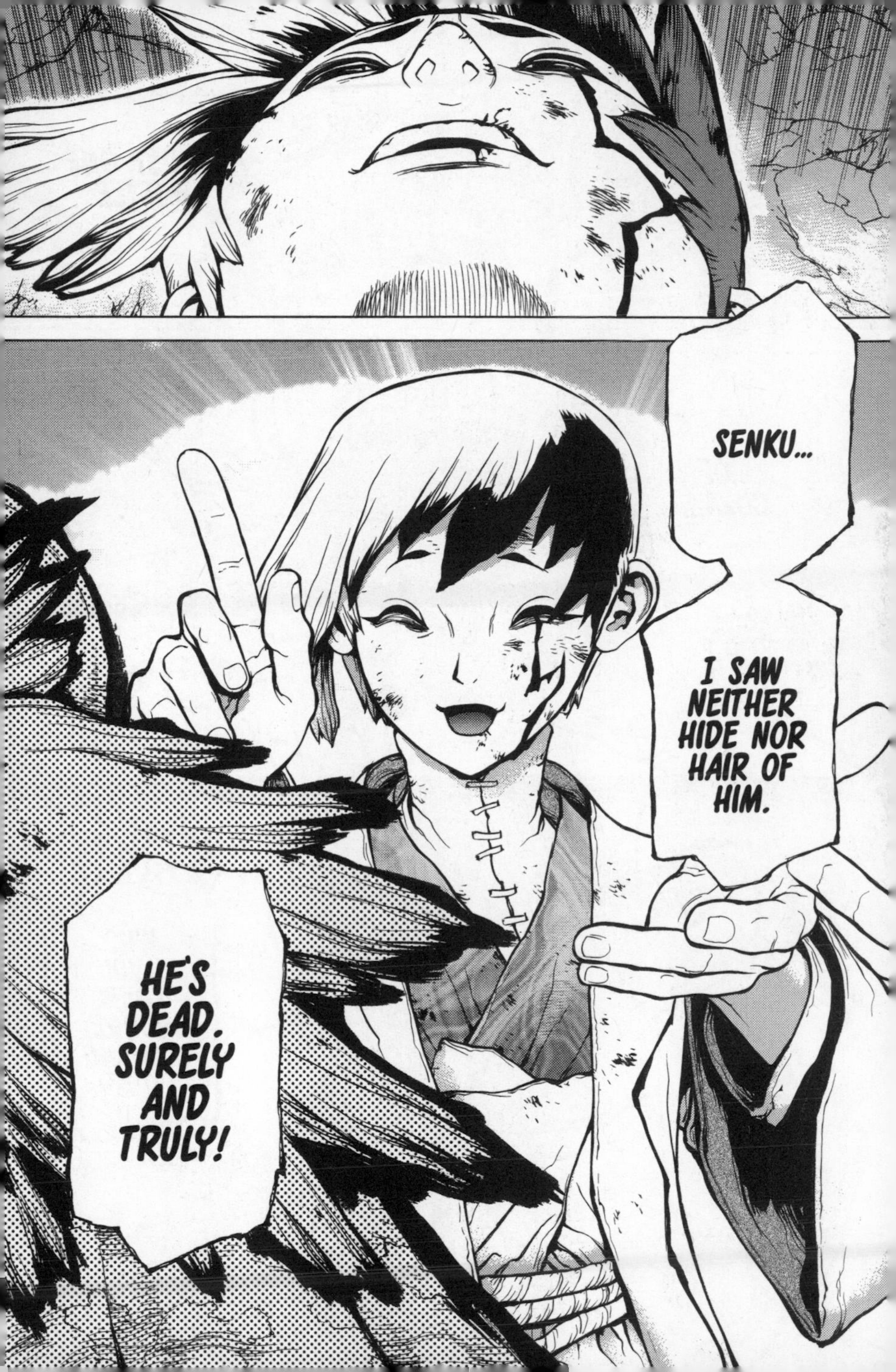
SENKU...
I SAW NEITHER HIDE NOR HAIR OF HIM.
HE'S DEAD. SURELY AND TRULY!

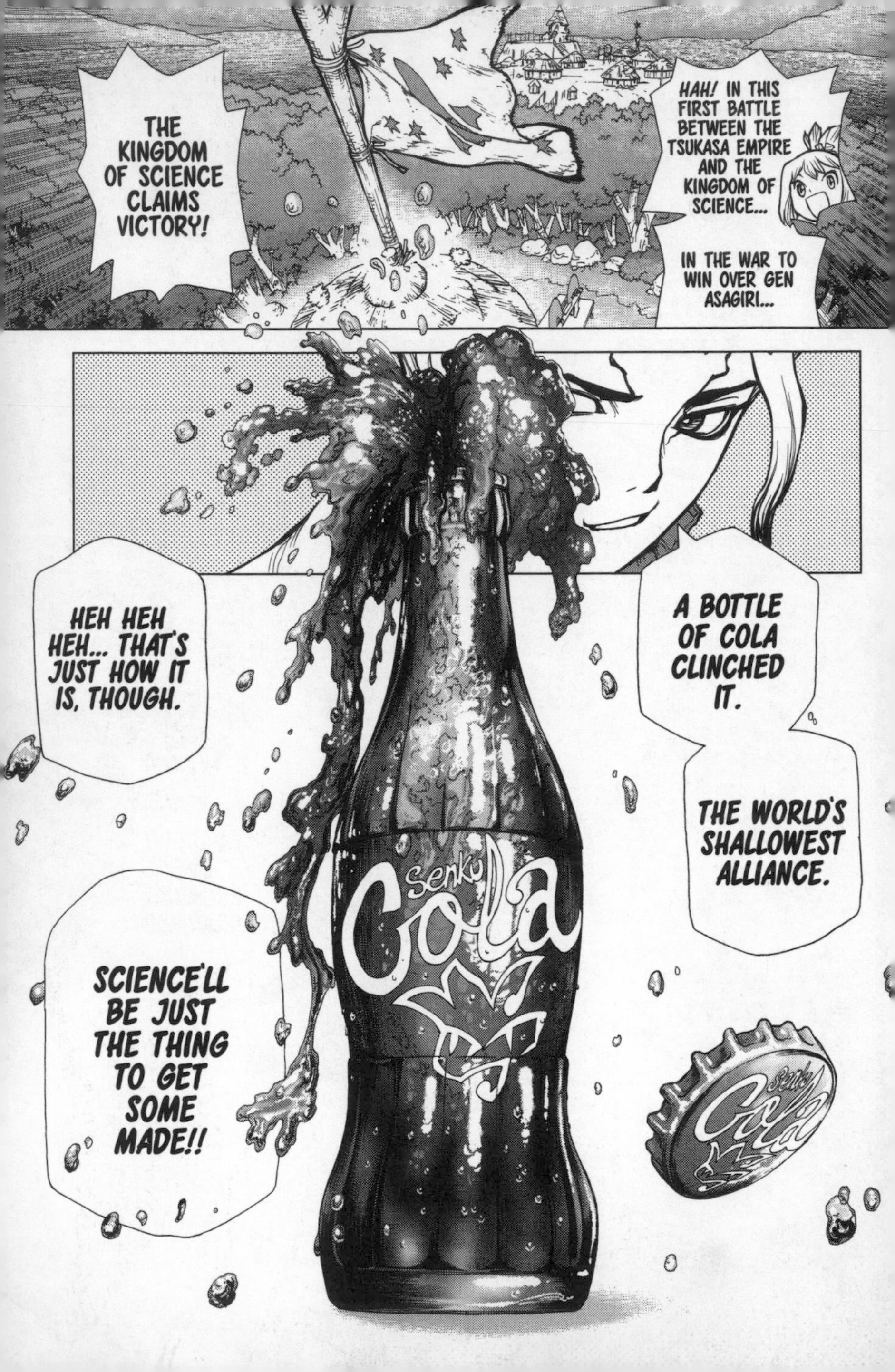
HAH! IN THIS FIRST BATTLE BETWEEN THE TSUKASA EMPIRE AND THE KINGDOM OF SCIENCE...
IN THE WAR TO WIN OVER GEN ASAGIRI...
THE KINGDOM OF SCIENCE CLAIMS VICTORY!
A BOTTLE OF COLA CLINCHED IT.
THE WORLD'S SHALLOWEST ALLIANCE.
HEH HEH HEH... THAT'S JUST HOW IT IS, THOUGH.
SCIENCE'LL BE JUST THE THING TO GET SOME MADE!!
senku Cola
senku Cola

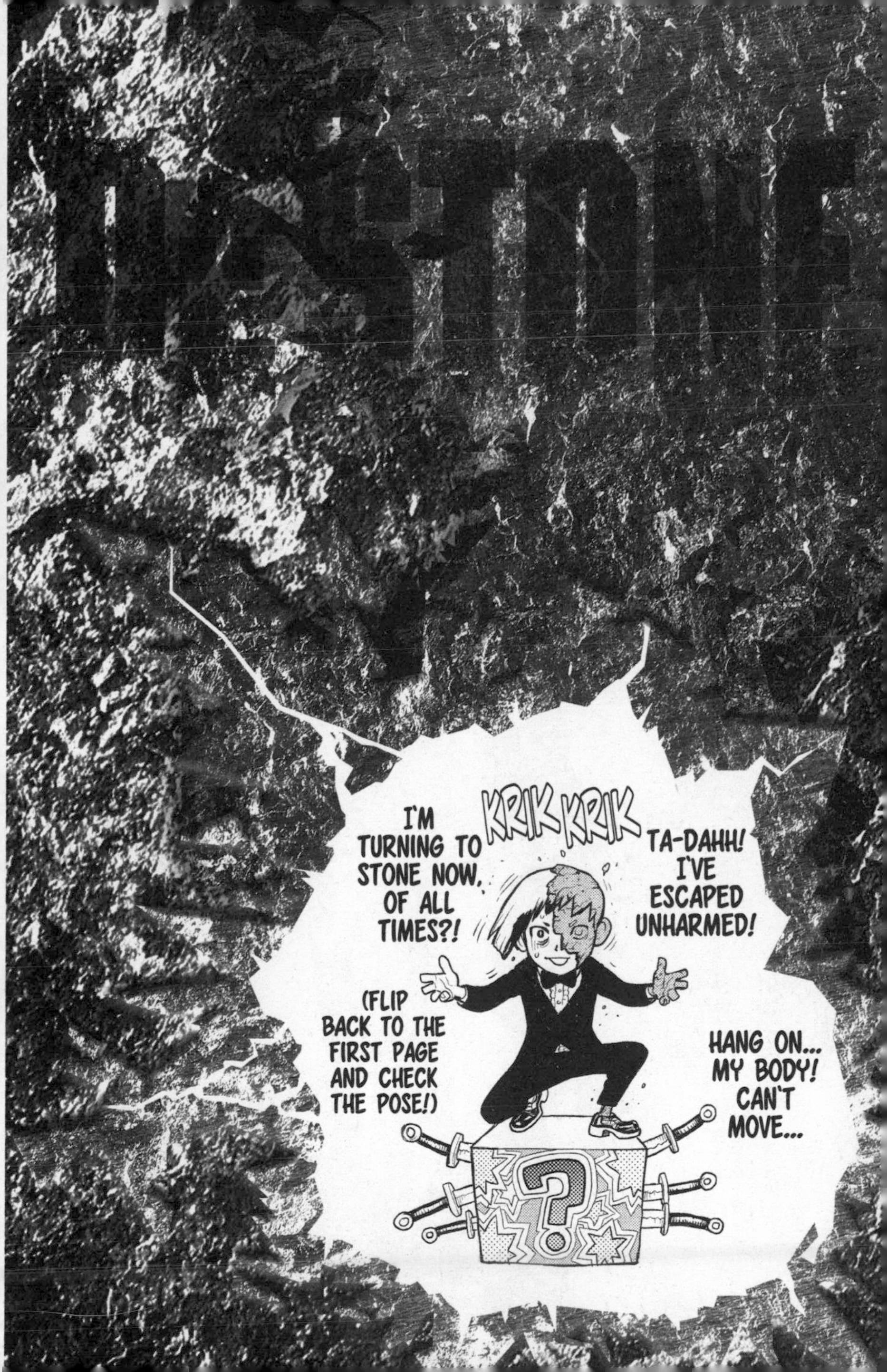

TA-DAHH! I'VE ESCAPED UNHARMED!
KRIK KRIK
I'M TURNING TO STONE NOW, OF ALL TIMES?!
HANG ON... MY BODY! CAN'T MOVE...
(FLIP BACK TO THE FIRST PAGE AND CHECK THE POSE!)

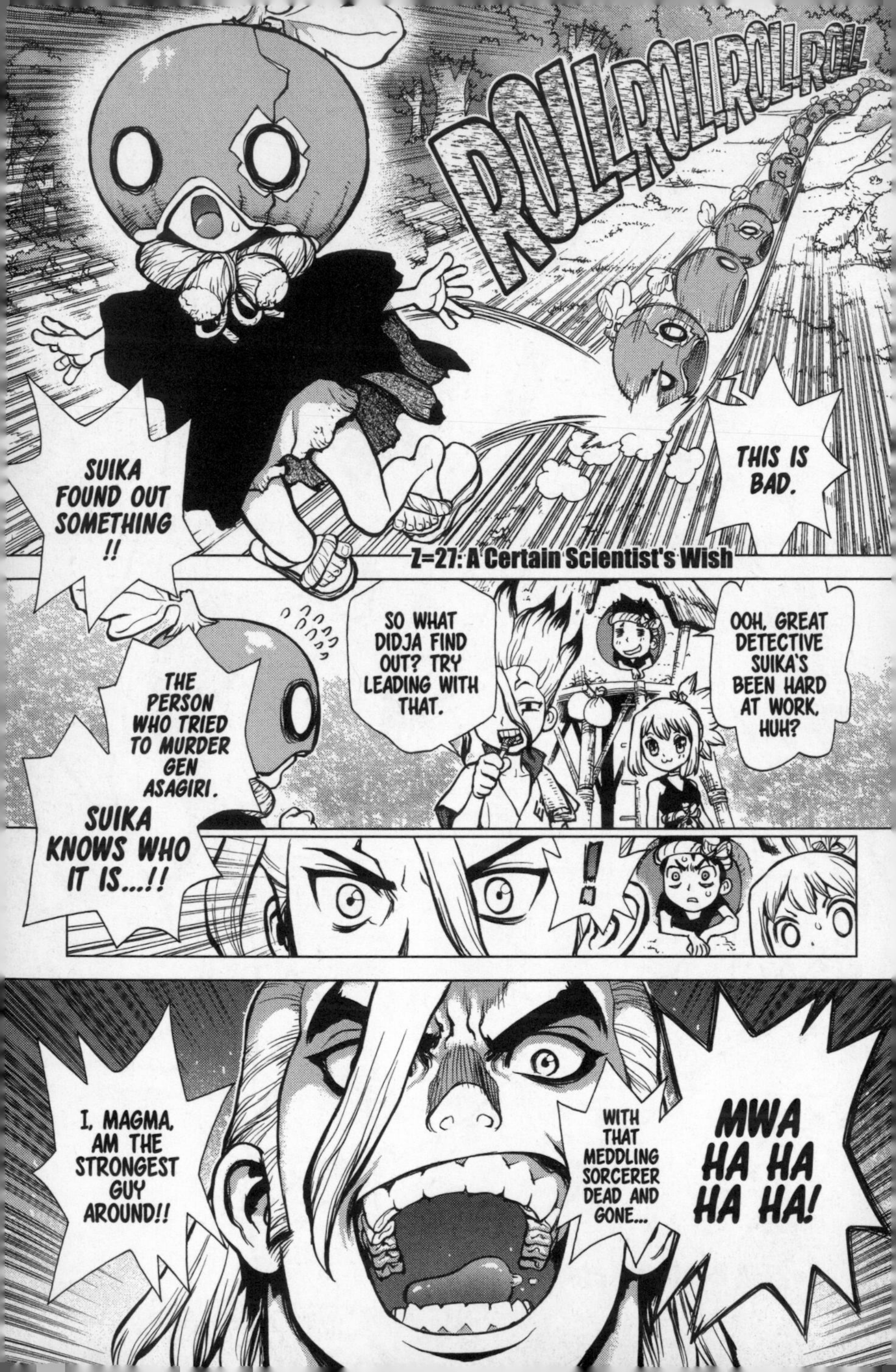
ROLL ROLL ROLL ROLL
THIS IS BAD.
SUIKA FOUND OUT SOMETHING!!
Z=27: A Certain Scientist's Wish
OOH, GREAT DETECTIVE SUIKA'S BEEN HARD AT WORK, HUH?
SO WHAT DIDJA FIND OUT? TRY LEADING WITH THAT.
THE PERSON WHO TRIED TO MURDER GEN ASAGIRI.
SUIKA KNOWS WHO IT IS...!!
!
MWA HA HA HA HA!
WITH THAT MEDDLING SORCERER DEAD AND GONE...
I, MAGMA, AM THE STRONGEST GUY AROUND!!

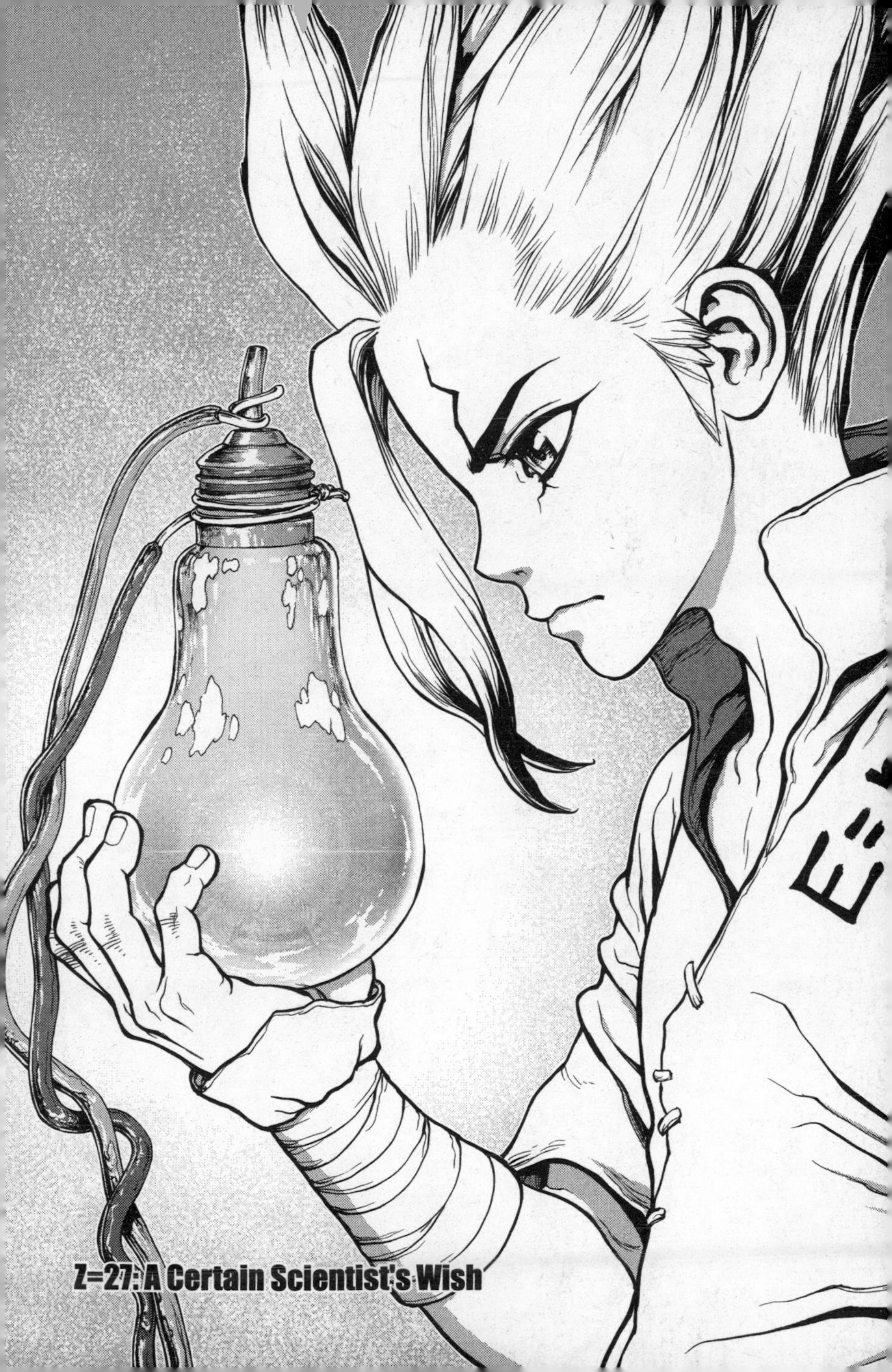

Z=27: A Certain Scientist's Wish

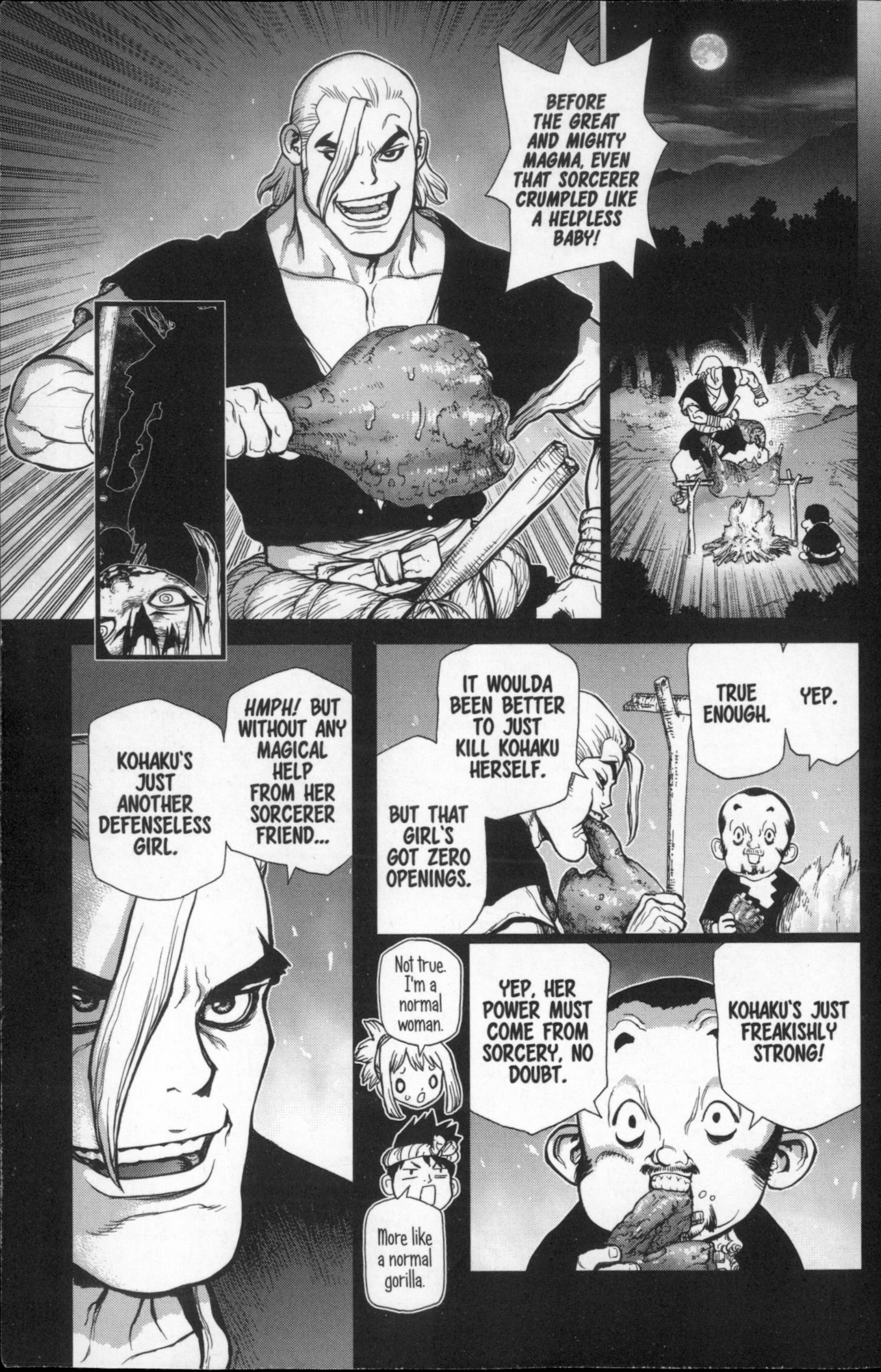
BEFORE THE GREAT AND MIGHTY MAGMA, EVEN THAT SORCERER CRUMPLED LIKE A HELPLESS BABY!
YEP.
TRUE ENOUGH.
IT WOULDA BEEN BETTER TO JUST KILL KOHAKU HERSELF.
BUT THAT GIRL'S GOT ZERO OPENINGS.
KOHAKU'S JUST FREAKISHLY STRONG!
YEP, HER POWER MUST COME FROM SORCERY, NO DOUBT.
Not true. I'm a normal woman.
More like a normal gorilla.
HMPH! BUT WITHOUT ANY MAGICAL HELP FROM HER SORCERER FRIEND...
KOHAKU'S JUST ANOTHER DEFENSELESS GIRL.

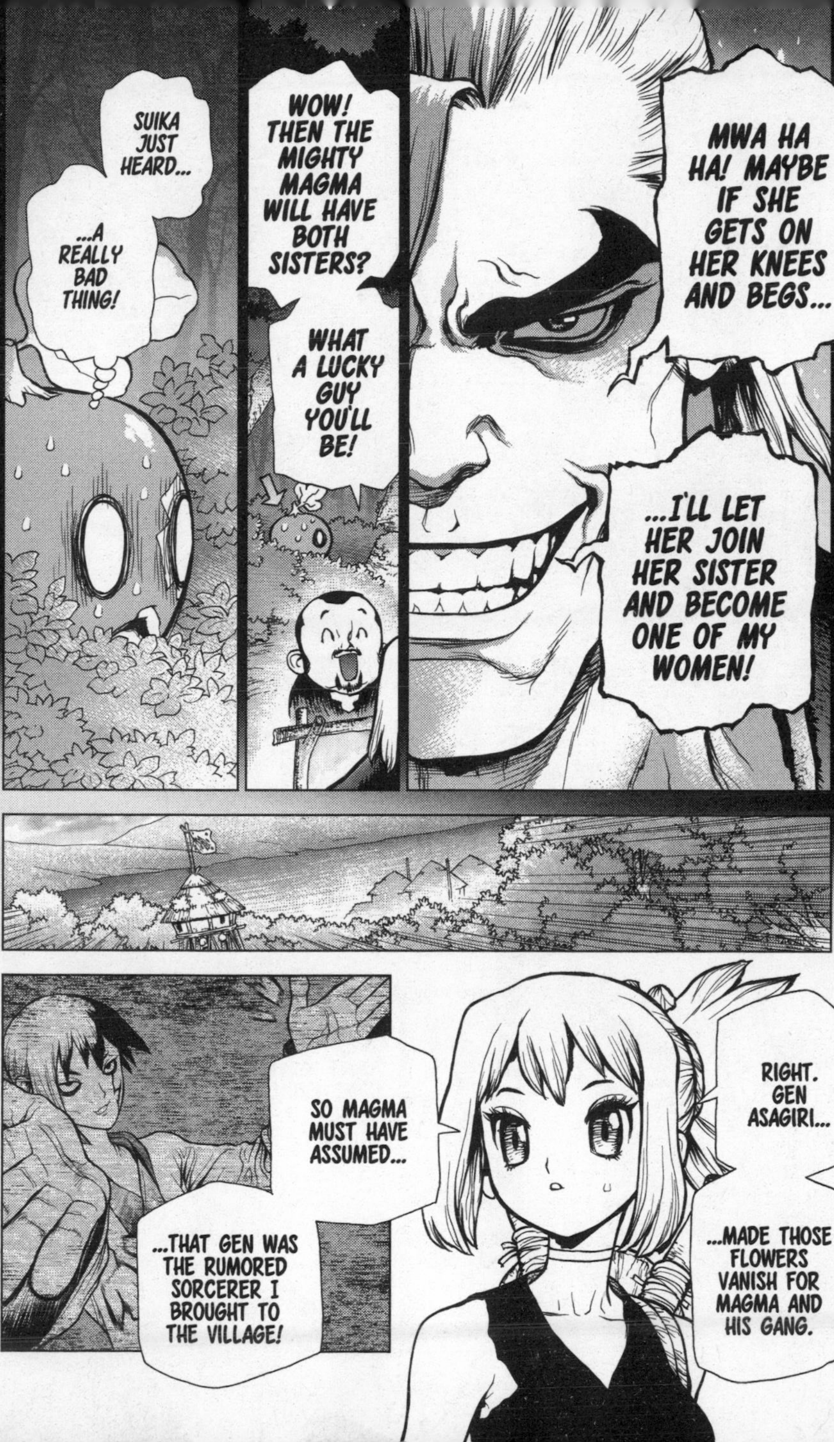
MWA HA HA! MAYBE IF SHE GETS ON HER KNEES AND BEGS...
...I'LL LET HER JOIN HER SISTER AND BECOME ONE OF MY WOMEN!
WOW! THEN THE MIGHTY MAGMA WILL HAVE BOTH SISTERS?
WHAT A LUCKY GUY YOU'LL BE!
SUIKA JUST HEARD...
...A REALLY BAD THING!
RIGHT. GEN ASAGIRI...
...MADE THOSE FLOWERS VANISH FOR MAGMA AND HIS GANG.
SO MAGMA MUST HAVE ASSUMED...
...THAT GEN WAS THE RUMORED SORCERER I BROUGHT TO THE VILLAGE!

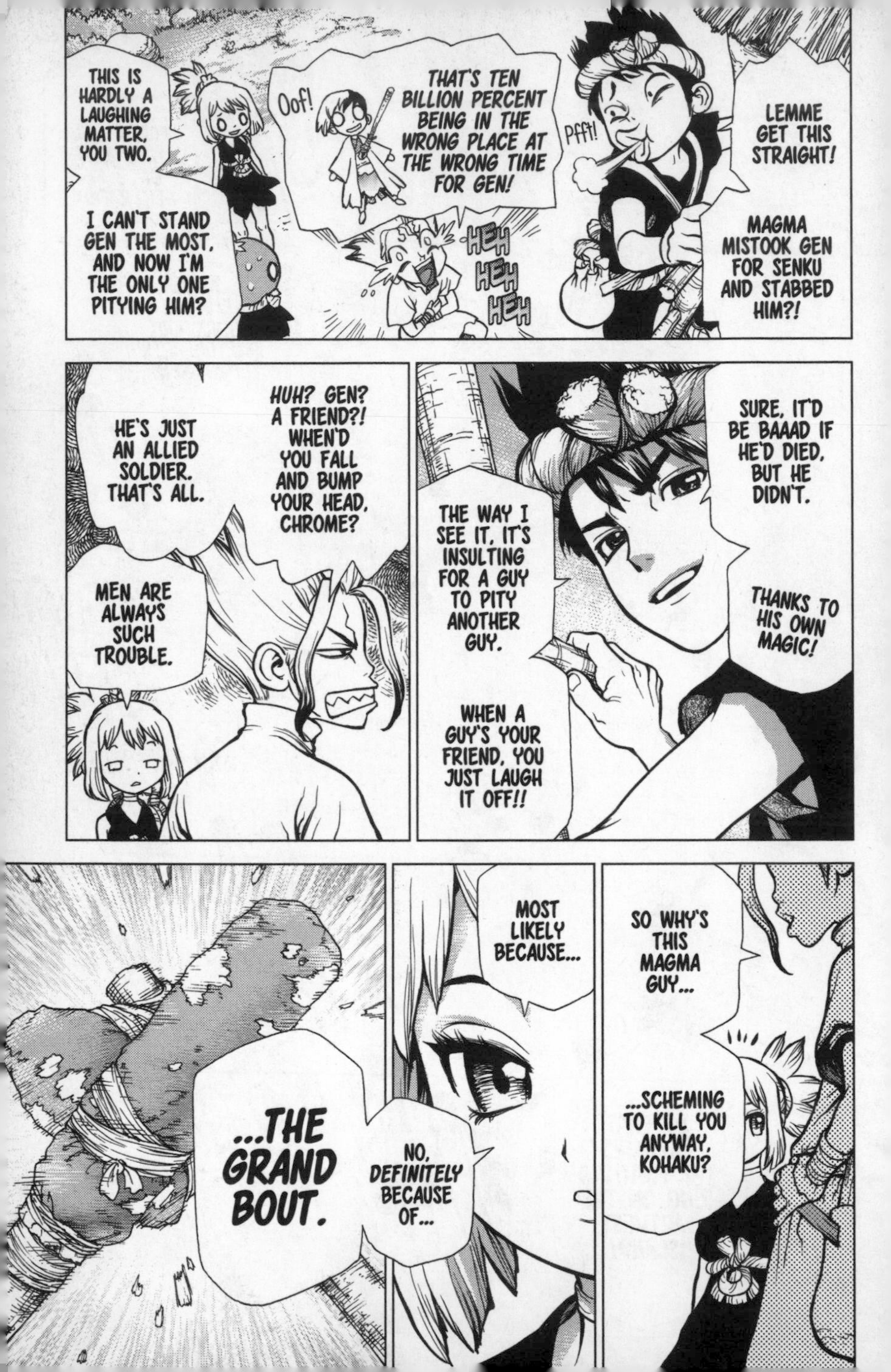
LEMME GET THIS STRAIGHT!
MAGMA MISTOOK GEN FOR SENKU AND STABBED HIM?!
Pffft!
THAT'S TEN BILLION PERCENT BEING IN THE WRONG PLACE AT THE WRONG TIME FOR GEN!
Oof!
HEH HEH HEH
THIS IS HARDLY A LAUGHING MATTER, YOU TWO.
I CAN'T STAND GEN THE MOST, AND NOW I'M THE ONLY ONE PITYING HIM?
SURE, IT'D BE BAAAD IF HE'D DIED, BUT HE DIDN'T.
THANKS TO HIS OWN MAGIC!
THE WAY I SEE IT, IT'S INSULTING FOR A GUY TO PITY ANOTHER GUY.
WHEN A GUY'S YOUR FRIEND, YOU JUST LAUGH IT OFF!!
HUH? GEN? A FRIEND?! WHEN'D YOU FALL AND BUMP YOUR HEAD, CHROME?
HE'S JUST AN ALLIED SOLDIER. THAT'S ALL.
MEN ARE ALWAYS SUCH TROUBLE.
SO WHY'S THIS MAGMA GUY...
...SCHEMING TO KILL YOU ANYWAY, KOHAKU?
MOST LIKELY BECAUSE...
NO, DEFINITELY BECAUSE OF...
...THE GRAND BOUT.

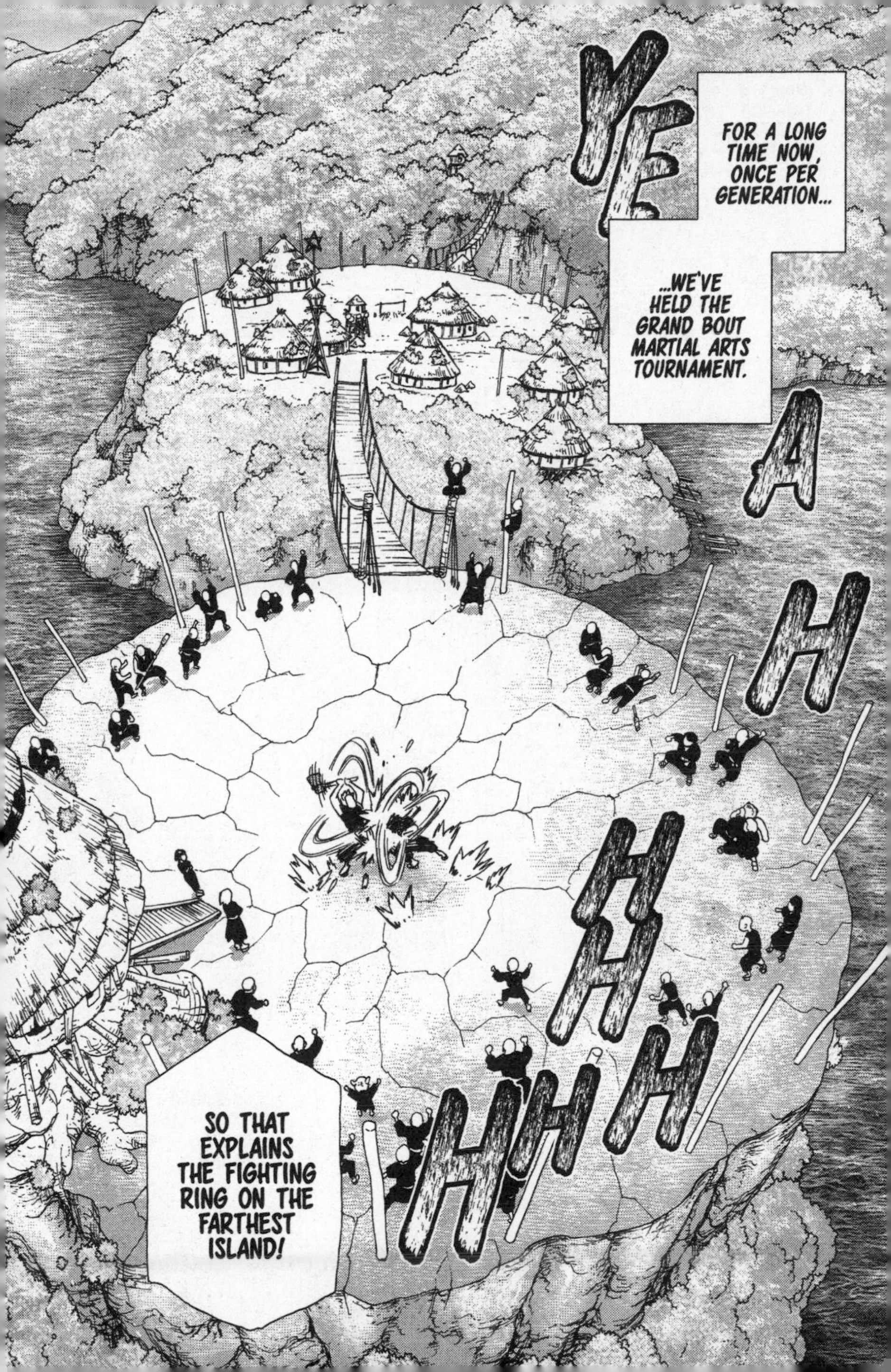
FOR A LONG TIME NOW, ONCE PER GENERATION...
...WE'VE HELD THE GRAND BOUT MARTIAL ARTS TOURNAMENT.
YEAHHHHHHHH
SO THAT EXPLAINS THE FIGHTING RING ON THE FARTHEST ISLAND!

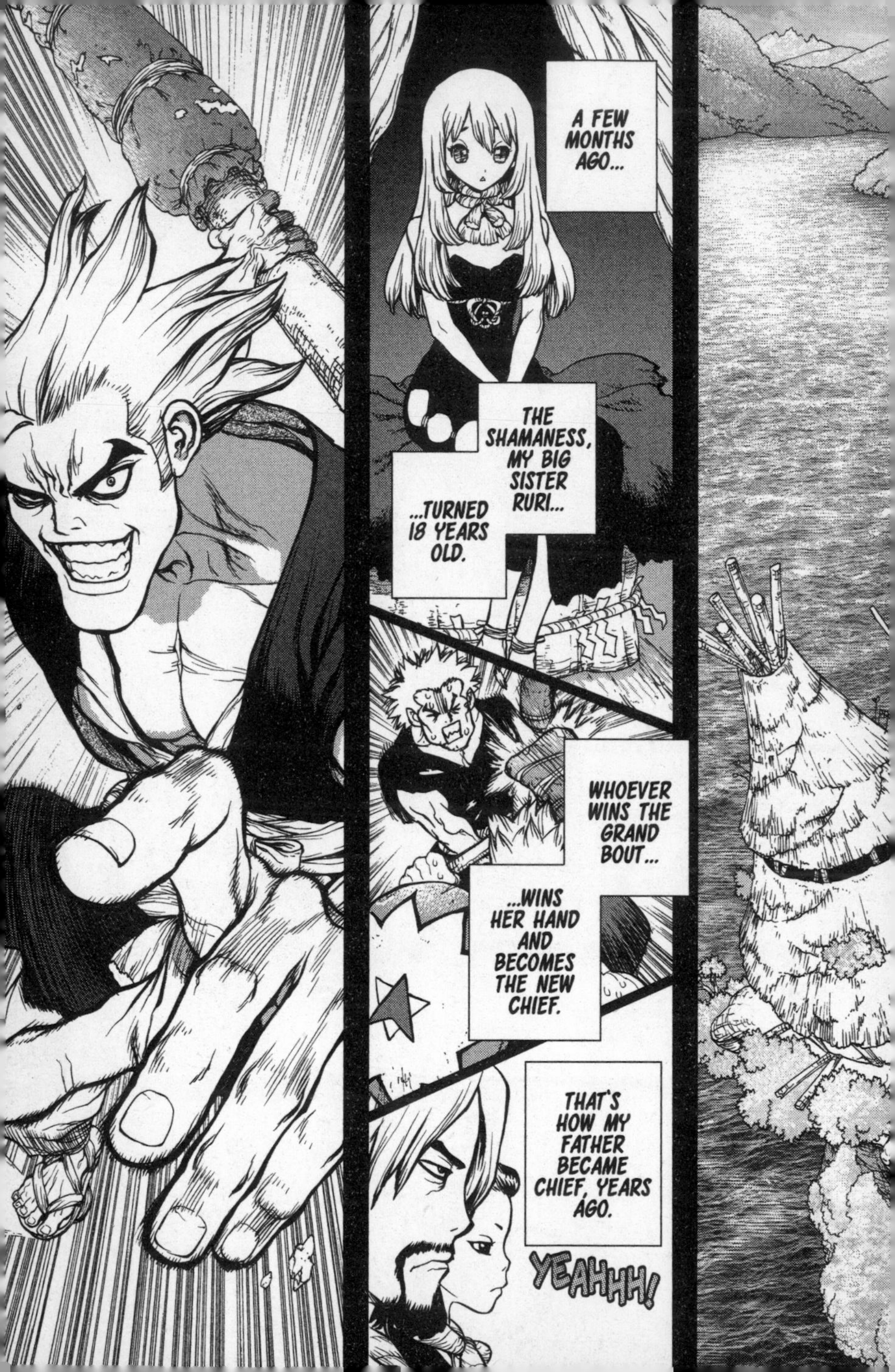
A FEW MONTHS AGO...
THE SHAMANESS, MY BIG SISTER RURI...
...TURNED 18 YEARS OLD.
WHOEVER WINS THE GRAND BOUT...
...WINS HER HAND AND BECOMES THE NEW CHIEF.
THAT'S HOW MY FATHER BECAME CHIEF, YEARS AGO.
YEAHHH!

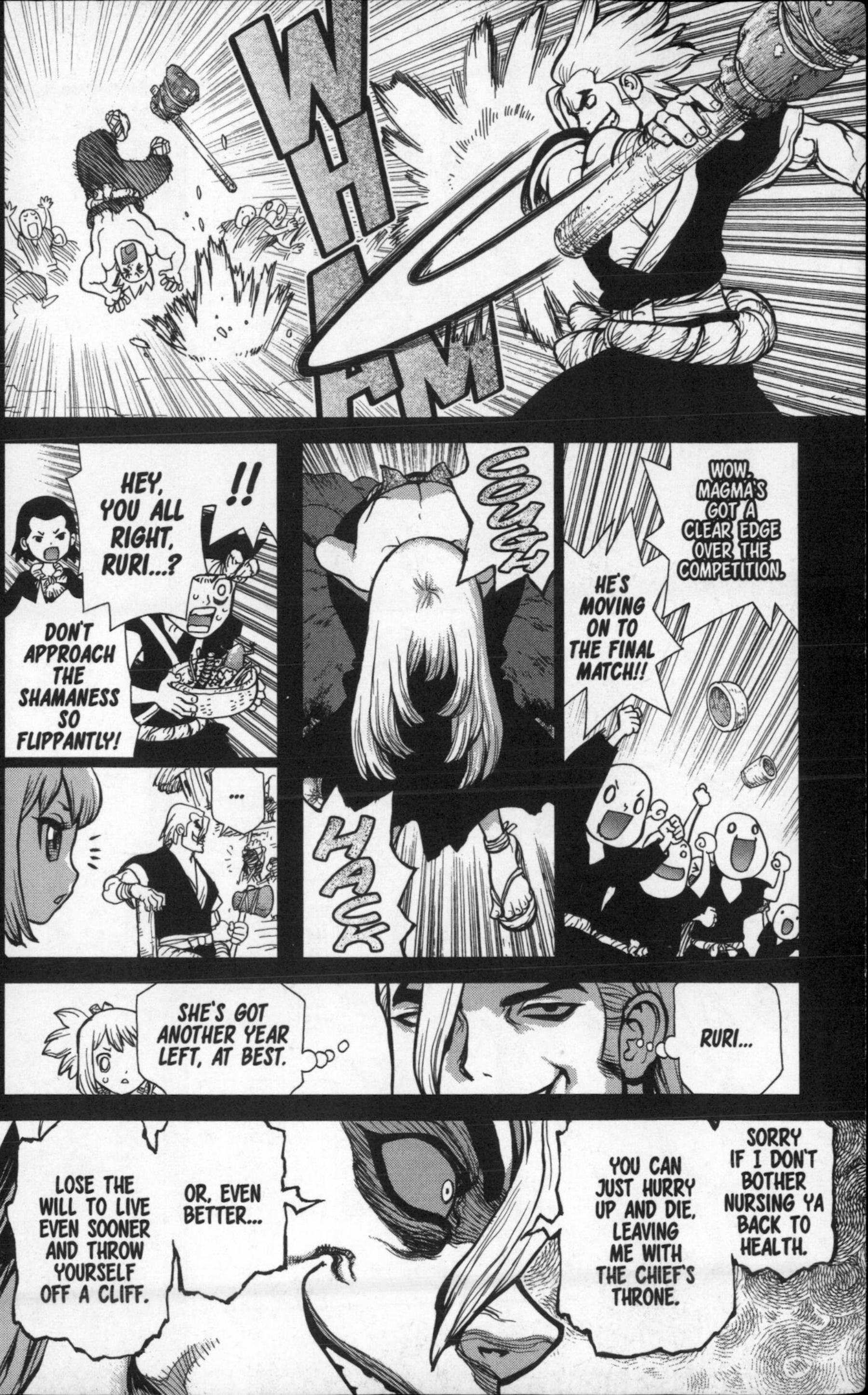
WHAM
WOW, MAGMA'S GOT A CLEAR EDGE OVER THE COMPETITION.
HE'S MOVING ON TO THE FINAL MATCH!!
COUGH
HACK
HEY, YOU ALL RIGHT, RURI...?
!!
DON'T APPROACH THE SHAMANESS SO FLIPPANTLY!
...
RURI...
SHE'S GOT ANOTHER YEAR LEFT, AT BEST.
SORRY IF I DON'T BOTHER NURSING YA BACK TO HEALTH.
YOU CAN JUST HURRY UP AND DIE, LEAVING ME WITH THE CHIEF'S THRONE.
OR, EVEN BETTER...
LOSE THE WILL TO LIVE EVEN SOONER AND THROW YOURSELF OFF A CLIFF.

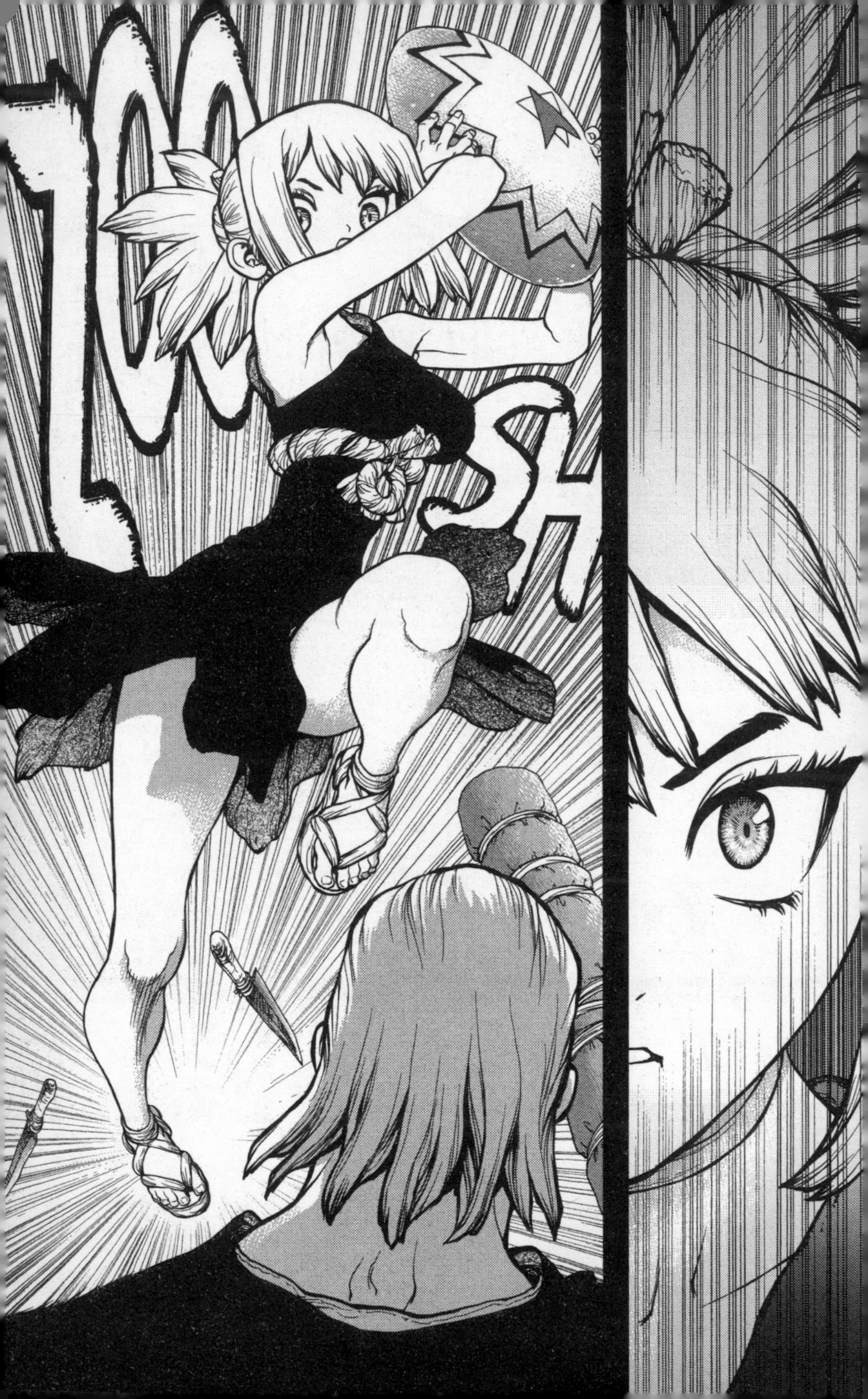

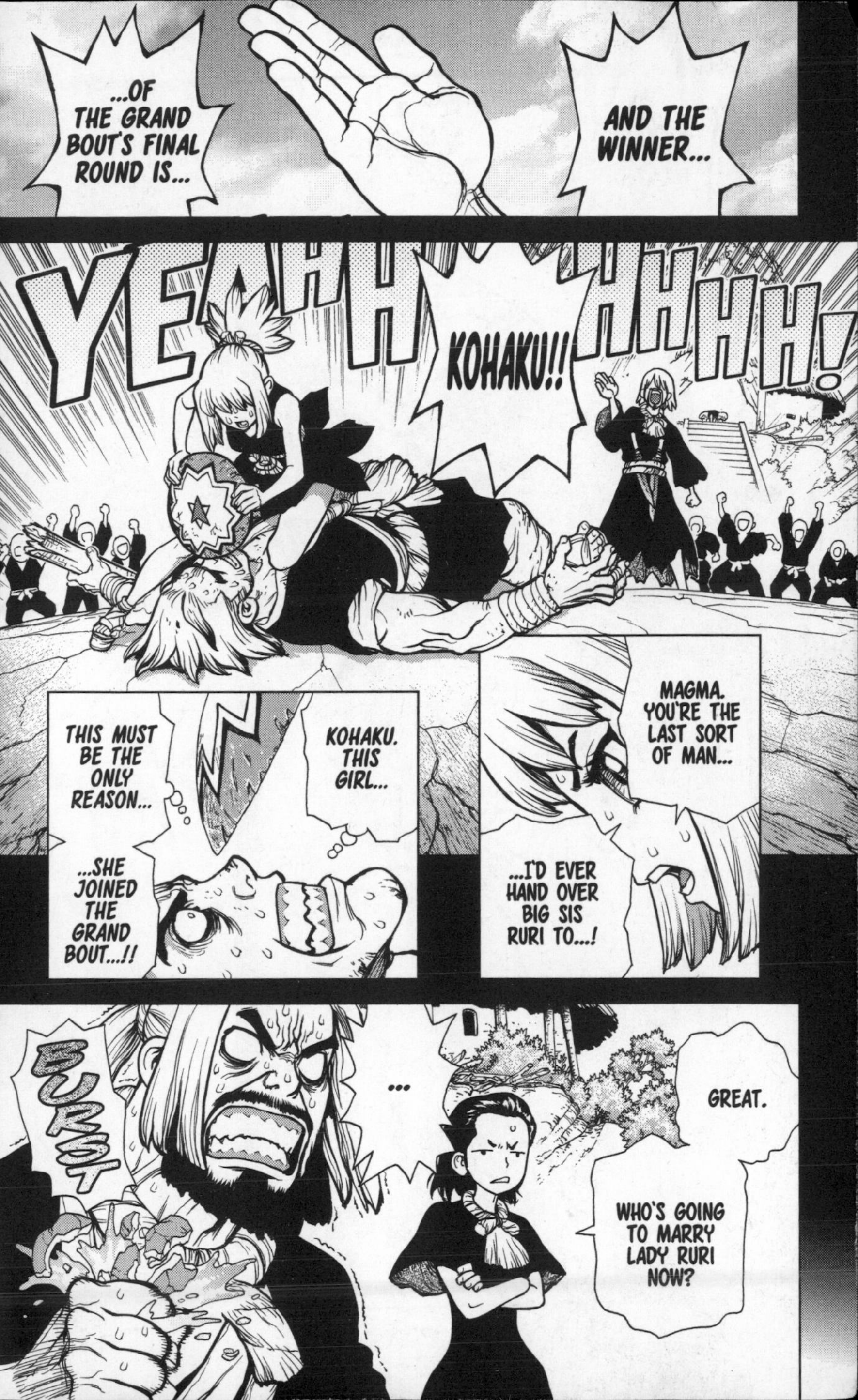
AND THE WINNER...
...OF THE GRAND BOUT'S FINAL ROUND IS...
YEAHHHHHHHH!
KOHAKU!!
MAGMA. YOU'RE THE LAST SORT OF MAN...
...I'D EVER HAND OVER BIG SIS RURI TO...!
KOHAKU. THIS GIRL...
THIS MUST BE THE ONLY REASON...
...SHE JOINED THE GRAND BOUT...!!
GREAT.
WHO'S GOING TO MARRY LADY RURI NOW?
...
BURST

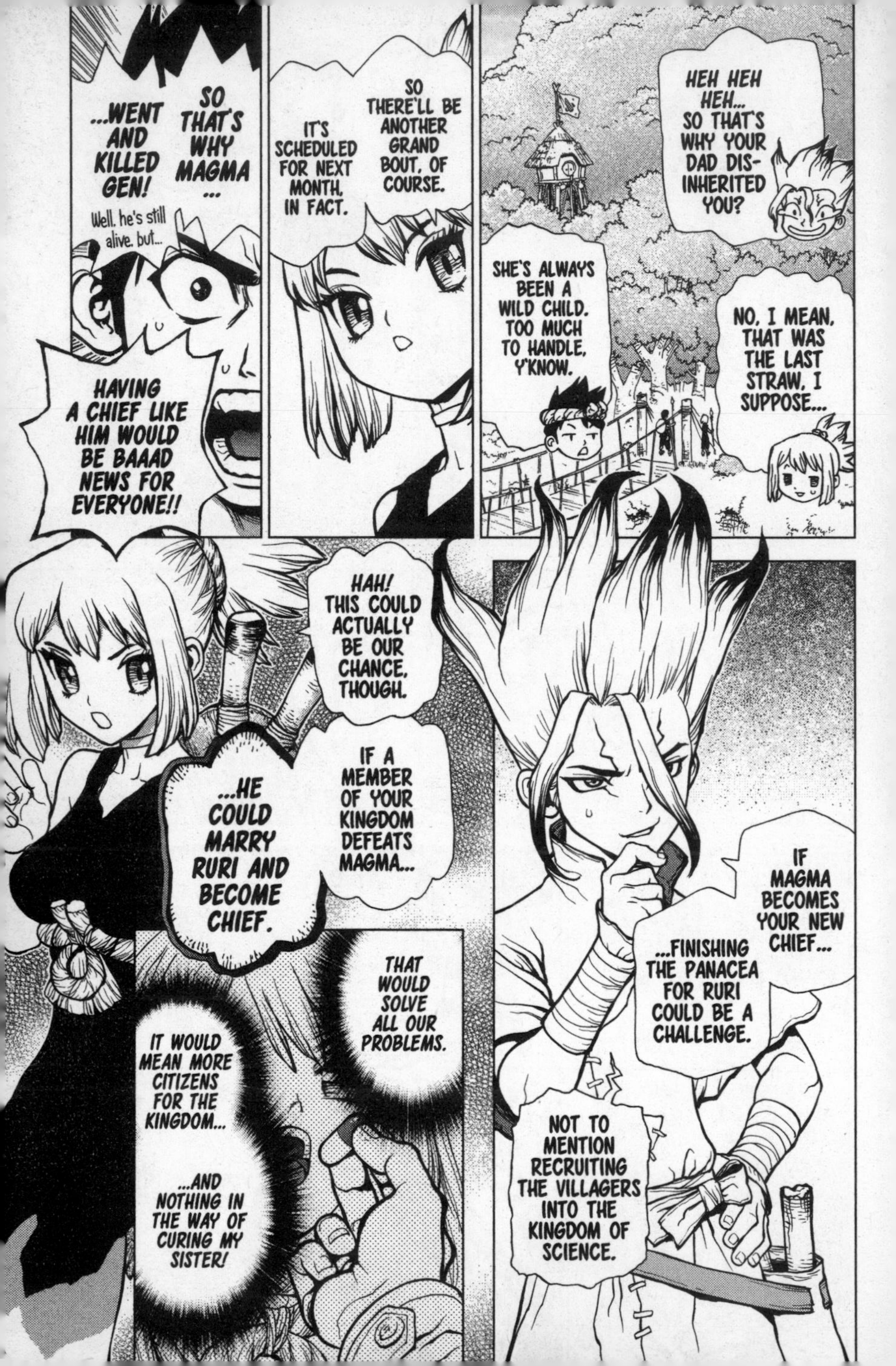
HEH HEH HEH... SO THAT'S WHY YOUR DAD DIS-INHERITED YOU?
SHE'S ALWAYS BEEN A WILD CHILD. TOO MUCH TO HANDLE, Y'KNOW.
NO, I MEAN, THAT WAS THE LAST STRAW, I SUPPOSE...
SO THERE'LL BE ANOTHER GRAND BOUT, OF COURSE.
IT'S SCHEDULED FOR NEXT MONTH, IN FACT.
SO THAT'S WHY MAGMA...
...WENT AND KILLED GEN!
Well, he's still alive, but...
HAVING A CHIEF LIKE HIM WOULD BE BAAAD NEWS FOR EVERYONE!!
IF MAGMA BECOMES YOUR NEW CHIEF...
...FINISHING THE PANACEA FOR RURI COULD BE A CHALLENGE.
NOT TO MENTION RECRUITING THE VILLAGERS INTO THE KINGDOM OF SCIENCE.
HAH! THIS COULD ACTUALLY BE OUR CHANCE, THOUGH.
IF A MEMBER OF YOUR KINGDOM DEFEATS MAGMA...
...HE COULD MARRY RURI AND BECOME CHIEF.
THAT WOULD SOLVE ALL OUR PROBLEMS.
IT WOULD MEAN MORE CITIZENS FOR THE KINGDOM...
...AND NOTHING IN THE WAY OF CURING MY SISTER!

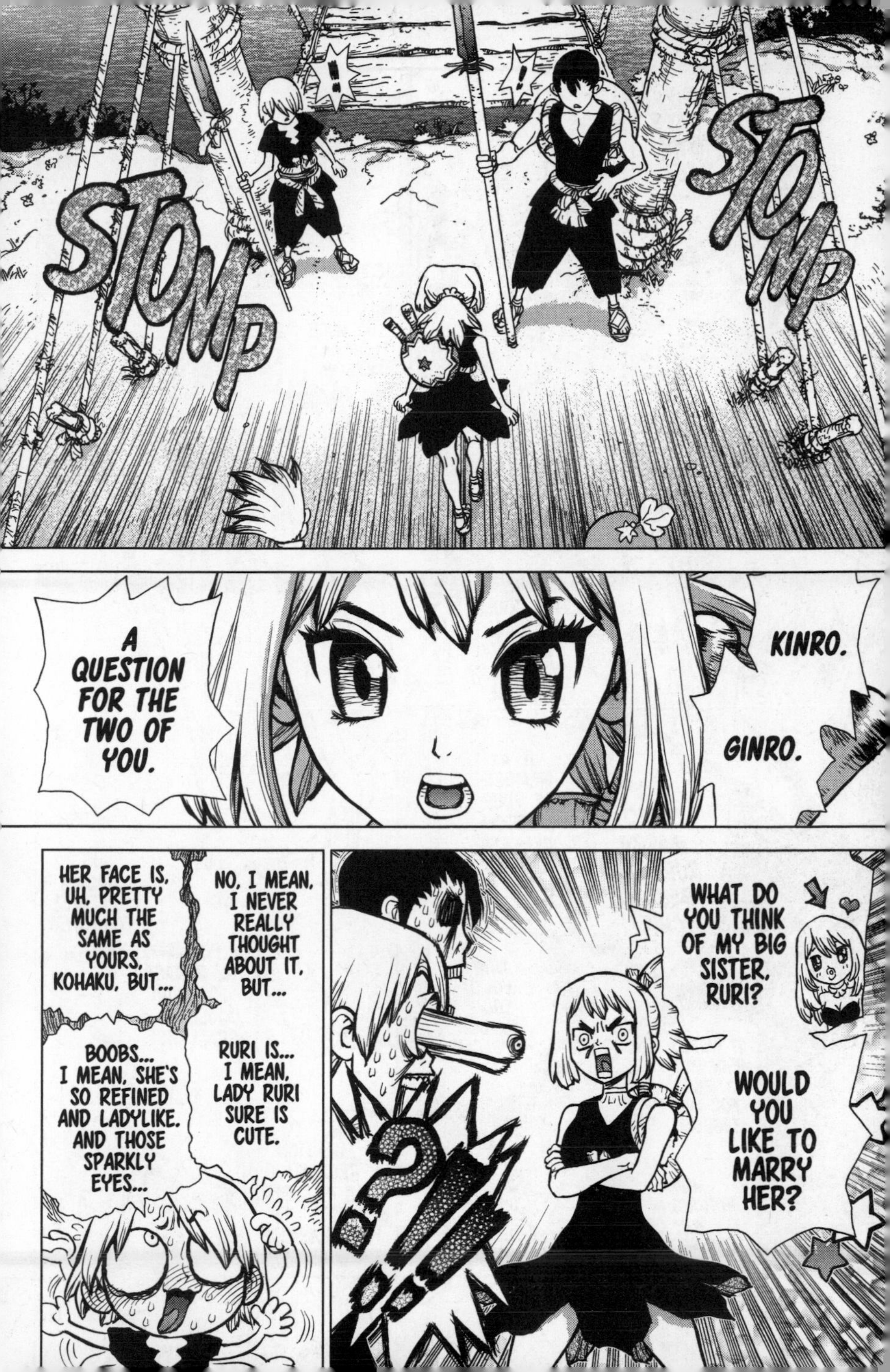
STOMP
STOMP
!!
!
KINRO.
GINRO.
A QUESTION FOR THE TWO OF YOU.
WHAT DO YOU THINK OF MY BIG SISTER, RURI?
WOULD YOU LIKE TO MARRY HER?
?!
NO, I MEAN, I NEVER REALLY THOUGHT ABOUT IT, BUT...
HER FACE IS, UH, PRETTY MUCH THE SAME AS YOURS, KOHAKU, BUT...
RURI IS... I MEAN, LADY RURI SURE IS CUTE.
BOOBS... I MEAN, SHE'S SO REFINED AND LADYLIKE. AND THOSE SPARKLY EYES...

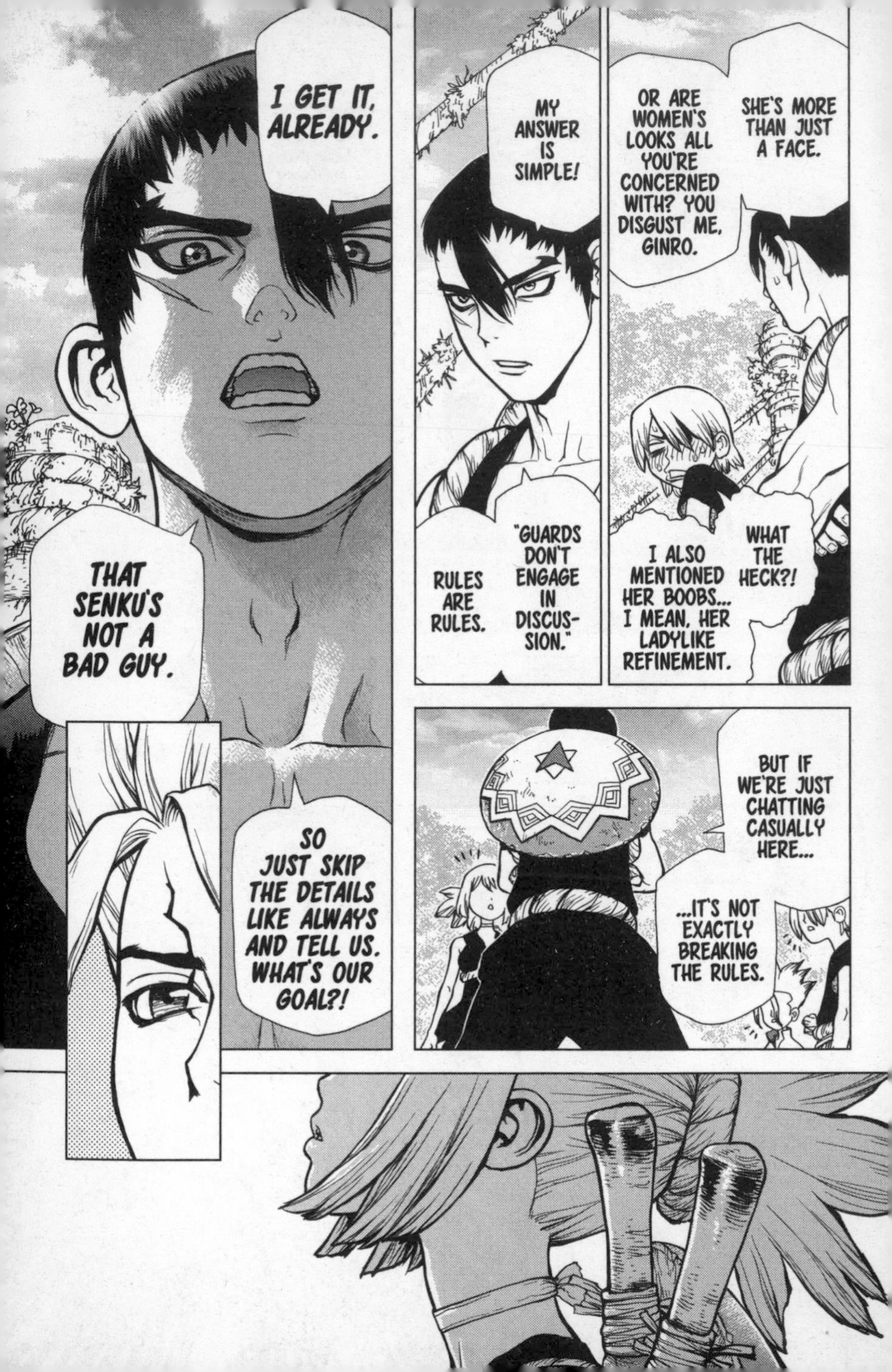

SHE'S MORE THAN JUST A FACE.
OR ARE WOMEN'S LOOKS ALL YOU'RE CONCERNED WITH? YOU DISGUST ME, GINRO.
WHAT THE HECK?!
I ALSO MENTIONED HER BOOBS... I MEAN, HER LADYLIKE REFINEMENT.
MY ANSWER IS SIMPLE!
"GUARDS DON'T ENGAGE IN DISCUSSION."
RULES ARE RULES.
BUT IF WE'RE JUST CHATTING CASUALLY HERE...
...IT'S NOT EXACTLY BREAKING THE RULES.
I GET IT, ALREADY.
THAT SENKU'S NOT A BAD GUY.
SO JUST SKIP THE DETAILS LIKE ALWAYS AND TELL US. WHAT'S OUR GOAL?!

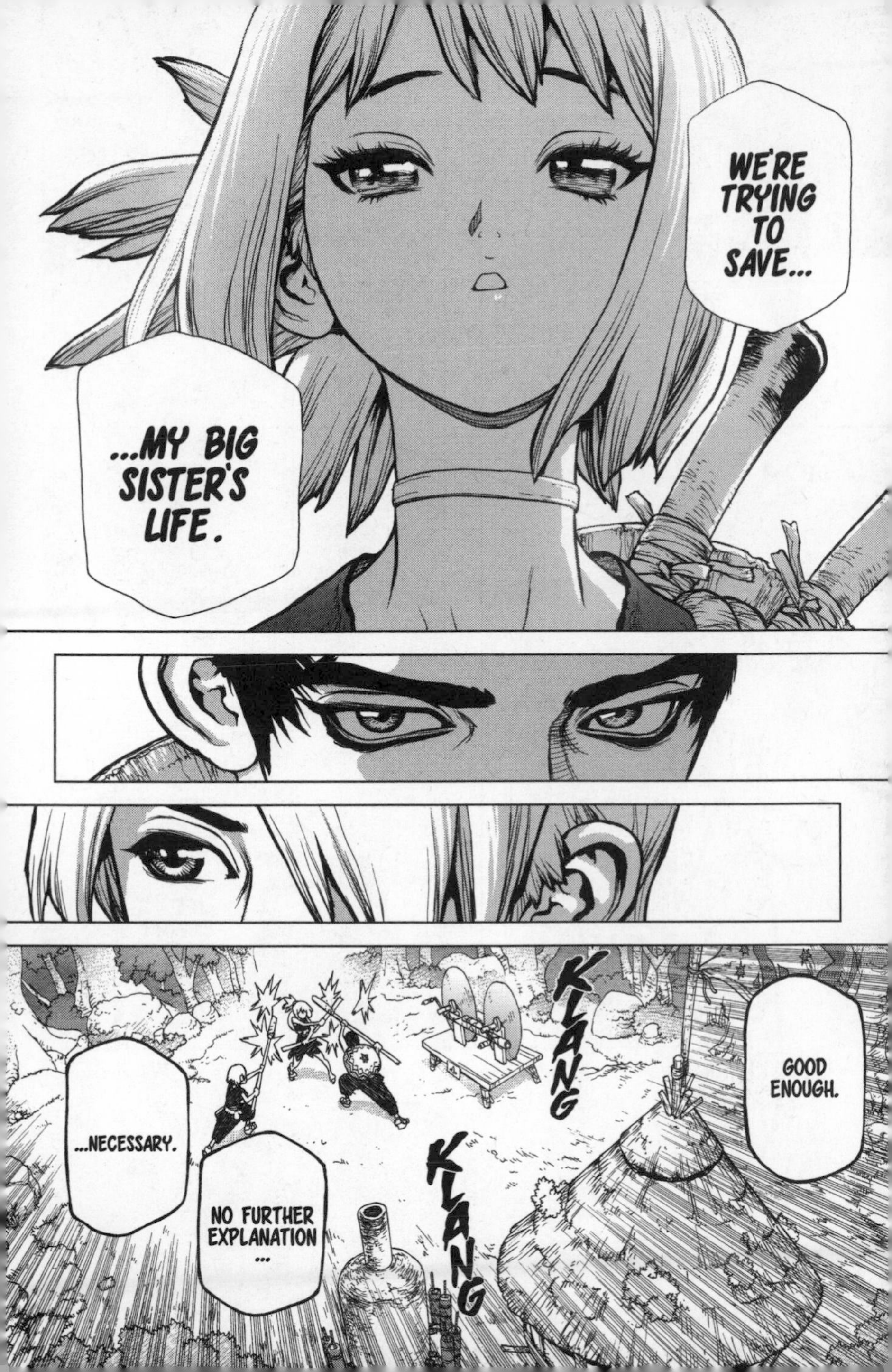
WE'RE TRYING TO SAVE...
...MY BIG SISTER'S LIFE.
GOOD ENOUGH.
KLANG
KLANG
NO FURTHER EXPLANATION ...
...NECESSARY.

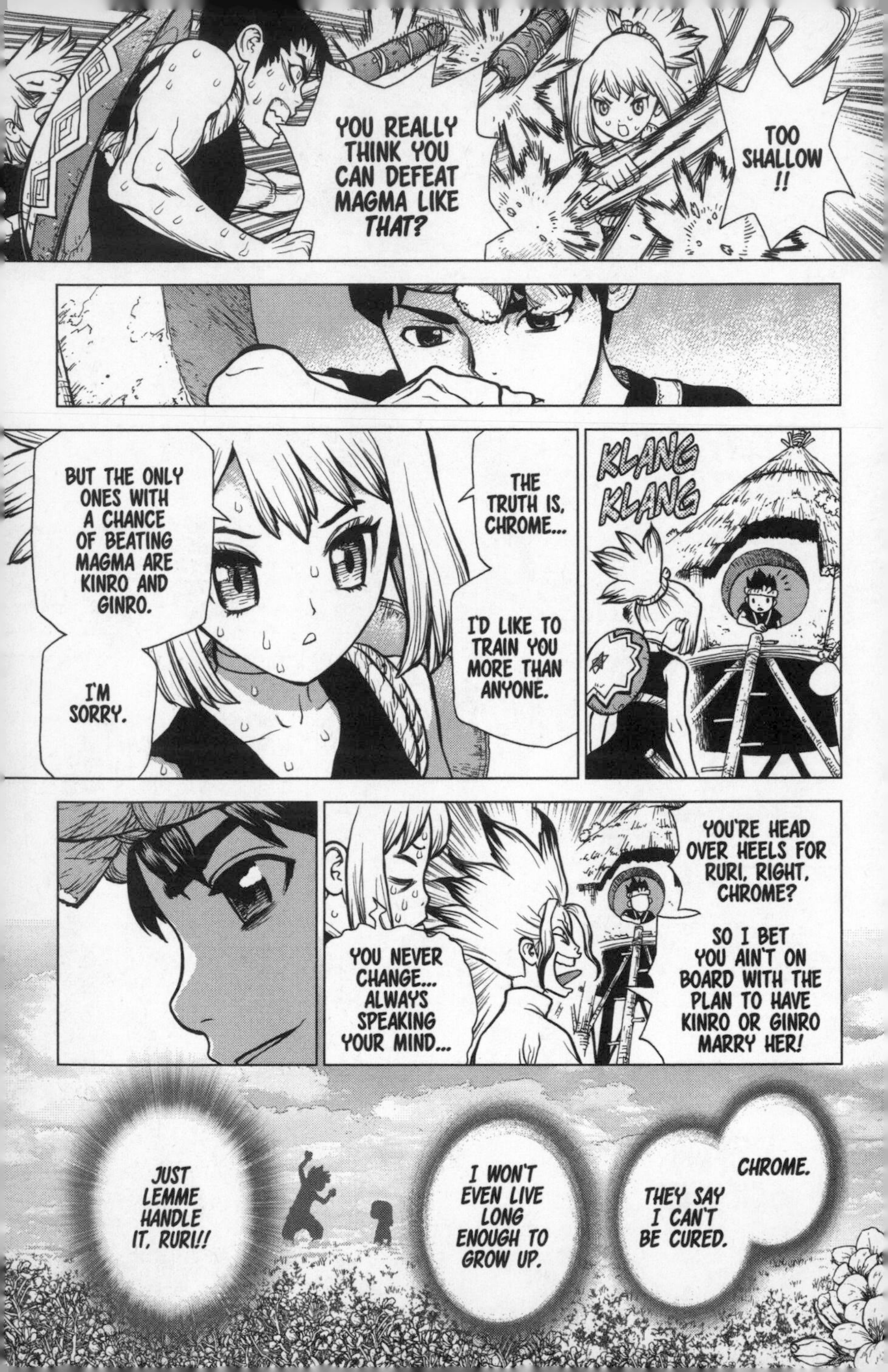
TOO SHALLOW !!
YOU REALLY THINK YOU CAN DEFEAT MAGMA LIKE THAT?
KLANG KLANG
THE TRUTH IS, CHROME...
I'D LIKE TO TRAIN YOU MORE THAN ANYONE.
BUT THE ONLY ONES WITH A CHANCE OF BEATING MAGMA ARE KINRO AND GINRO.
I'M SORRY.
YOU'RE HEAD OVER HEELS FOR RURI, RIGHT, CHROME?
SO I BET YOU AIN'T ON BOARD WITH THE PLAN TO HAVE KINRO OR GINRO MARRY HER!
YOU NEVER CHANGE... ALWAYS SPEAKING YOUR MIND...
CHROME.
THEY SAY I CAN'T BE CURED.
I WON'T EVEN LIVE LONG ENOUGH TO GROW UP.
JUST LEMME HANDLE IT, RURI!!

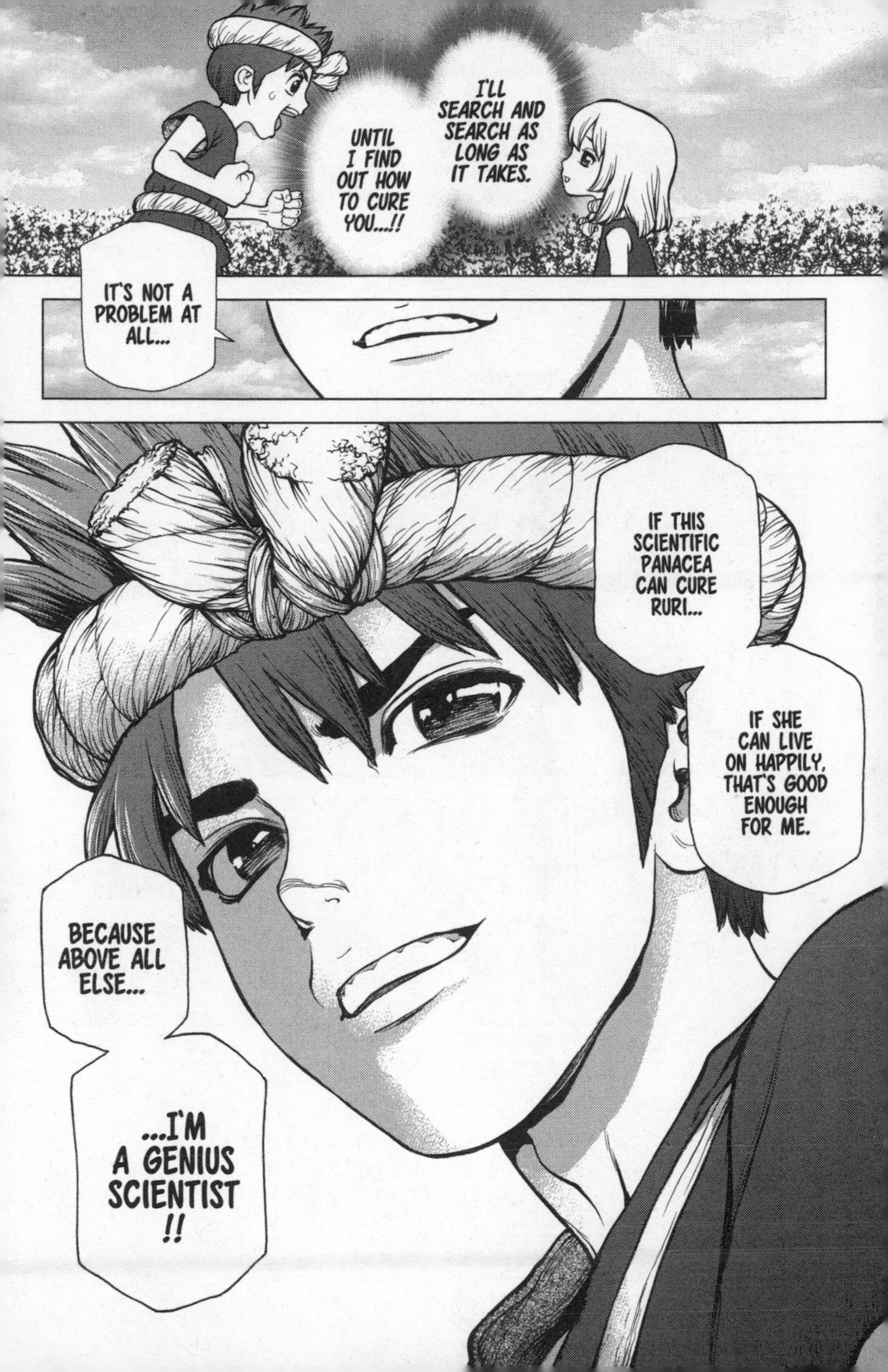
I'LL SEARCH AND SEARCH AS LONG AS IT TAKES.
UNTIL I FIND OUT HOW TO CURE YOU...!!
IT'S NOT A PROBLEM AT ALL...
IF THIS SCIENTIFIC PANACEA CAN CURE RURI...
IF SHE CAN LIVE ON HAPPILY, THAT'S GOOD ENOUGH FOR ME.
BECAUSE ABOVE ALL ELSE...
...I'M A GENIUS SCIENTIST!!

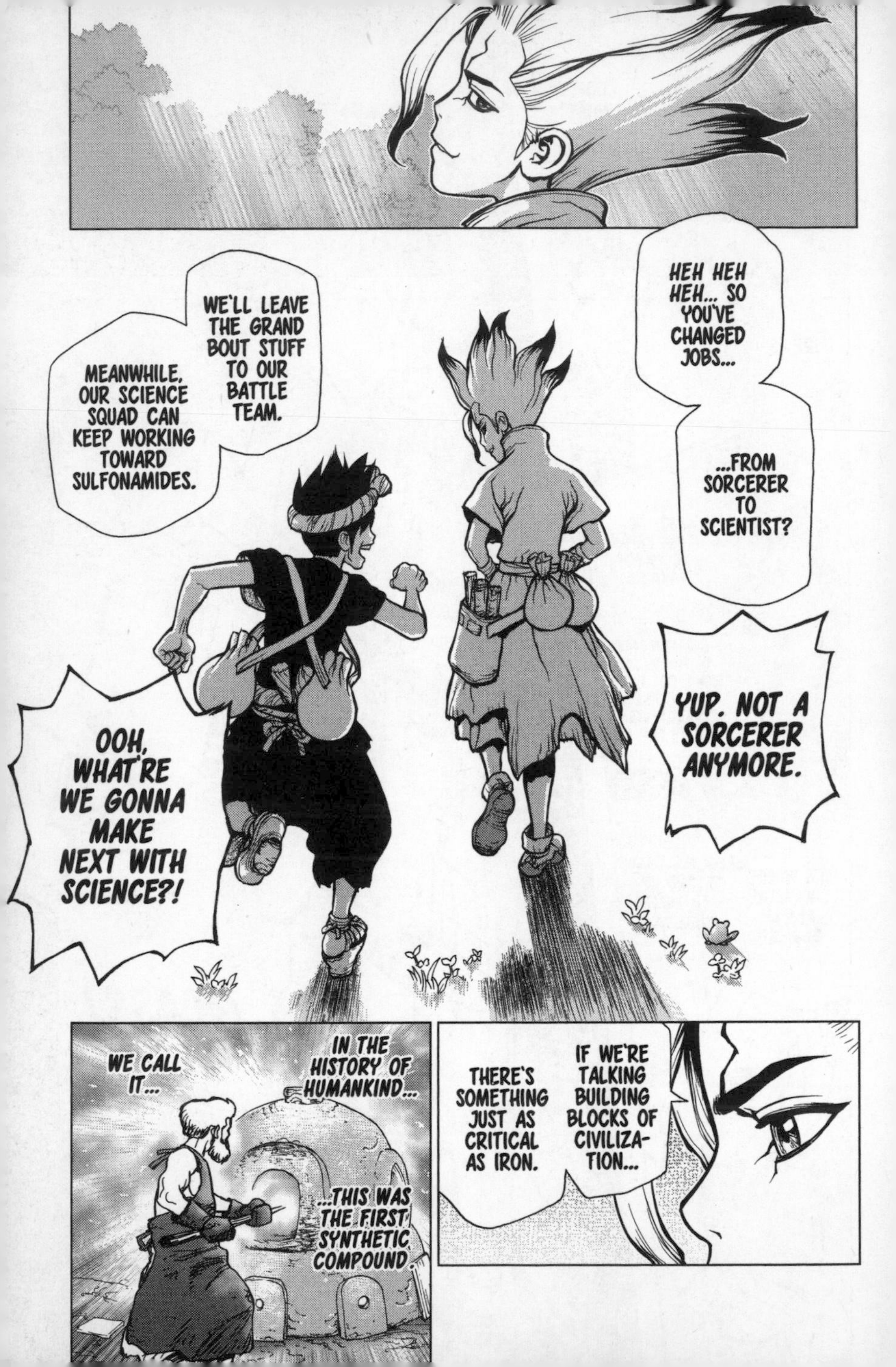
HEH HEH HEH... SO YOU'VE CHANGED JOBS...
...FROM SORCERER TO SCIENTIST?
WE'LL LEAVE THE GRAND BOUT STUFF TO OUR BATTLE TEAM.
MEANWHILE, OUR SCIENCE SQUAD CAN KEEP WORKING TOWARD SULFONAMIDES.
YUP. NOT A SORCERER ANYMORE.
OOH, WHAT'RE WE GONNA MAKE NEXT WITH SCIENCE?!
IF WE'RE TALKING BUILDING BLOCKS OF CIVILIZA-TION...
THERE'S SOMETHING JUST AS CRITICAL AS IRON.
IN THE HISTORY OF HUMANKIND...
WE CALL IT...
...THIS WAS THE FIRST SYNTHETIC COMPOUND.

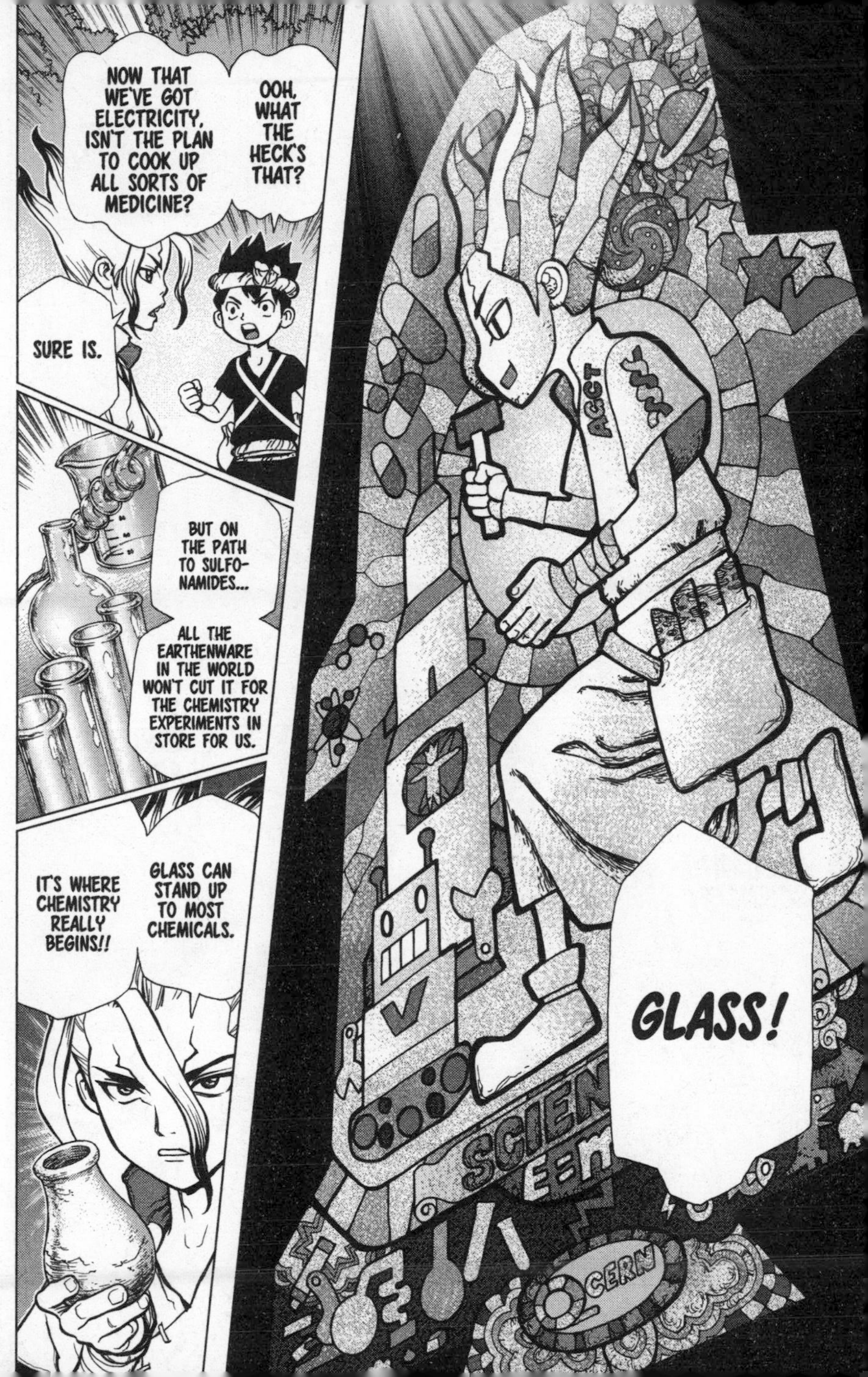

GLASS!
ACGT
CERN
NOW THAT WE'VE GOT ELECTRICITY, ISN'T THE PLAN TO COOK UP ALL SORTS OF MEDICINE?
OOH, WHAT THE HECK'S THAT?
SURE IS.
BUT ON THE PATH TO SULFONAMIDES...
ALL THE EARTHENWARE IN THE WORLD WON'T CUT IT FOR THE CHEMISTRY EXPERIMENTS IN STORE FOR US.
GLASS CAN STAND UP TO MOST CHEMICALS.
IT'S WHERE CHEMISTRY REALLY BEGINS!!

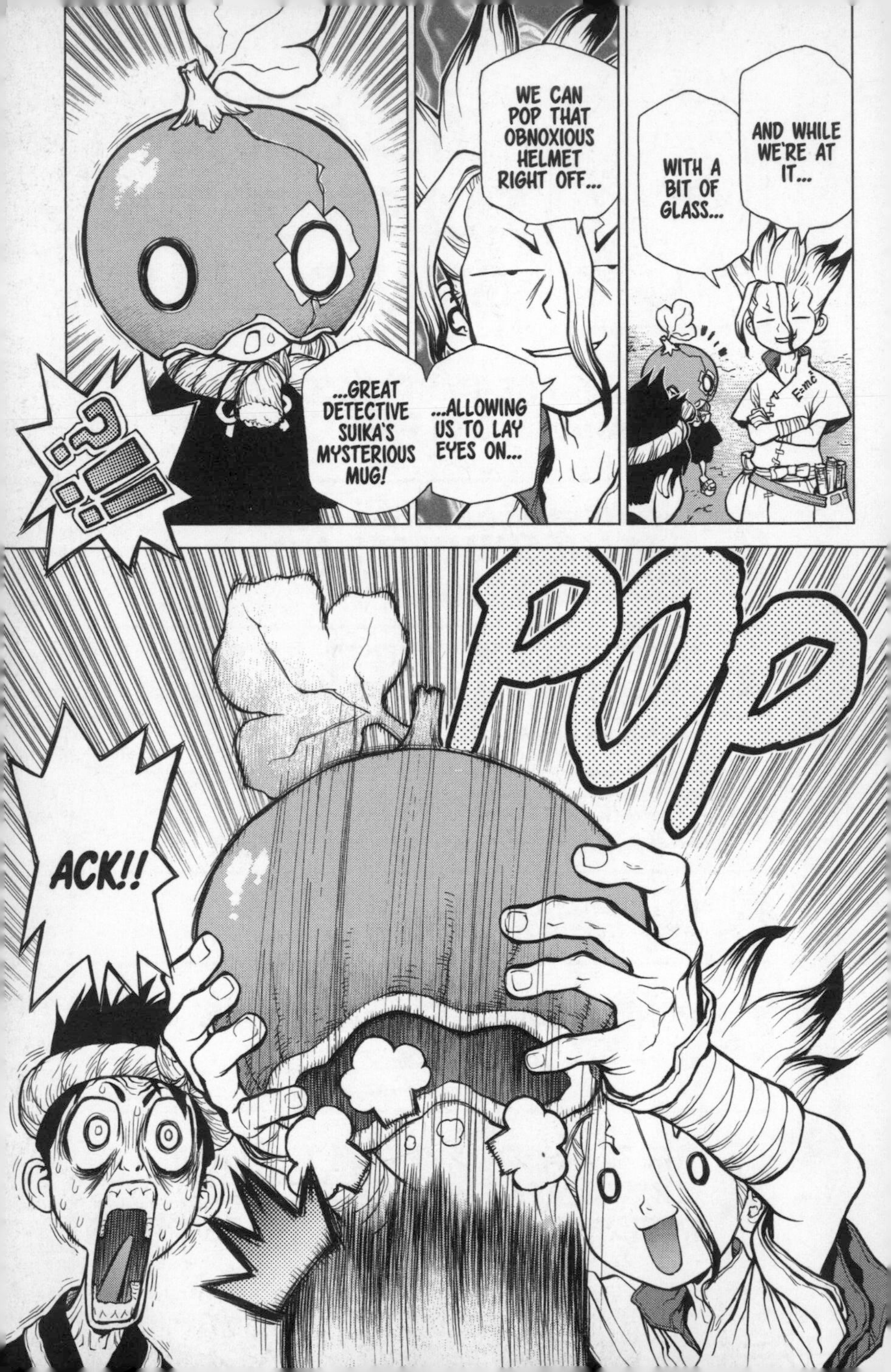
AND WHILE WE'RE AT IT...
WITH A BIT OF GLASS...
WE CAN POP THAT OBNOXIOUS HELMET RIGHT OFF...
...ALLOWING US TO LAY EYES ON...
...GREAT DETECTIVE SUIKA'S MYSTERIOUS MUG!
?!!
POP
ACK!!

THE SEVEN RULES OF THE GRAND BOUT

1. ANYONE AGE 14 OR OLDER AND UNMARRIED CAN PARTICIPATE

2. THE WINNER MARRIES THE CURRENT SHAMANESS AND BECOMES VILLAGE CHIEF

3. MATCHES ARE DECIDED BY SURRENDER, RING OUT OR WHEN ONE COMBATANT IS INCAPACITATED

4. BLADED WEAPONS AND PROJECTILES ARE FORBIDDEN

5. ATTACKS FROM SPECTATORS ARE FORBIDDEN

6. PUNISHMENT FOR INFRACTIONS WILL FIT THE CRIME

7. THE RUNNER-UP FROM THE LAST TOURNAMENT WILL SERVE AS REFEREE AND ENFORCE THESE RULES

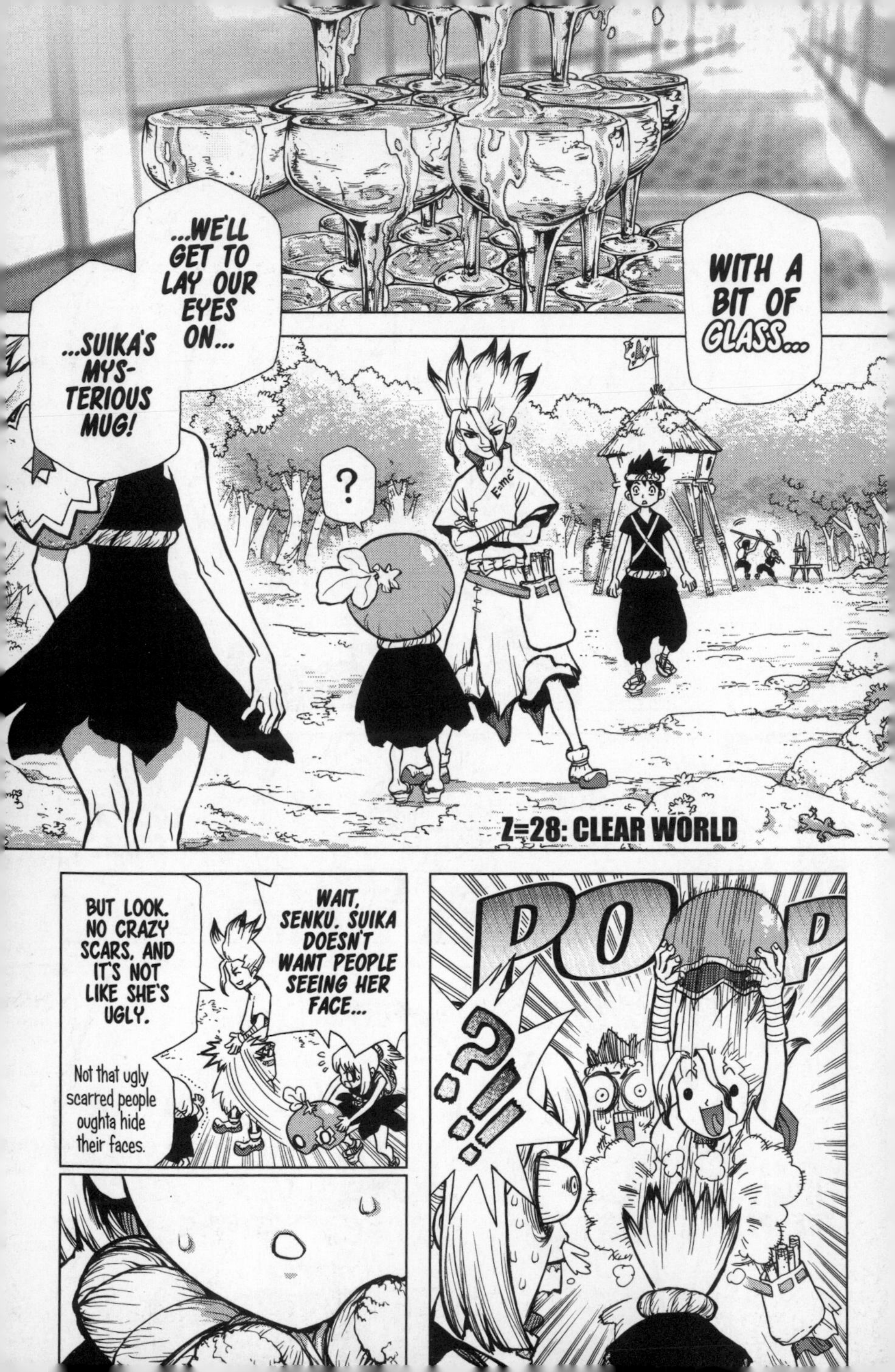
WITH A BIT OF GLASS...
...WE'LL GET TO LAY OUR EYES ON...
...SUIKA'S MYS-TERIOUS MUG!
?
Z=28: CLEAR WORLD
POP
?!!
WAIT, SENKU. SUIKA DOESN'T WANT PEOPLE SEEING HER FACE...
BUT LOOK. NO CRAZY SCARS, AND IT'S NOT LIKE SHE'S UGLY.
Not that ugly scarred people oughta hide their faces.

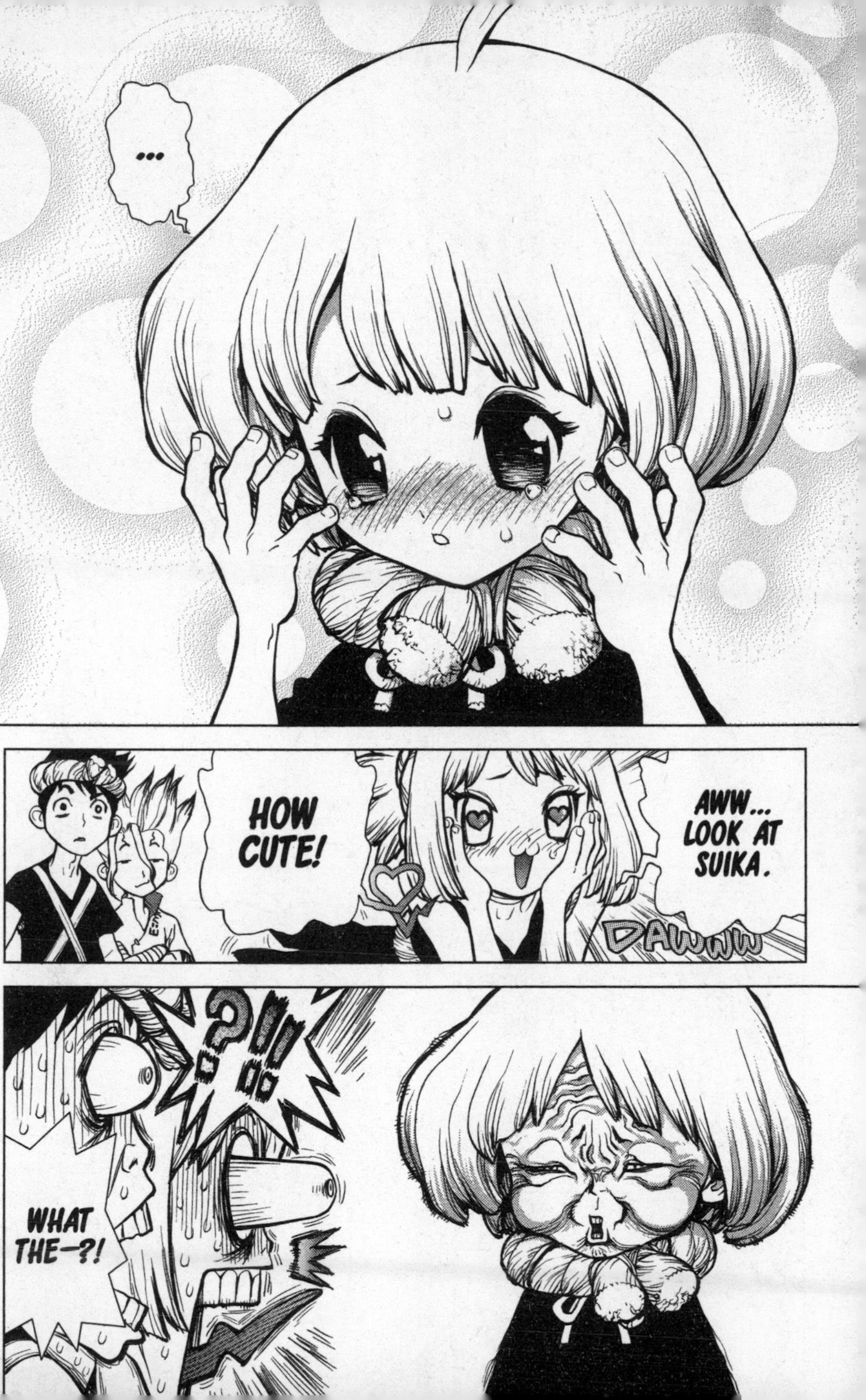
...
AWW... LOOK AT SUIKA.
HOW CUTE!
DAWWW
?!!
WHAT THE—?!

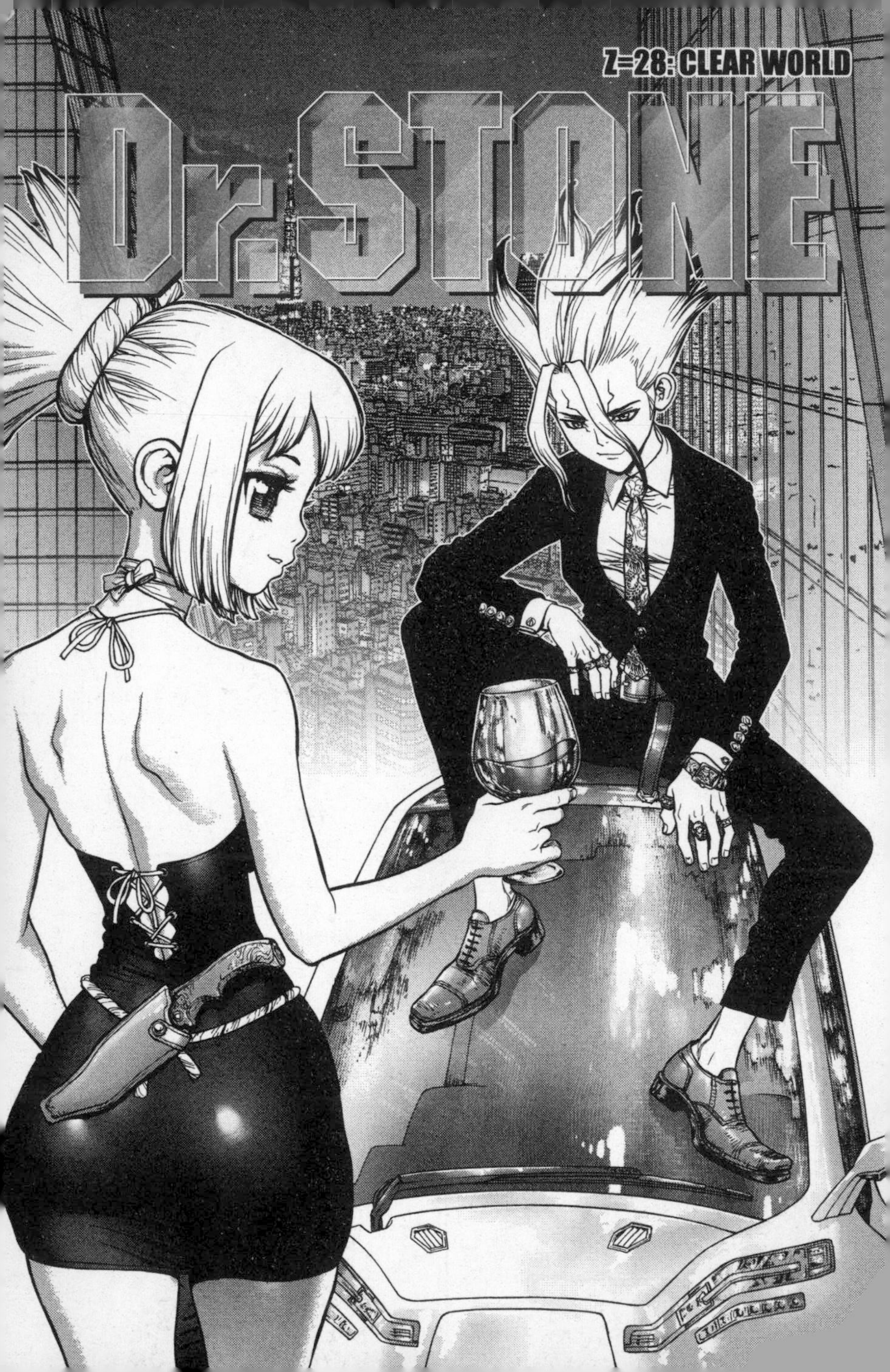
Z=28: CLEAR WORLD
Dr.STONE

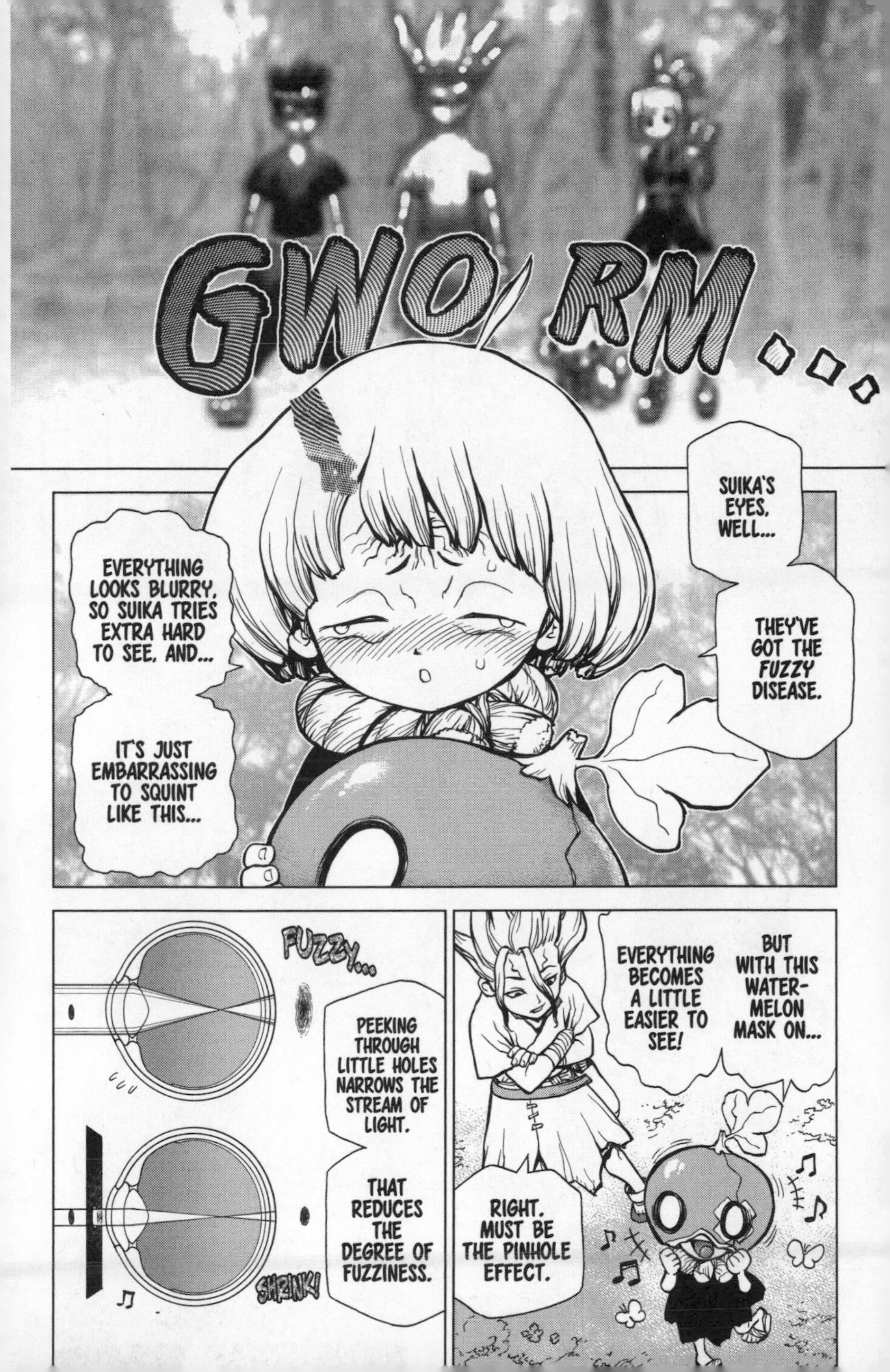
GWORM...
SUIKA'S EYES, WELL...
THEY'VE GOT THE FUZZY DISEASE.
EVERYTHING LOOKS BLURRY, SO SUIKA TRIES EXTRA HARD TO SEE, AND...
IT'S JUST EMBARRASSING TO SQUINT LIKE THIS...
BUT WITH THIS WATER-MELON MASK ON...
EVERYTHING BECOMES A LITTLE EASIER TO SEE!
RIGHT. MUST BE THE PINHOLE EFFECT.
FUZZY...
PEEKING THROUGH LITTLE HOLES NARROWS THE STREAM OF LIGHT.
THAT REDUCES THE DEGREE OF FUZZINESS.
SHRINK!

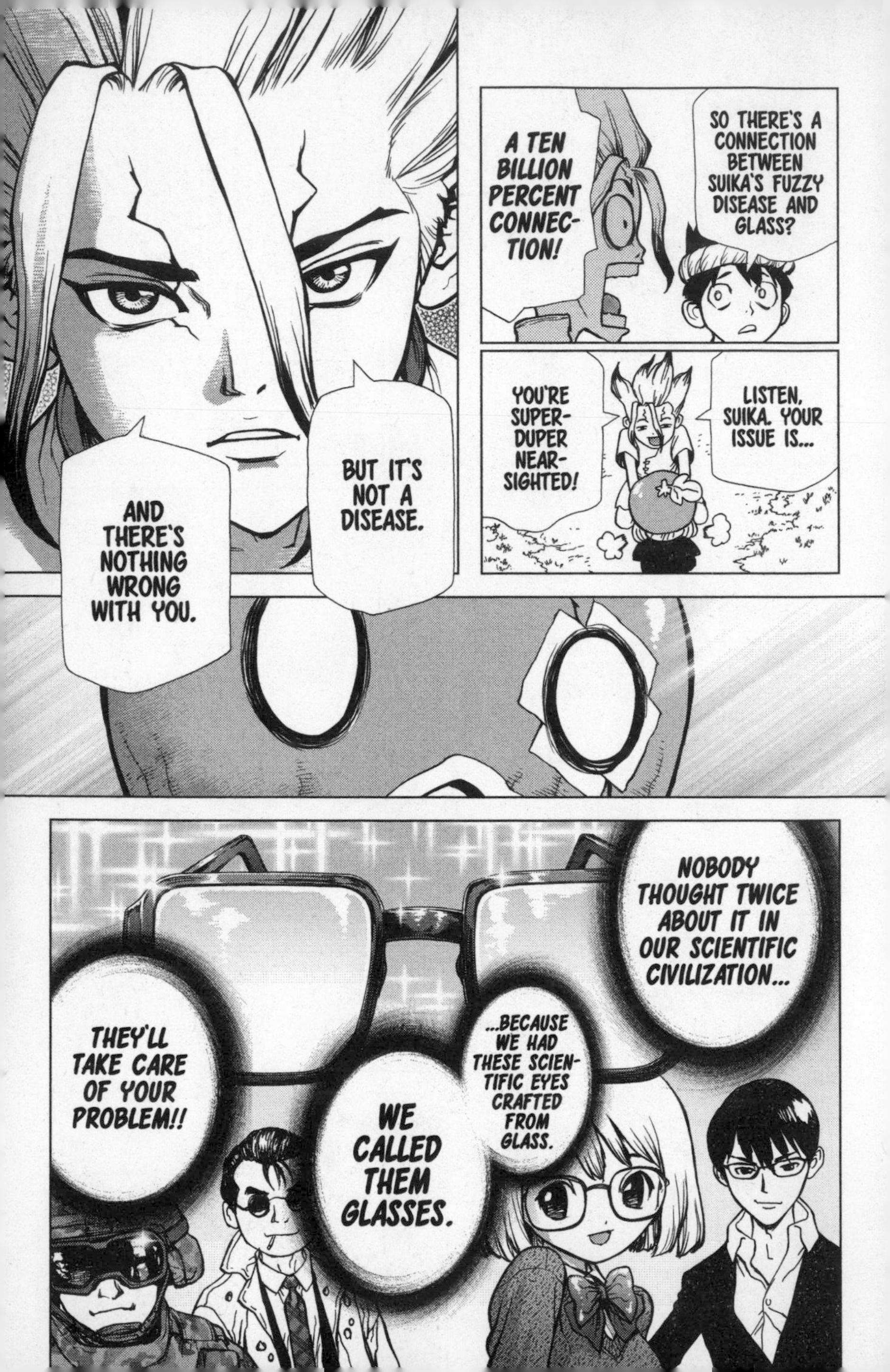
SO THERE'S A CONNECTION BETWEEN SUIKA'S FUZZY DISEASE AND GLASS?
A TEN BILLION PERCENT CONNECTION!
LISTEN, SUIKA. YOUR ISSUE IS...
YOU'RE SUPER-DUPER NEARSIGHTED!
BUT IT'S NOT A DISEASE.
AND THERE'S NOTHING WRONG WITH YOU.
NOBODY THOUGHT TWICE ABOUT IT IN OUR SCIENTIFIC CIVILIZATION...
...BECAUSE WE HAD THESE SCIENTIFIC EYES CRAFTED FROM GLASS.
WE CALLED THEM GLASSES.
THEY'LL TAKE CARE OF YOUR PROBLEM!!

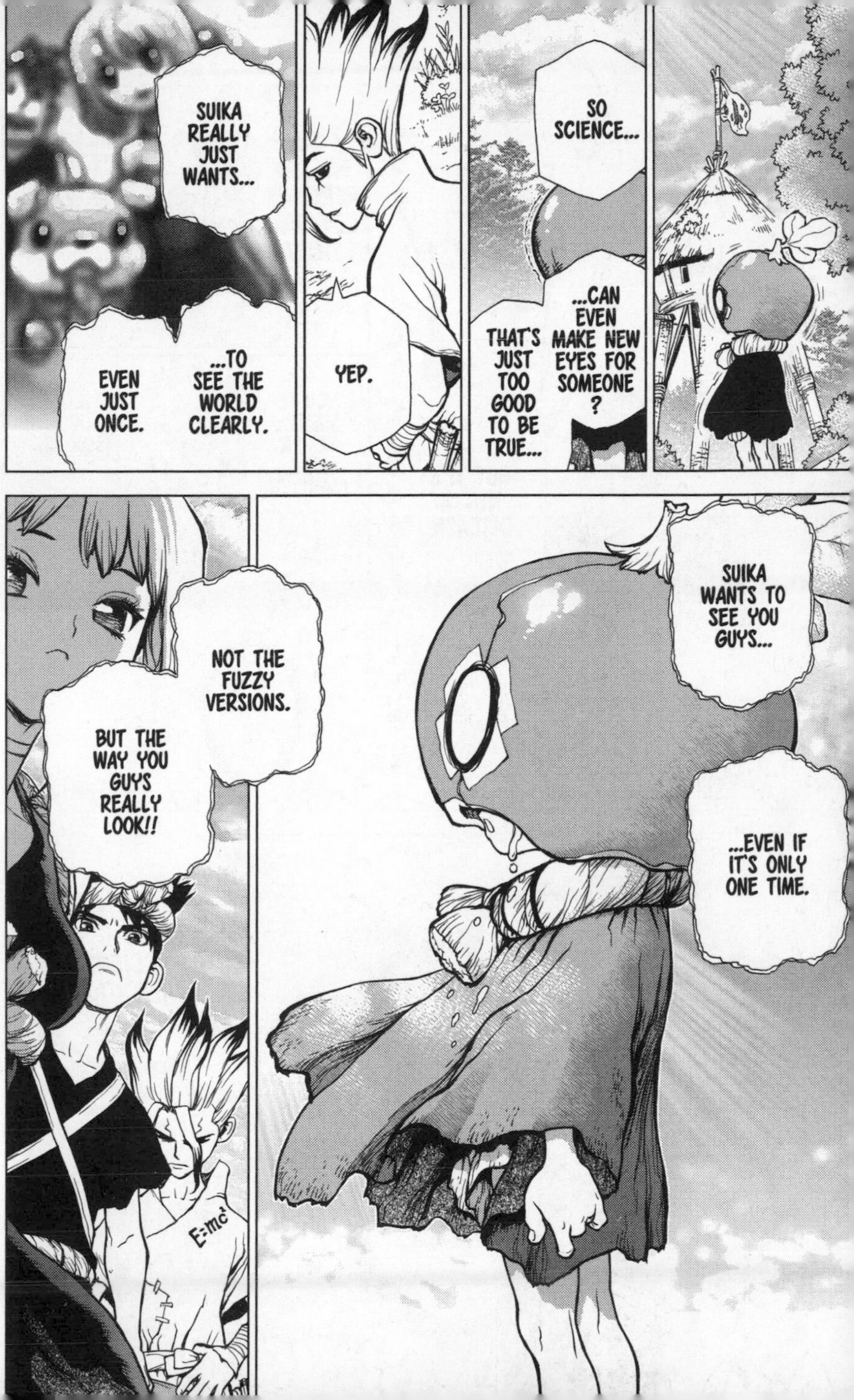
SO SCIENCE...
...CAN EVEN MAKE NEW EYES FOR SOMEONE?
THAT'S JUST TOO GOOD TO BE TRUE...
YEP.
SUIKA REALLY JUST WANTS...
...TO SEE THE WORLD CLEARLY.
EVEN JUST ONCE.
SUIKA WANTS TO SEE YOU GUYS...
...EVEN IF IT'S ONLY ONE TIME.
NOT THE FUZZY VERSIONS.
BUT THE WAY YOU GUYS REALLY LOOK!!
$E=mc^2$

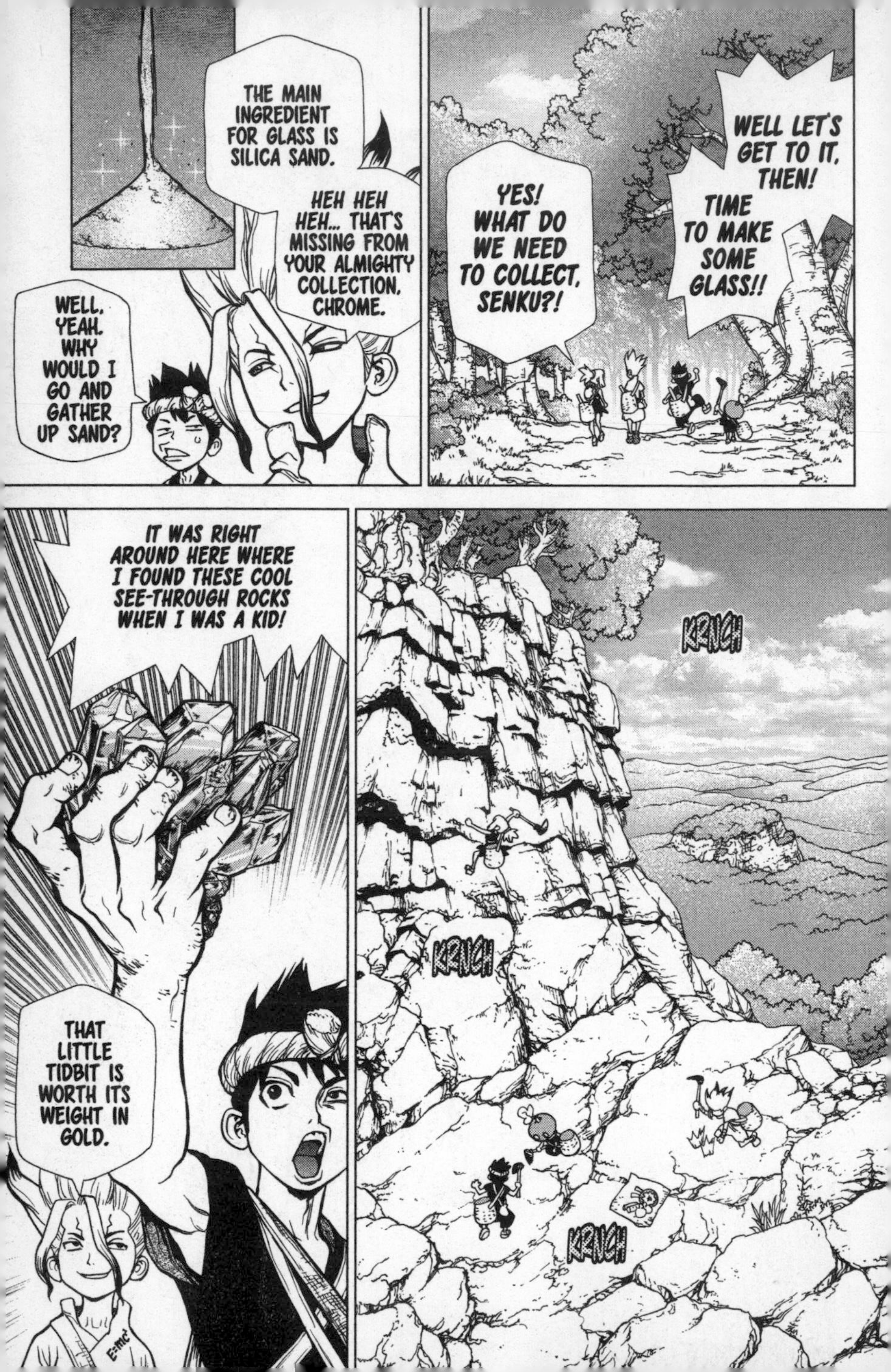
WELL LET'S GET TO IT, THEN!
TIME TO MAKE SOME GLASS!!
YES! WHAT DO WE NEED TO COLLECT, SENKU?!
THE MAIN INGREDIENT FOR GLASS IS SILICA SAND.
HEH HEH HEH... THAT'S MISSING FROM YOUR ALMIGHTY COLLECTION, CHROME.
WELL, YEAH. WHY WOULD I GO AND GATHER UP SAND?
KRNCH
KRNCH
KRNCH
IT WAS RIGHT AROUND HERE WHERE I FOUND THESE COOL SEE-THROUGH ROCKS WHEN I WAS A KID!
THAT LITTLE TIDBIT IS WORTH ITS WEIGHT IN GOLD.
E=mc²

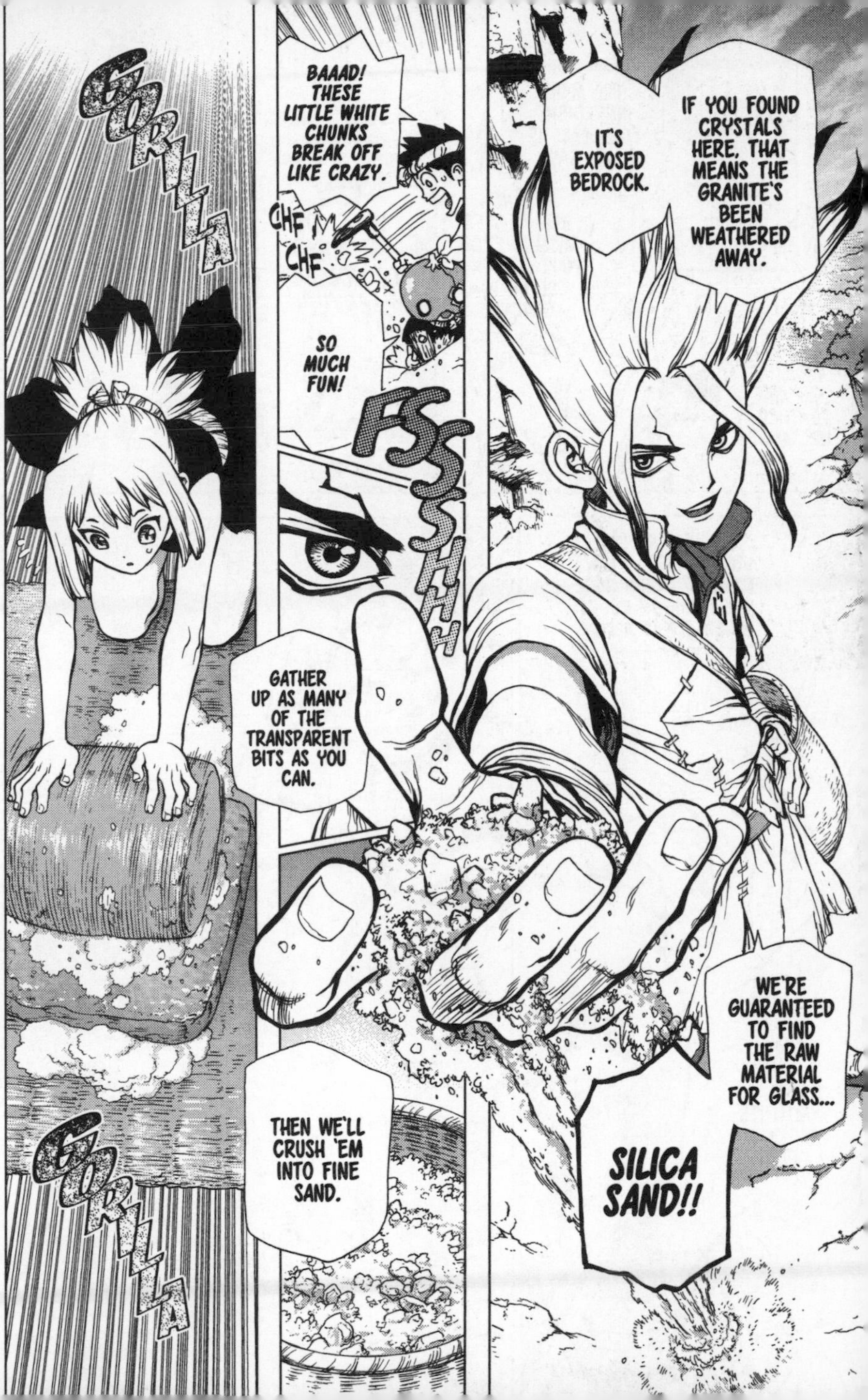
IF YOU FOUND CRYSTALS HERE, THAT MEANS THE GRANITE'S BEEN WEATHERED AWAY.
IT'S EXPOSED BEDROCK.
WE'RE GUARANTEED TO FIND THE RAW MATERIAL FOR GLASS...
SILICA SAND!!
BAAAD! THESE LITTLE WHITE CHUNKS BREAK OFF LIKE CRAZY.
CHF
CHF
SO MUCH FUN!
FSSSHHHH
GATHER UP AS MANY OF THE TRANSPARENT BITS AS YOU CAN.
THEN WE'LL CRUSH 'EM INTO FINE SAND.
GORILLA
GORILLA

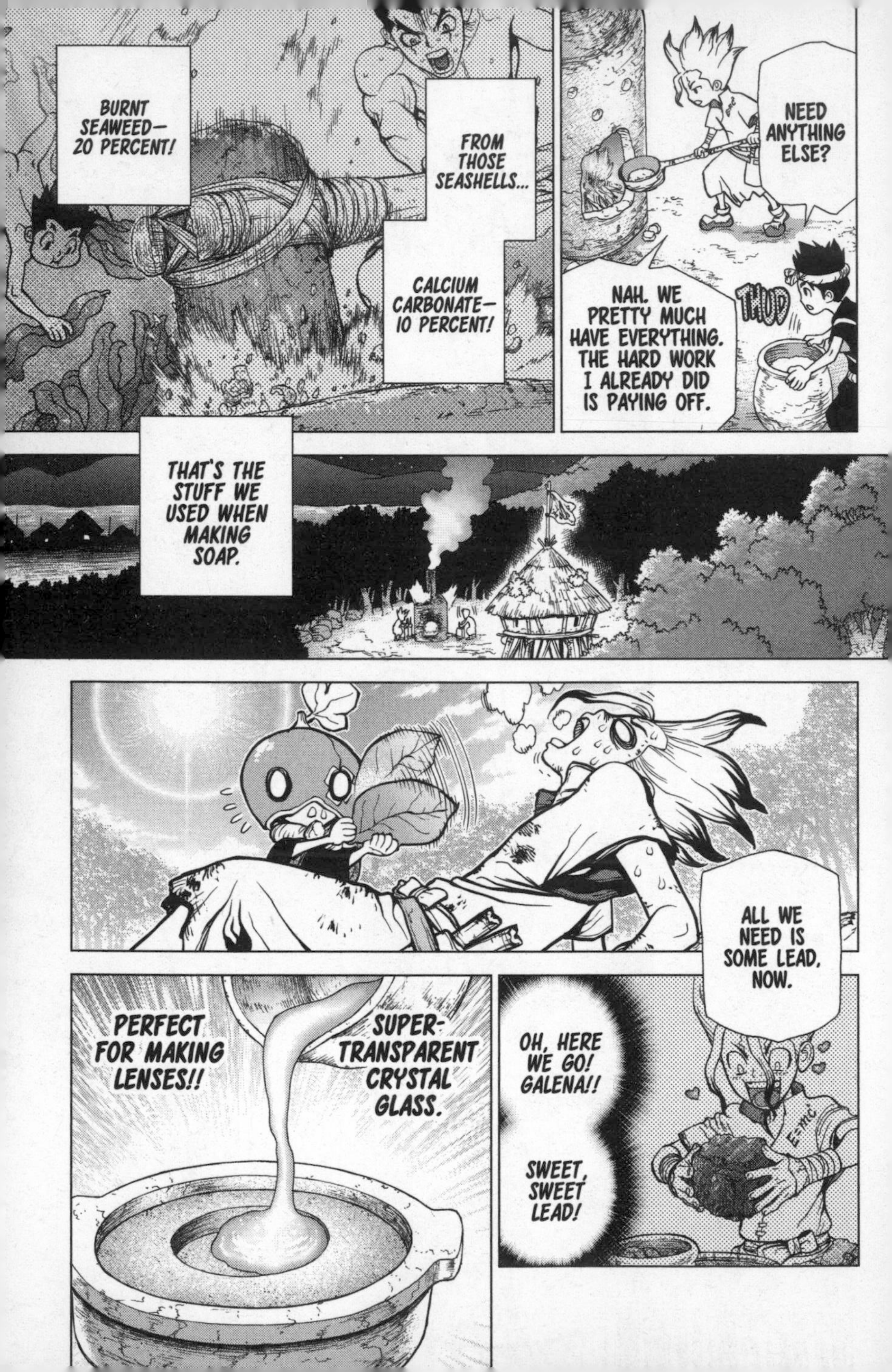
NEED ANYTHING ELSE?
THUD
NAH. WE PRETTY MUCH HAVE EVERYTHING. THE HARD WORK I ALREADY DID IS PAYING OFF.
BURNT SEAWEED—20 PERCENT!
FROM THOSE SEASHELLS...
CALCIUM CARBONATE—10 PERCENT!
THAT'S THE STUFF WE USED WHEN MAKING SOAP.
ALL WE NEED IS SOME LEAD, NOW.
OH, HERE WE GO! GALENA!!
SWEET, SWEET LEAD!
SUPER-TRANSPARENT CRYSTAL GLASS.
PERFECT FOR MAKING LENSES!!

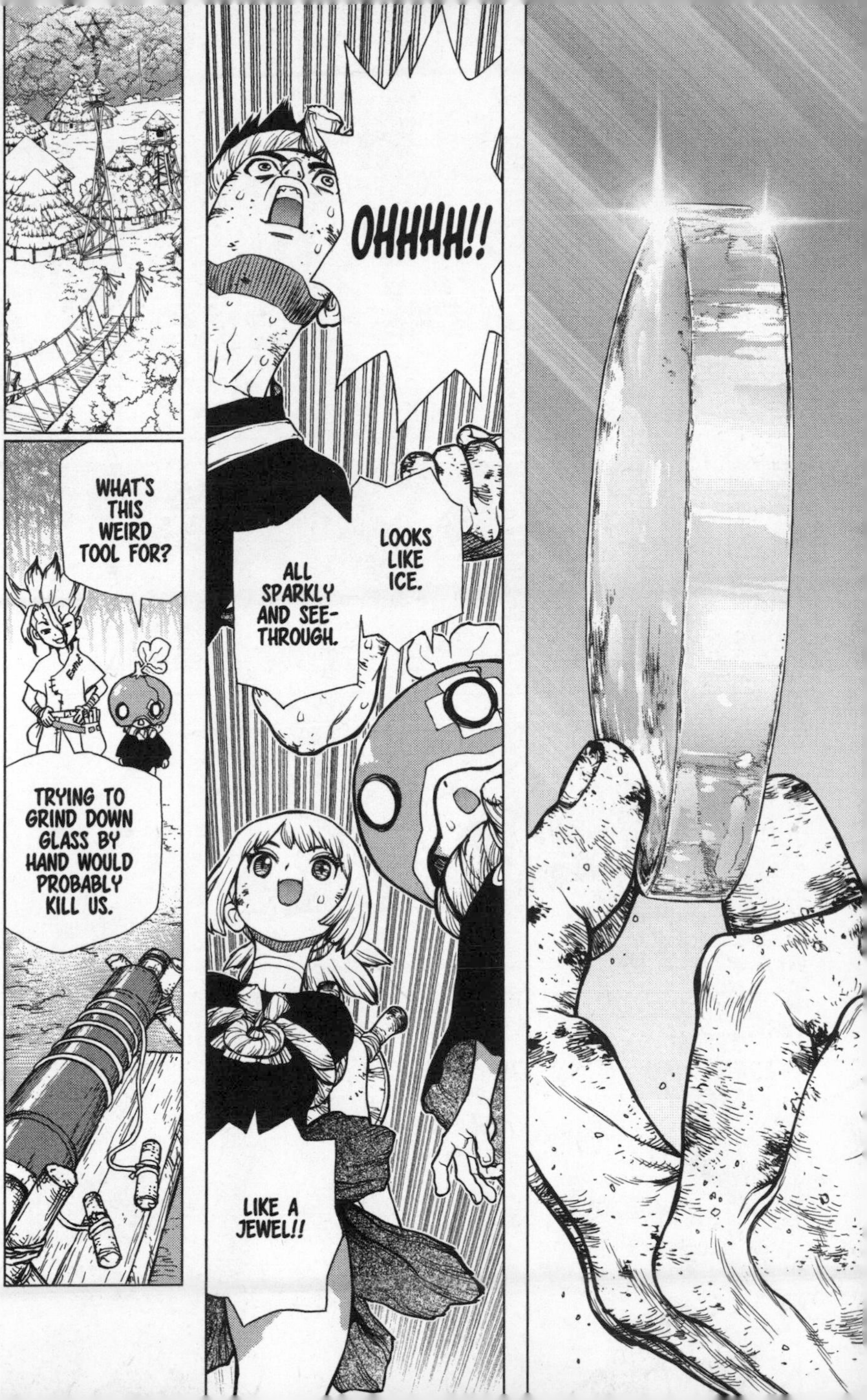

OHHHH!!
LOOKS LIKE ICE.
ALL SPARKLY AND SEE-THROUGH.
LIKE A JEWEL!!
WHAT'S THIS WEIRD TOOL FOR?
TRYING TO GRIND DOWN GLASS BY HAND WOULD PROBABLY KILL US.

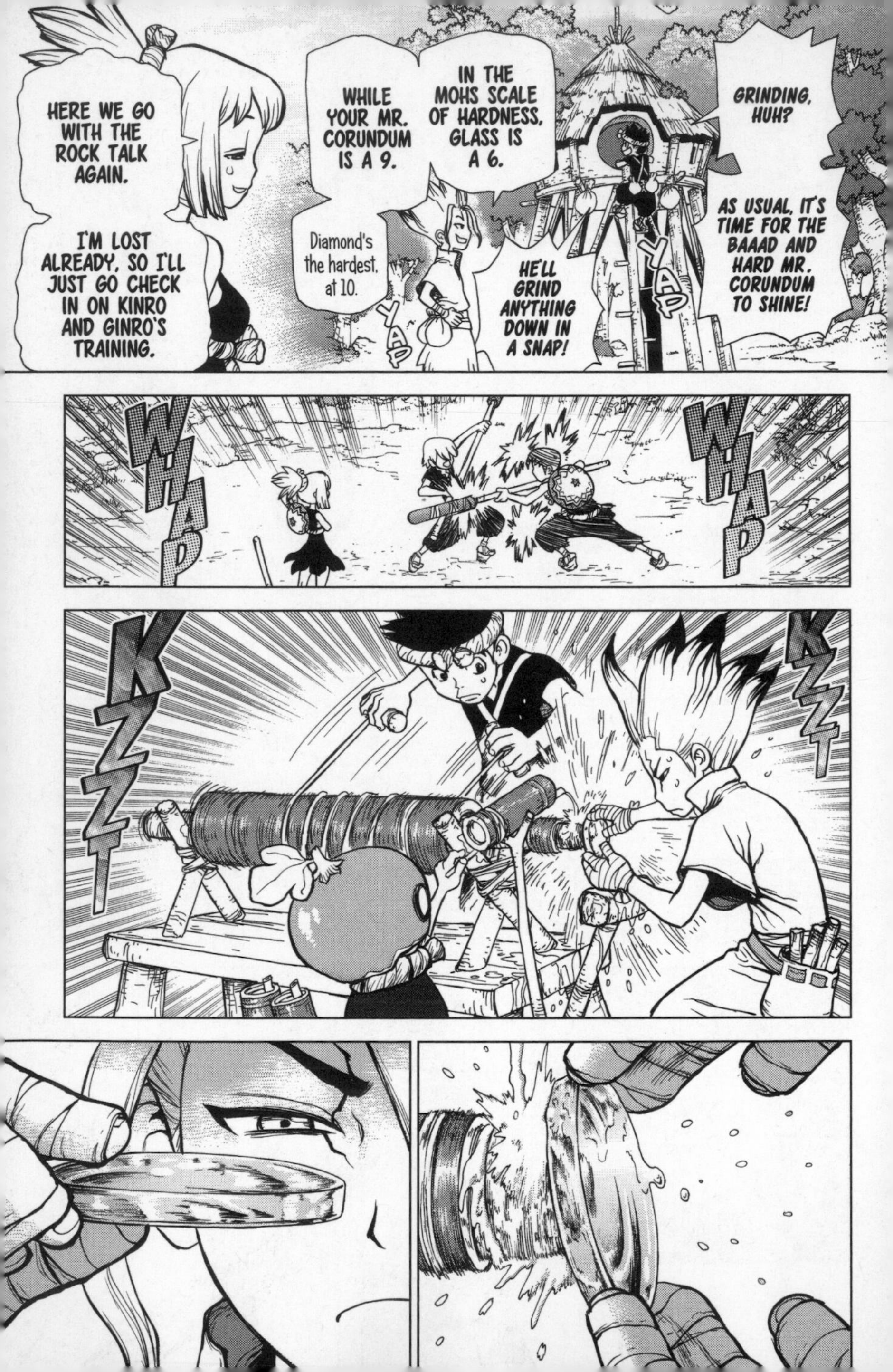
GRINDING, HUH?
AS USUAL, IT'S TIME FOR THE BAAAD AND HARD MR. CORUNDUM TO SHINE!
YAP
HE'LL GRIND ANYTHING DOWN IN A SNAP!
IN THE MOHS SCALE OF HARDNESS, GLASS IS A 6.
WHILE YOUR MR. CORUNDUM IS A 9.
Diamond's the hardest, at 10.
YAP
HERE WE GO WITH THE ROCK TALK AGAIN.
I'M LOST ALREADY, SO I'LL JUST GO CHECK IN ON KINRO AND GINRO'S TRAINING.
WHAP
WHAP
KZZZT
KZZZT

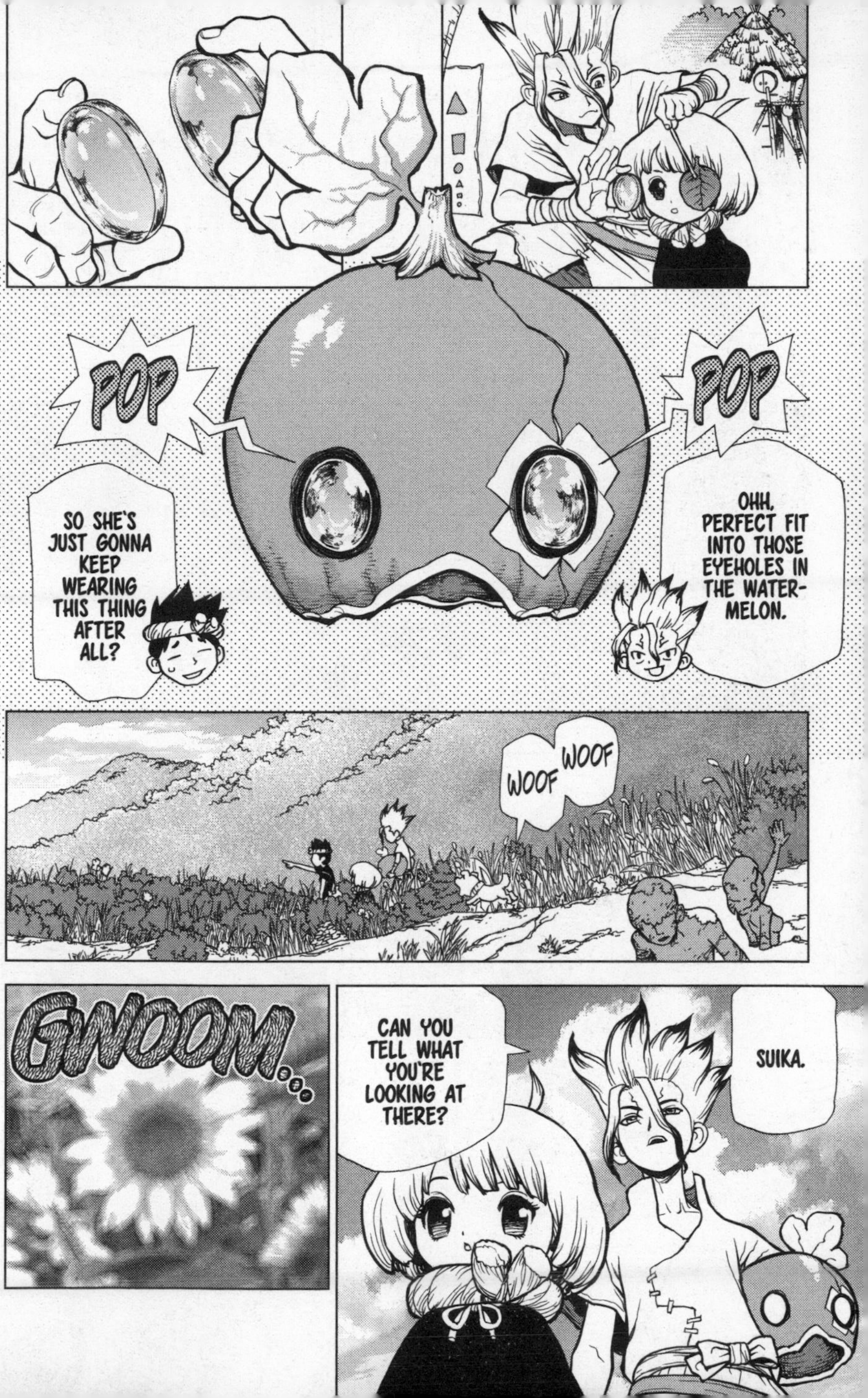
POP
POP
OHH, PERFECT FIT INTO THOSE EYEHOLES IN THE WATER-MELON.
SO SHE'S JUST GONNA KEEP WEARING THIS THING AFTER ALL?
WOOF
WOOF
SUIKA.
CAN YOU TELL WHAT YOU'RE LOOKING AT THERE?
GWOOM...

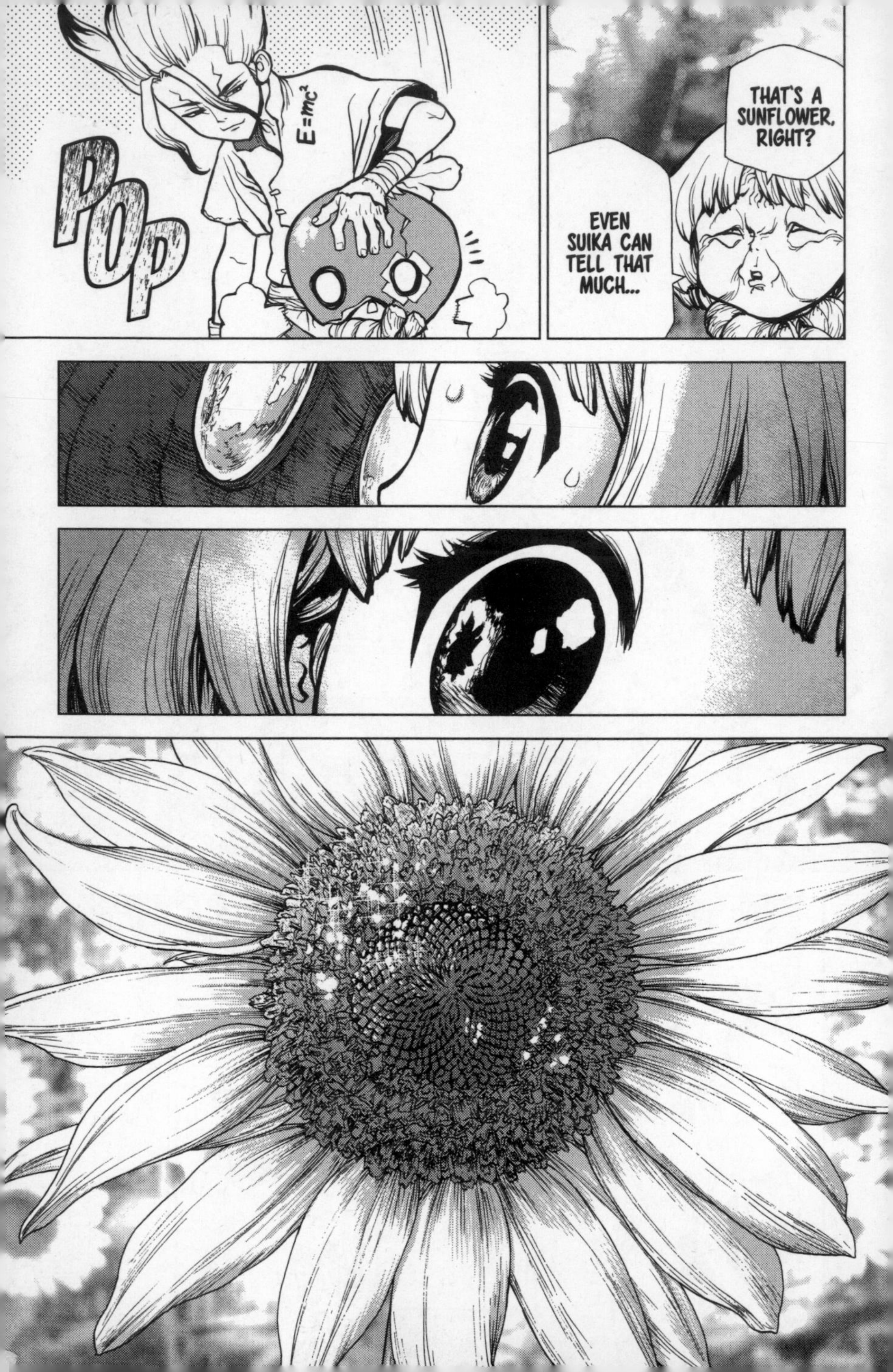
THAT'S A SUNFLOWER, RIGHT?
EVEN SUIKA CAN TELL THAT MUCH...
E=mc²
POP

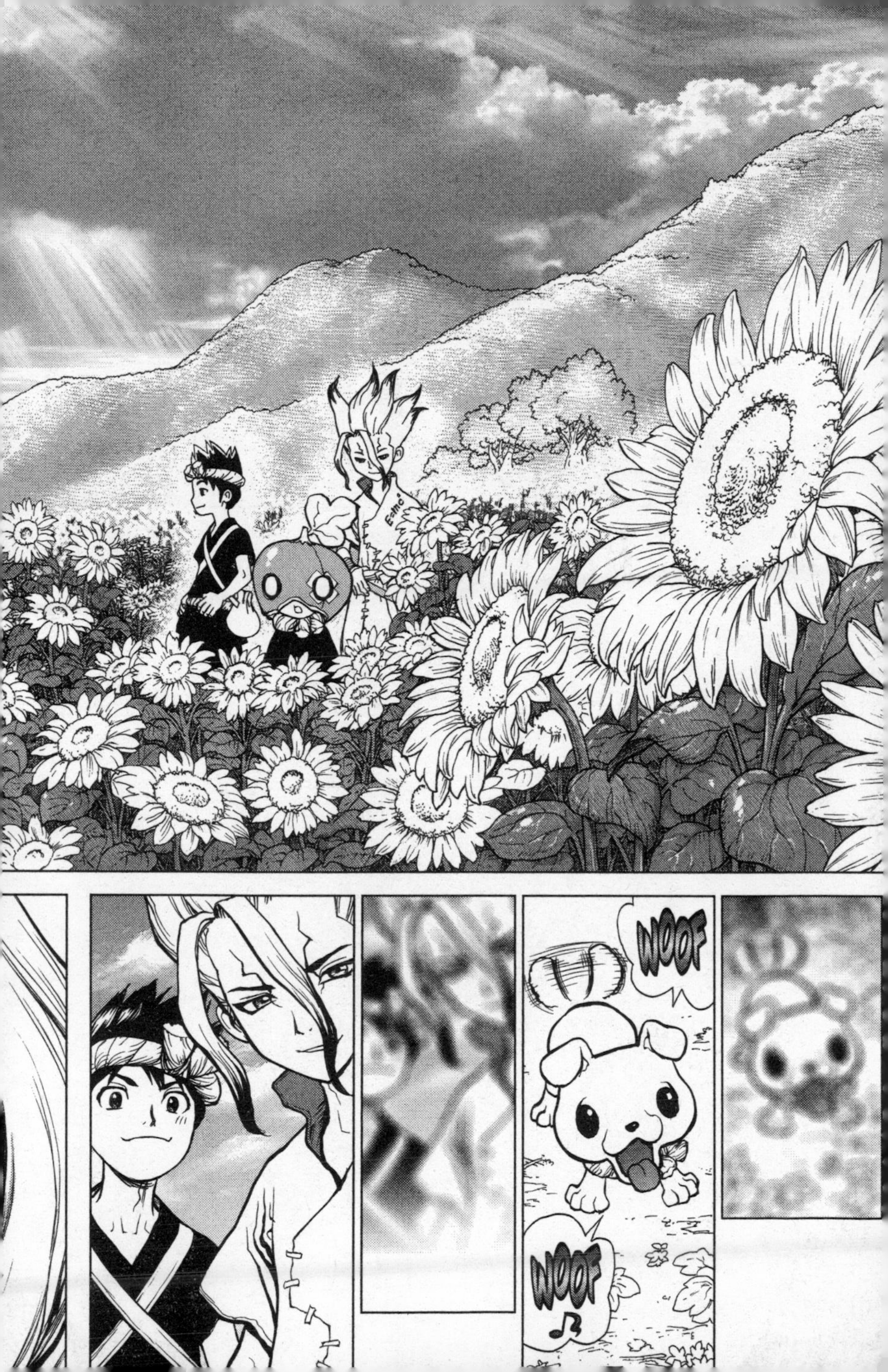
E=mc²
WOOF
WOOF ♪

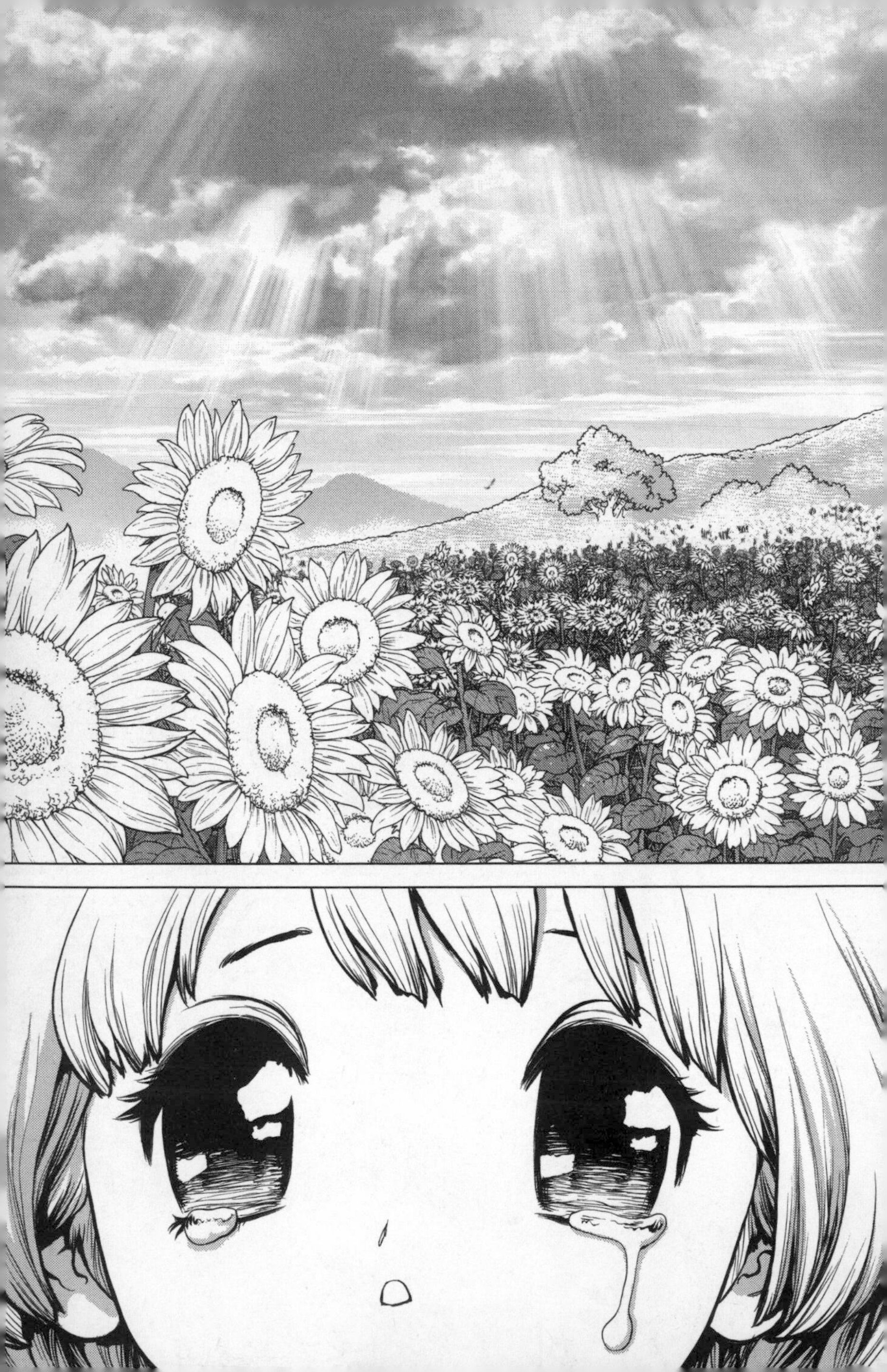

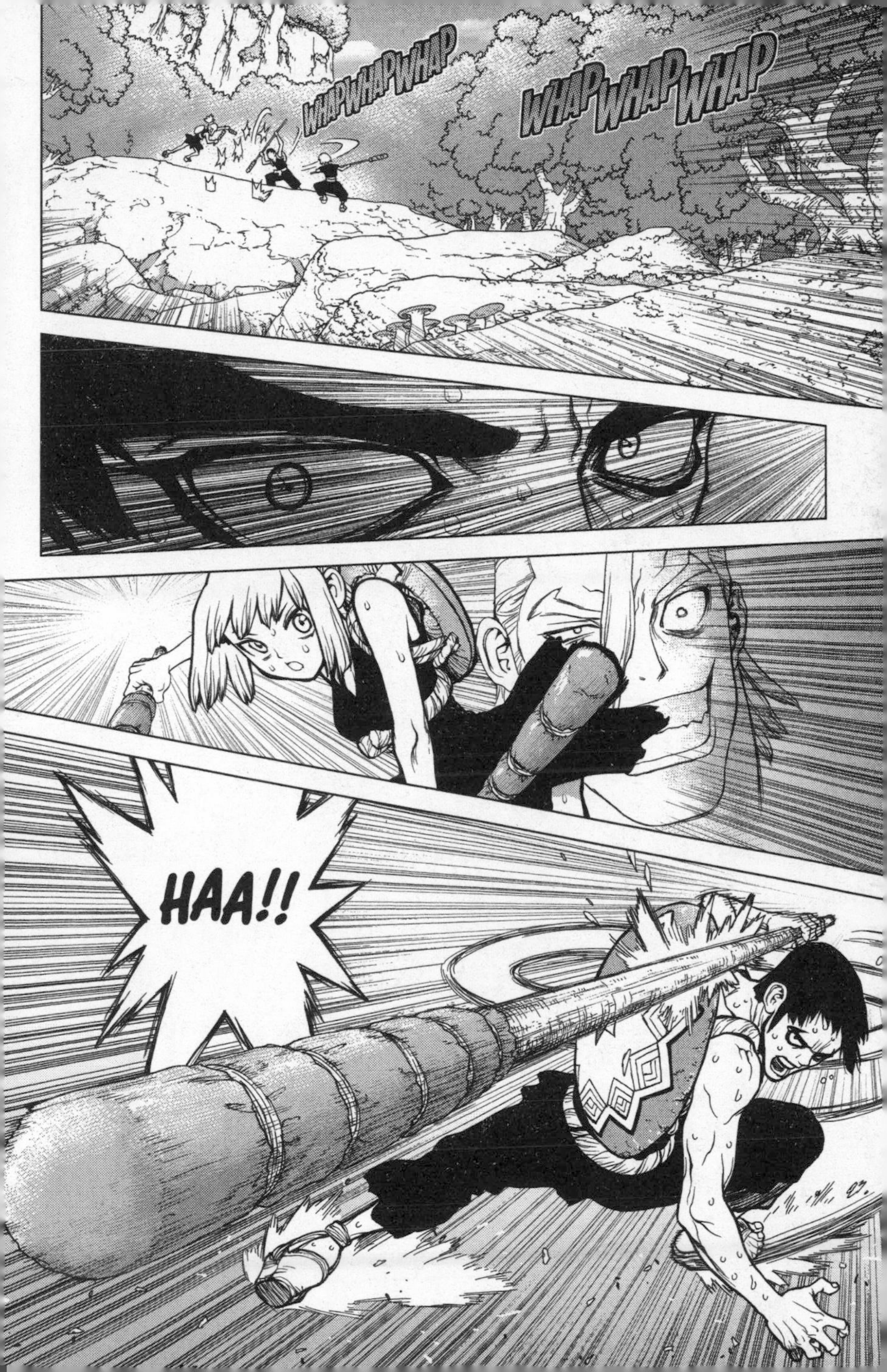
WHAPWHAPWHAP
WHAPWHAPWHAP
HAA!!

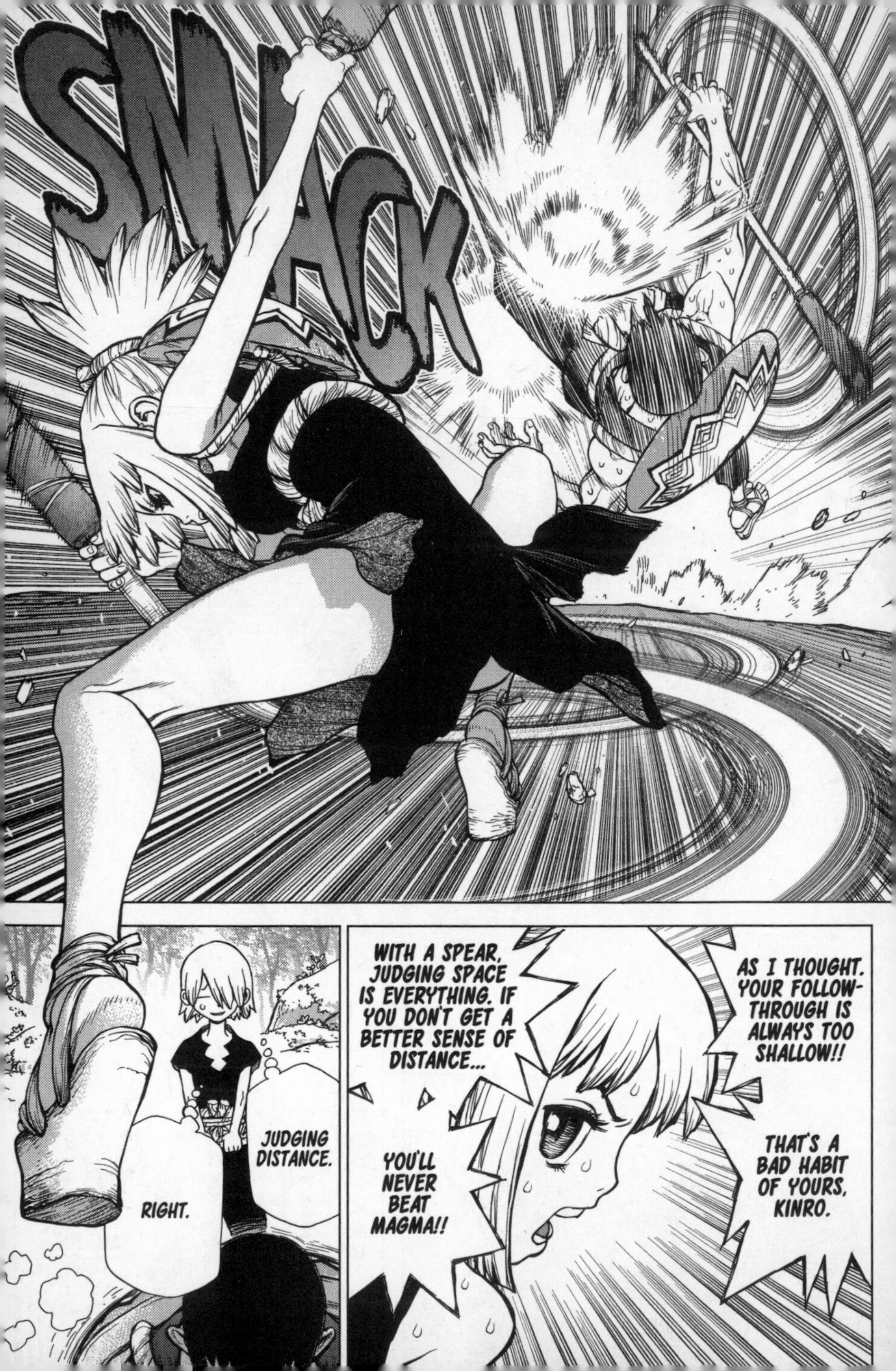
SMACK
AS I THOUGHT. YOUR FOLLOW-THROUGH IS ALWAYS TOO SHALLOW!!
WITH A SPEAR, JUDGING SPACE IS EVERYTHING. IF YOU DON'T GET A BETTER SENSE OF DISTANCE...
THAT'S A BAD HABIT OF YOURS, KINRO.
YOU'LL NEVER BEAT MAGMA!!
JUDGING DISTANCE.
RIGHT.

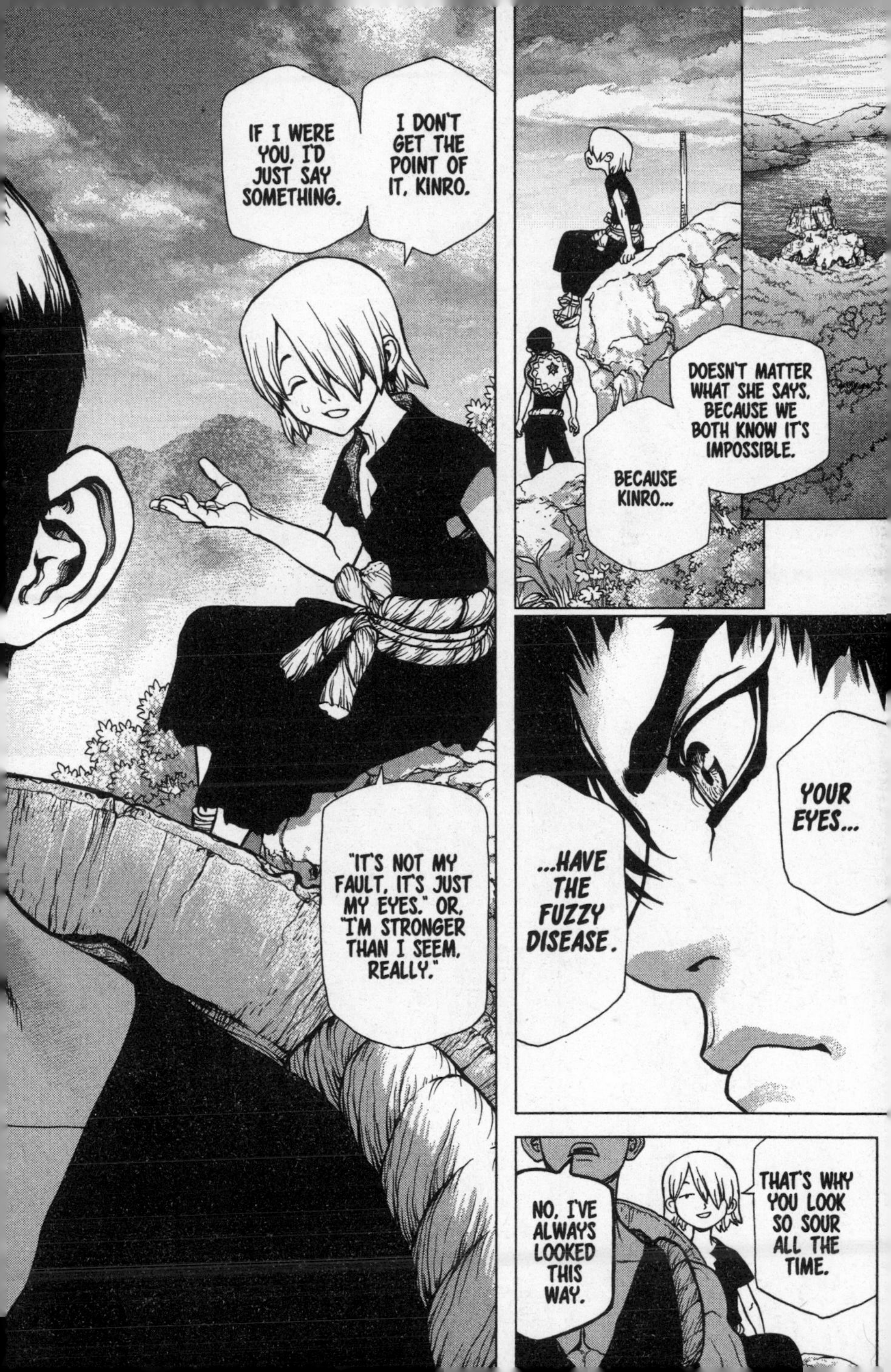
DOESN'T MATTER WHAT SHE SAYS, BECAUSE WE BOTH KNOW IT'S IMPOSSIBLE.
BECAUSE KINRO...
YOUR EYES...
...HAVE THE FUZZY DISEASE.
THAT'S WHY YOU LOOK SO SOUR ALL THE TIME.
NO, I'VE ALWAYS LOOKED THIS WAY.
I DON'T GET THE POINT OF IT, KINRO.
IF I WERE YOU, I'D JUST SAY SOMETHING.
"IT'S NOT MY FAULT, IT'S JUST MY EYES." OR, "I'M STRONGER THAN I SEEM, REALLY."

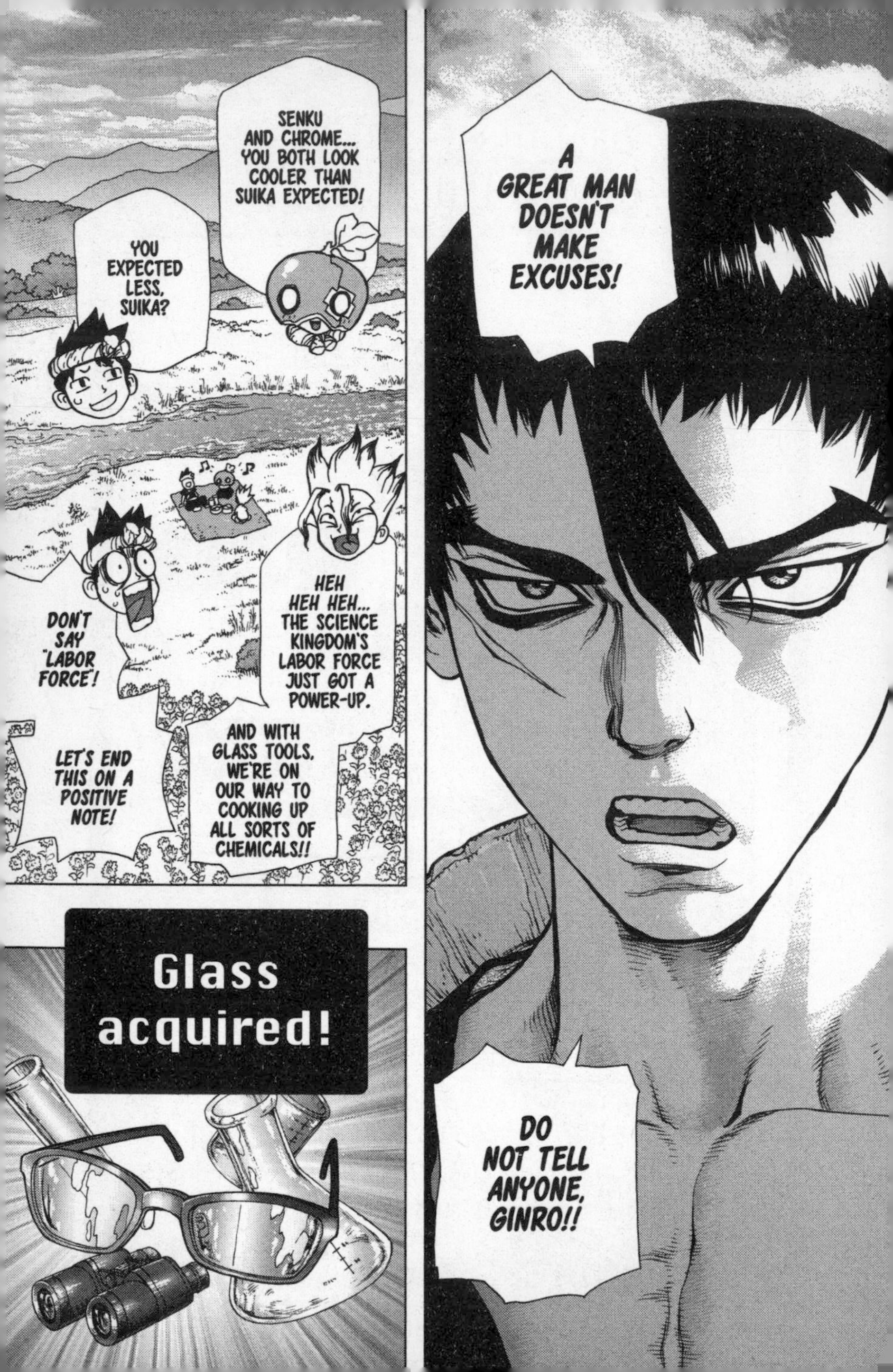
A GREAT MAN DOESN'T MAKE EXCUSES!
DO NOT TELL ANYONE, GINRO!!
SENKU AND CHROME... YOU BOTH LOOK COOLER THAN SUIKA EXPECTED!
YOU EXPECTED LESS, SUIKA?
HEH HEH HEH... THE SCIENCE KINGDOM'S LABOR FORCE JUST GOT A POWER-UP.
DON'T SAY "LABOR FORCE"!
AND WITH GLASS TOOLS, WE'RE ON OUR WAY TO COOKING UP ALL SORTS OF CHEMICALS!!
LET'S END THIS ON A POSITIVE NOTE!
Glass acquired!

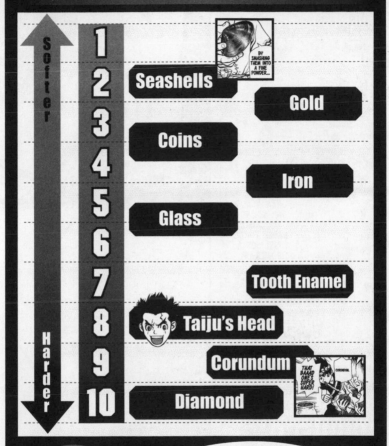

Mohs Scale of Mineral Hardness

Softer

1

BY SMASHING THEM INTO A FINE POWDER...

2 — Seashells

Gold

3 — Coins

4

Iron

5 — Glass

6

7 — Tooth Enamel

8 — Taiju's Head

9 — Corundum

CORUNDUM.
THAT BAAAD ONE'S SUPER HARD!

10 — Diamond

Harder

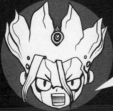

This scale indicates how difficult it is to scratch a given material! By no means should you attempt to chew on iron!

Z=29: SENKU'S LAB

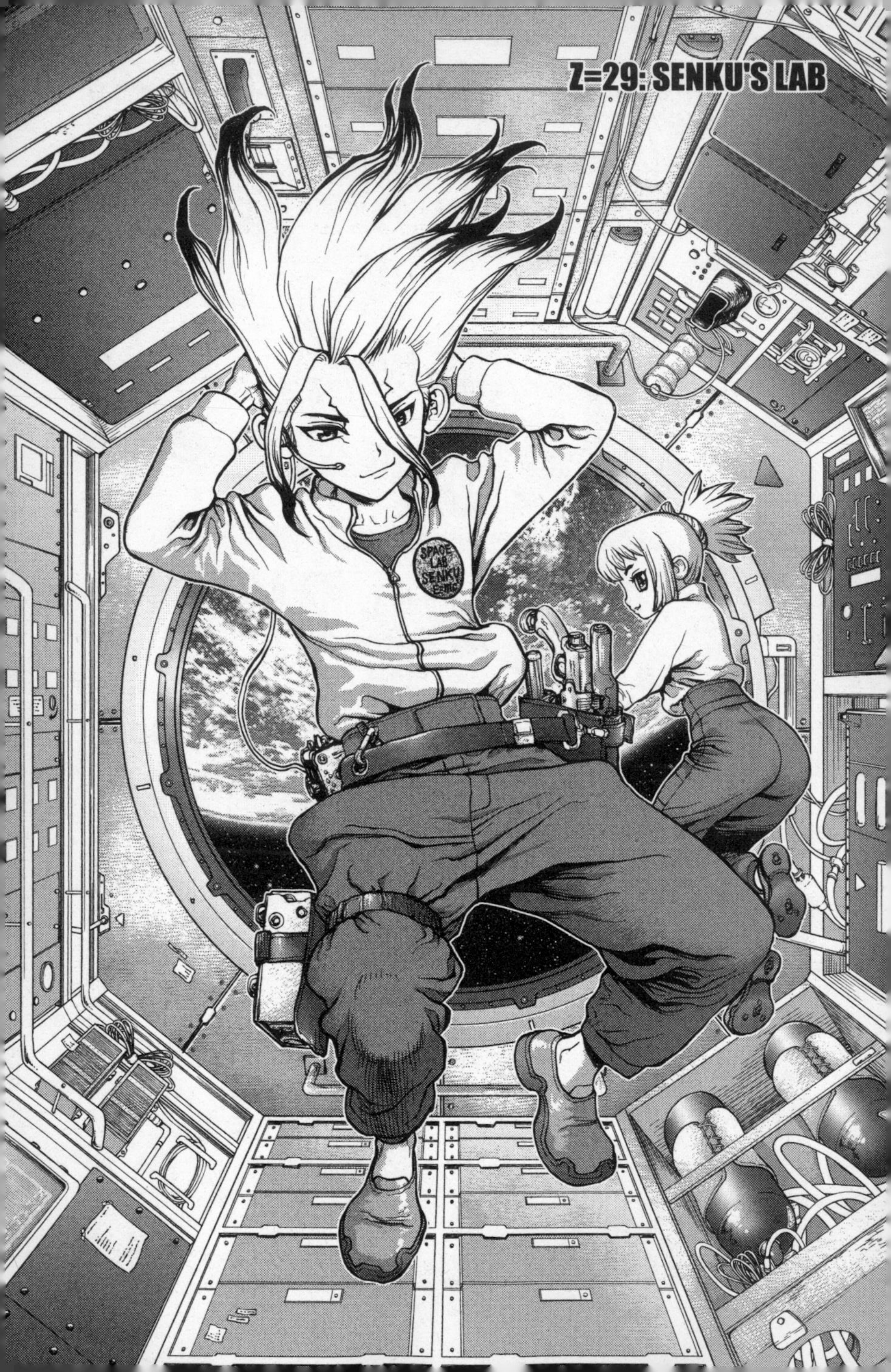
SPACE LAB SENKU

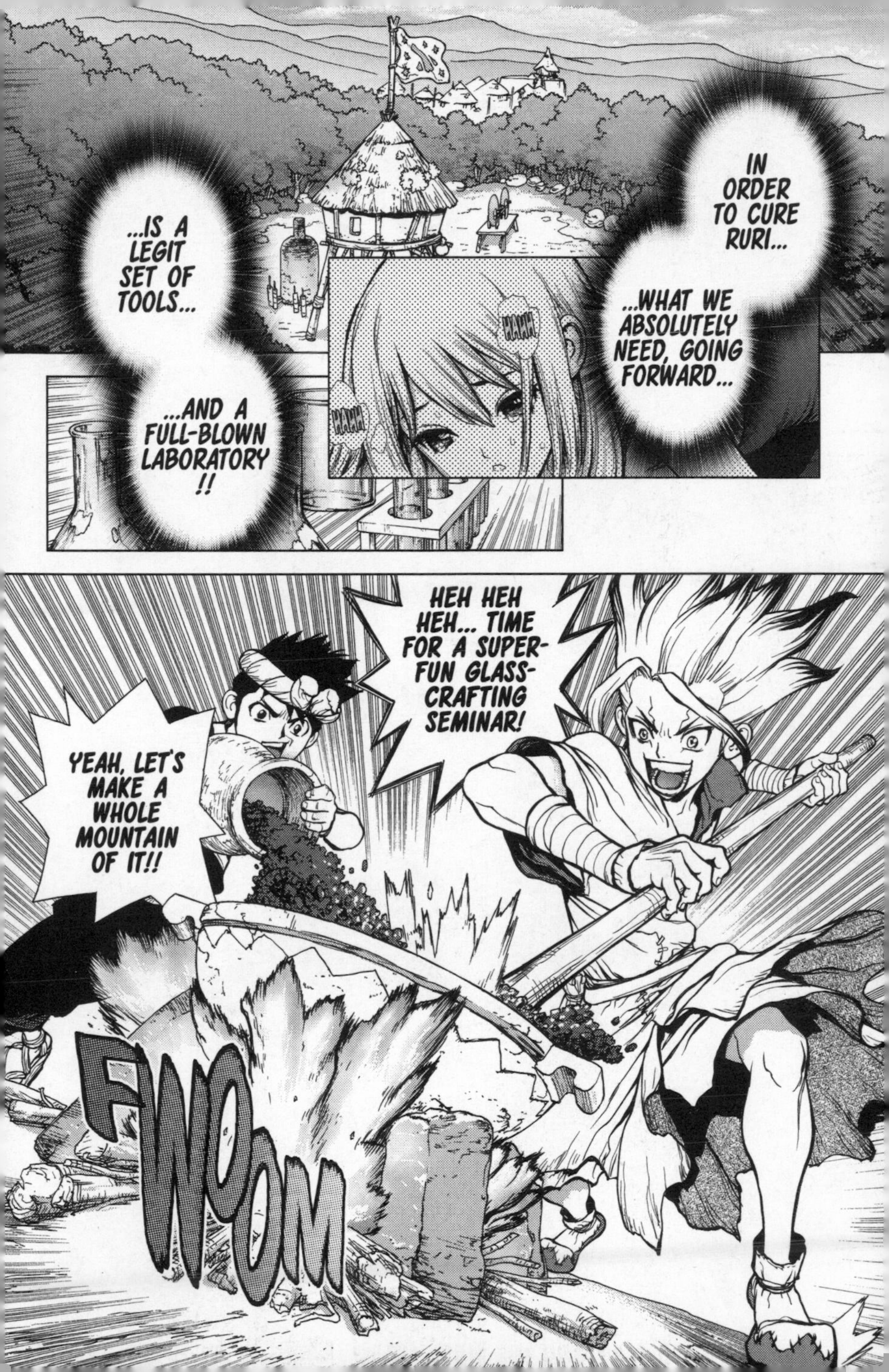
IN ORDER TO CURE RURI...
...WHAT WE ABSOLUTELY NEED, GOING FORWARD...
HAHH
HAHH
...IS A LEGIT SET OF TOOLS...
...AND A FULL-BLOWN LABORATORY !!
HEH HEH HEH... TIME FOR A SUPER-FUN GLASS-CRAFTING SEMINAR!
YEAH, LET'S MAKE A WHOLE MOUNTAIN OF IT!!
FWOOM

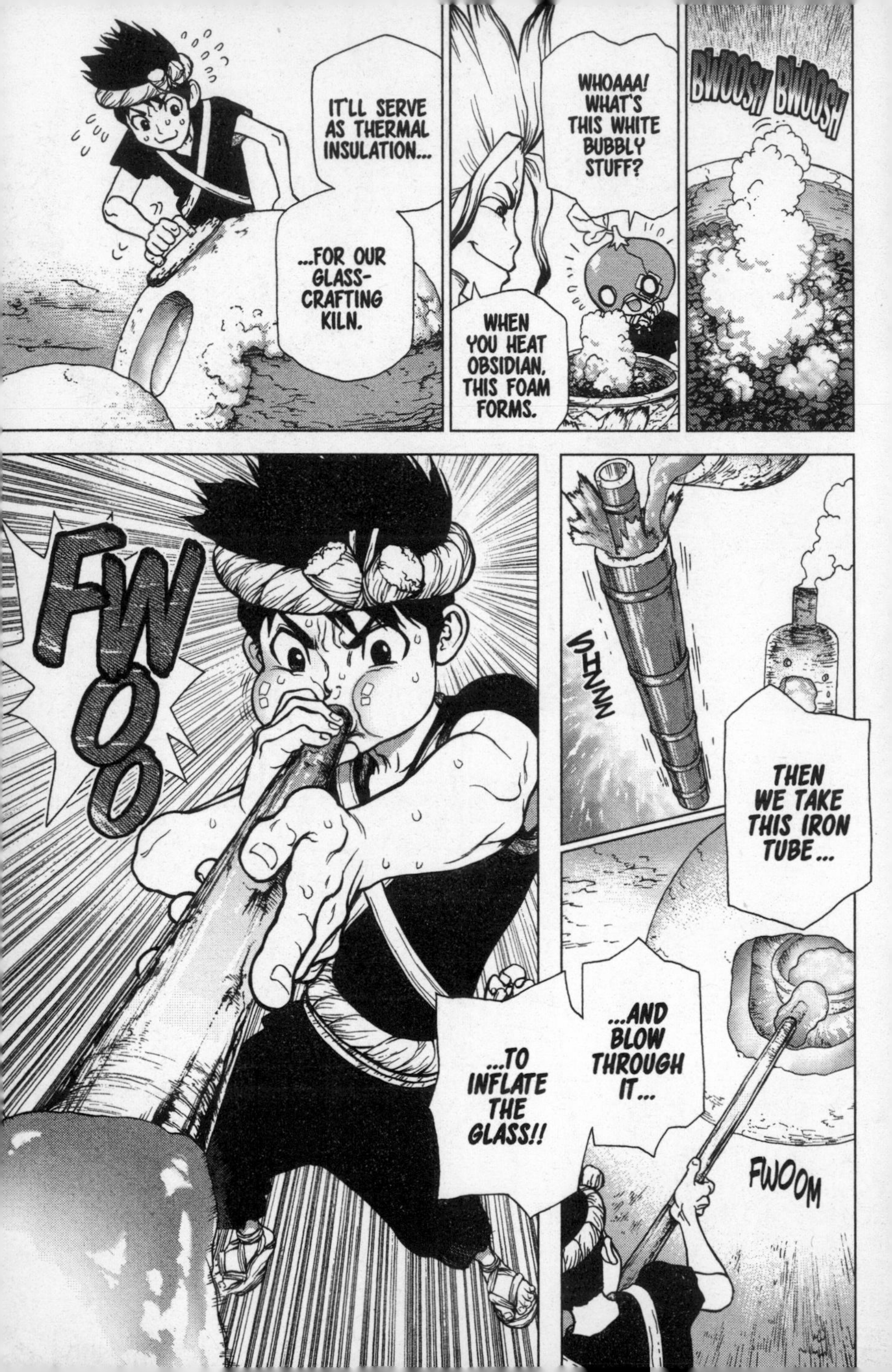
BWOOSH BWOOSH
WHOAAA! WHAT'S THIS WHITE BUBBLY STUFF?
WHEN YOU HEAT OBSIDIAN, THIS FOAM FORMS.
IT'LL SERVE AS THERMAL INSULATION...
...FOR OUR GLASS-CRAFTING KILN.
SHZZZ
THEN WE TAKE THIS IRON TUBE...
FWOOM
...AND BLOW THROUGH IT...
FWOO
...TO INFLATE THE GLASS!!

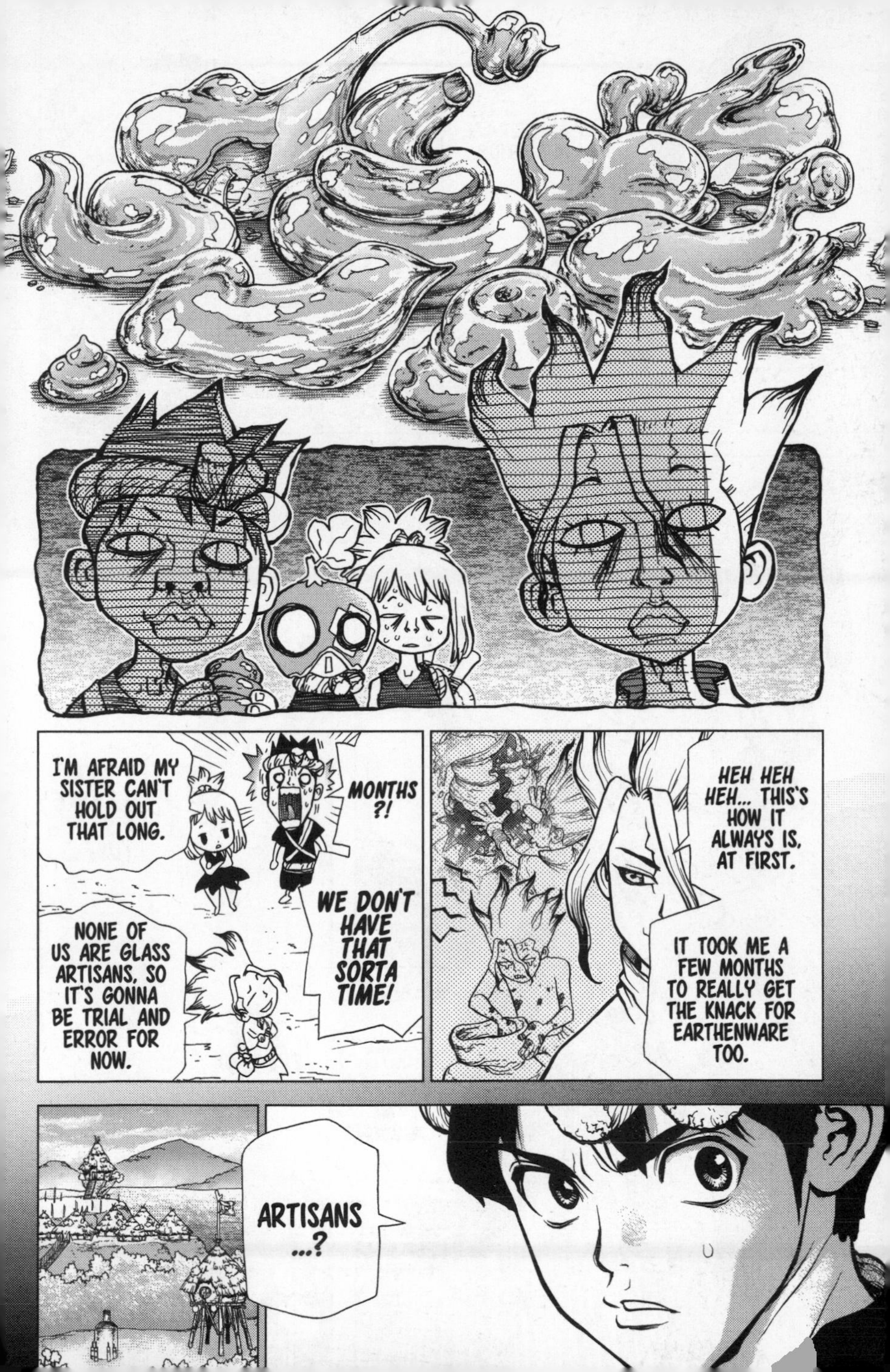
HEH HEH HEH... THIS'S HOW IT ALWAYS IS, AT FIRST.
IT TOOK ME A FEW MONTHS TO REALLY GET THE KNACK FOR EARTHENWARE TOO.
MONTHS ?!
I'M AFRAID MY SISTER CAN'T HOLD OUT THAT LONG.
WE DON'T HAVE THAT SORTA TIME!
NONE OF US ARE GLASS ARTISANS, SO IT'S GONNA BE TRIAL AND ERROR FOR NOW.
ARTISANS ...?

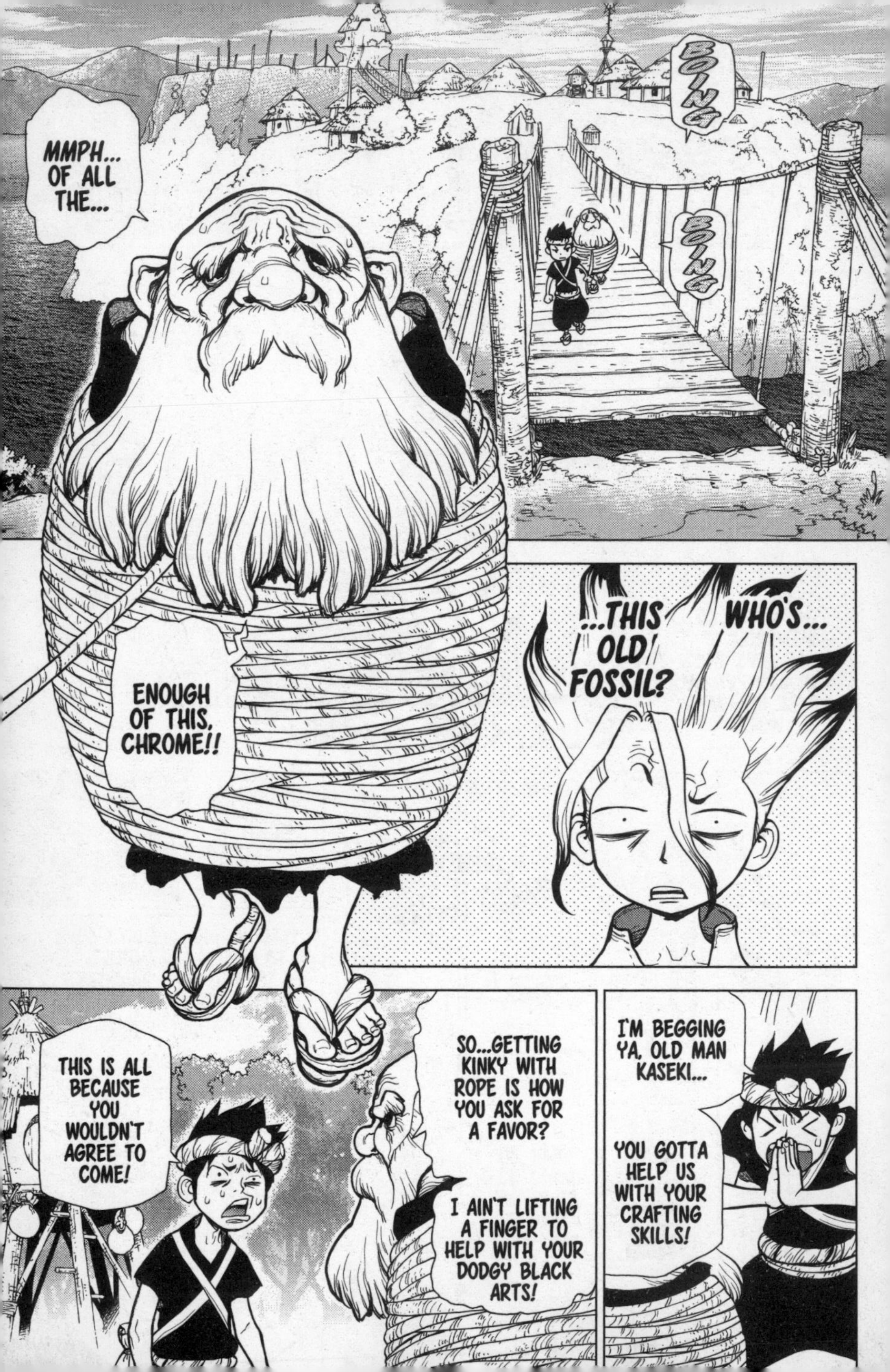
BOING
BOING
WHO'S...
...THIS OLD FOSSIL?
MMPH... OF ALL THE...
ENOUGH OF THIS, CHROME!!
I'M BEGGING YA, OLD MAN KASEKI...
YOU GOTTA HELP US WITH YOUR CRAFTING SKILLS!
SO...GETTING KINKY WITH ROPE IS HOW YOU ASK FOR A FAVOR?
I AIN'T LIFTING A FINGER TO HELP WITH YOUR DODGY BLACK ARTS!
THIS IS ALL BECAUSE YOU WOULDN'T AGREE TO COME!

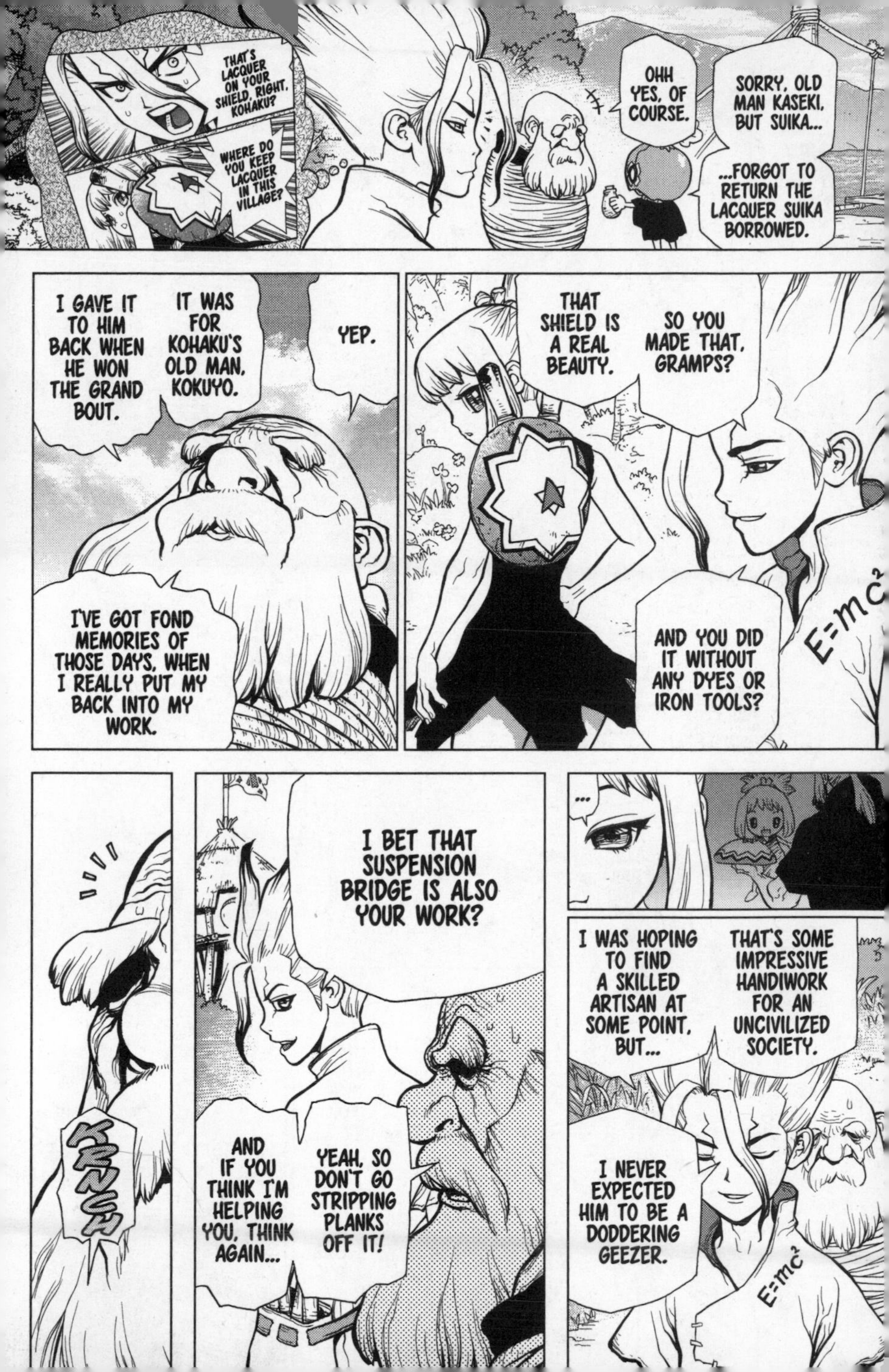
SORRY, OLD MAN KASEKI, BUT SUIKA...
...FORGOT TO RETURN THE LACQUER SUIKA BORROWED.
OHH YES, OF COURSE.
THAT'S LACQUER ON YOUR SHIELD, RIGHT, KOHAKU?
WHERE DO YOU KEEP LACQUER IN THIS VILLAGE?
SO YOU MADE THAT, GRAMPS?
THAT SHIELD IS A REAL BEAUTY.
AND YOU DID IT WITHOUT ANY DYES OR IRON TOOLS?
E=mc²
YEP.
IT WAS FOR KOHAKU'S OLD MAN, KOKUYO.
I GAVE IT TO HIM BACK WHEN HE WON THE GRAND BOUT.
I'VE GOT FOND MEMORIES OF THOSE DAYS, WHEN I REALLY PUT MY BACK INTO MY WORK.
...
THAT'S SOME IMPRESSIVE HANDIWORK FOR AN UNCIVILIZED SOCIETY.
I WAS HOPING TO FIND A SKILLED ARTISAN AT SOME POINT, BUT...
I NEVER EXPECTED HIM TO BE A DODDERING GEEZER.
E=mc²
I BET THAT SUSPENSION BRIDGE IS ALSO YOUR WORK?
YEAH, SO DON'T GO STRIPPING PLANKS OFF IT!
AND IF YOU THINK I'M HELPING YOU, THINK AGAIN...
KRNCH

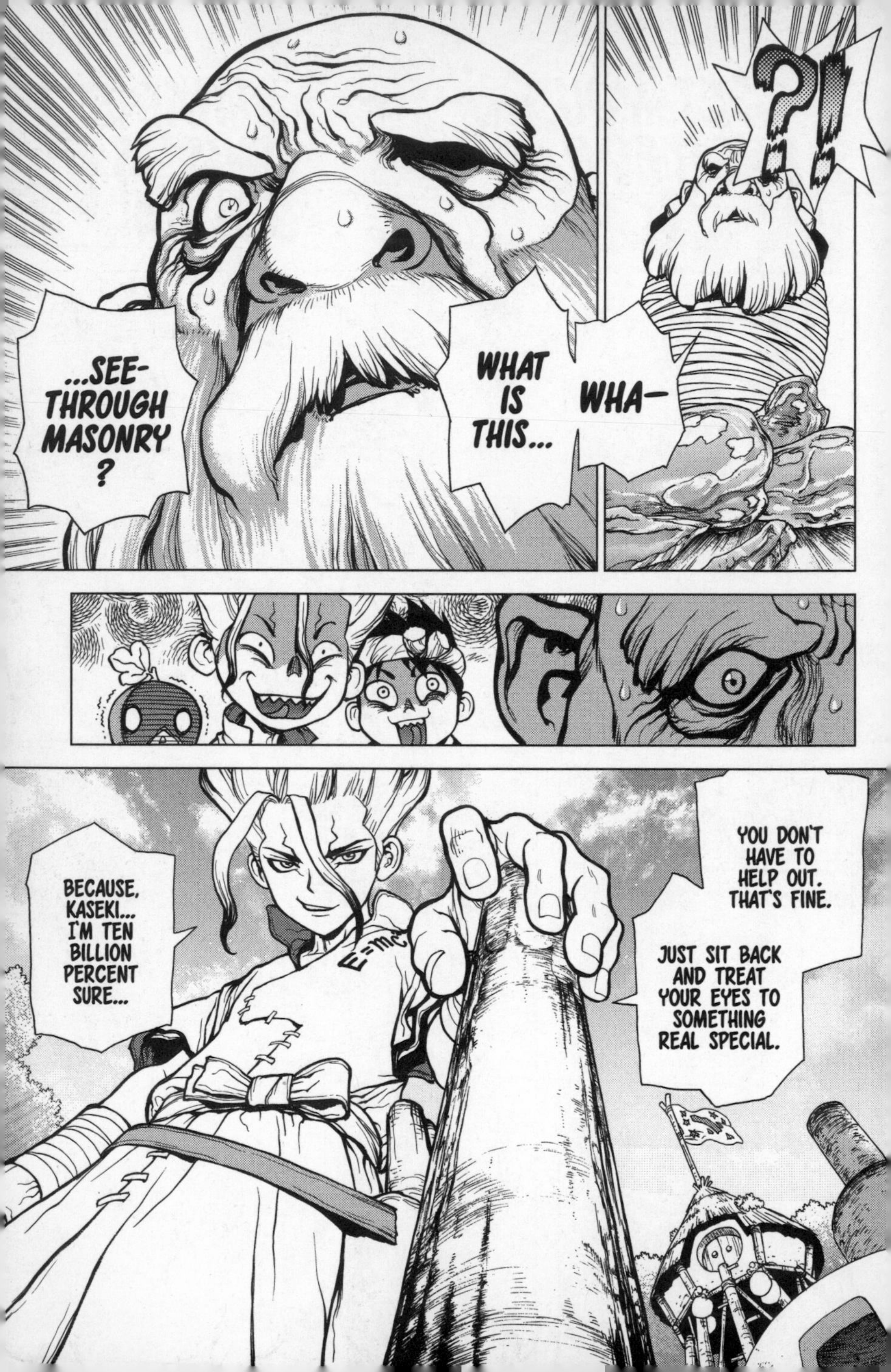
?!
WHA-
WHAT IS THIS...
...SEE-THROUGH MASONRY?
YOU DON'T HAVE TO HELP OUT. THAT'S FINE.
JUST SIT BACK AND TREAT YOUR EYES TO SOMETHING REAL SPECIAL.
BECAUSE, KASEKI... I'M TEN BILLION PERCENT SURE...

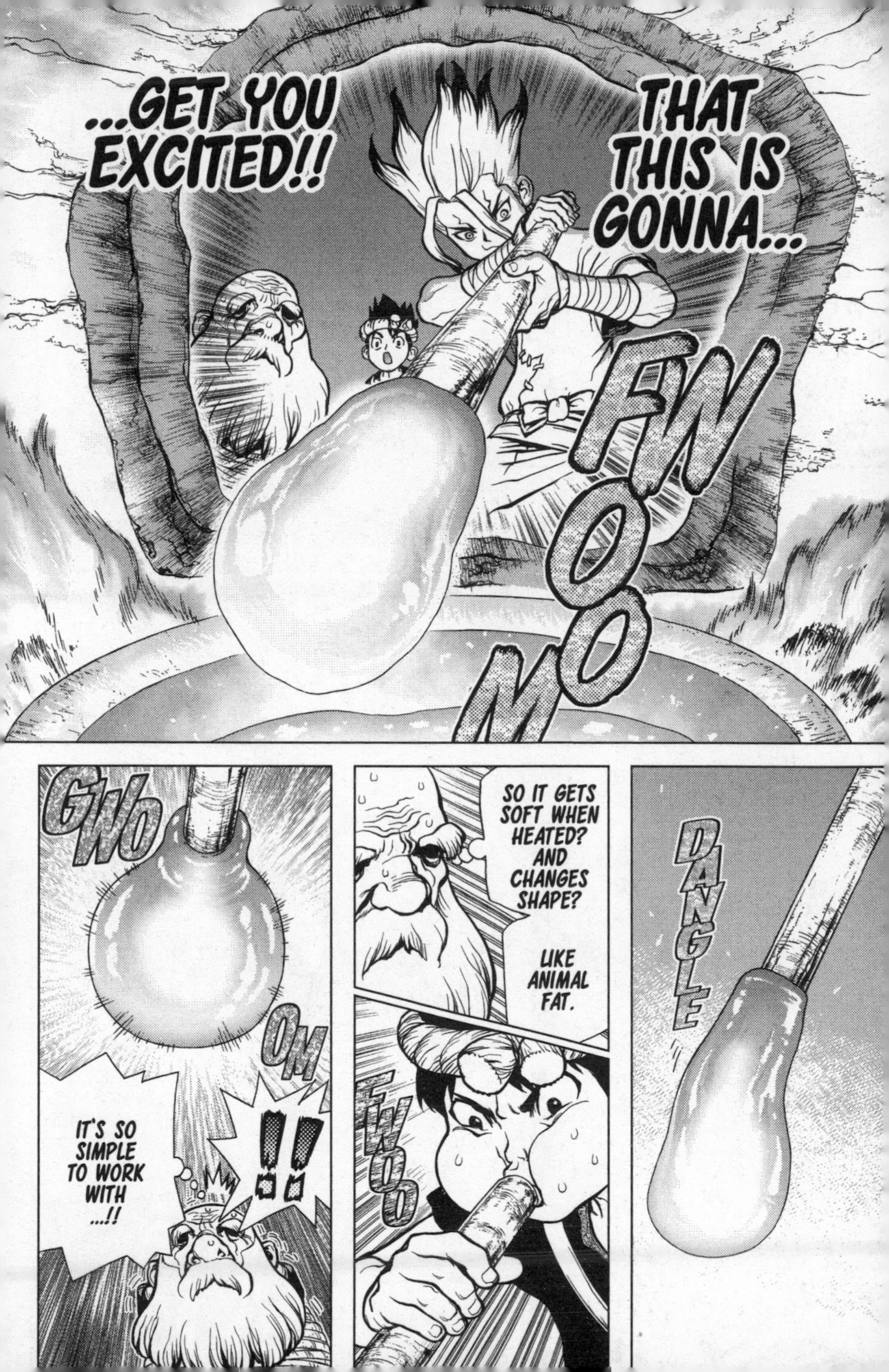
THAT THIS IS GONNA...
...GET YOU EXCITED!!
FWOOM
DANGLE
SO IT GETS SOFT WHEN HEATED? AND CHANGES SHAPE?
LIKE ANIMAL FAT.
FWOO
GWO
OM
!!
IT'S SO SIMPLE TO WORK WITH ...!!

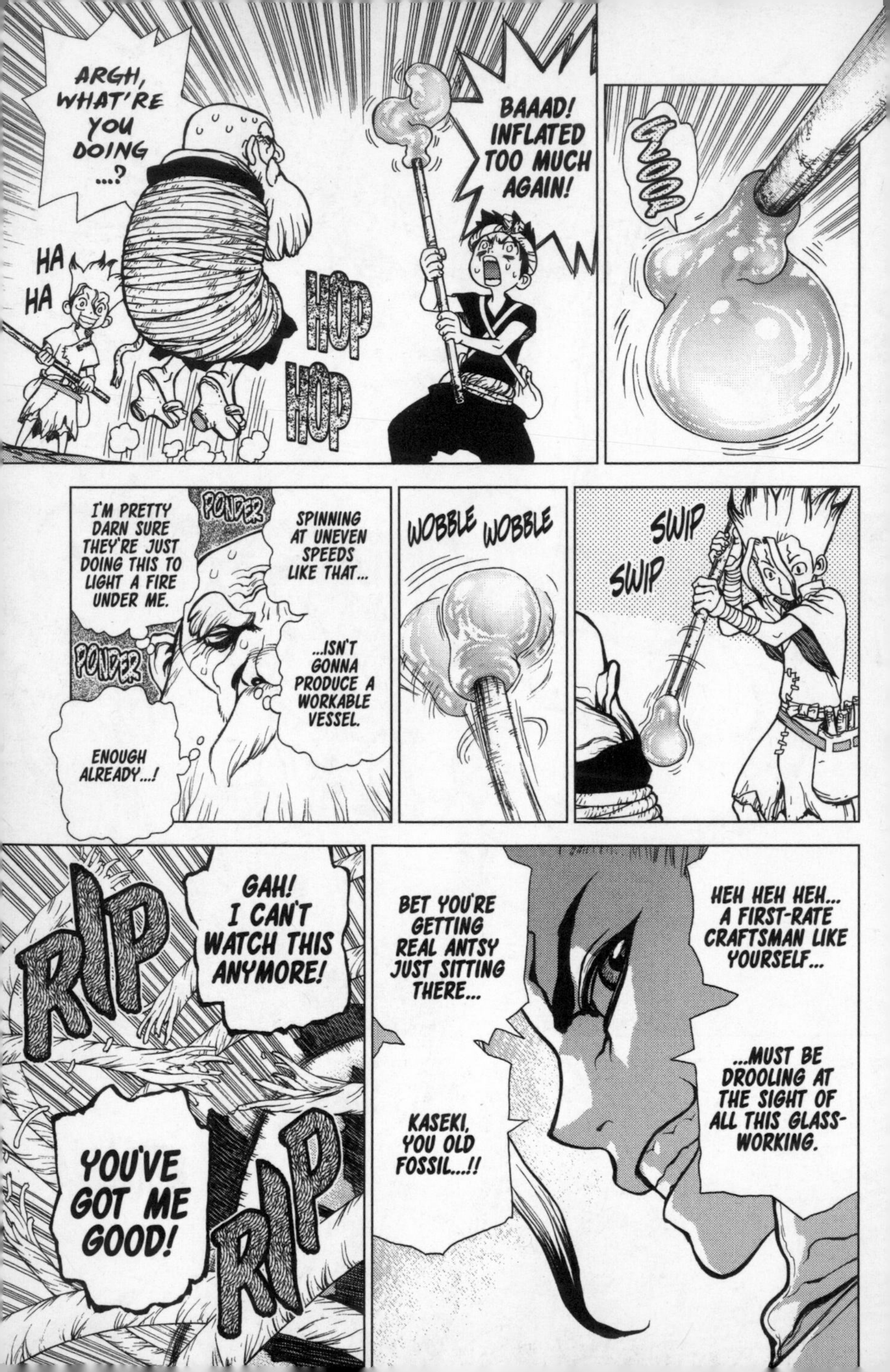
BAAAD! INFLATED TOO MUCH AGAIN!
ARGH, WHAT'RE YOU DOING ...?
HOP HOP
HA HA
SWIP SWIP
WOBBLE WOBBLE
SPINNING AT UNEVEN SPEEDS LIKE THAT...
PONDER
I'M PRETTY DARN SURE THEY'RE JUST DOING THIS TO LIGHT A FIRE UNDER ME.
...ISN'T GONNA PRODUCE A WORKABLE VESSEL.
PONDER
ENOUGH ALREADY...!
HEH HEH HEH... A FIRST-RATE CRAFTSMAN LIKE YOURSELF...
BET YOU'RE GETTING REAL ANTSY JUST SITTING THERE...
...MUST BE DROOLING AT THE SIGHT OF ALL THIS GLASS-WORKING.
KASEKI, YOU OLD FOSSIL...!!
GAH! I CAN'T WATCH THIS ANYMORE!
RIP
RIP
YOU'VE GOT ME GOOD!

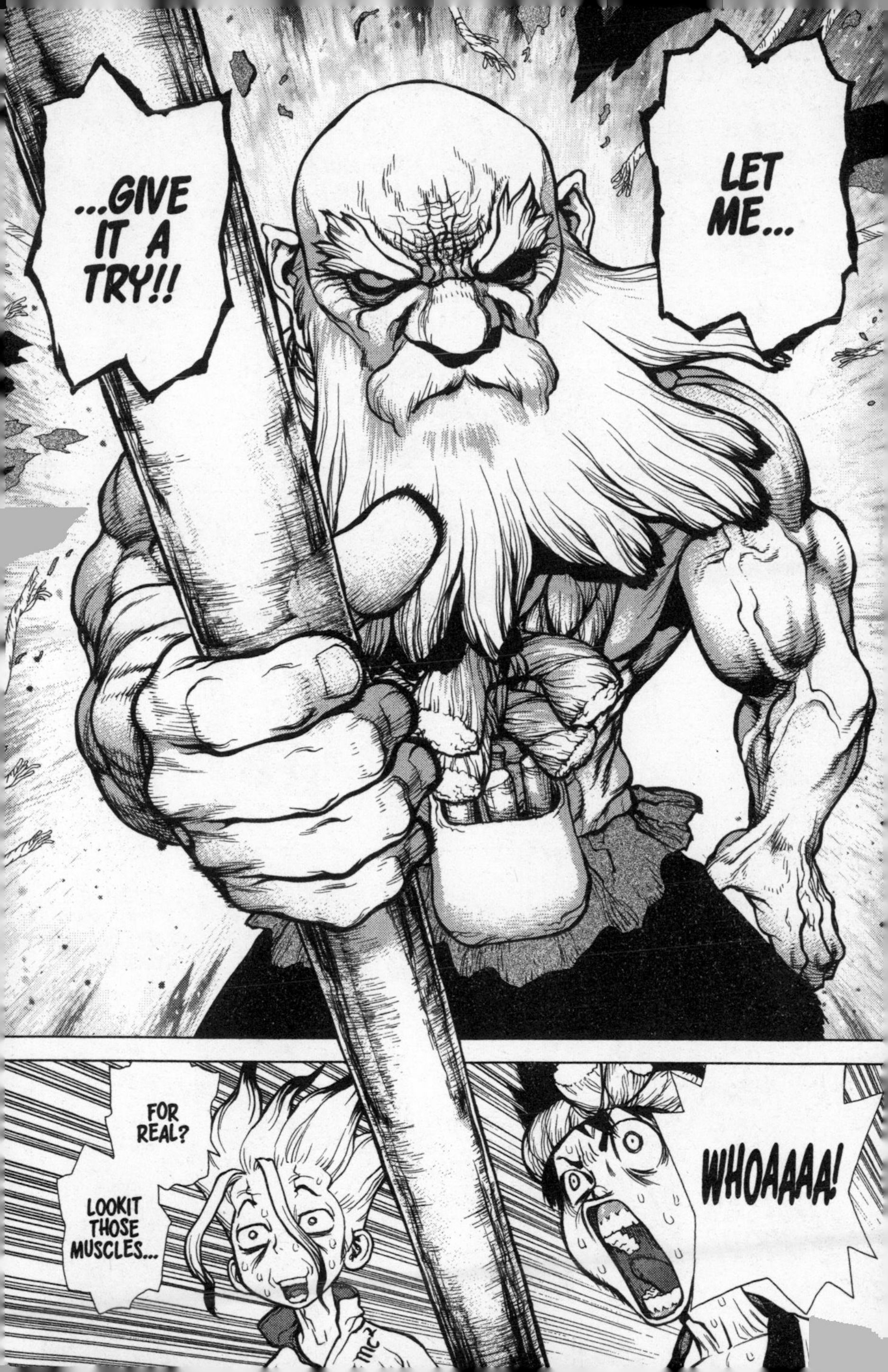
LET ME...
...GIVE IT A TRY!!
WHOAAAA!
FOR REAL?
LOOKIT THOSE MUSCLES...

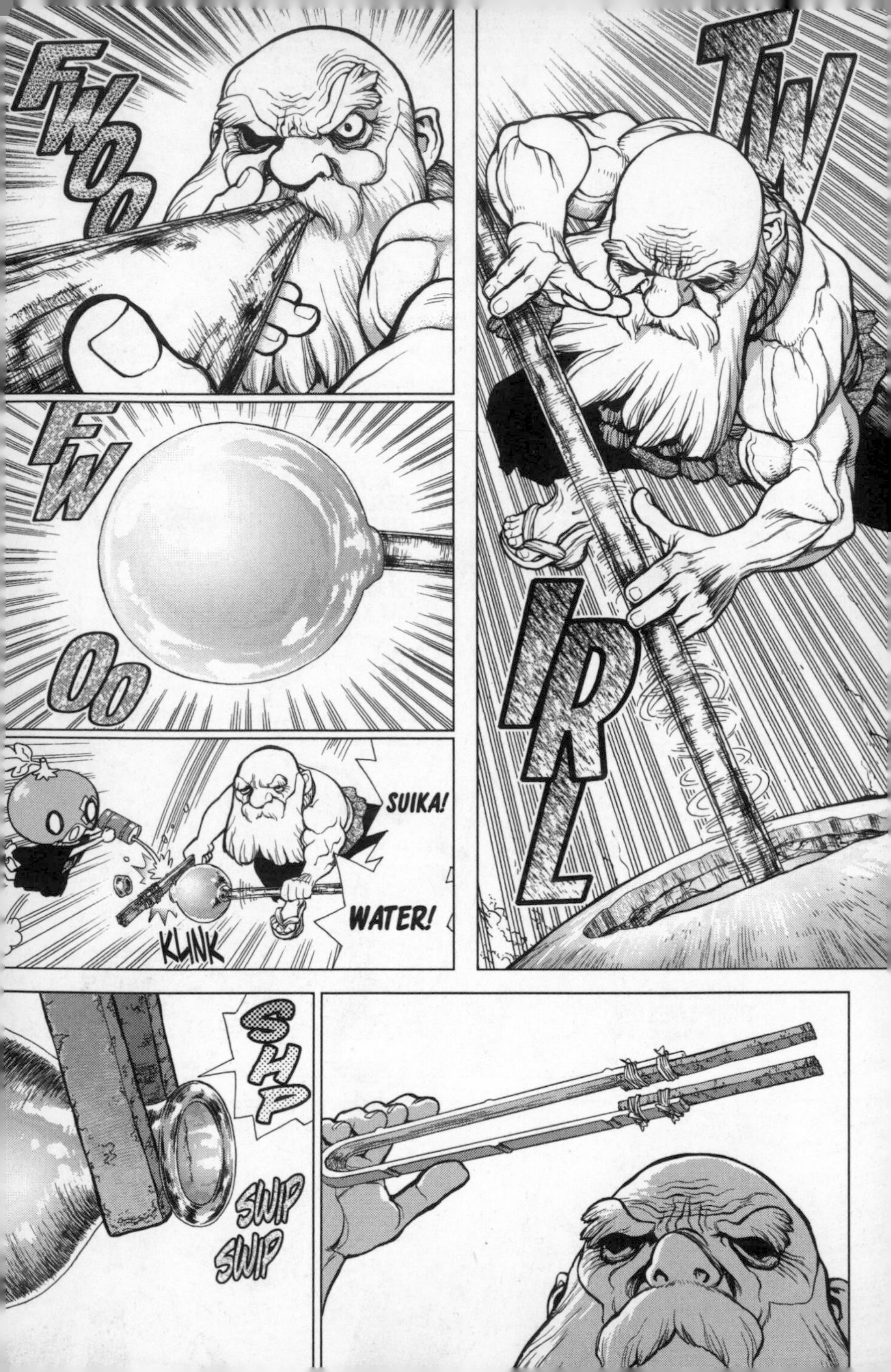
TWIRL
FWOO
FWOO
SUIKA!
WATER!
KLUNK
SHP
SWIP
SWIP

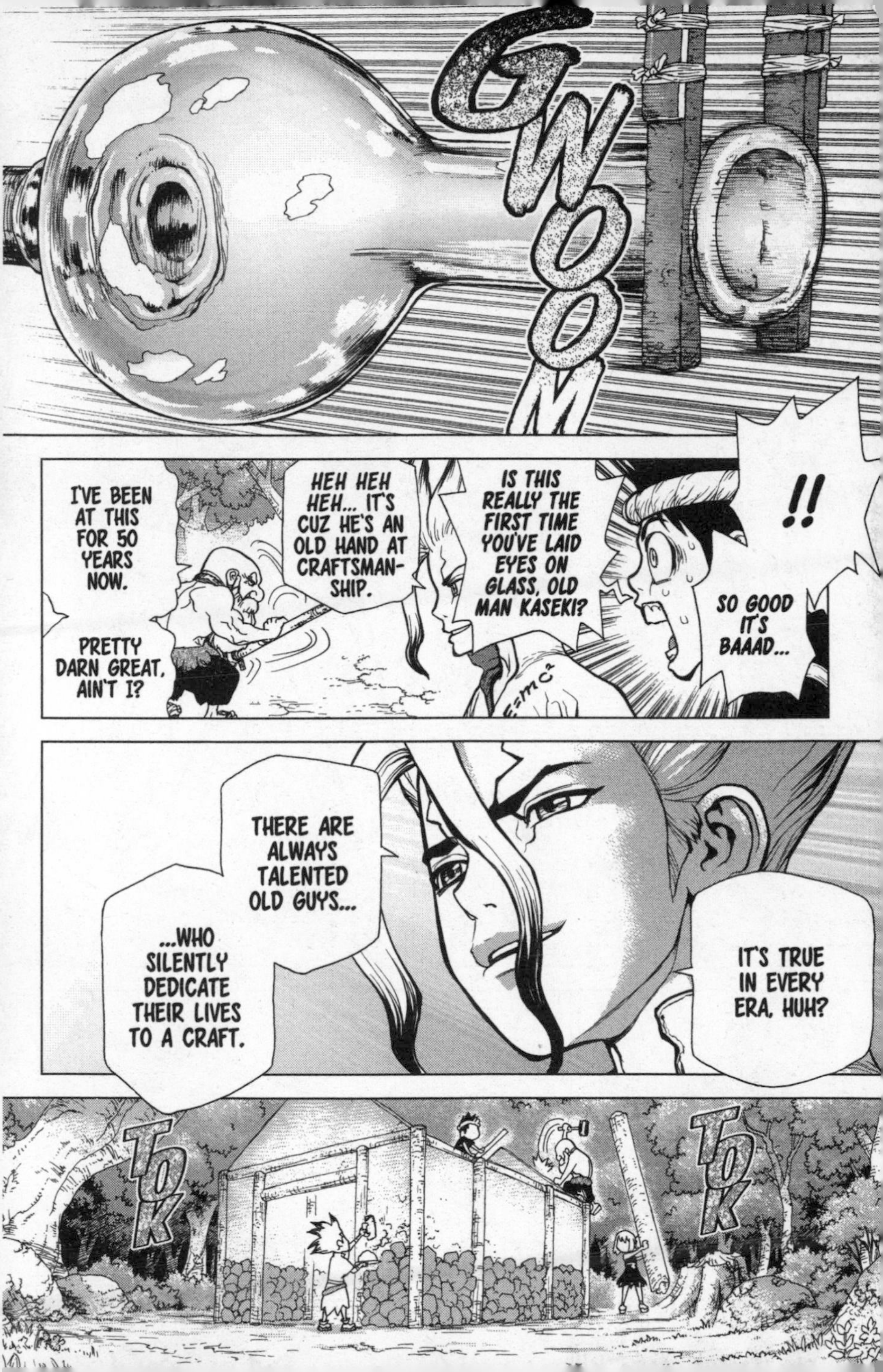
GWOOOM
!!
SO GOOD IT'S BAAAD...
IS THIS REALLY THE FIRST TIME YOU'VE LAID EYES ON GLASS, OLD MAN KASEKI?
HEH HEH HEH... IT'S CUZ HE'S AN OLD HAND AT CRAFTSMAN-SHIP.
I'VE BEEN AT THIS FOR 50 YEARS NOW.
PRETTY DARN GREAT, AIN'T I?
IT'S TRUE IN EVERY ERA, HUH?
THERE ARE ALWAYS TALENTED OLD GUYS...
...WHO SILENTLY DEDICATE THEIR LIVES TO A CRAFT.
TOK
TOK

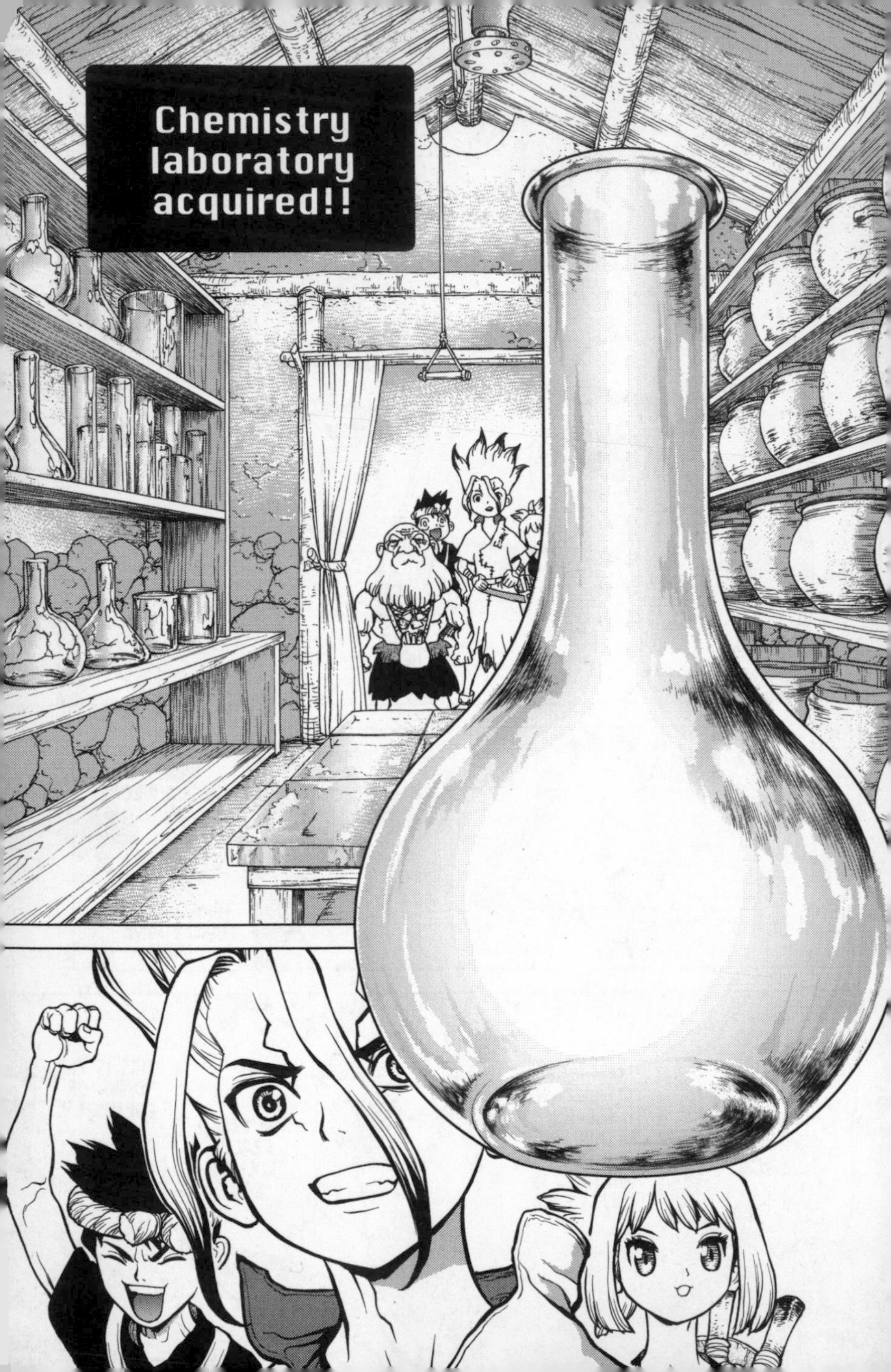
Chemistry laboratory acquired!!

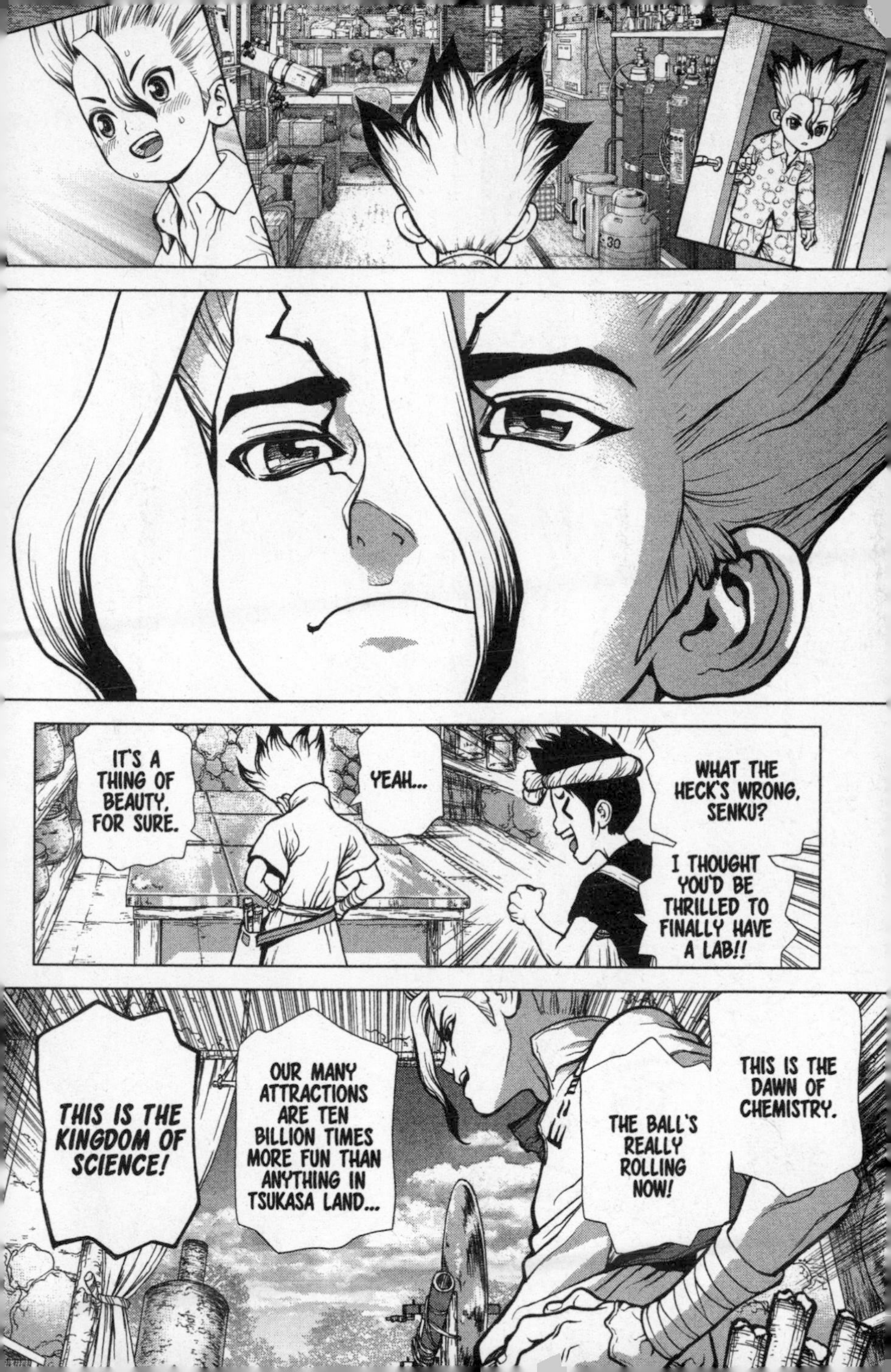
WHAT THE HECK'S WRONG, SENKU?
I THOUGHT YOU'D BE THRILLED TO FINALLY HAVE A LAB!!
YEAH...
IT'S A THING OF BEAUTY, FOR SURE.
THIS IS THE DAWN OF CHEMISTRY.
THE BALL'S REALLY ROLLING NOW!
OUR MANY ATTRACTIONS ARE TEN BILLION TIMES MORE FUN THAN ANYTHING IN TSUKASA LAND...
THIS IS THE KINGDOM OF SCIENCE!

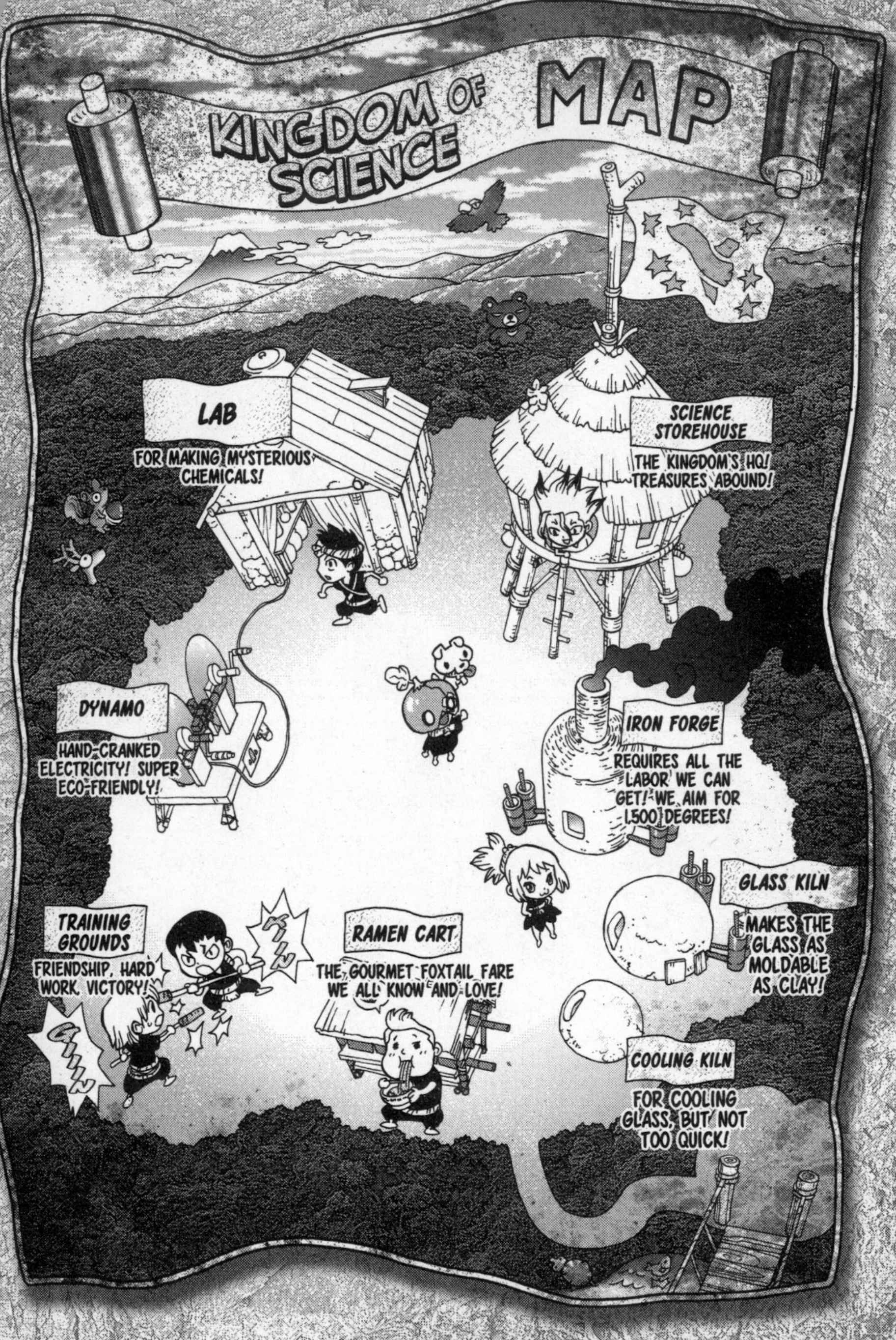
KINGDOM OF SCIENCE MAP
SCIENCE STOREHOUSE
THE KINGDOM'S HQ! TREASURES ABOUND!
LAB
FOR MAKING MYSTERIOUS CHEMICALS!
IRON FORGE
REQUIRES ALL THE LABOR WE CAN GET! WE AIM FOR 1,500 DEGREES!
DYNAMO
HAND-CRANKED ELECTRICITY! SUPER ECO-FRIENDLY!
GLASS KILN
MAKES THE GLASS AS MOLDABLE AS CLAY!
RAMEN CART
THE GOURMET FOXTAIL FARE WE ALL KNOW AND LOVE!
TRAINING GROUNDS
FRIENDSHIP, HARD WORK, VICTORY!
COOLING KILN
FOR COOLING GLASS, BUT NOT TOO QUICK!

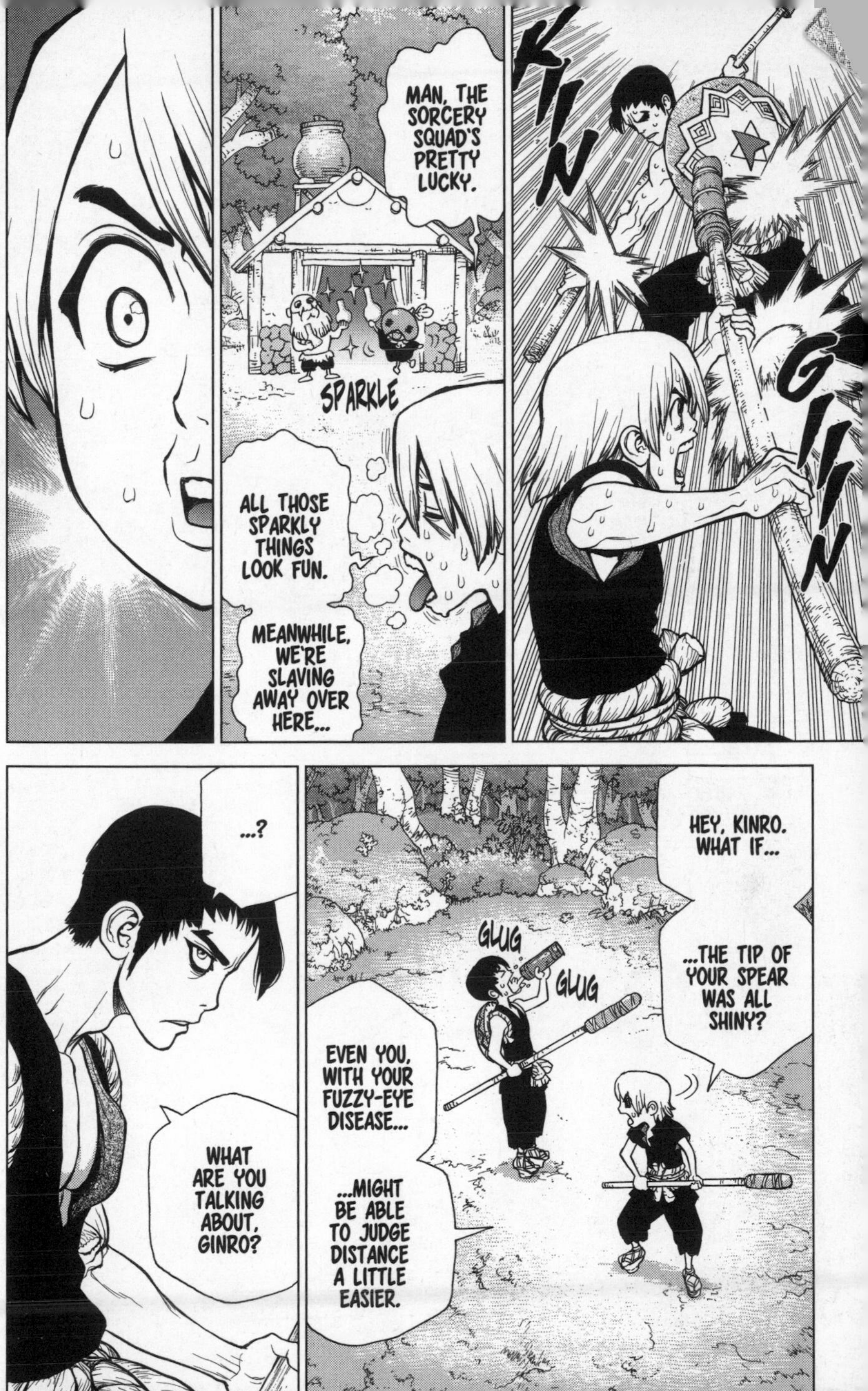
KIN
GIIIN
MAN, THE SORCERY SQUAD'S PRETTY LUCKY.
SPARKLE
ALL THOSE SPARKLY THINGS LOOK FUN.
MEANWHILE, WE'RE SLAVING AWAY OVER HERE...
HEY, KINRO. WHAT IF...
...THE TIP OF YOUR SPEAR WAS ALL SHINY?
GLUG
GLUG
EVEN YOU, WITH YOUR FUZZY-EYE DISEASE...
...MIGHT BE ABLE TO JUDGE DISTANCE A LITTLE EASIER.
...?
WHAT ARE YOU TALKING ABOUT, GINRO?

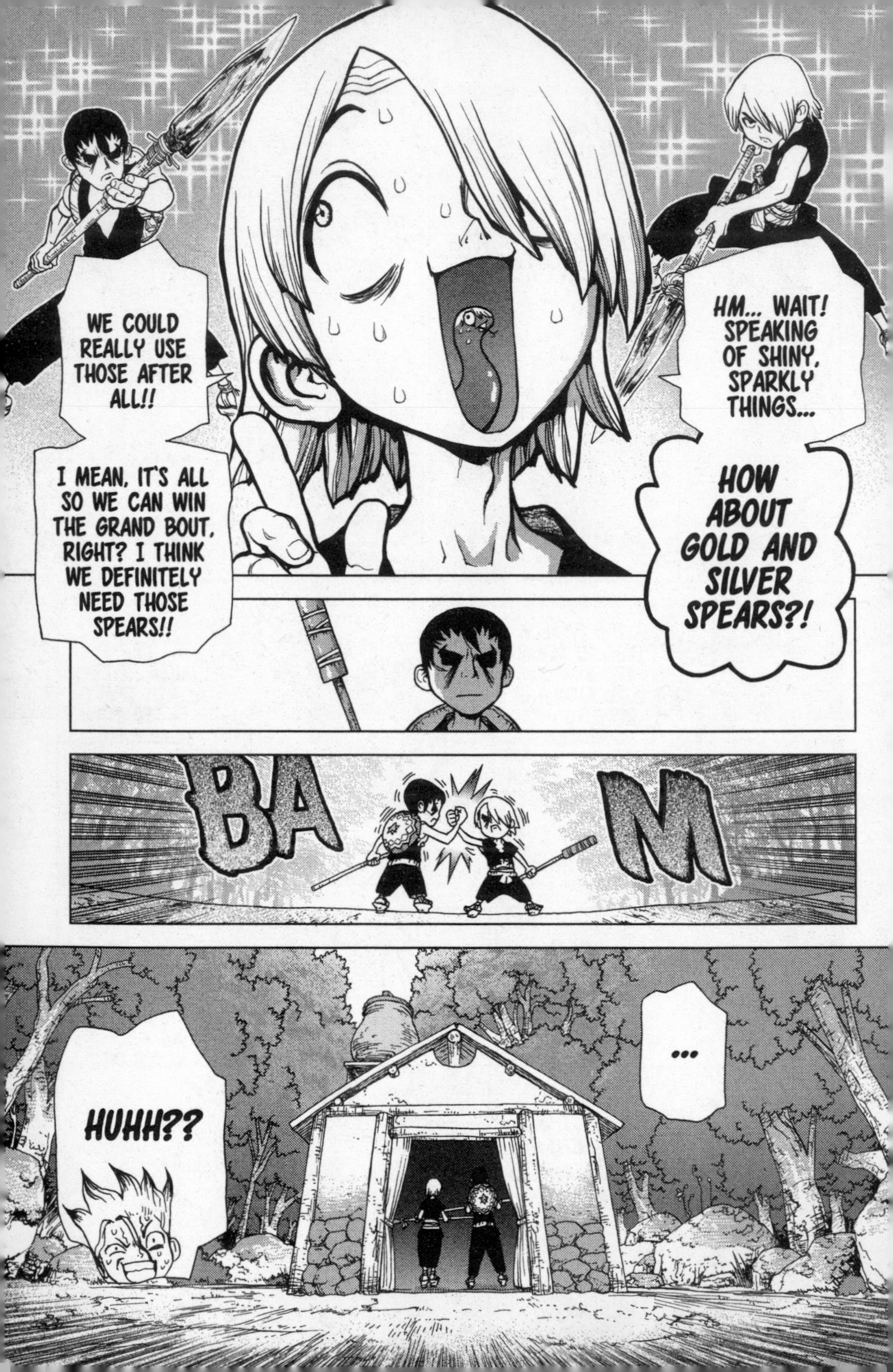
HM... WAIT! SPEAKING OF SHINY, SPARKLY THINGS...
HOW ABOUT GOLD AND SILVER SPEARS?!
WE COULD REALLY USE THOSE AFTER ALL!!
I MEAN, IT'S ALL SO WE CAN WIN THE GRAND BOUT, RIGHT? I THINK WE DEFINITELY NEED THOSE SPEARS!!
BAM
...
HUHH??

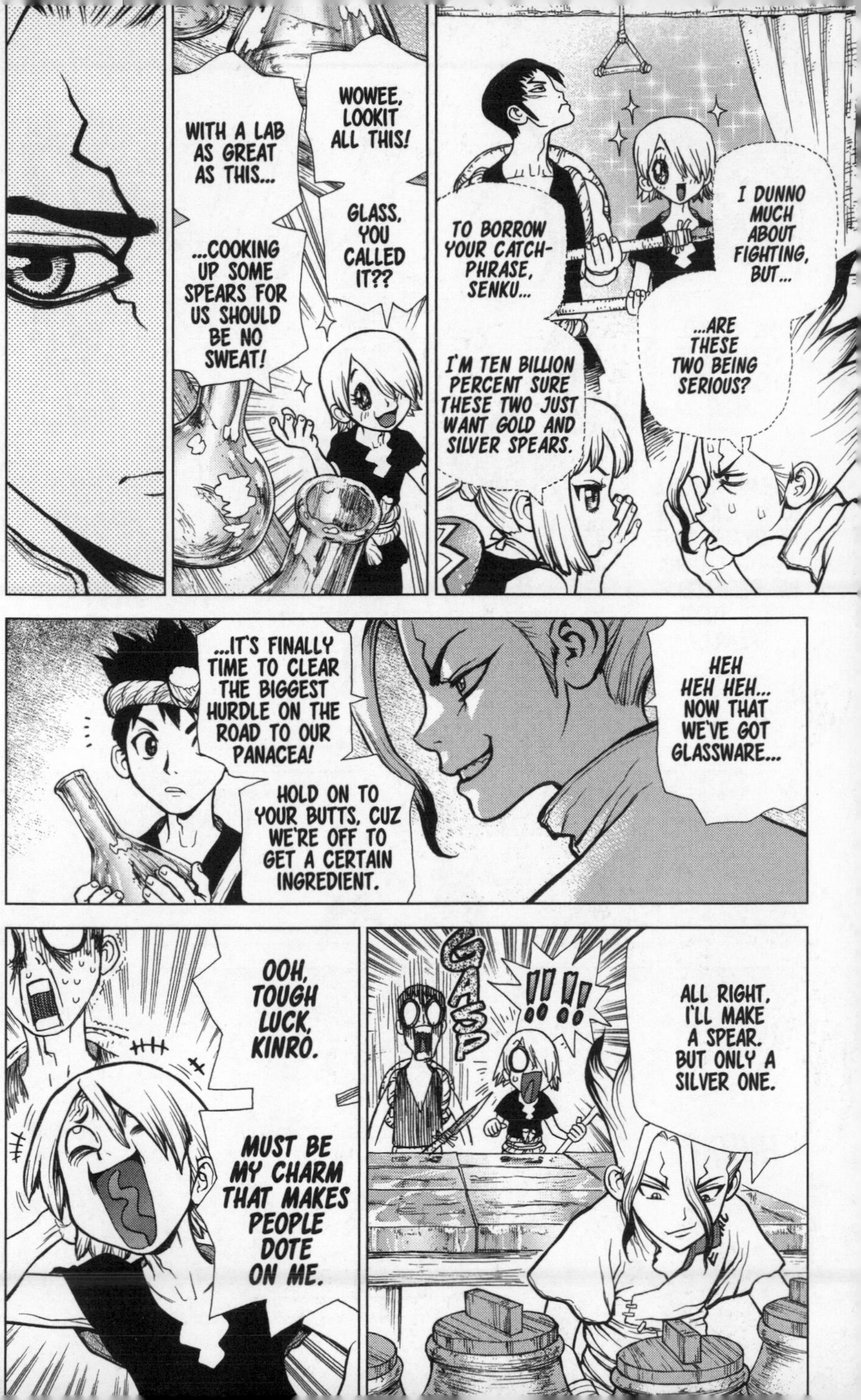
I DUNNO MUCH ABOUT FIGHTING, BUT...
...ARE THESE TWO BEING SERIOUS?
TO BORROW YOUR CATCH-PHRASE, SENKU...
I'M TEN BILLION PERCENT SURE THESE TWO JUST WANT GOLD AND SILVER SPEARS.
WOWEE, LOOKIT ALL THIS!
GLASS, YOU CALLED IT??
WITH A LAB AS GREAT AS THIS...
...COOKING UP SOME SPEARS FOR US SHOULD BE NO SWEAT!
HEH HEH HEH... NOW THAT WE'VE GOT GLASSWARE...
...IT'S FINALLY TIME TO CLEAR THE BIGGEST HURDLE ON THE ROAD TO OUR PANACEA!
HOLD ON TO YOUR BUTTS, CUZ WE'RE OFF TO GET A CERTAIN INGREDIENT.
ALL RIGHT, I'LL MAKE A SPEAR. BUT ONLY A SILVER ONE.
!! !!
GASP
OOH, TOUGH LUCK, KINRO.
MUST BE MY CHARM THAT MAKES PEOPLE DOTE ON ME.

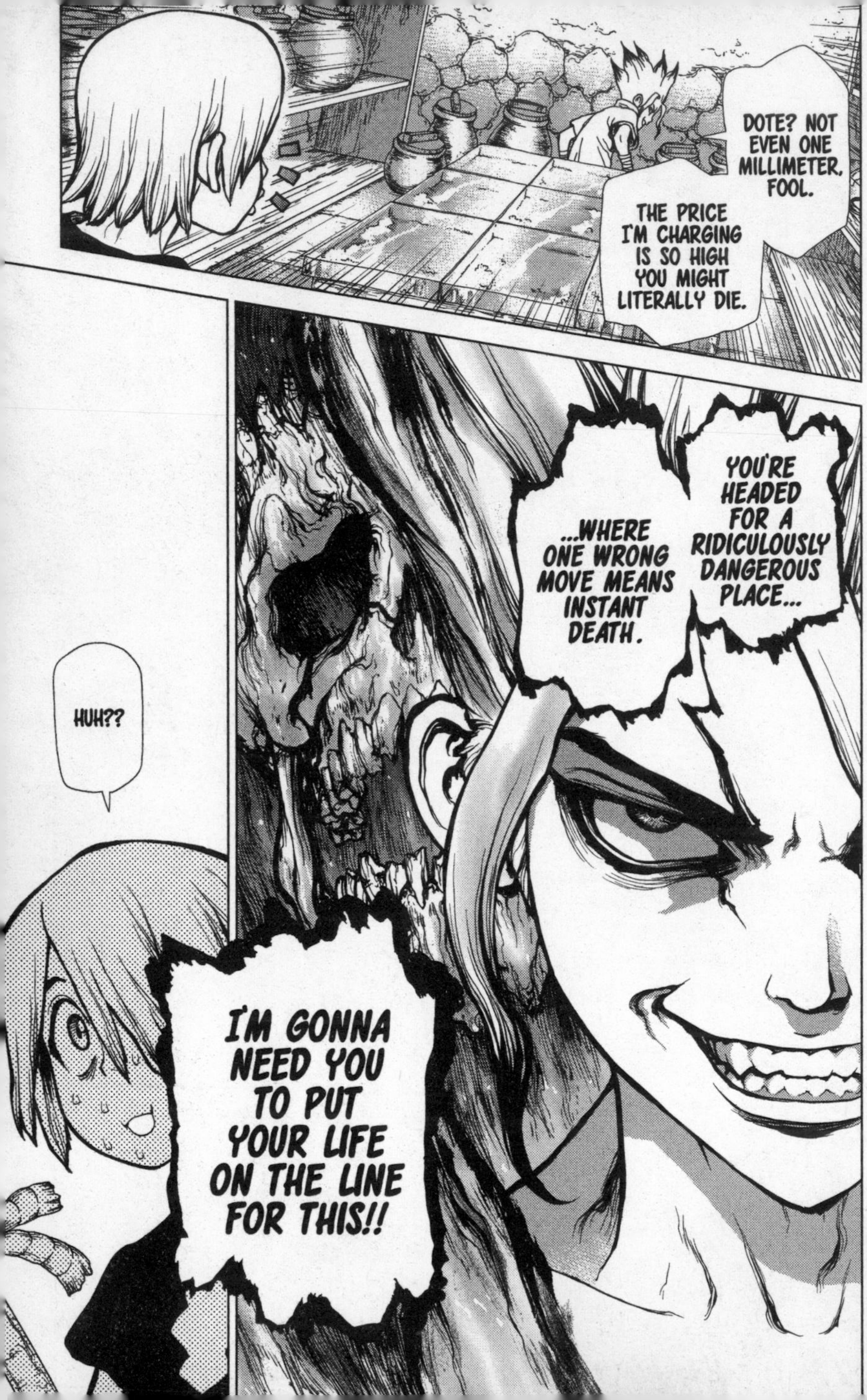
DOTE? NOT EVEN ONE MILLIMETER, FOOL.
THE PRICE I'M CHARGING IS SO HIGH YOU MIGHT LITERALLY DIE.
YOU'RE HEADED FOR A RIDICULOUSLY DANGEROUS PLACE...
...WHERE ONE WRONG MOVE MEANS INSTANT DEATH.
I'M GONNA NEED YOU TO PUT YOUR LIFE ON THE LINE FOR THIS!!
HUH??

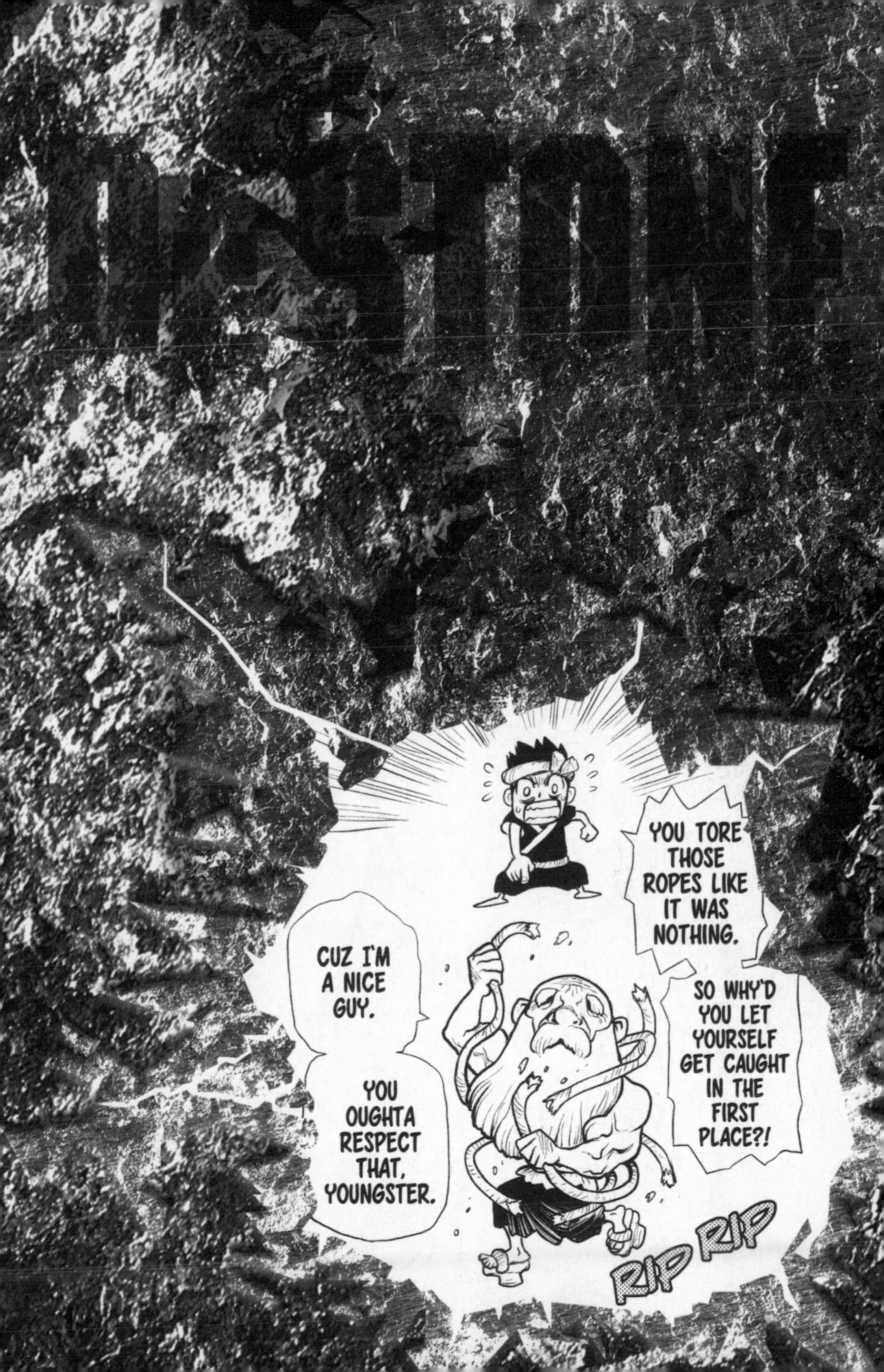
YOU TORE THOSE ROPES LIKE IT WAS NOTHING.
SO WHY'D YOU LET YOURSELF GET CAUGHT IN THE FIRST PLACE?!
CUZ I'M A NICE GUY.
YOU OUGHTA RESPECT THAT, YOUNGSTER.
RIP RIP

Z=30: DEATH GREEN

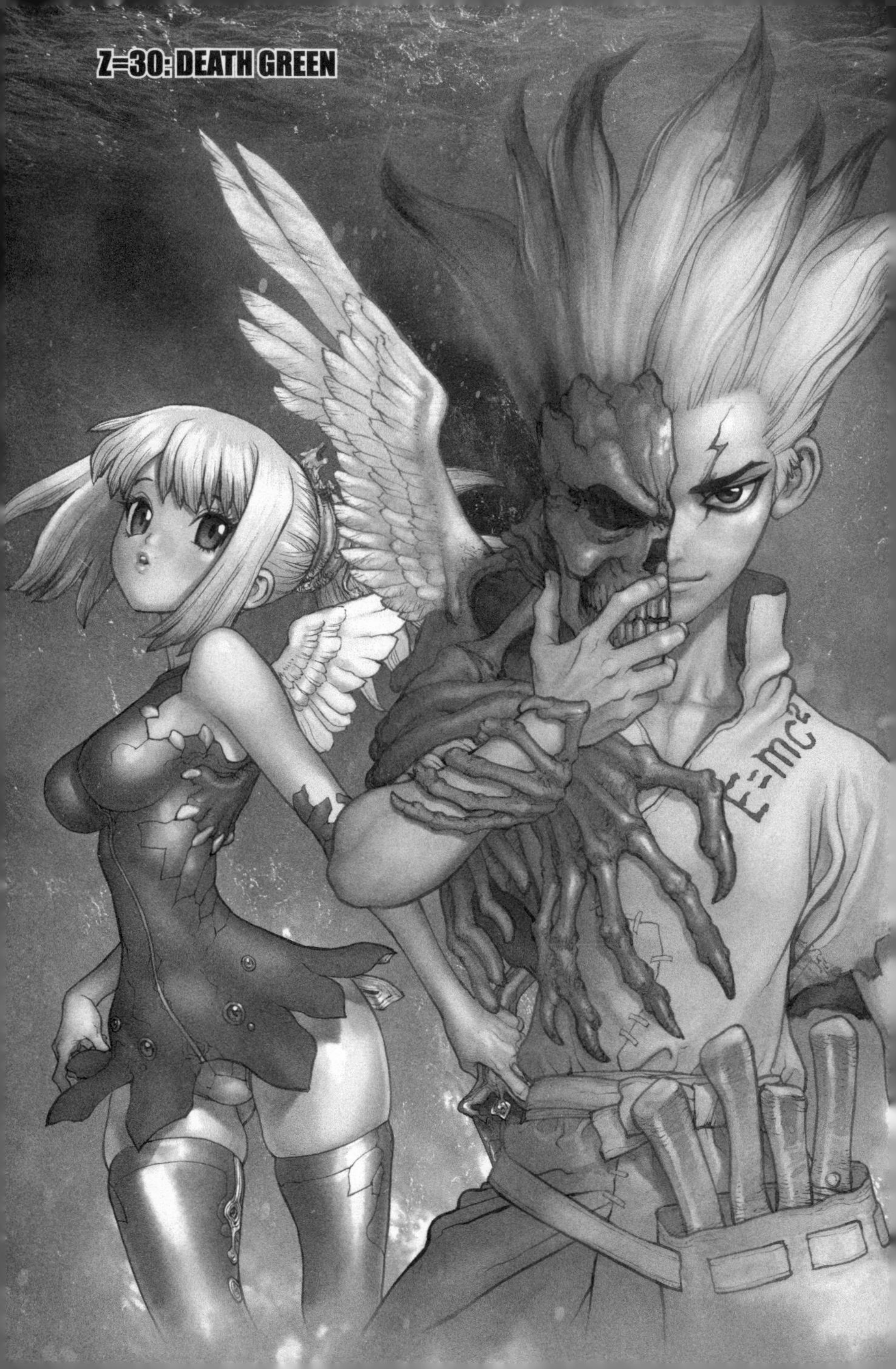
E=MC²

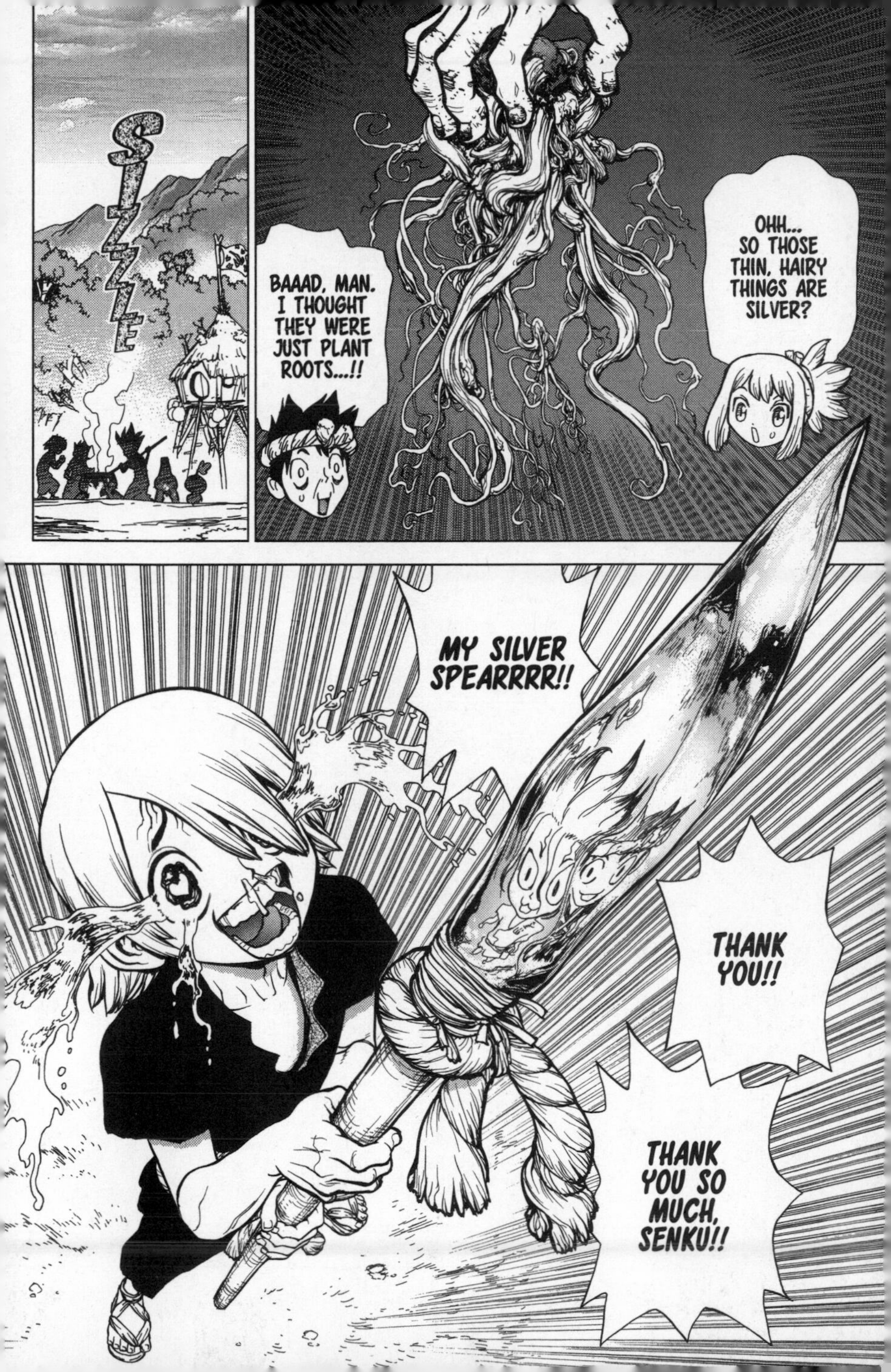
OHH... SO THOSE THIN, HAIRY THINGS ARE SILVER?
BAAAD, MAN. I THOUGHT THEY WERE JUST PLANT ROOTS...!!
SIZZLE
MY SILVER SPEARRRR!!
THANK YOU!!
THANK YOU SO MUCH, SENKU!!

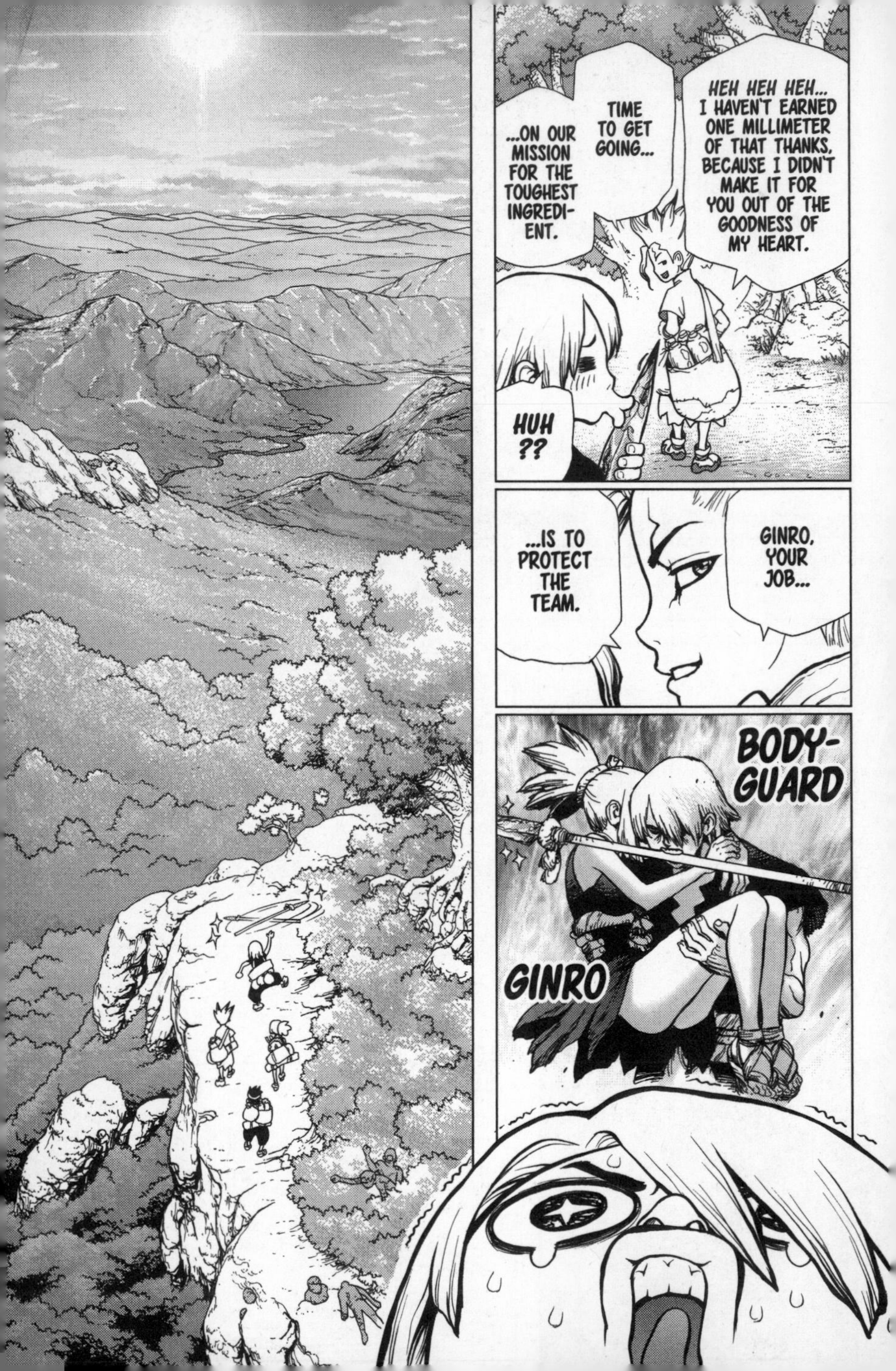
HEH HEH HEH... I HAVEN'T EARNED ONE MILLIMETER OF THAT THANKS, BECAUSE I DIDN'T MAKE IT FOR YOU OUT OF THE GOODNESS OF MY HEART.
TIME TO GET GOING...
...ON OUR MISSION FOR THE TOUGHEST INGREDI-ENT.
HUH ??
GINRO, YOUR JOB...
...IS TO PROTECT THE TEAM.
BODY-GUARD
GINRO

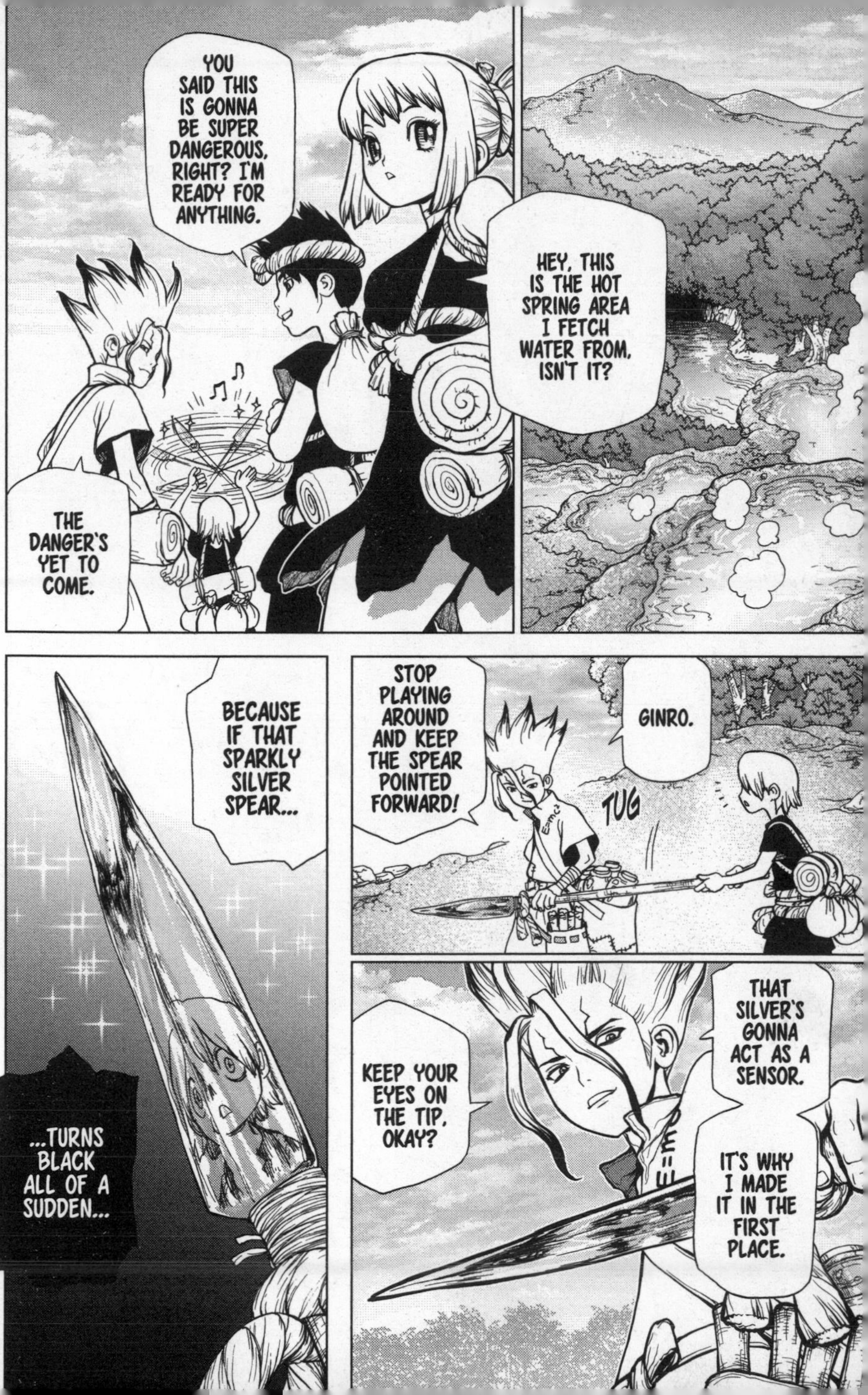
HEY, THIS IS THE HOT SPRING AREA I FETCH WATER FROM, ISN'T IT?
YOU SAID THIS IS GONNA BE SUPER DANGEROUS, RIGHT? I'M READY FOR ANYTHING.
THE DANGER'S YET TO COME.
GINRO.
STOP PLAYING AROUND AND KEEP THE SPEAR POINTED FORWARD!
TUG
THAT SILVER'S GONNA ACT AS A SENSOR.
IT'S WHY I MADE IT IN THE FIRST PLACE.
KEEP YOUR EYES ON THE TIP, OKAY?
BECAUSE IF THAT SPARKLY SILVER SPEAR...
...TURNS BLACK ALL OF A SUDDEN...

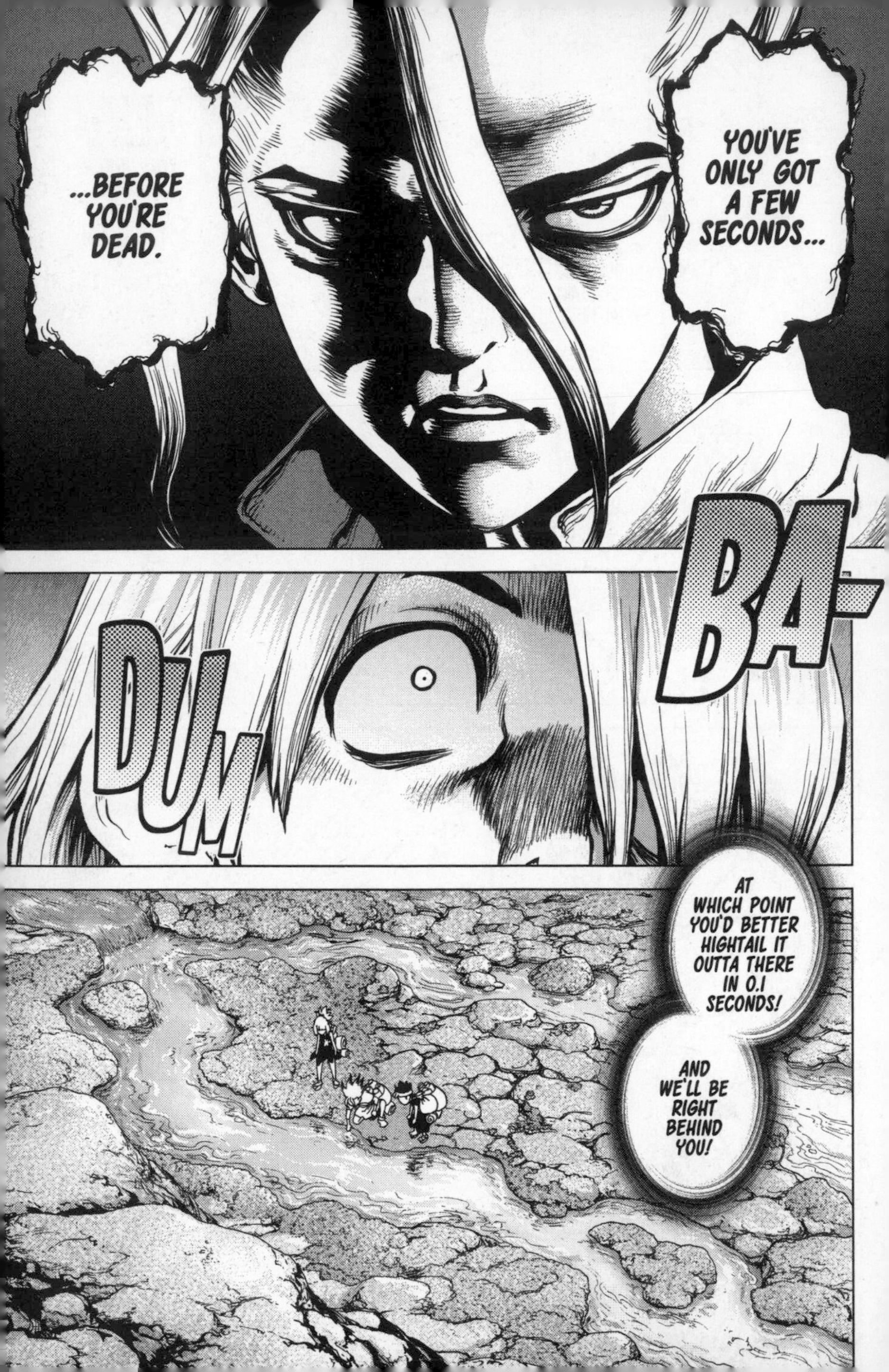
YOU'VE ONLY GOT A FEW SECONDS...
...BEFORE YOU'RE DEAD.
BA-
DUM
AT WHICH POINT YOU'D BETTER HIGHTAIL IT OUTTA THERE IN 0.1 SECONDS!
AND WE'LL BE RIGHT BEHIND YOU!

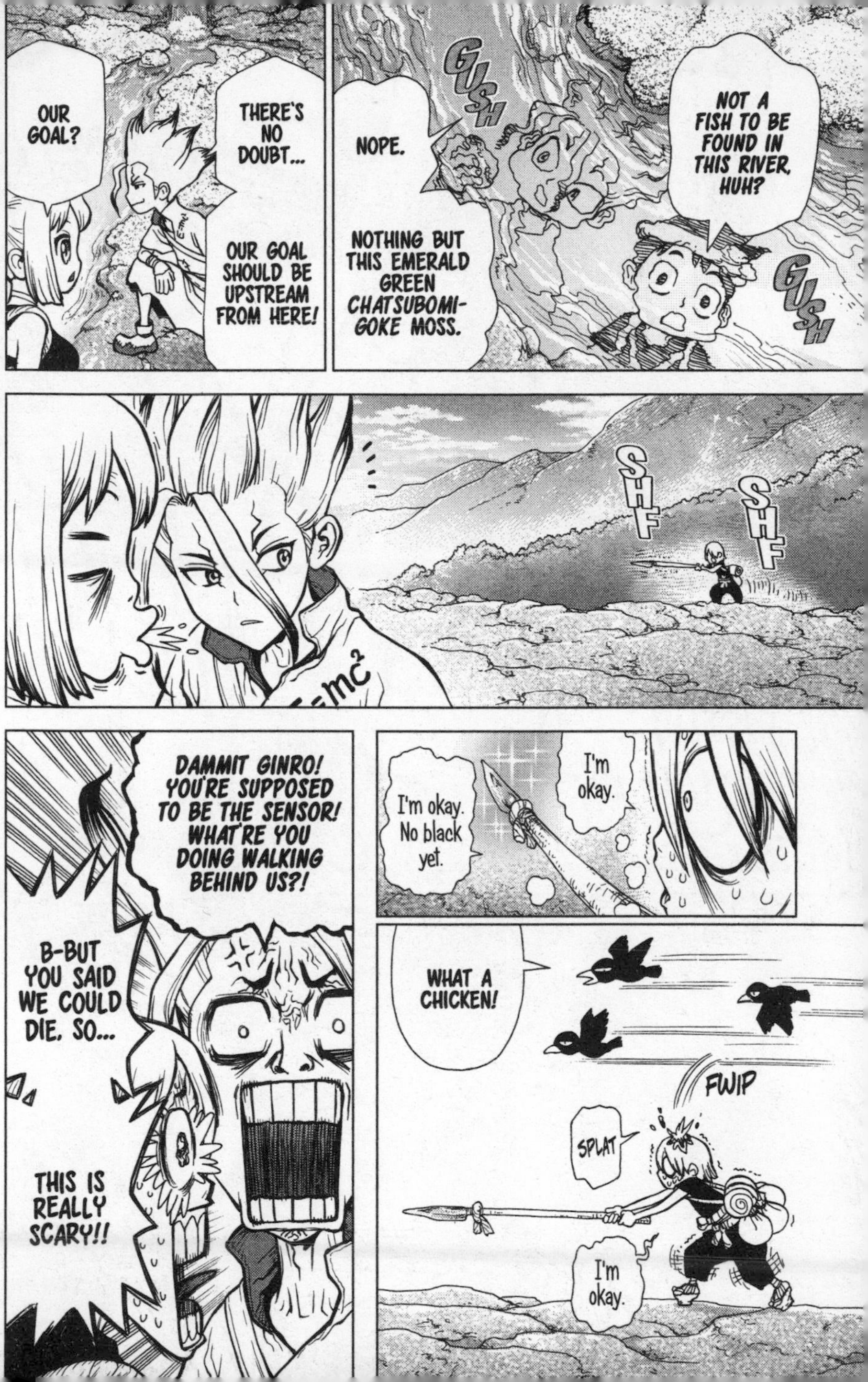
NOT A FISH TO BE FOUND IN THIS RIVER, HUH?
GUSH
GUSH
NOPE.
NOTHING BUT THIS EMERALD GREEN CHATSUBOMI-GOKE MOSS.
THERE'S NO DOUBT...
OUR GOAL SHOULD BE UPSTREAM FROM HERE!
OUR GOAL?
SHF
SHF
I'm okay.
I'm okay. No black yet.
WHAT A CHICKEN!
FWIP
SPLAT
I'm okay.
DAMMIT GINRO! YOU'RE SUPPOSED TO BE THE SENSOR! WHAT'RE YOU DOING WALKING BEHIND US?!
B-BUT YOU SAID WE COULD DIE, SO...
THIS IS REALLY SCARY!!

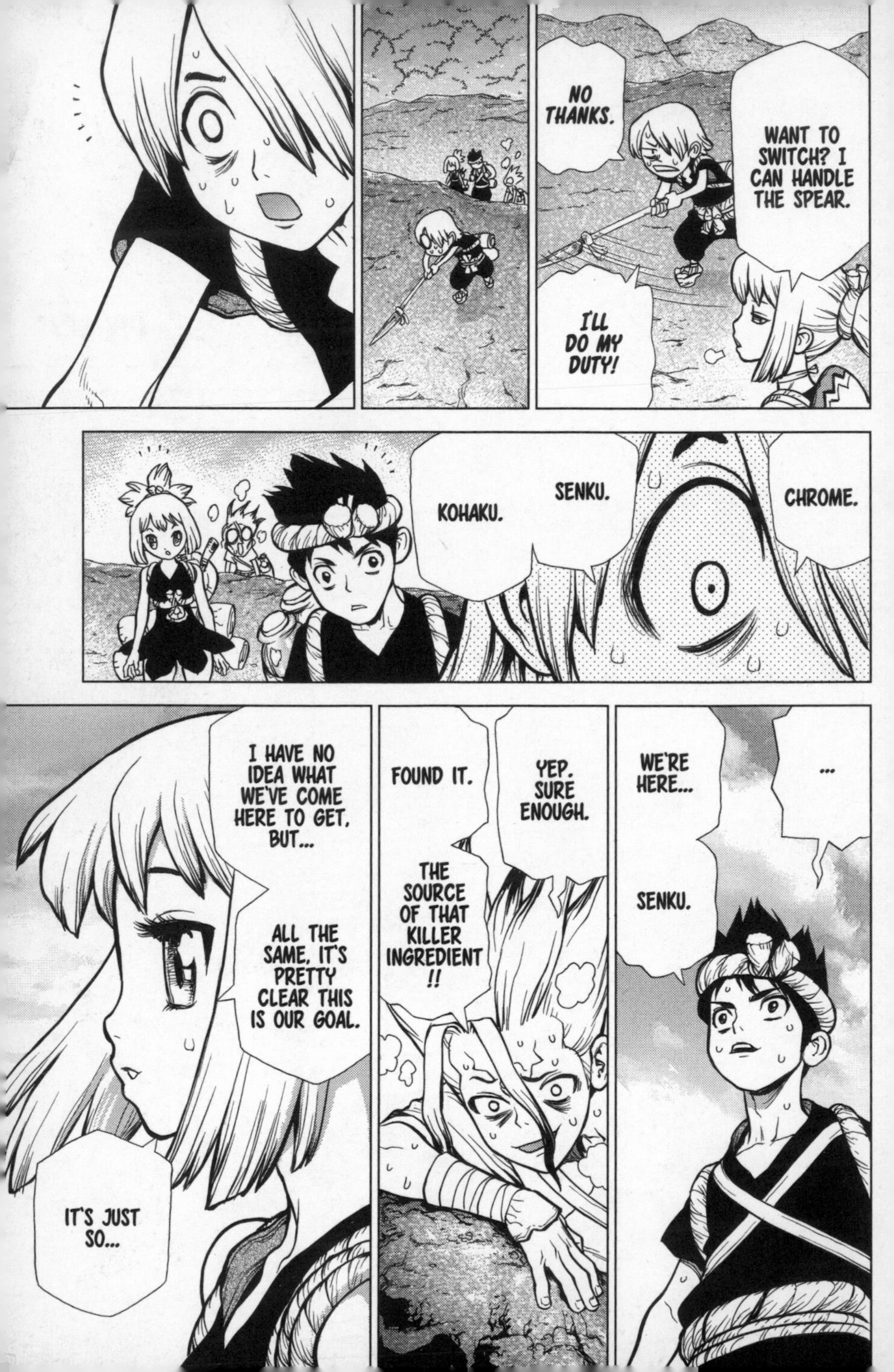
WANT TO SWITCH? I CAN HANDLE THE SPEAR.
NO THANKS.
I'LL DO MY DUTY!
CHROME.
SENKU.
KOHAKU.
...
WE'RE HERE...
SENKU.
YEP. SURE ENOUGH.
FOUND IT.
THE SOURCE OF THAT KILLER INGREDIENT!!
I HAVE NO IDEA WHAT WE'VE COME HERE TO GET, BUT...
ALL THE SAME, IT'S PRETTY CLEAR THIS IS OUR GOAL.
IT'S JUST SO...

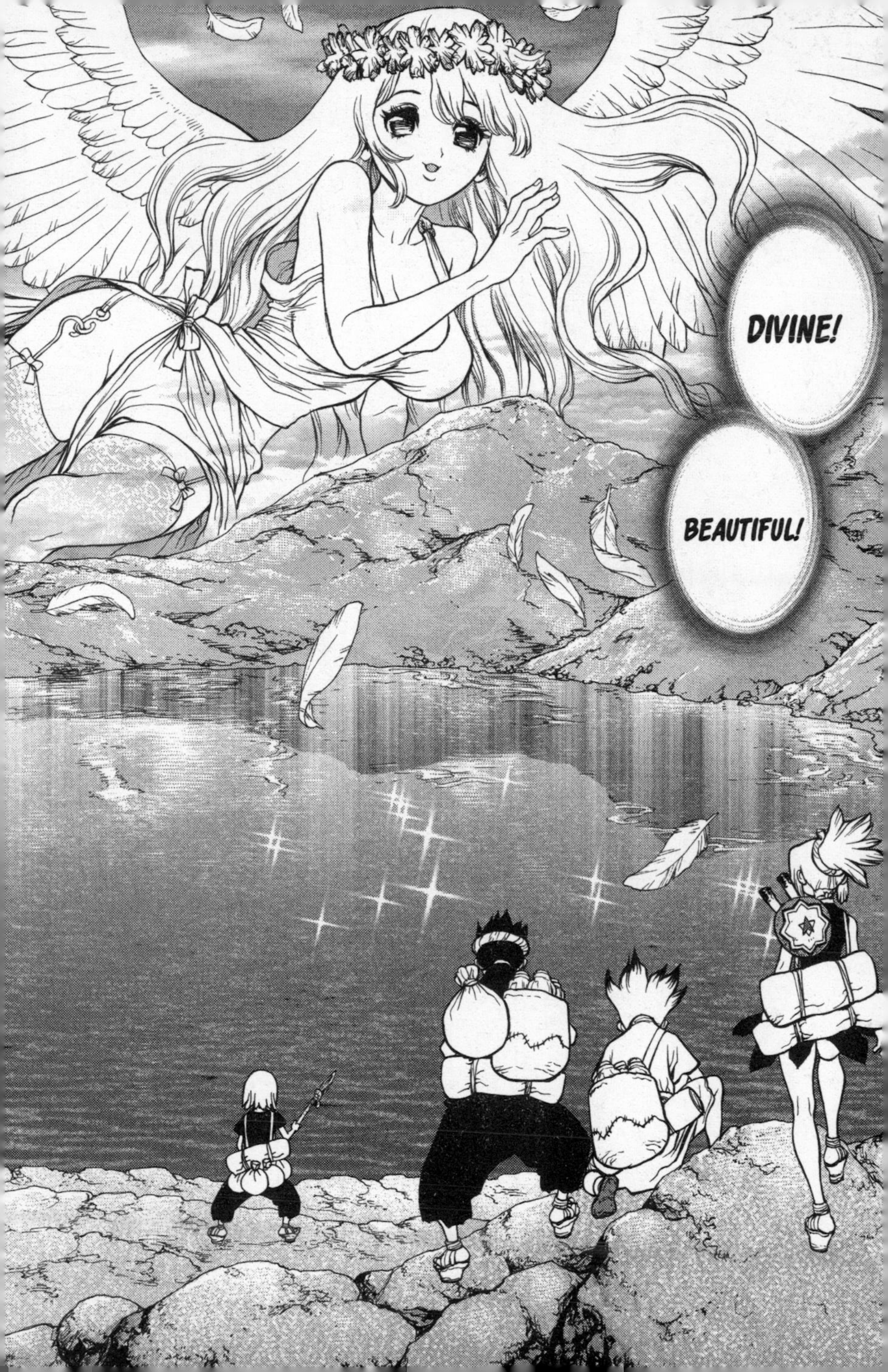
DIVINE!
BEAUTIFUL!

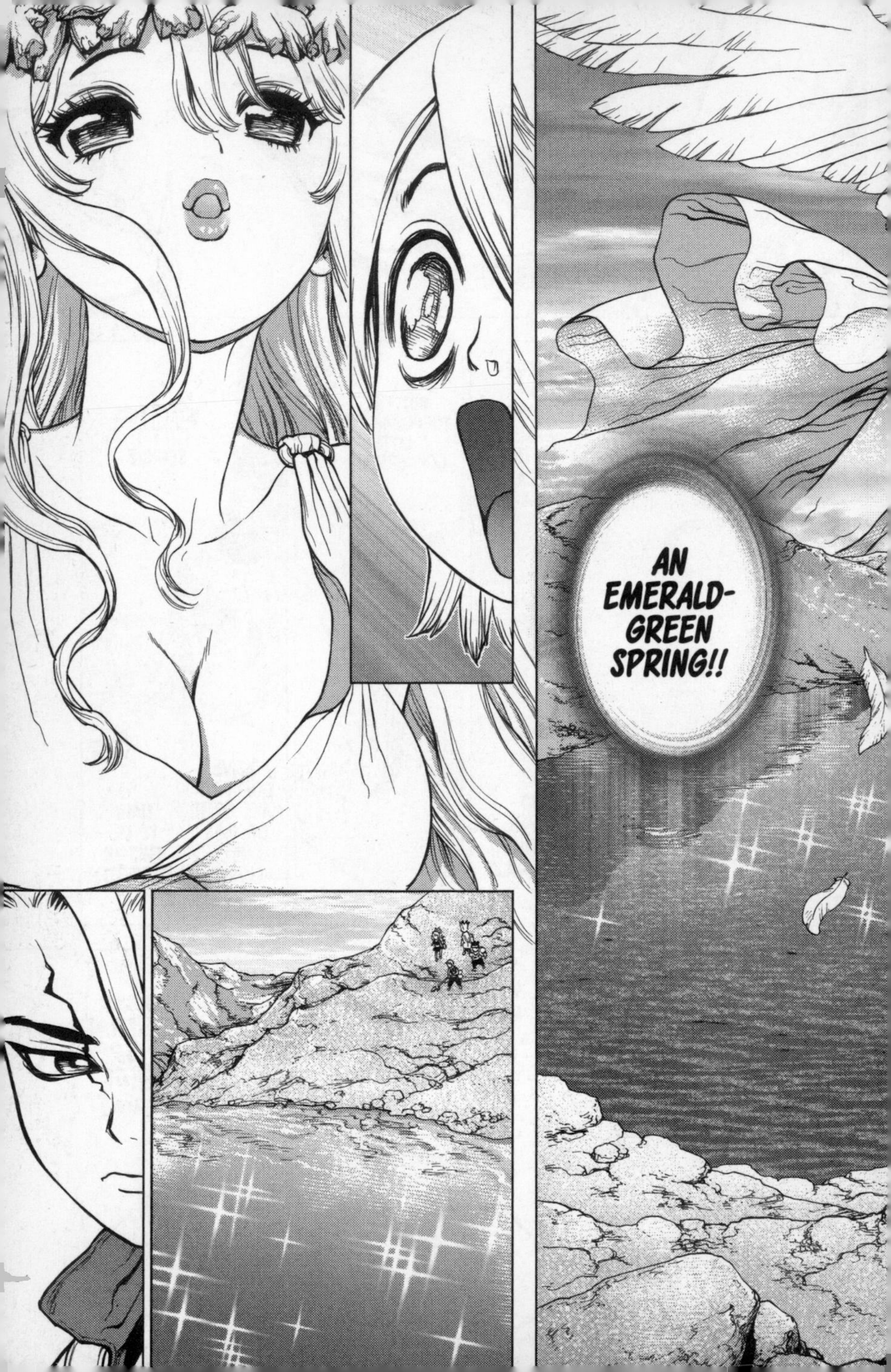
AN EMERALD-GREEN SPRING!!

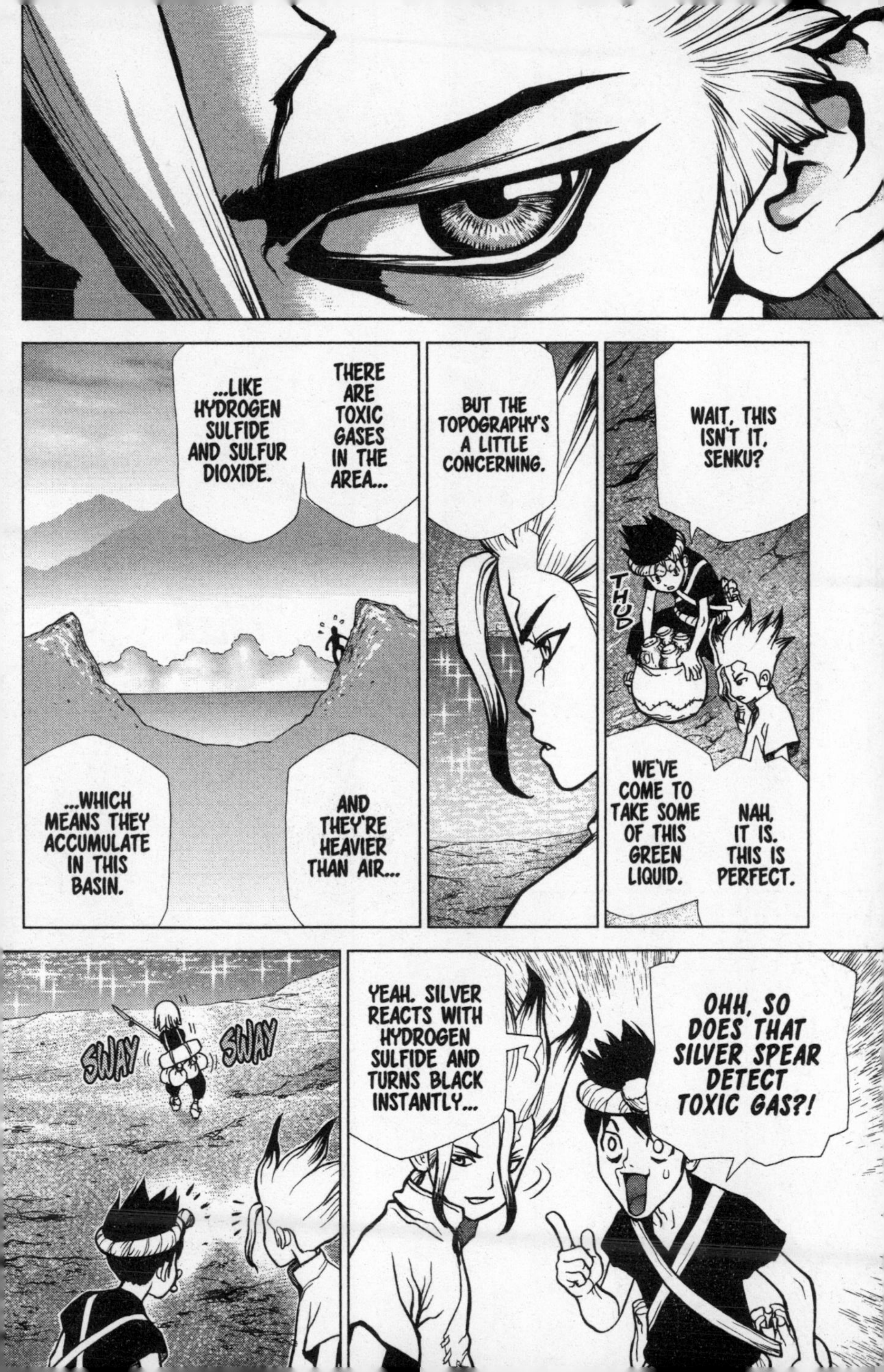
WAIT, THIS ISN'T IT, SENKU?
THUD
NAH, IT IS. THIS IS PERFECT.
WE'VE COME TO TAKE SOME OF THIS GREEN LIQUID.
BUT THE TOPOGRAPHY'S A LITTLE CONCERNING.
THERE ARE TOXIC GASES IN THE AREA...
...LIKE HYDROGEN SULFIDE AND SULFUR DIOXIDE.
AND THEY'RE HEAVIER THAN AIR...
...WHICH MEANS THEY ACCUMULATE IN THIS BASIN.
OHH, SO DOES THAT SILVER SPEAR DETECT TOXIC GAS?!
YEAH. SILVER REACTS WITH HYDROGEN SULFIDE AND TURNS BLACK INSTANTLY...
SWAY
SWAY

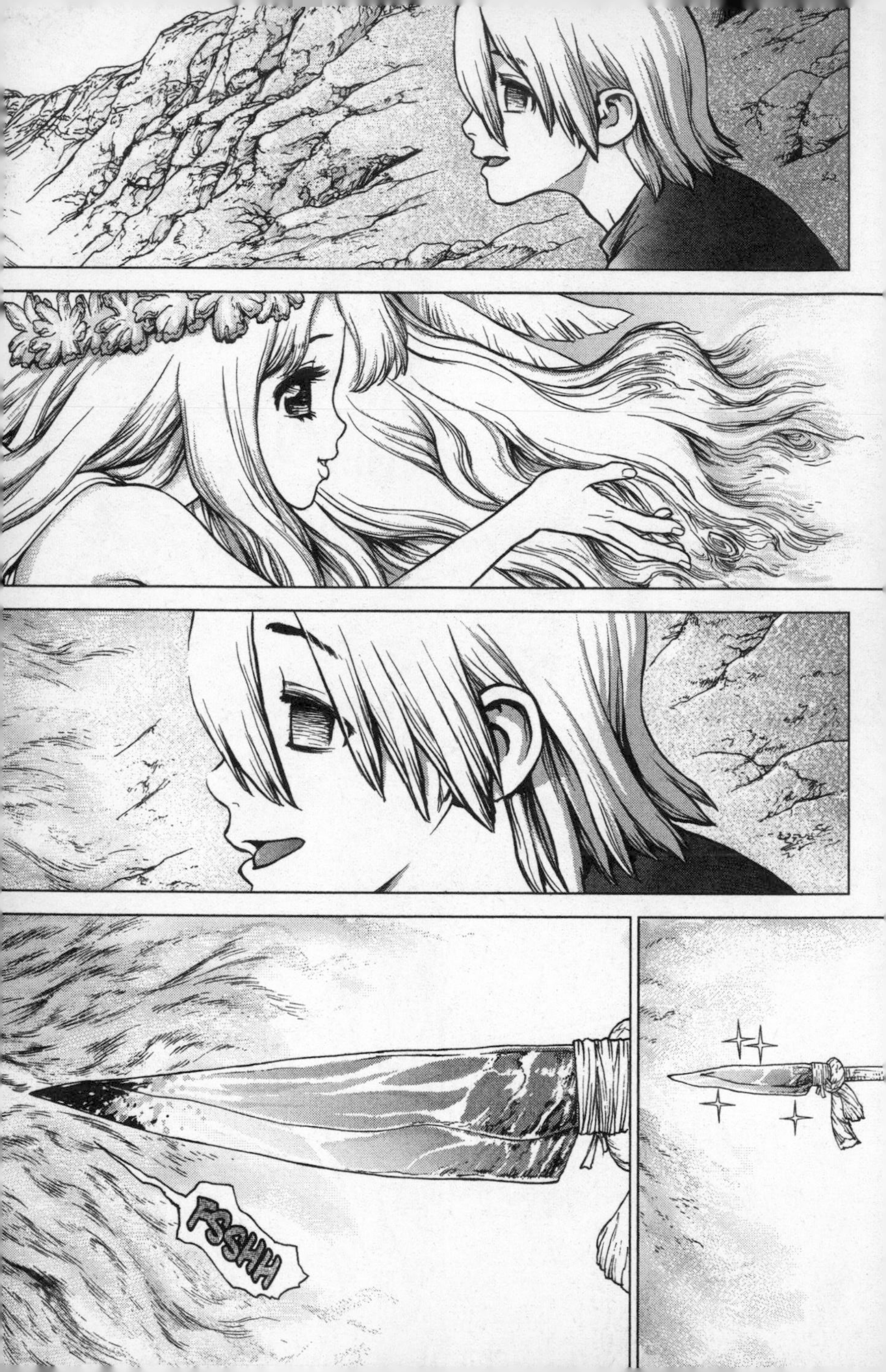
FSSHH

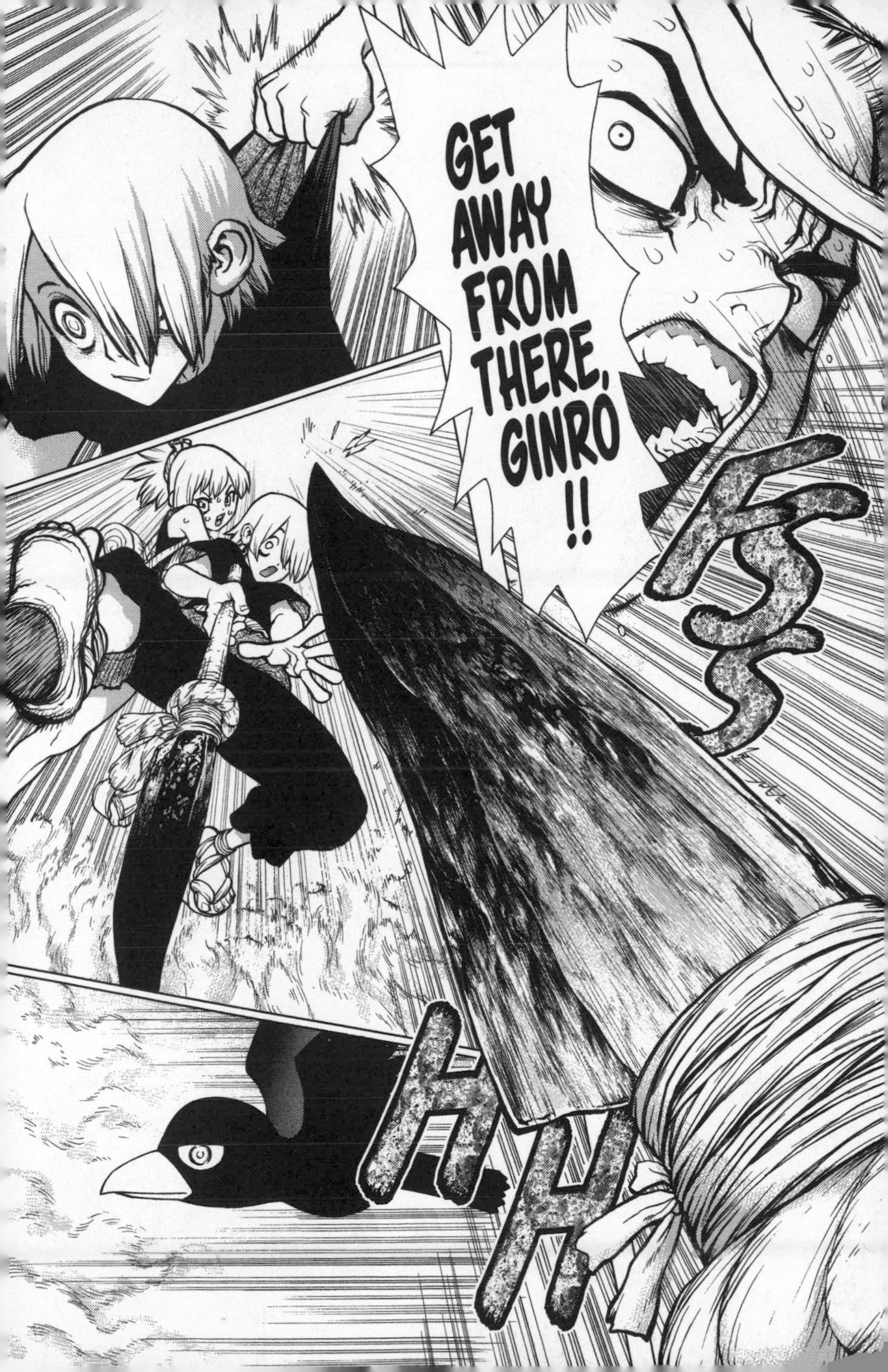
GET AWAY FROM THERE, GINRO!!
FSS

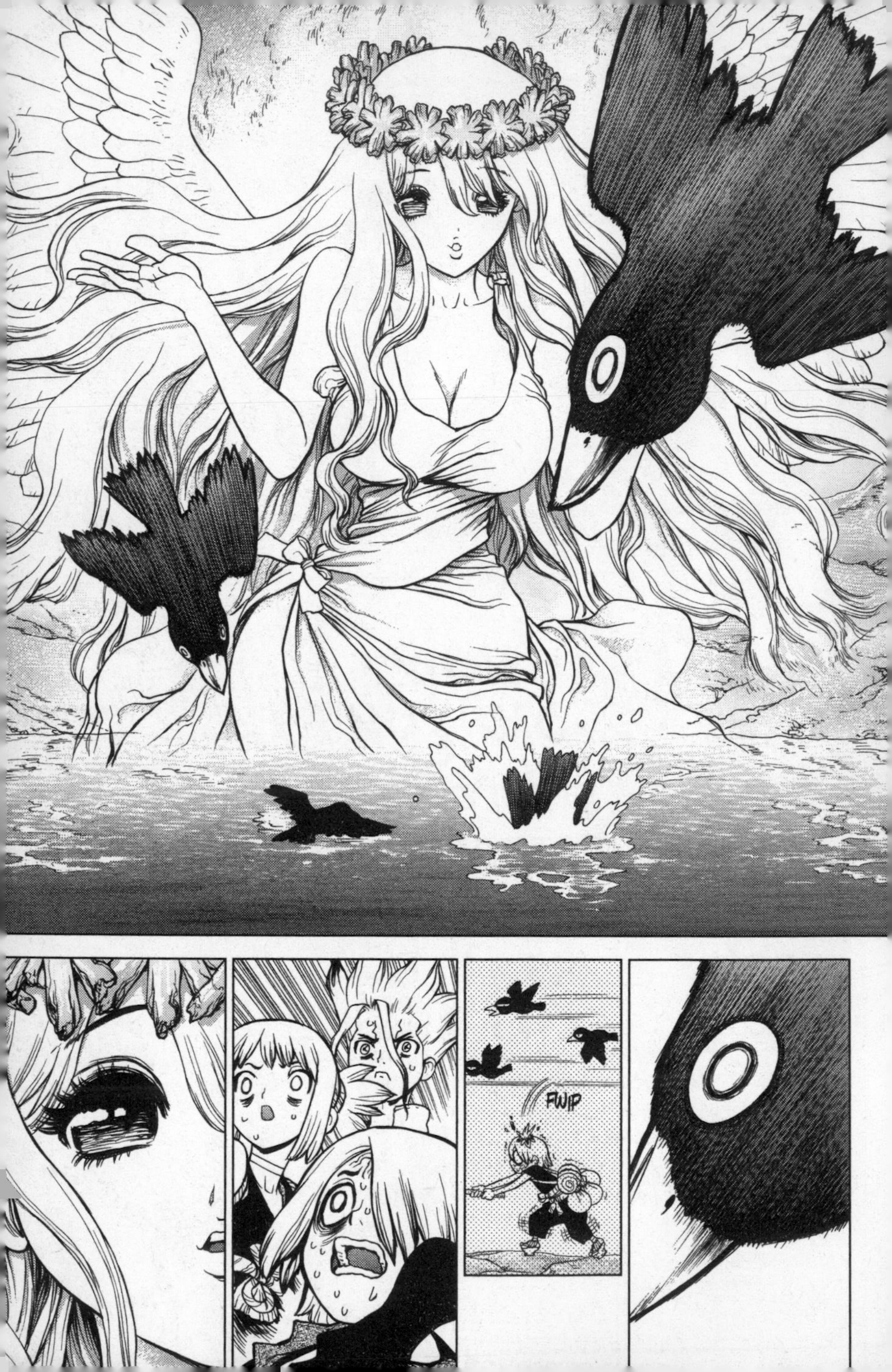
FWIP

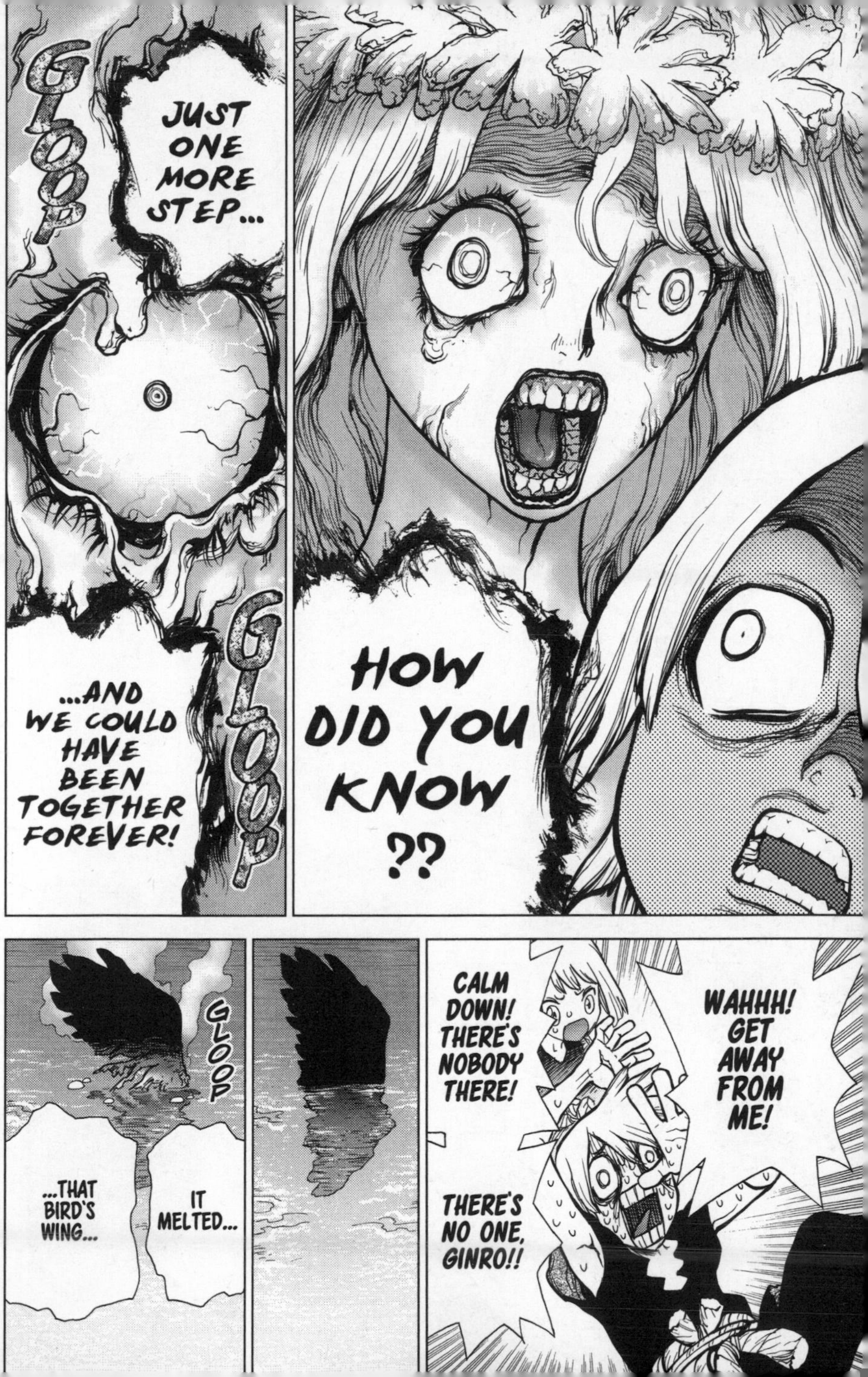
HOW DID YOU KNOW ??
JUST ONE MORE STEP...
GLOOP
GLOOP
...AND WE COULD HAVE BEEN TOGETHER FOREVER!
WAHHH! GET AWAY FROM ME!
CALM DOWN! THERE'S NOBODY THERE!
THERE'S NO ONE, GINRO!!
GLOOP
IT MELTED...
...THAT BIRD'S WING...

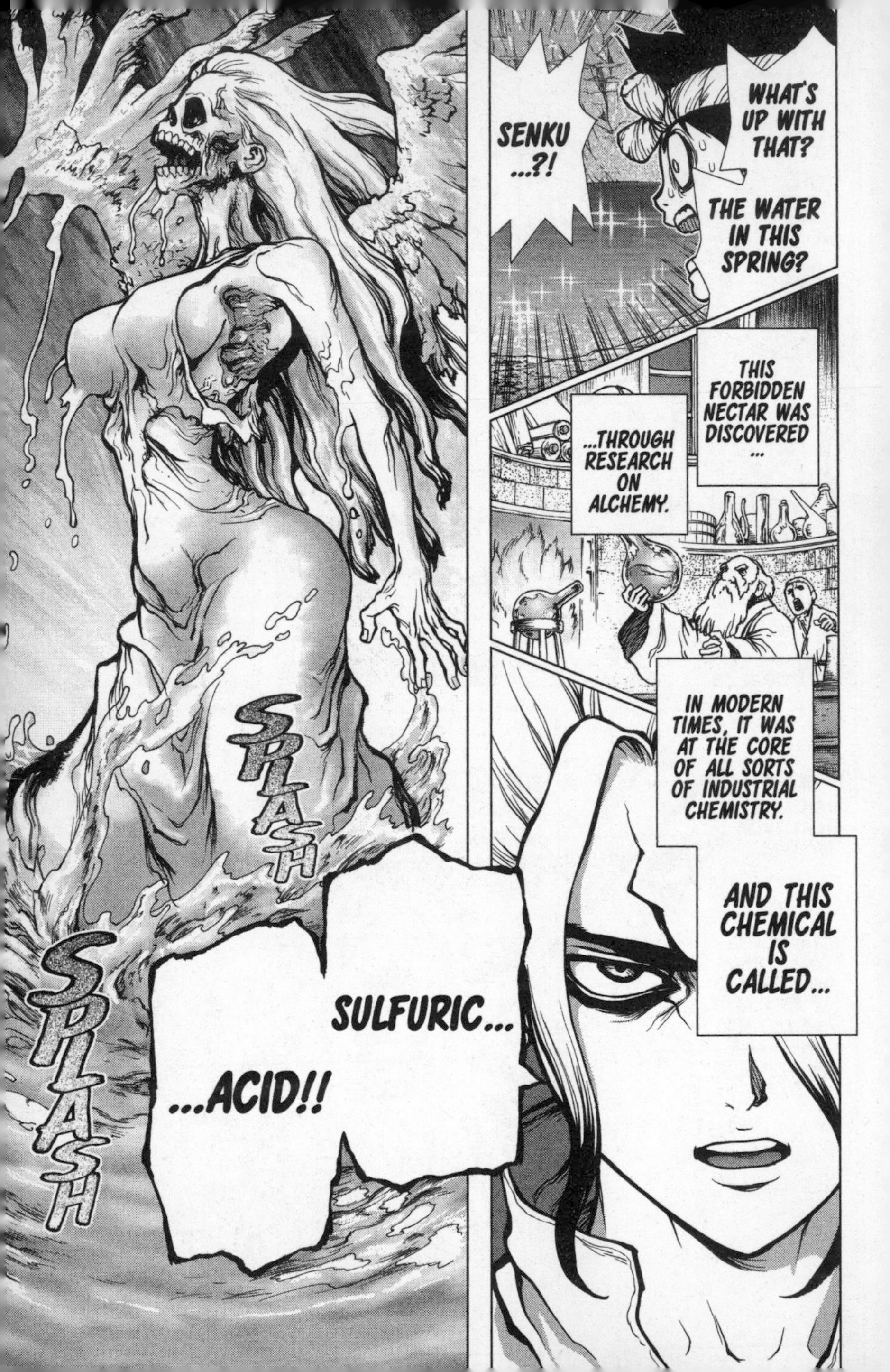

WHAT'S UP WITH THAT?
THE WATER IN THIS SPRING?
SENKU ...?!
THIS FORBIDDEN NECTAR WAS DISCOVERED ...
...THROUGH RESEARCH ON ALCHEMY.
IN MODERN TIMES, IT WAS AT THE CORE OF ALL SORTS OF INDUSTRIAL CHEMISTRY.
AND THIS CHEMICAL IS CALLED...
SULFURIC...
...ACID!!
SPLASH
SPLASH

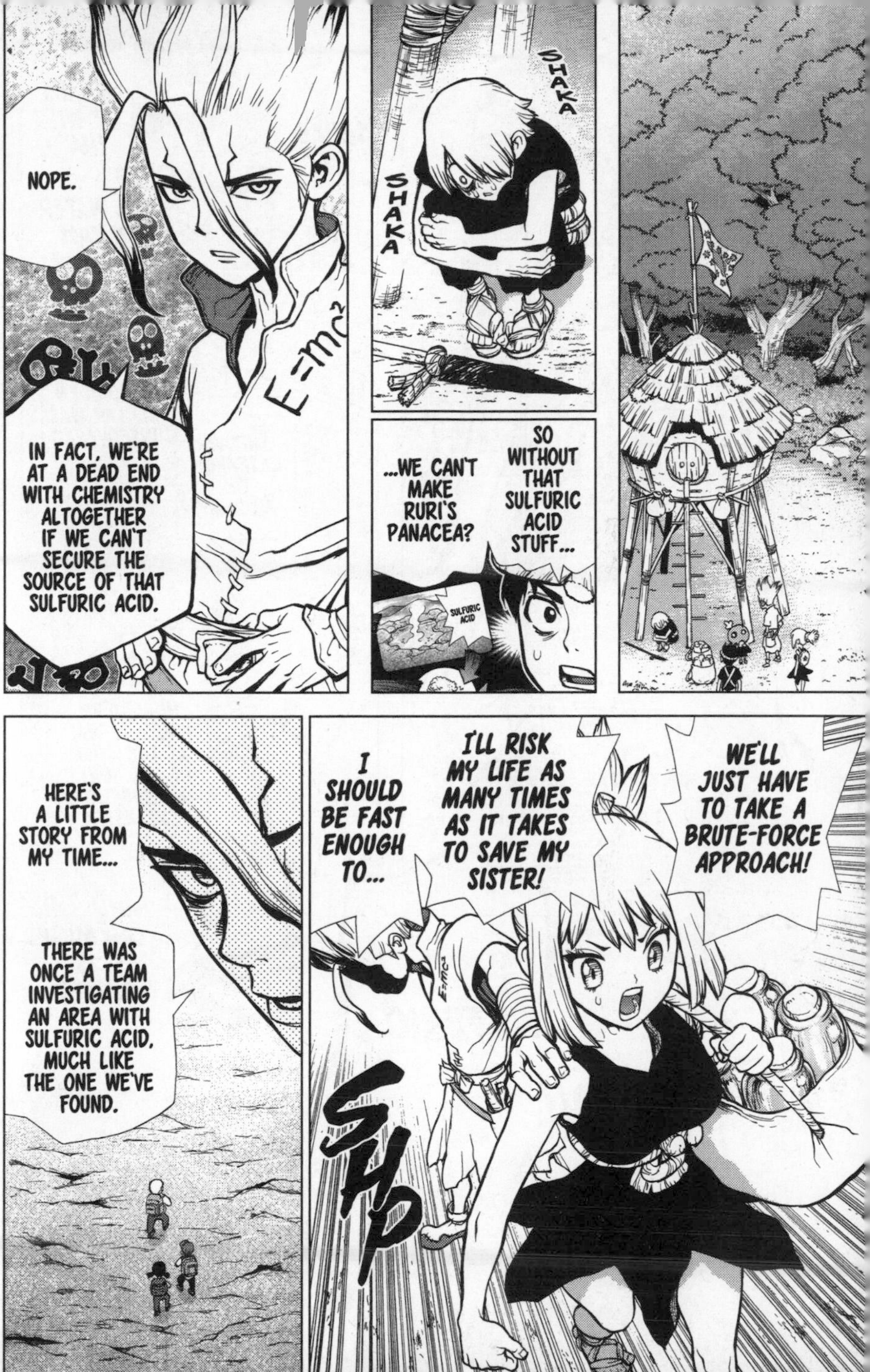
SHAKA
SHAKA
SO WITHOUT THAT SULFURIC ACID STUFF...
...WE CAN'T MAKE RURI'S PANACEA?
SULFURIC ACID
NOPE.
IN FACT, WE'RE AT A DEAD END WITH CHEMISTRY ALTOGETHER IF WE CAN'T SECURE THE SOURCE OF THAT SULFURIC ACID.
E=mc²
WE'LL JUST HAVE TO TAKE A BRUTE-FORCE APPROACH!
I'LL RISK MY LIFE AS MANY TIMES AS IT TAKES TO SAVE MY SISTER!
I SHOULD BE FAST ENOUGH TO...
SHP
HERE'S A LITTLE STORY FROM MY TIME...
THERE WAS ONCE A TEAM INVESTIGATING AN AREA WITH SULFURIC ACID, MUCH LIKE THE ONE WE'VE FOUND.

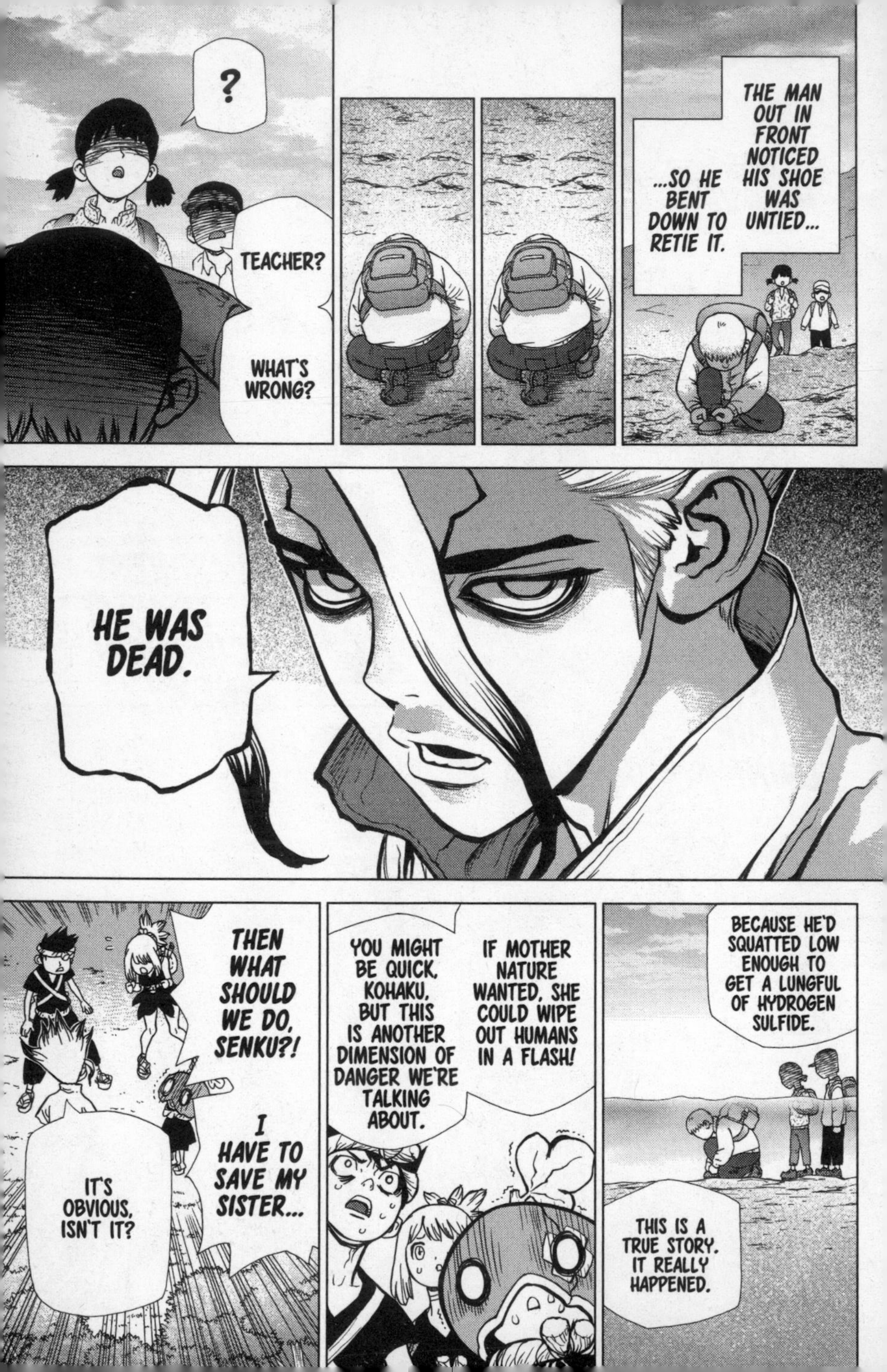
THE MAN OUT IN FRONT NOTICED HIS SHOE WAS UNTIED...
...SO HE BENT DOWN TO RETIE IT.
?
TEACHER?
WHAT'S WRONG?
HE WAS DEAD.
BECAUSE HE'D SQUATTED LOW ENOUGH TO GET A LUNGFUL OF HYDROGEN SULFIDE.
THIS IS A TRUE STORY. IT REALLY HAPPENED.
IF MOTHER NATURE WANTED, SHE COULD WIPE OUT HUMANS IN A FLASH!
YOU MIGHT BE QUICK, KOHAKU, BUT THIS IS ANOTHER DIMENSION OF DANGER WE'RE TALKING ABOUT.
THEN WHAT SHOULD WE DO, SENKU?!
I HAVE TO SAVE MY SISTER...
IT'S OBVIOUS, ISN'T IT?

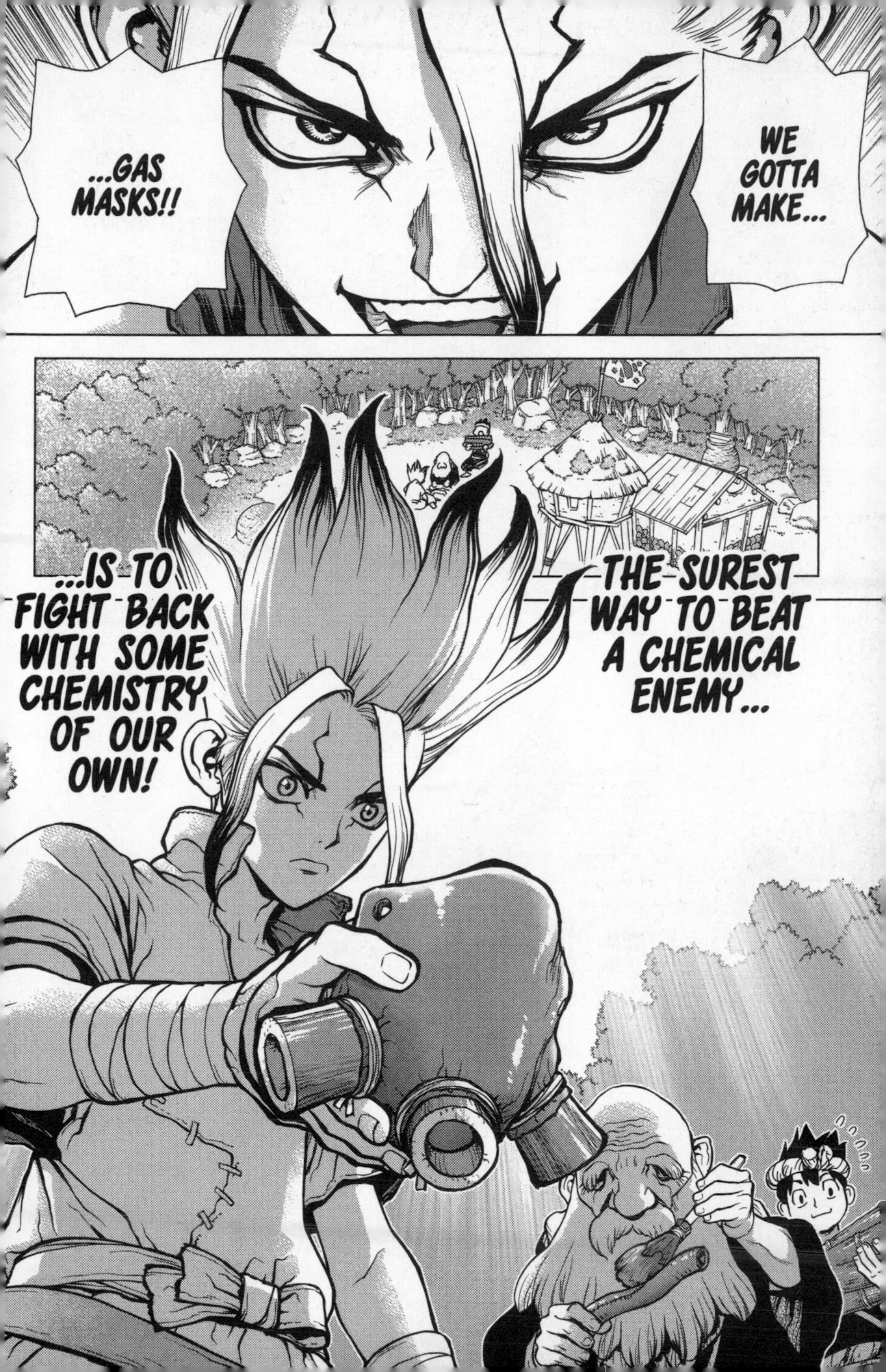
WE GOTTA MAKE...
...GAS MASKS!!
THE SUREST WAY TO BEAT A CHEMICAL ENEMY...
...IS TO FIGHT BACK WITH SOME CHEMISTRY OF OUR OWN!

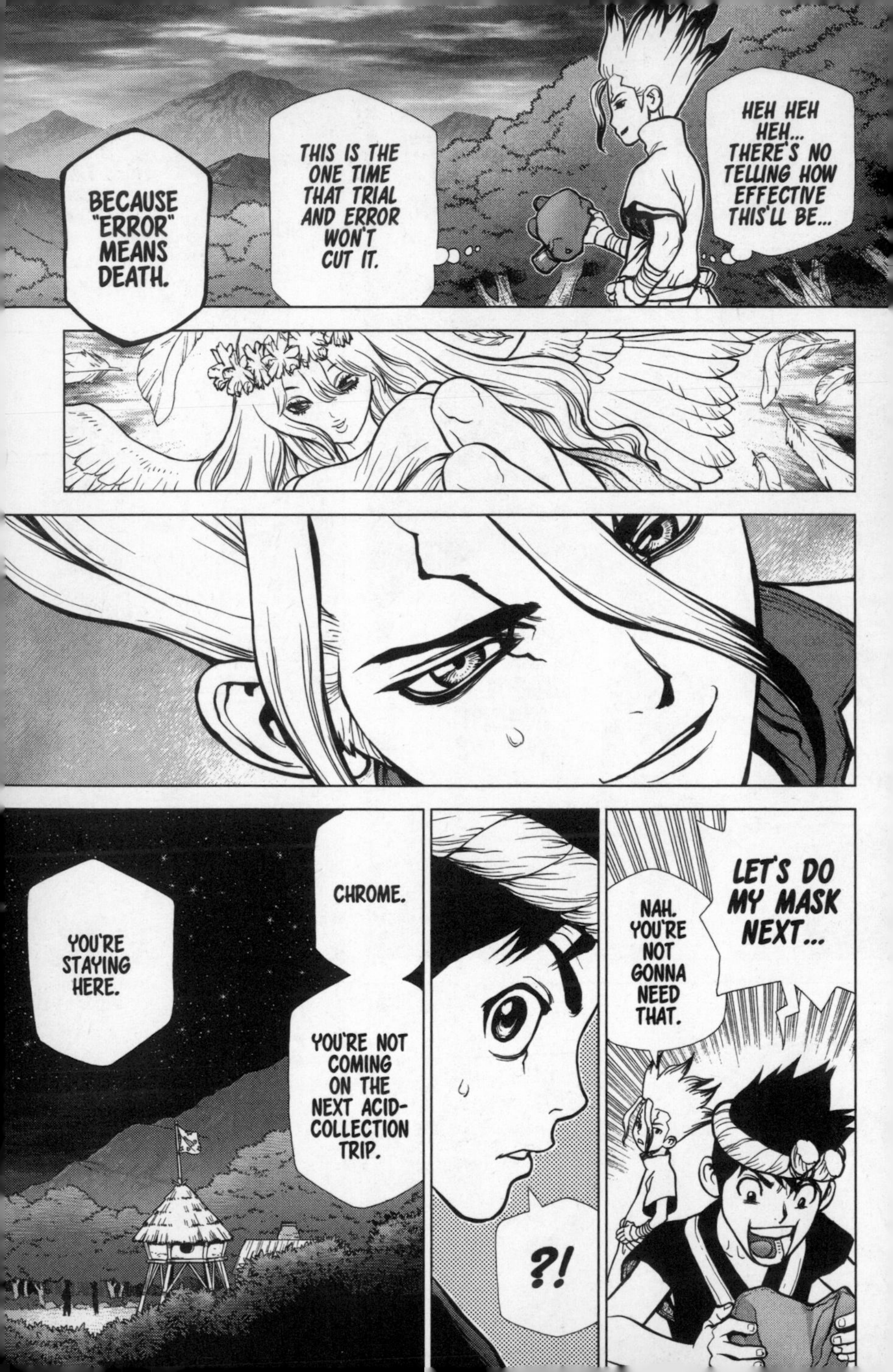
HEH HEH HEH... THERE'S NO TELLING HOW EFFECTIVE THIS'LL BE...
THIS IS THE ONE TIME THAT TRIAL AND ERROR WON'T CUT IT.
BECAUSE "ERROR" MEANS DEATH.
LET'S DO MY MASK NEXT...
NAH. YOU'RE NOT GONNA NEED THAT.
CHROME.
YOU'RE NOT COMING ON THE NEXT ACID-COLLECTION TRIP.
?!
YOU'RE STAYING HERE.

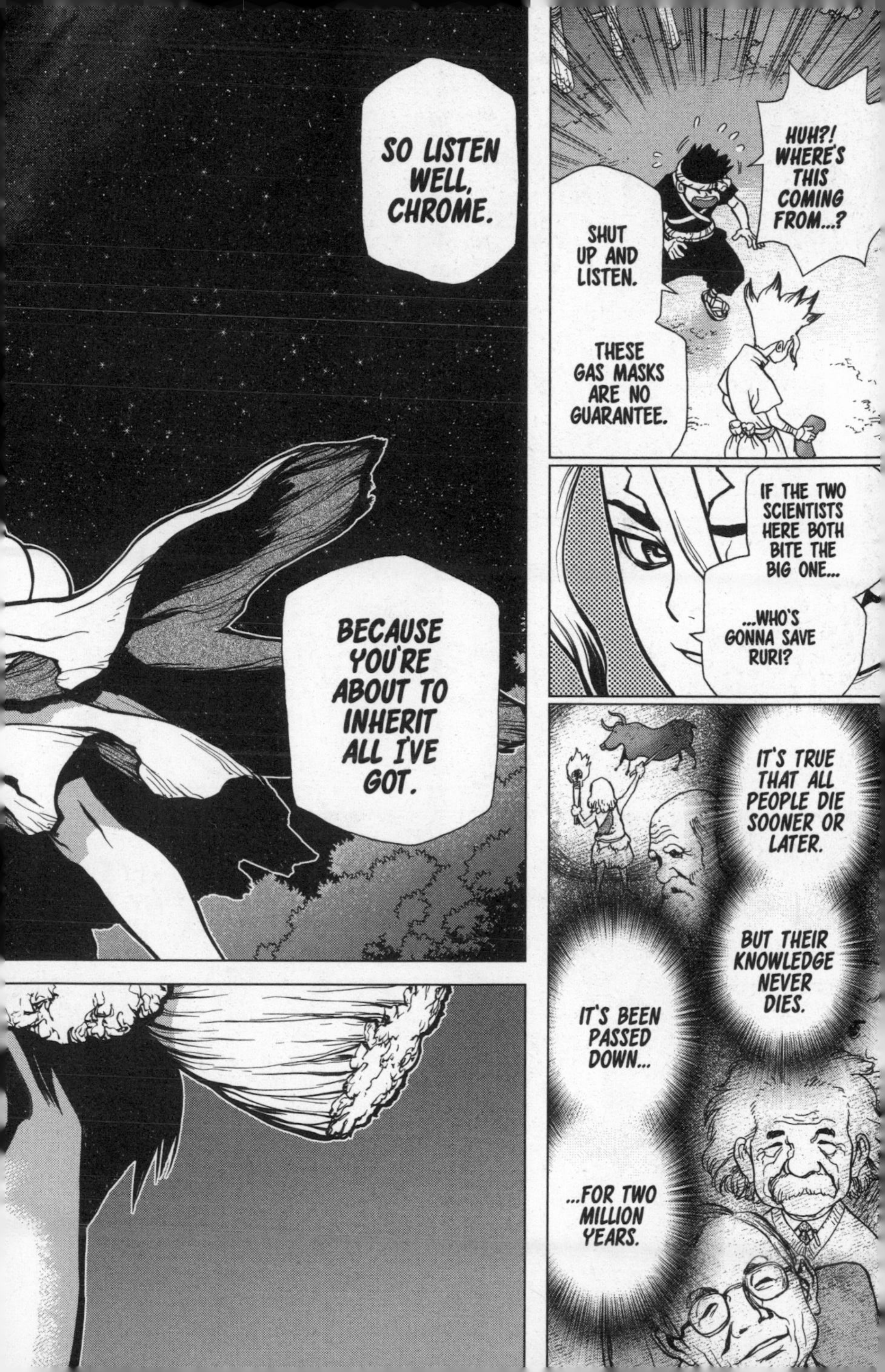
HUH?! WHERE'S THIS COMING FROM...?
SHUT UP AND LISTEN.
THESE GAS MASKS ARE NO GUARANTEE.
IF THE TWO SCIENTISTS HERE BOTH BITE THE BIG ONE...
...WHO'S GONNA SAVE RURI?
IT'S TRUE THAT ALL PEOPLE DIE SOONER OR LATER.
BUT THEIR KNOWLEDGE NEVER DIES.
IT'S BEEN PASSED DOWN...
...FOR TWO MILLION YEARS.
SO LISTEN WELL, CHROME.
BECAUSE YOU'RE ABOUT TO INHERIT ALL I'VE GOT.

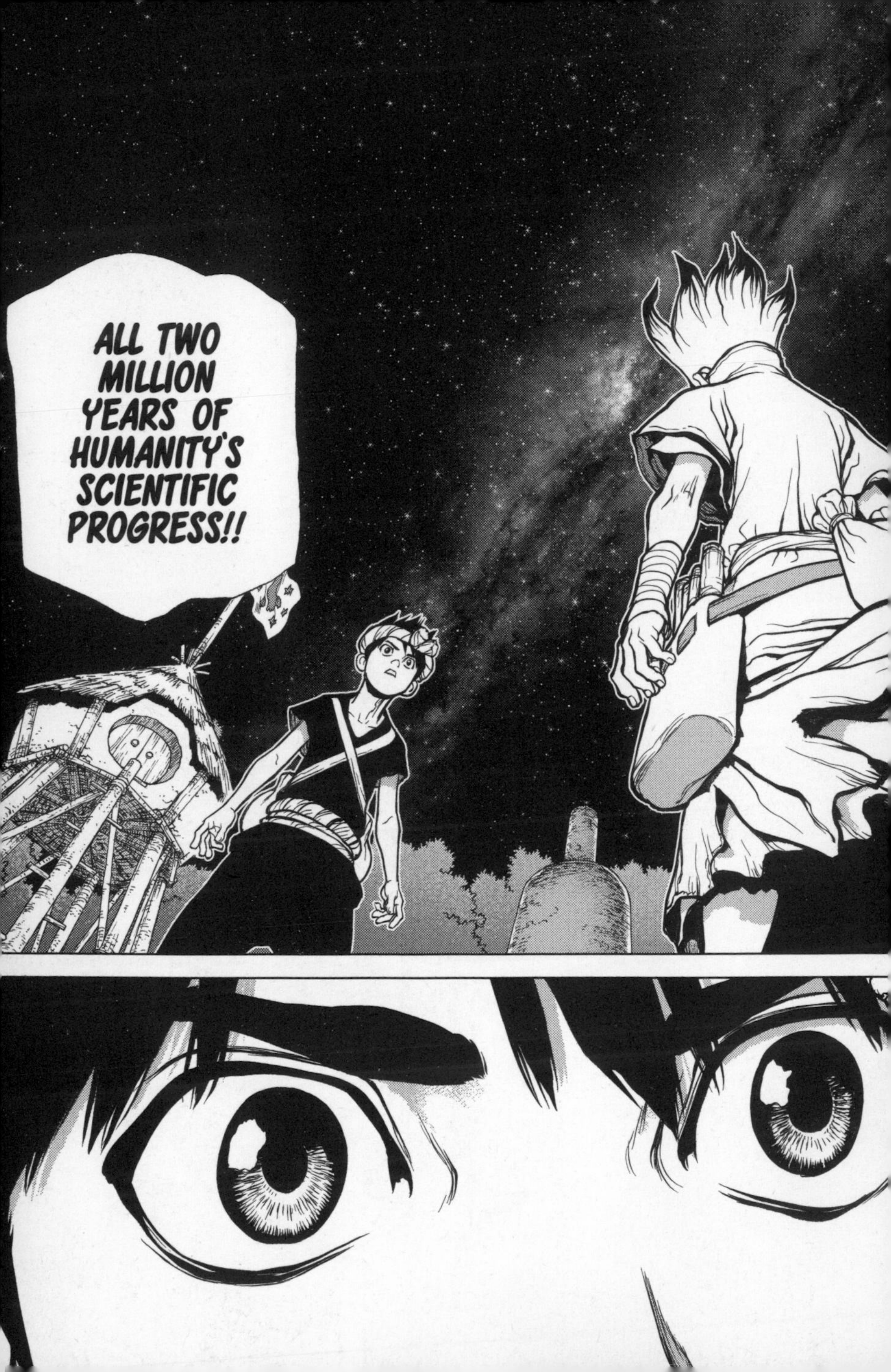
ALL TWO MILLION YEARS OF HUMANITY'S SCIENTIFIC PROGRESS!!

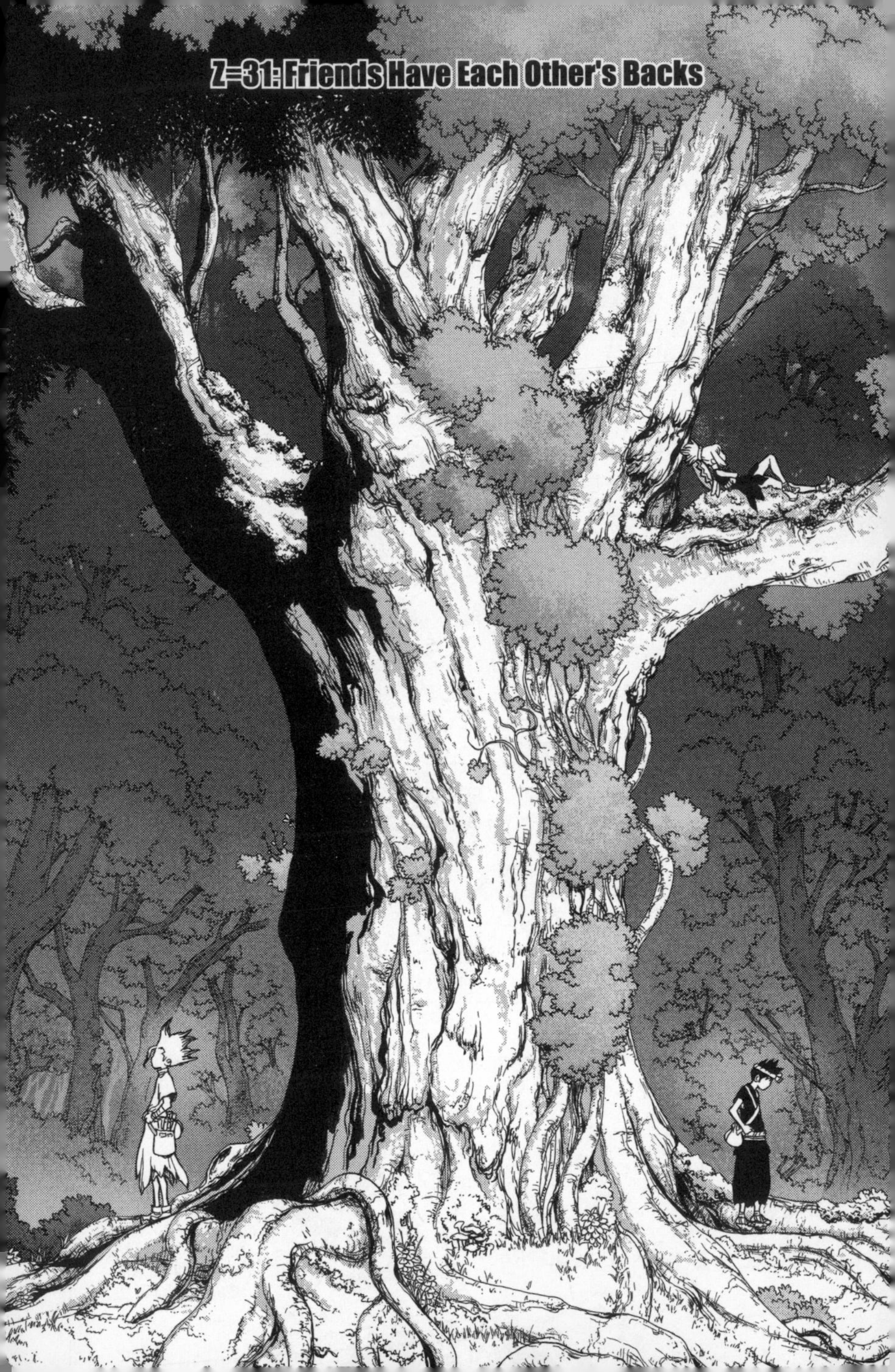
Z=31: Friends Have Each Other's Backs

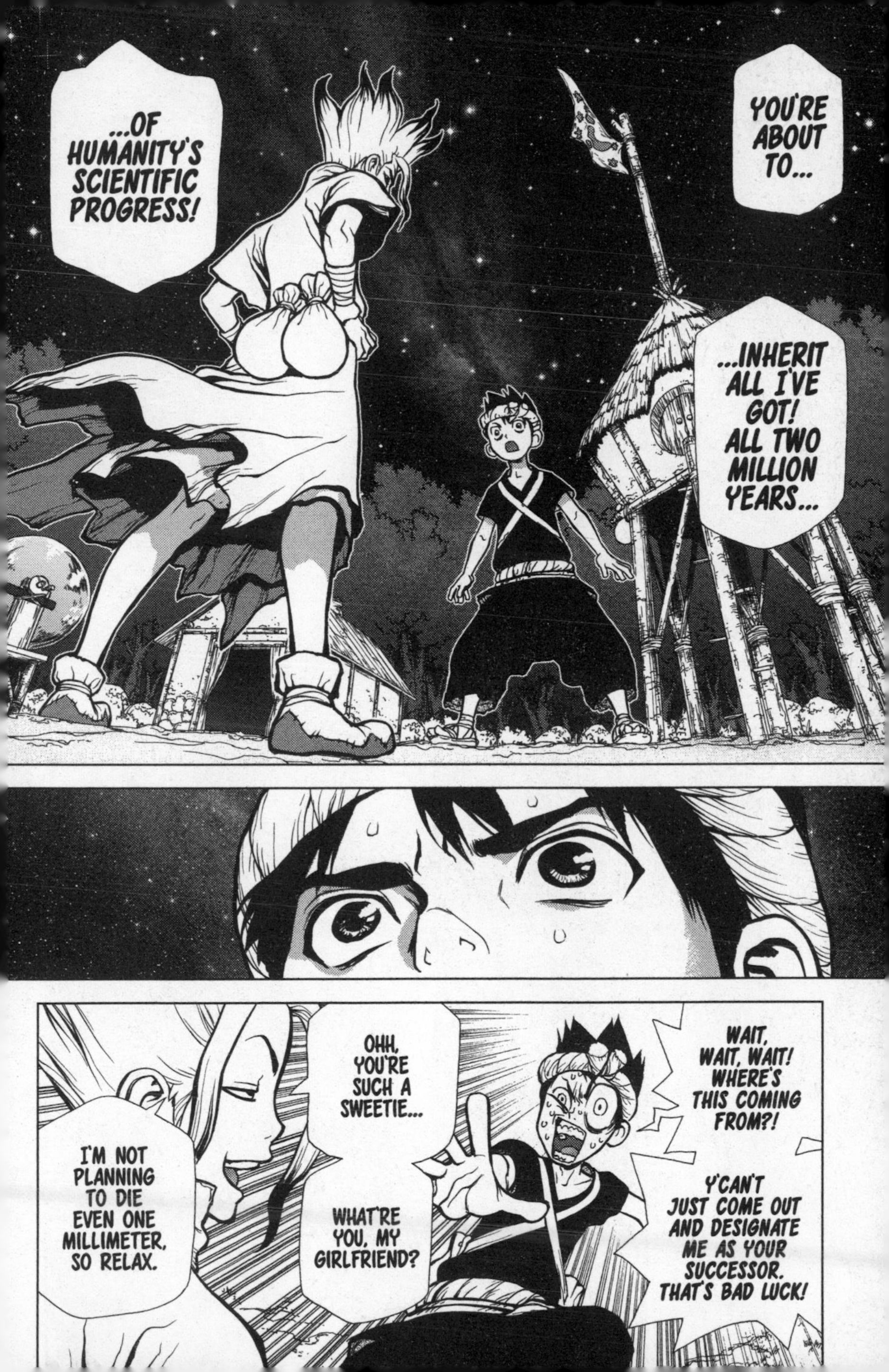

YOU'RE ABOUT TO...
...INHERIT ALL I'VE GOT! ALL TWO MILLION YEARS...
...OF HUMANITY'S SCIENTIFIC PROGRESS!
WAIT, WAIT, WAIT! WHERE'S THIS COMING FROM?!
Y'CAN'T JUST COME OUT AND DESIGNATE ME AS YOUR SUCCESSOR. THAT'S BAD LUCK!
OHH, YOU'RE SUCH A SWEETIE...
WHAT'RE YOU, MY GIRLFRIEND?
I'M NOT PLANNING TO DIE EVEN ONE MILLIMETER, SO RELAX.

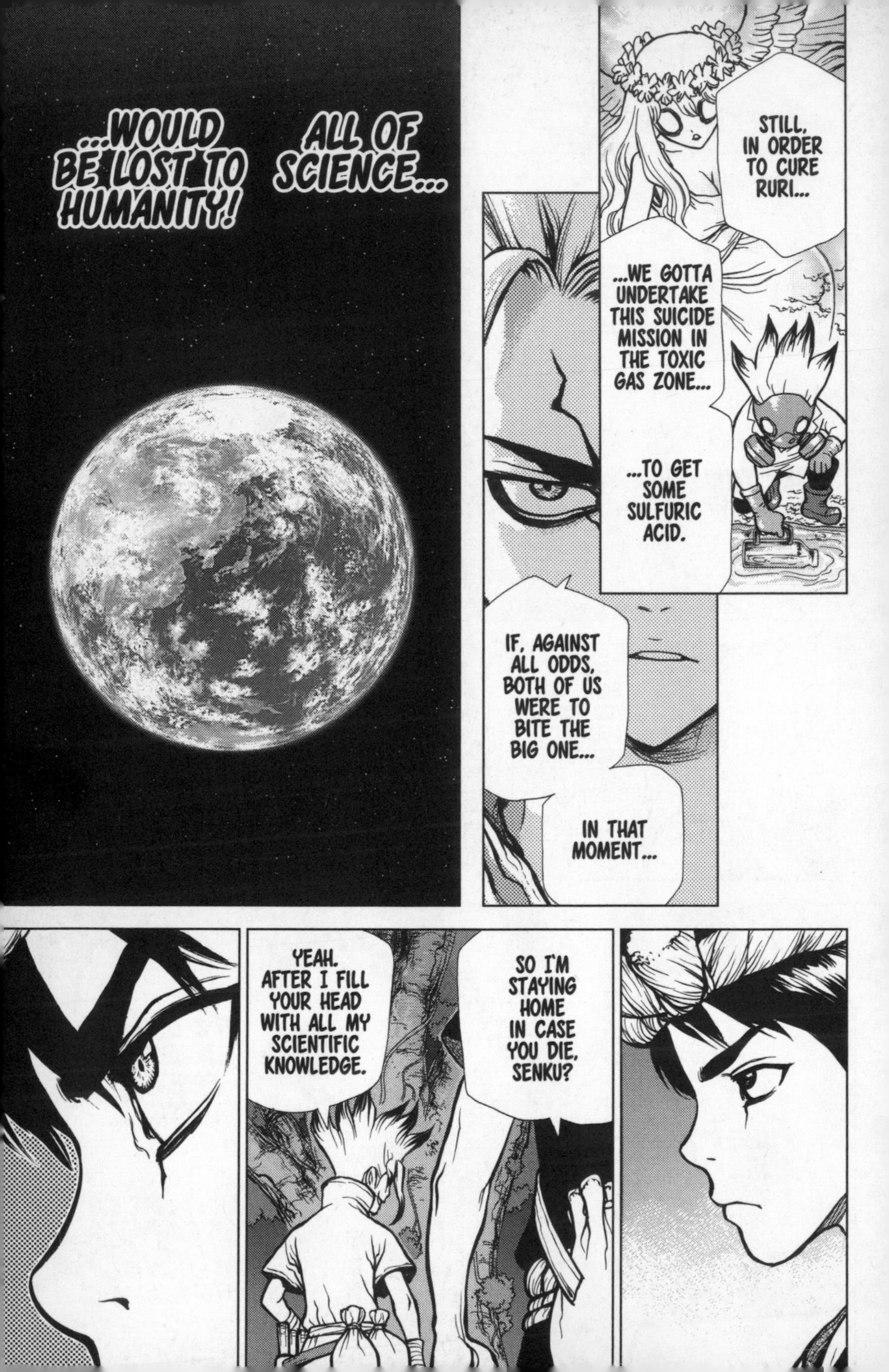
STILL, IN ORDER TO CURE RURI...
...WE GOTTA UNDERTAKE THIS SUICIDE MISSION IN THE TOXIC GAS ZONE...
...TO GET SOME SULFURIC ACID.
IF, AGAINST ALL ODDS, BOTH OF US WERE TO BITE THE BIG ONE...
IN THAT MOMENT...
ALL OF SCIENCE...
...WOULD BE LOST TO HUMANITY!
SO I'M STAYING HOME IN CASE YOU DIE, SENKU?
YEAH. AFTER I FILL YOUR HEAD WITH ALL MY SCIENTIFIC KNOWLEDGE.

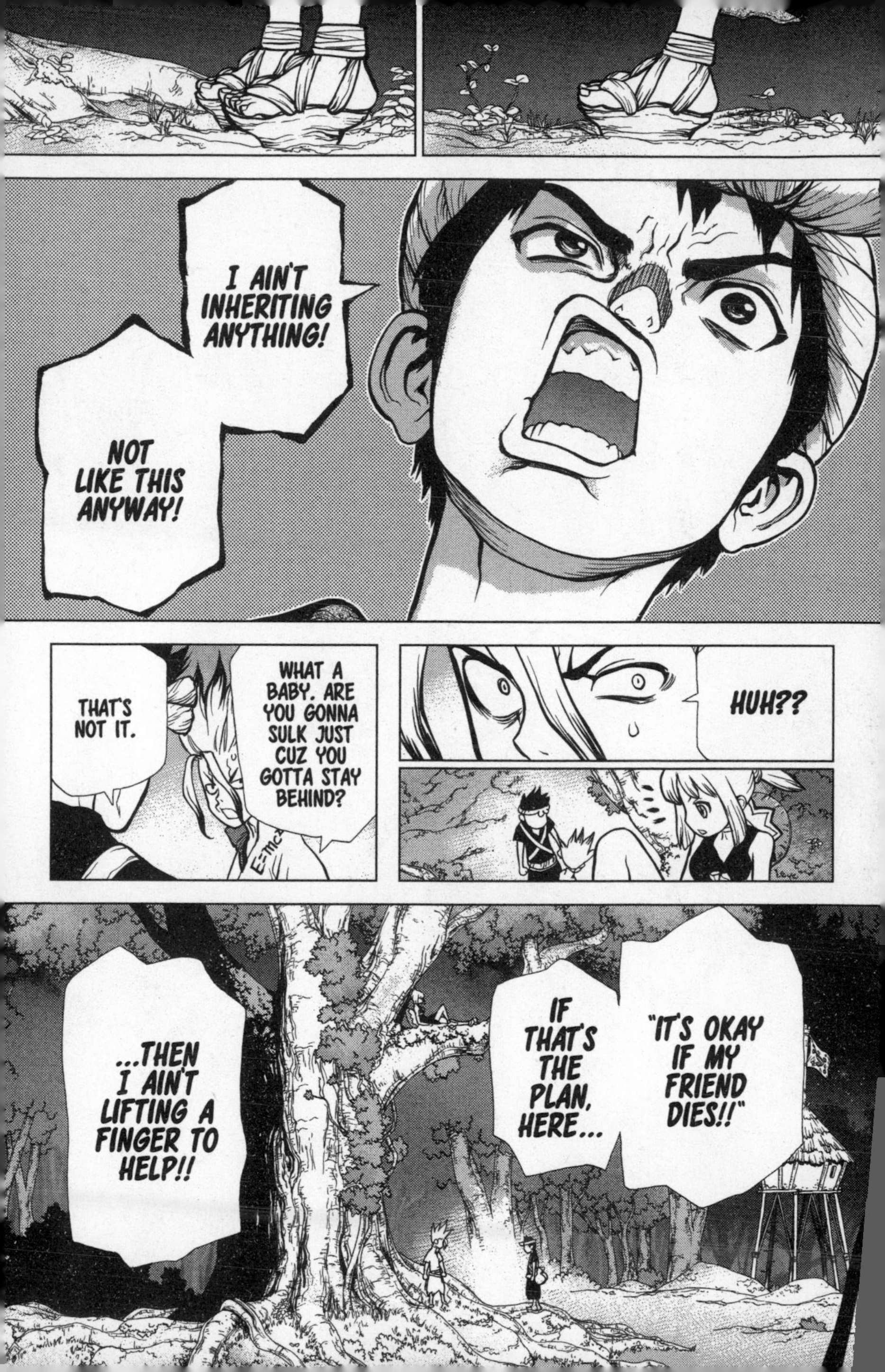
I AIN'T INHERITING ANYTHING!
NOT LIKE THIS ANYWAY!
HUH??
WHAT A BABY. ARE YOU GONNA SULK JUST CUZ YOU GOTTA STAY BEHIND?
THAT'S NOT IT.
E=mc
"IT'S OKAY IF MY FRIEND DIES!!"
IF THAT'S THE PLAN, HERE...
...THEN I AIN'T LIFTING A FINGER TO HELP!!

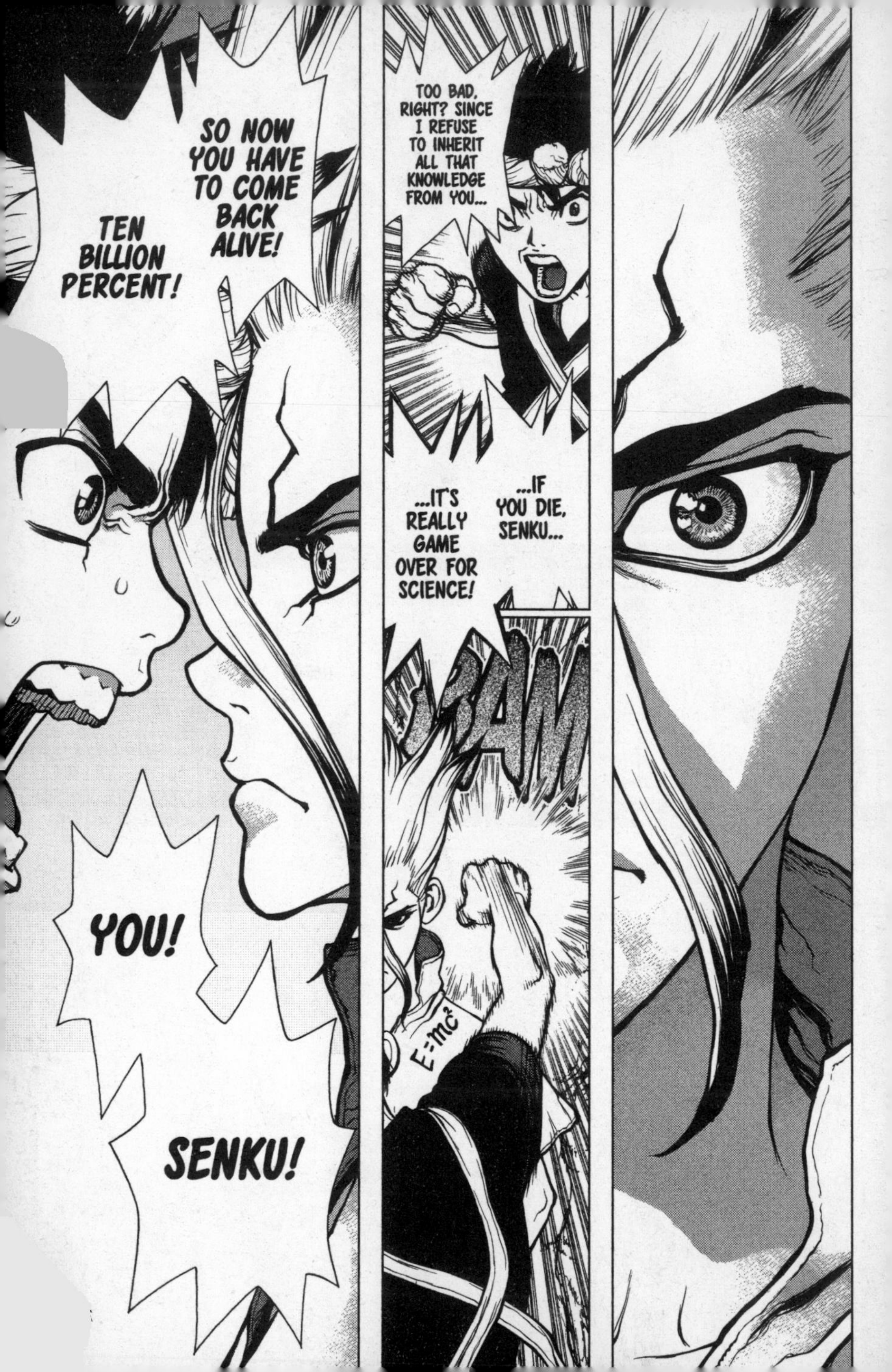
TOO BAD, RIGHT? SINCE I REFUSE TO INHERIT ALL THAT KNOWLEDGE FROM YOU...
...IF YOU DIE, SENKU...
...IT'S REALLY GAME OVER FOR SCIENCE!
$E=mc^2$
SO NOW YOU HAVE TO COME BACK ALIVE!
TEN BILLION PERCENT!
YOU!
SENKU!

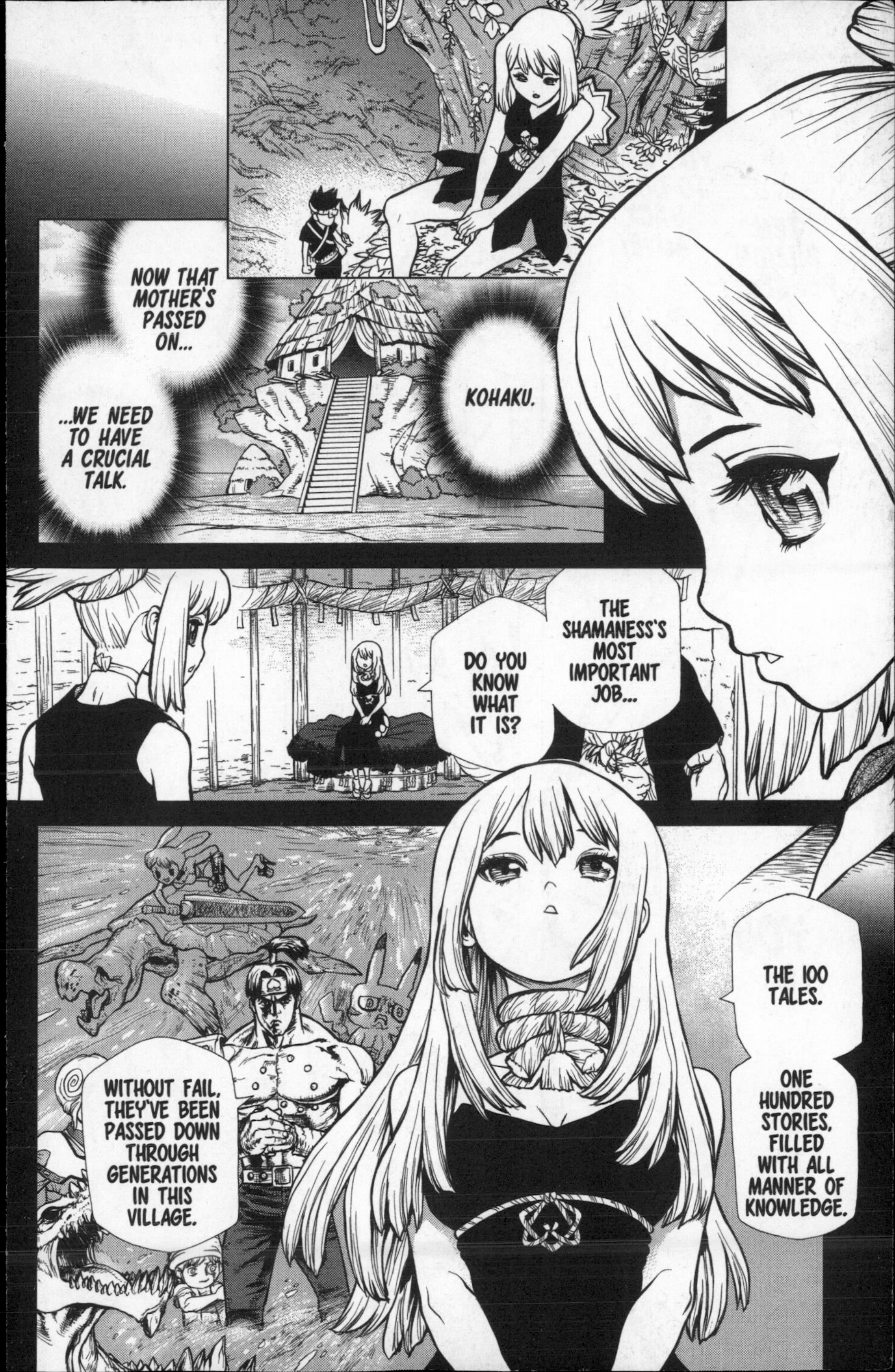
KOHAKU.
NOW THAT MOTHER'S PASSED ON...
...WE NEED TO HAVE A CRUCIAL TALK.
THE SHAMANESS'S MOST IMPORTANT JOB...
DO YOU KNOW WHAT IT IS?
THE 100 TALES.
ONE HUNDRED STORIES, FILLED WITH ALL MANNER OF KNOWLEDGE.
WITHOUT FAIL, THEY'VE BEEN PASSED DOWN THROUGH GENERATIONS IN THIS VILLAGE.

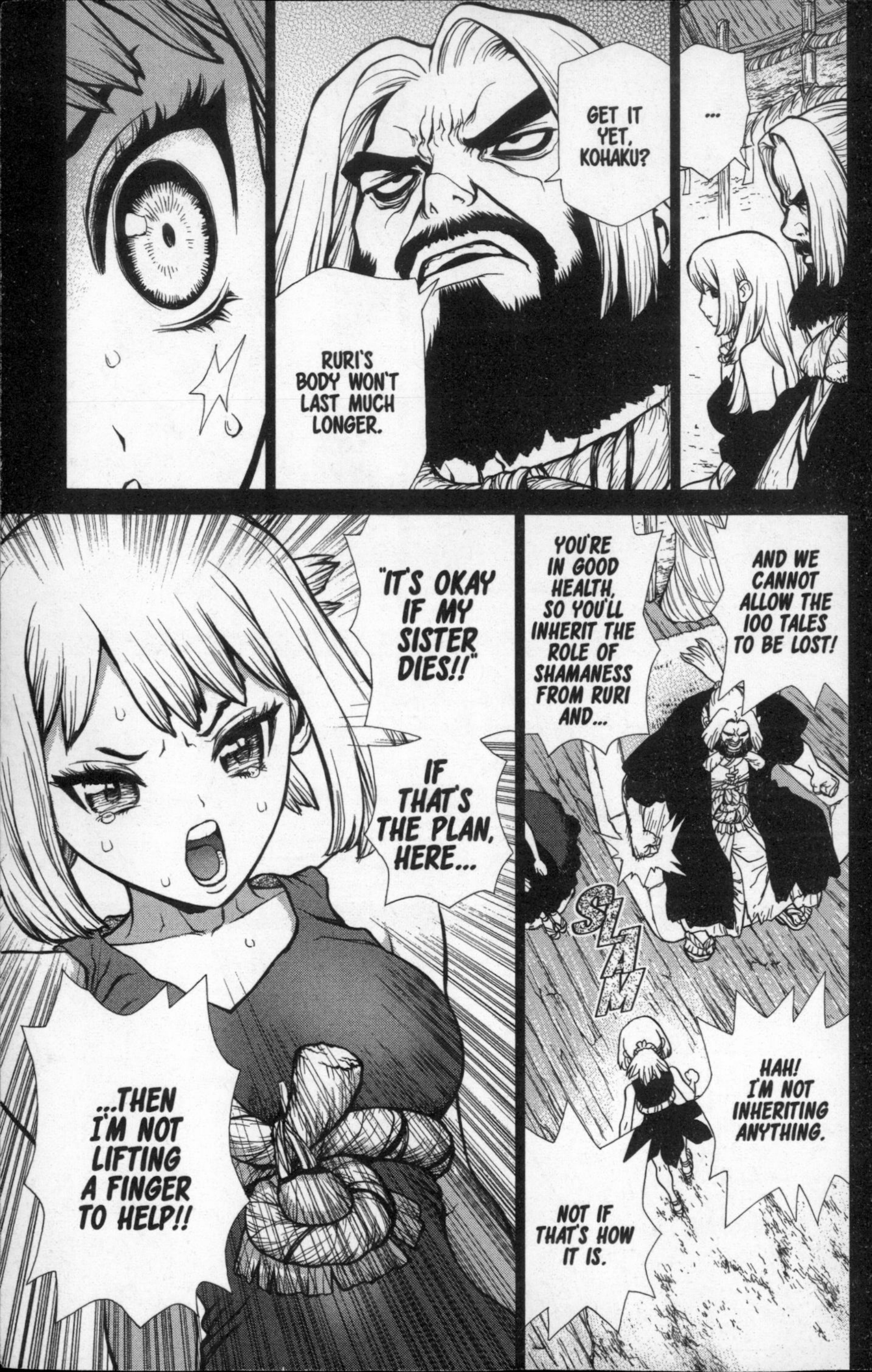
...
GET IT YET, KOHAKU?
RURI'S BODY WON'T LAST MUCH LONGER.
AND WE CANNOT ALLOW THE 100 TALES TO BE LOST!
YOU'RE IN GOOD HEALTH, SO YOU'LL INHERIT THE ROLE OF SHAMANESS FROM RURI AND...
SLAM
HAH! I'M NOT INHERITING ANYTHING.
NOT IF THAT'S HOW IT IS.
"IT'S OKAY IF MY SISTER DIES!!"
IF THAT'S THE PLAN, HERE...
...THEN I'M NOT LIFTING A FINGER TO HELP!!

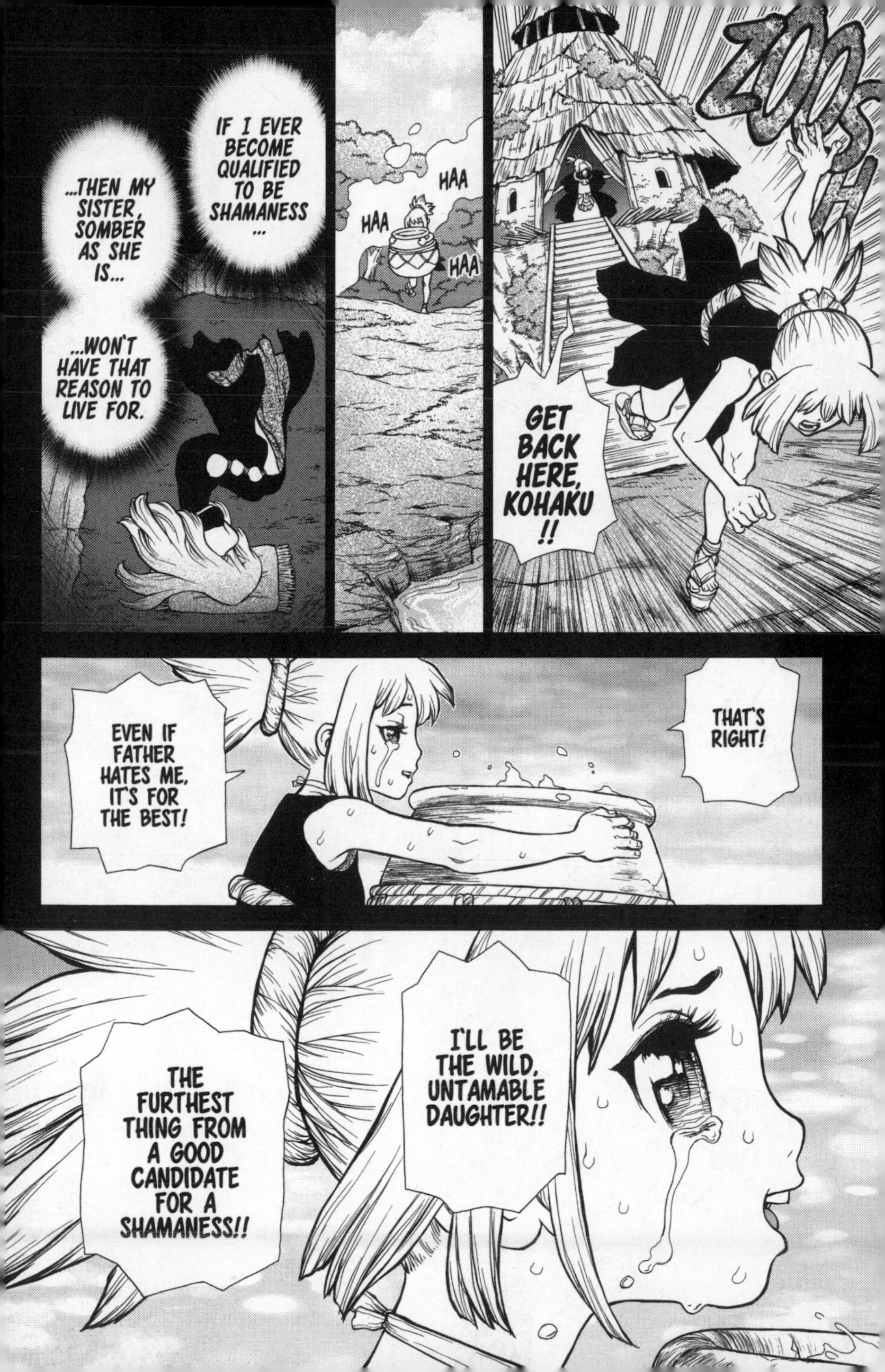
ZOOSH
GET BACK HERE, KOHAKU!!
HAA
HAA
HAA
IF I EVER BECOME QUALIFIED TO BE SHAMANESS...
...THEN MY SISTER, SOMBER AS SHE IS...
...WON'T HAVE THAT REASON TO LIVE FOR.
THAT'S RIGHT!
EVEN IF FATHER HATES ME, IT'S FOR THE BEST!
I'LL BE THE WILD, UNTAMABLE DAUGHTER!!
THE FURTHEST THING FROM A GOOD CANDIDATE FOR A SHAMANESS!!

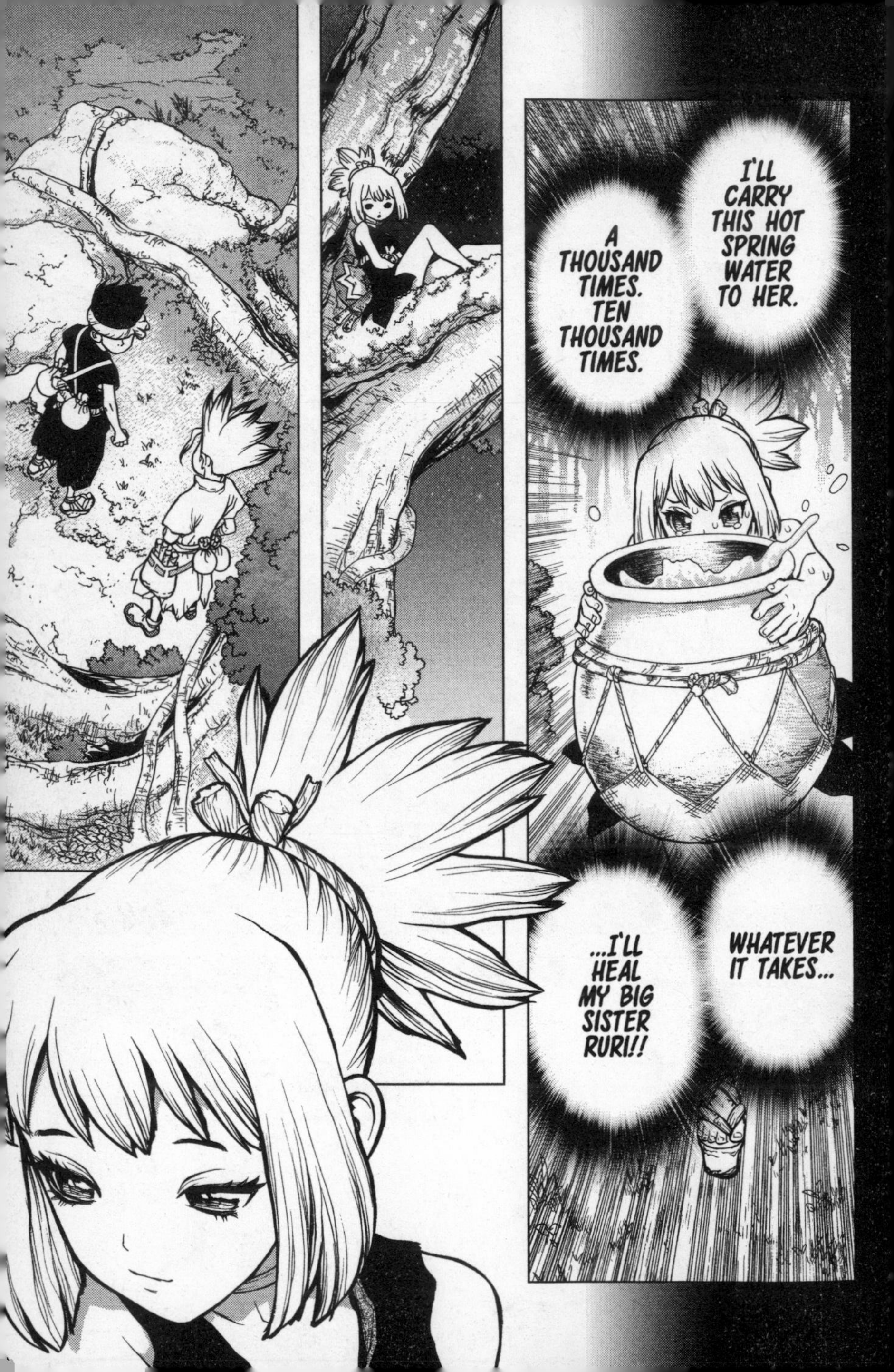
I'LL CARRY THIS HOT SPRING WATER TO HER.
A THOUSAND TIMES. TEN THOUSAND TIMES.
WHATEVER IT TAKES...
...I'LL HEAL MY BIG SISTER RURI!!

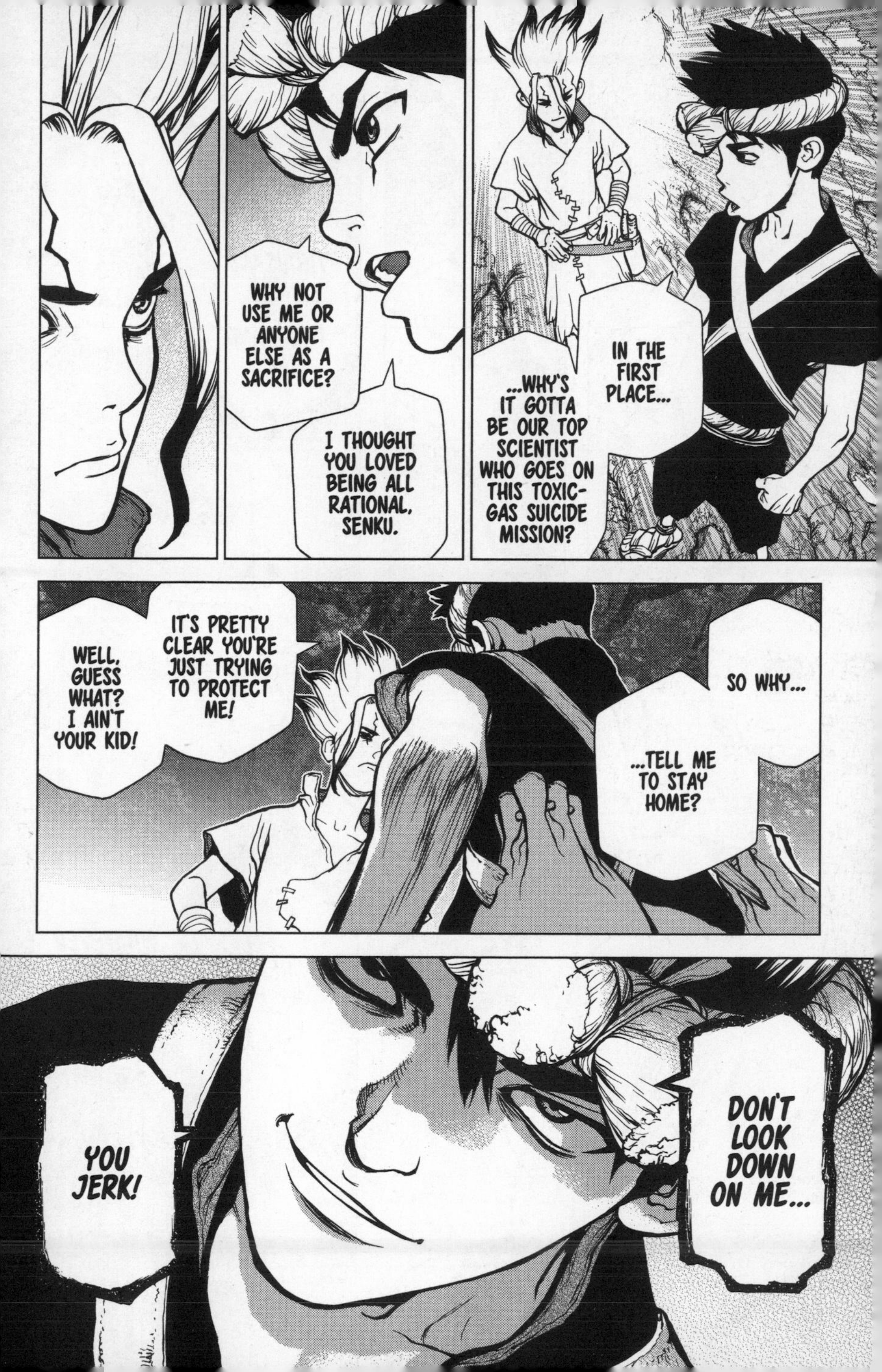
IN THE FIRST PLACE...
...WHY'S IT GOTTA BE OUR TOP SCIENTIST WHO GOES ON THIS TOXIC-GAS SUICIDE MISSION?
WHY NOT USE ME OR ANYONE ELSE AS A SACRIFICE?
I THOUGHT YOU LOVED BEING ALL RATIONAL, SENKU.
SO WHY...
...TELL ME TO STAY HOME?
IT'S PRETTY CLEAR YOU'RE JUST TRYING TO PROTECT ME!
WELL, GUESS WHAT? I AIN'T YOUR KID!
DON'T LOOK DOWN ON ME...
YOU JERK!

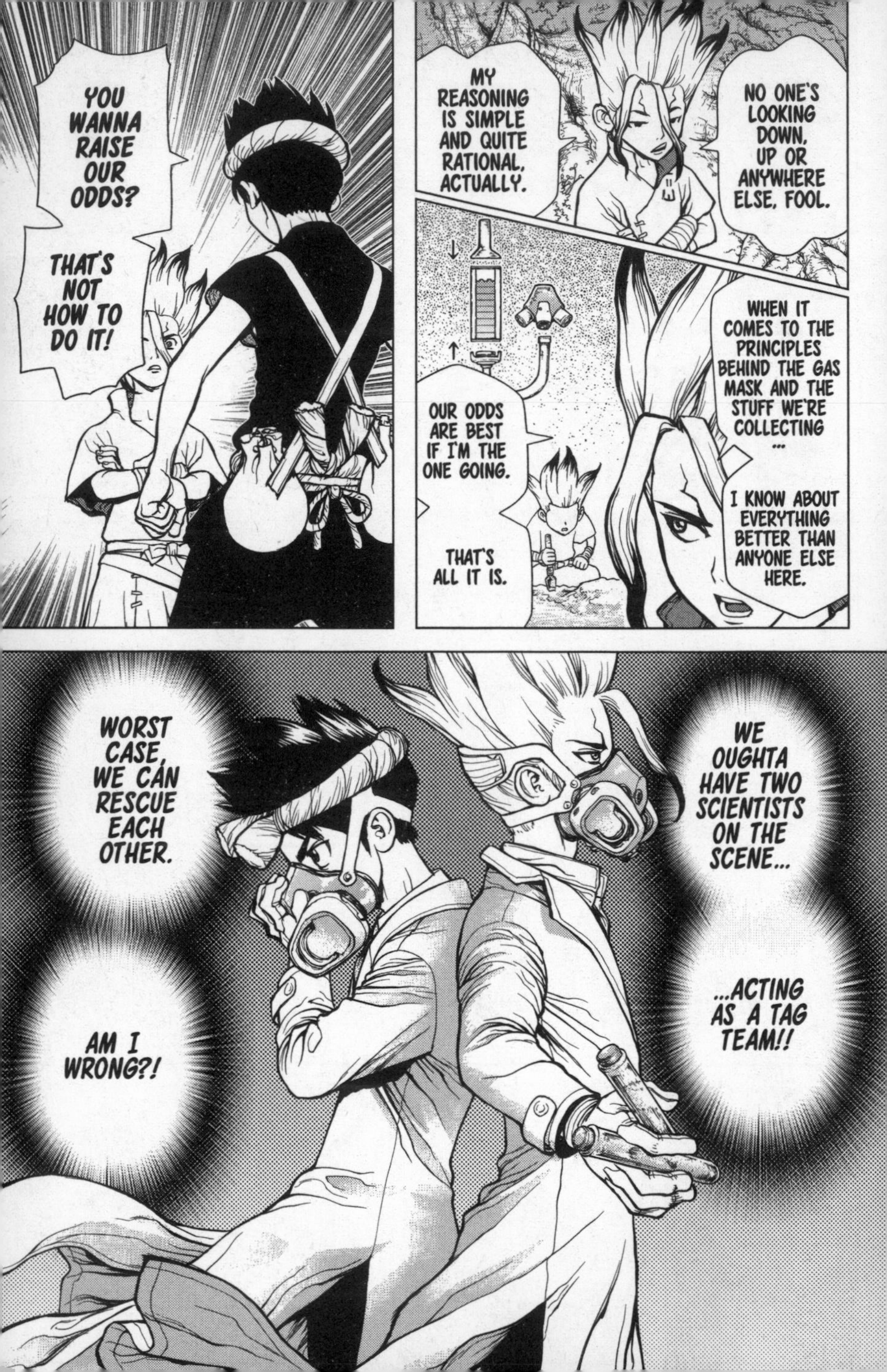
NO ONE'S LOOKING DOWN, UP OR ANYWHERE ELSE, FOOL.
MY REASONING IS SIMPLE AND QUITE RATIONAL, ACTUALLY.
WHEN IT COMES TO THE PRINCIPLES BEHIND THE GAS MASK AND THE STUFF WE'RE COLLECTING ...
I KNOW ABOUT EVERYTHING BETTER THAN ANYONE ELSE HERE.
OUR ODDS ARE BEST IF I'M THE ONE GOING.
THAT'S ALL IT IS.
YOU WANNA RAISE OUR ODDS?
THAT'S NOT HOW TO DO IT!
WE OUGHTA HAVE TWO SCIENTISTS ON THE SCENE...
...ACTING AS A TAG TEAM!!
WORST CASE, WE CAN RESCUE EACH OTHER.
AM I WRONG?!

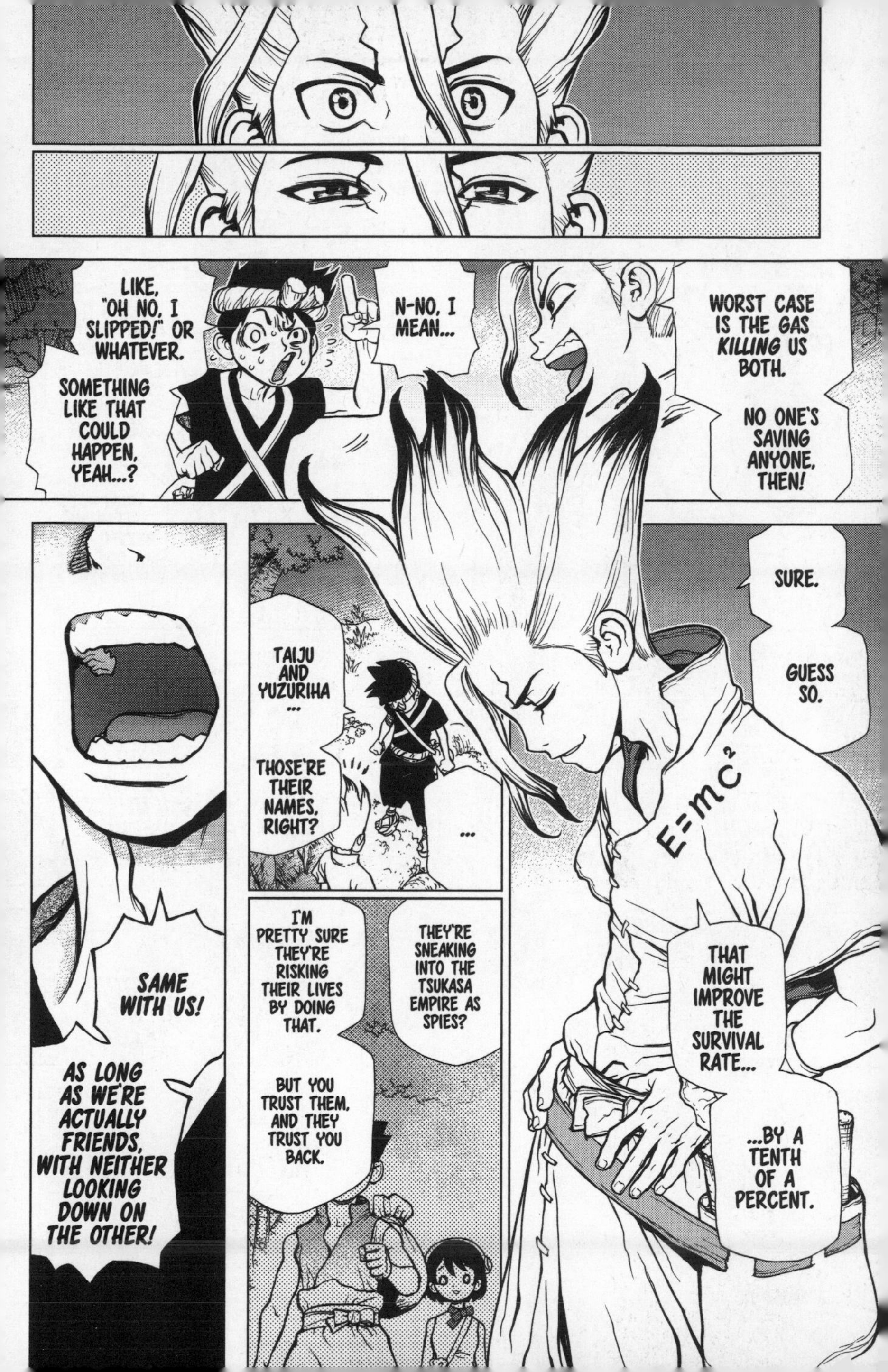
WORST CASE IS THE GAS KILLING US BOTH.
NO ONE'S SAVING ANYONE, THEN!
N-NO, I MEAN...
LIKE, "OH NO, I SLIPPED!" OR WHATEVER.
SOMETHING LIKE THAT COULD HAPPEN, YEAH...?
SURE.
GUESS SO.
$E=mc^2$
THAT MIGHT IMPROVE THE SURVIVAL RATE...
...BY A TENTH OF A PERCENT.
...
TAIJU AND YUZURIHA...
THOSE'RE THEIR NAMES, RIGHT?
THEY'RE SNEAKING INTO THE TSUKASA EMPIRE AS SPIES?
I'M PRETTY SURE THEY'RE RISKING THEIR LIVES BY DOING THAT.
BUT YOU TRUST THEM, AND THEY TRUST YOU BACK.
SAME WITH US!
AS LONG AS WE'RE ACTUALLY FRIENDS, WITH NEITHER LOOKING DOWN ON THE OTHER!

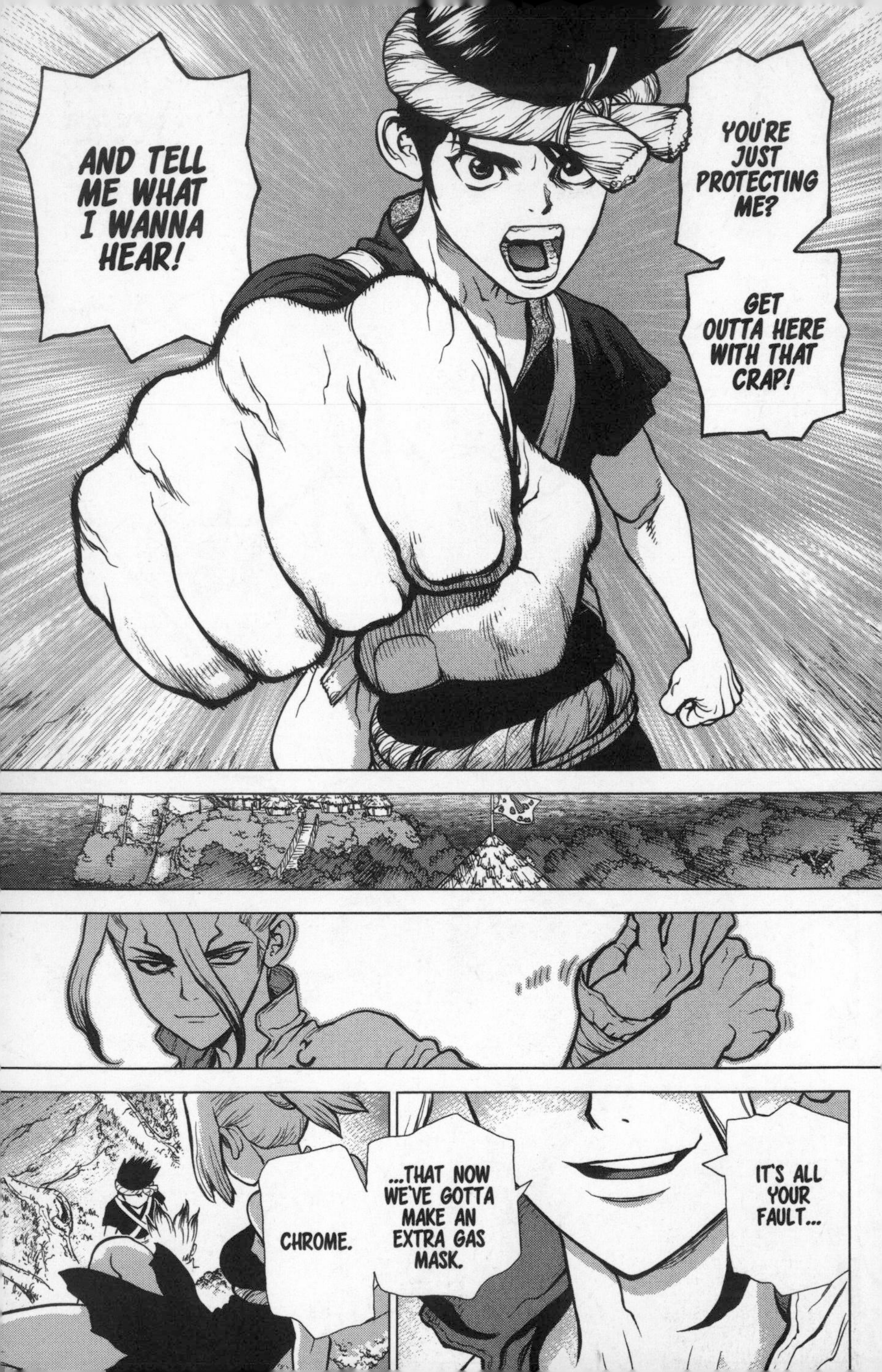
YOU'RE JUST PROTECTING ME?
GET OUTTA HERE WITH THAT CRAP!
AND TELL ME WHAT I WANNA HEAR!
IT'S ALL YOUR FAULT...
...THAT NOW WE'VE GOTTA MAKE AN EXTRA GAS MASK.
CHROME.

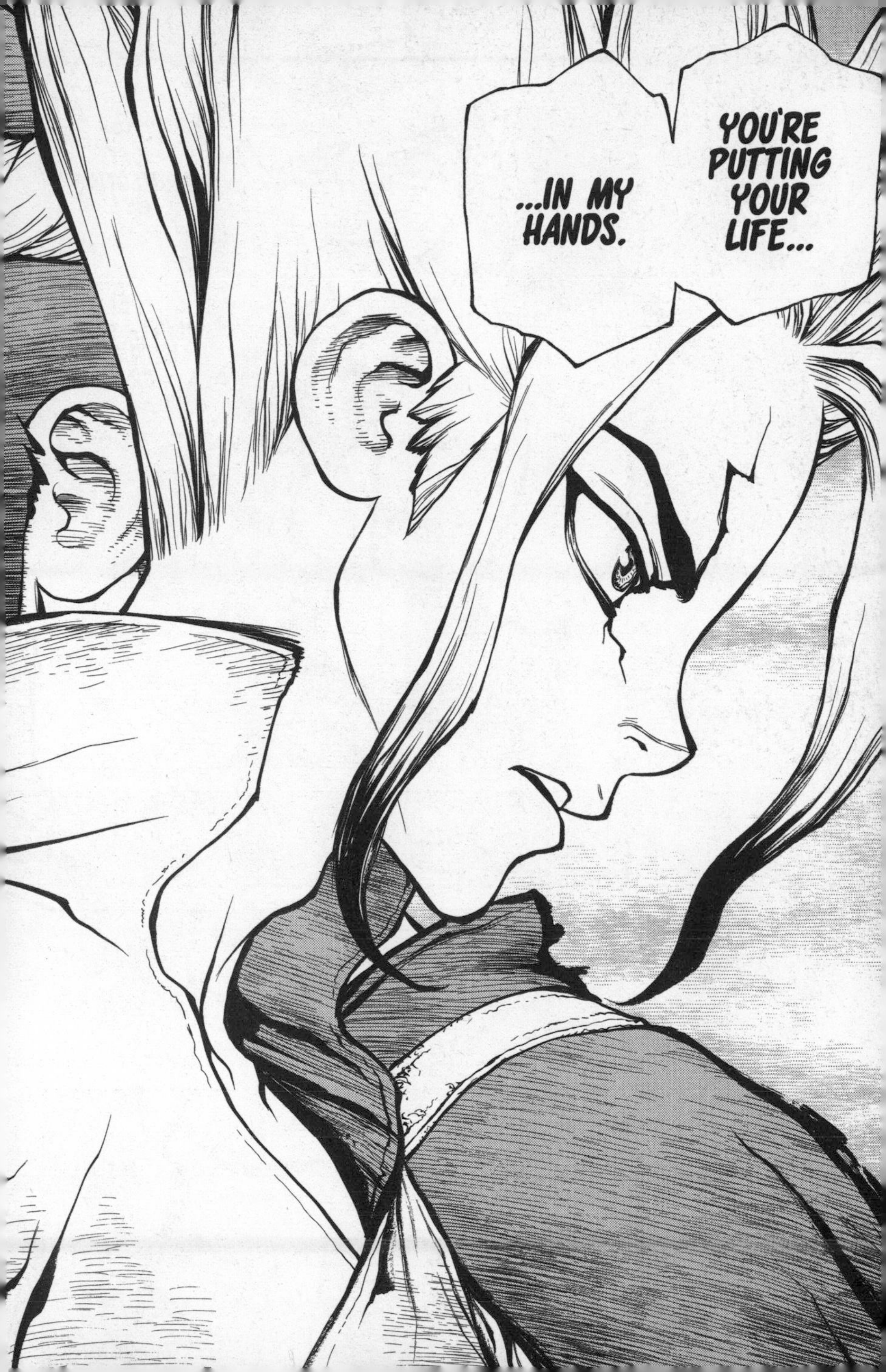
YOU'RE PUTTING YOUR LIFE...
...IN MY HANDS.

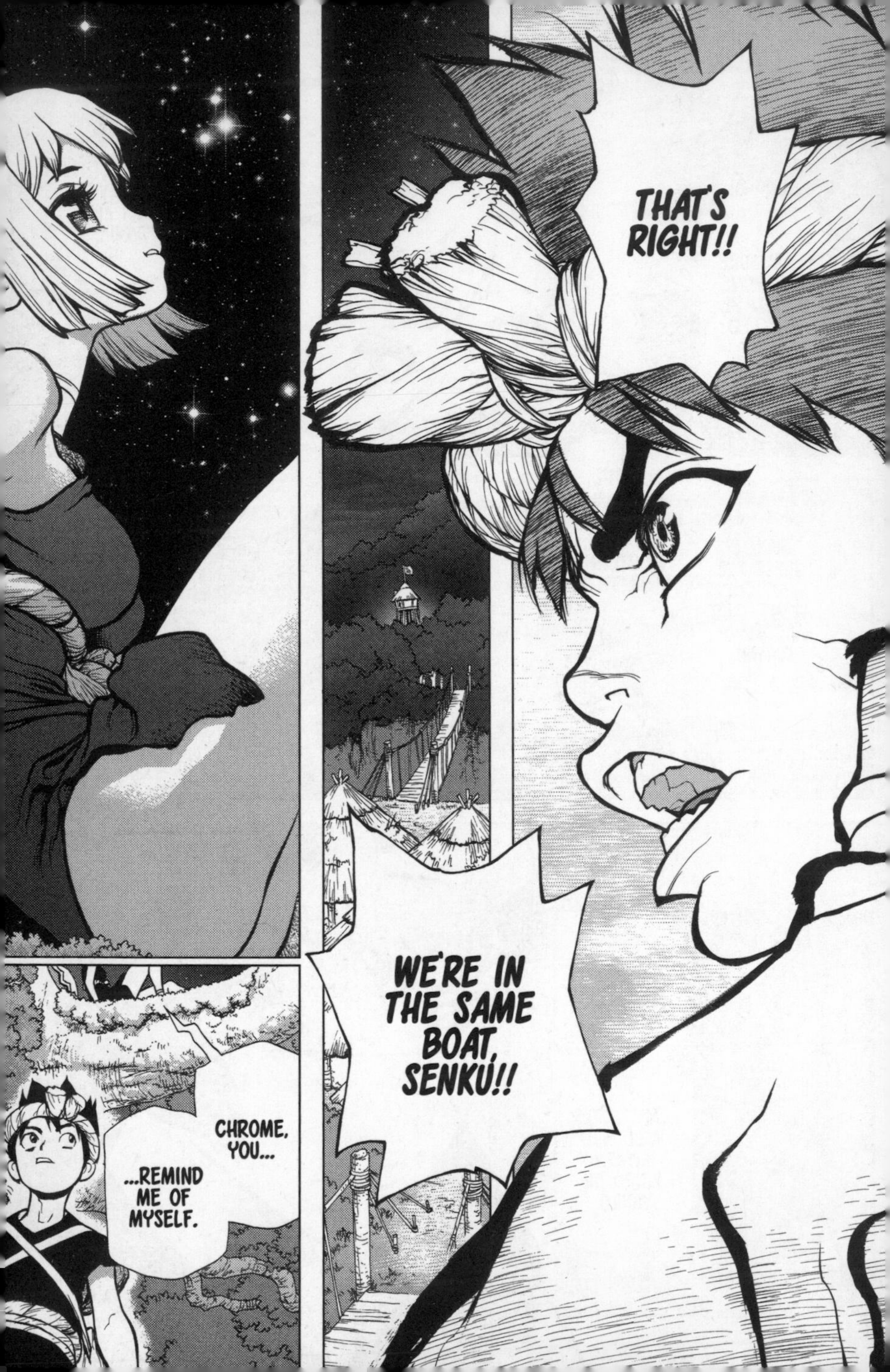
THAT'S RIGHT!!
WE'RE IN THE SAME BOAT, SENKU!!
CHROME, YOU...
...REMIND ME OF MYSELF.

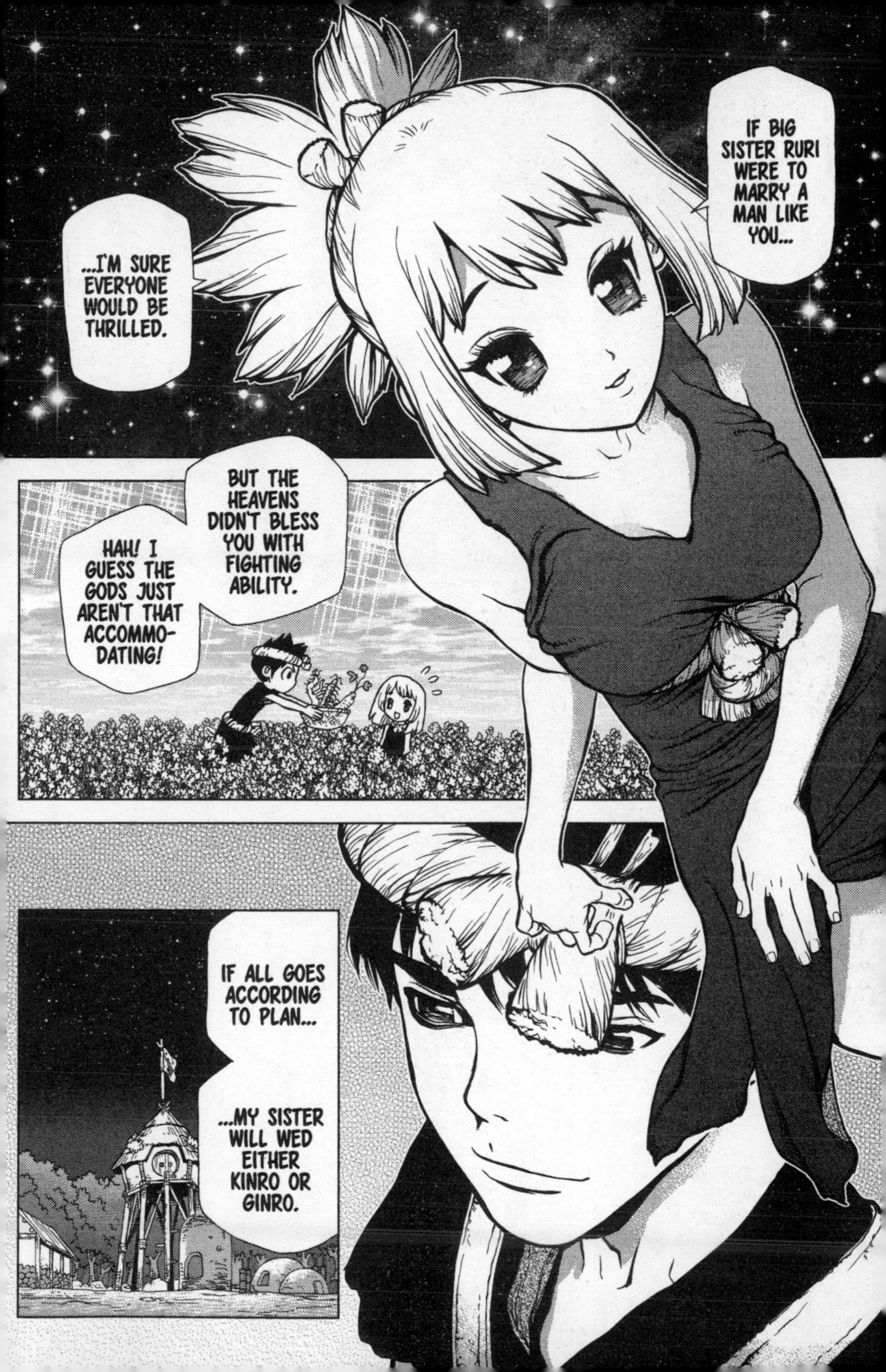
IF BIG SISTER RURI WERE TO MARRY A MAN LIKE YOU...
...I'M SURE EVERYONE WOULD BE THRILLED.
BUT THE HEAVENS DIDN'T BLESS YOU WITH FIGHTING ABILITY.
HAH! I GUESS THE GODS JUST AREN'T THAT ACCOMMO-DATING!
IF ALL GOES ACCORDING TO PLAN...
...MY SISTER WILL WED EITHER KINRO OR GINRO.

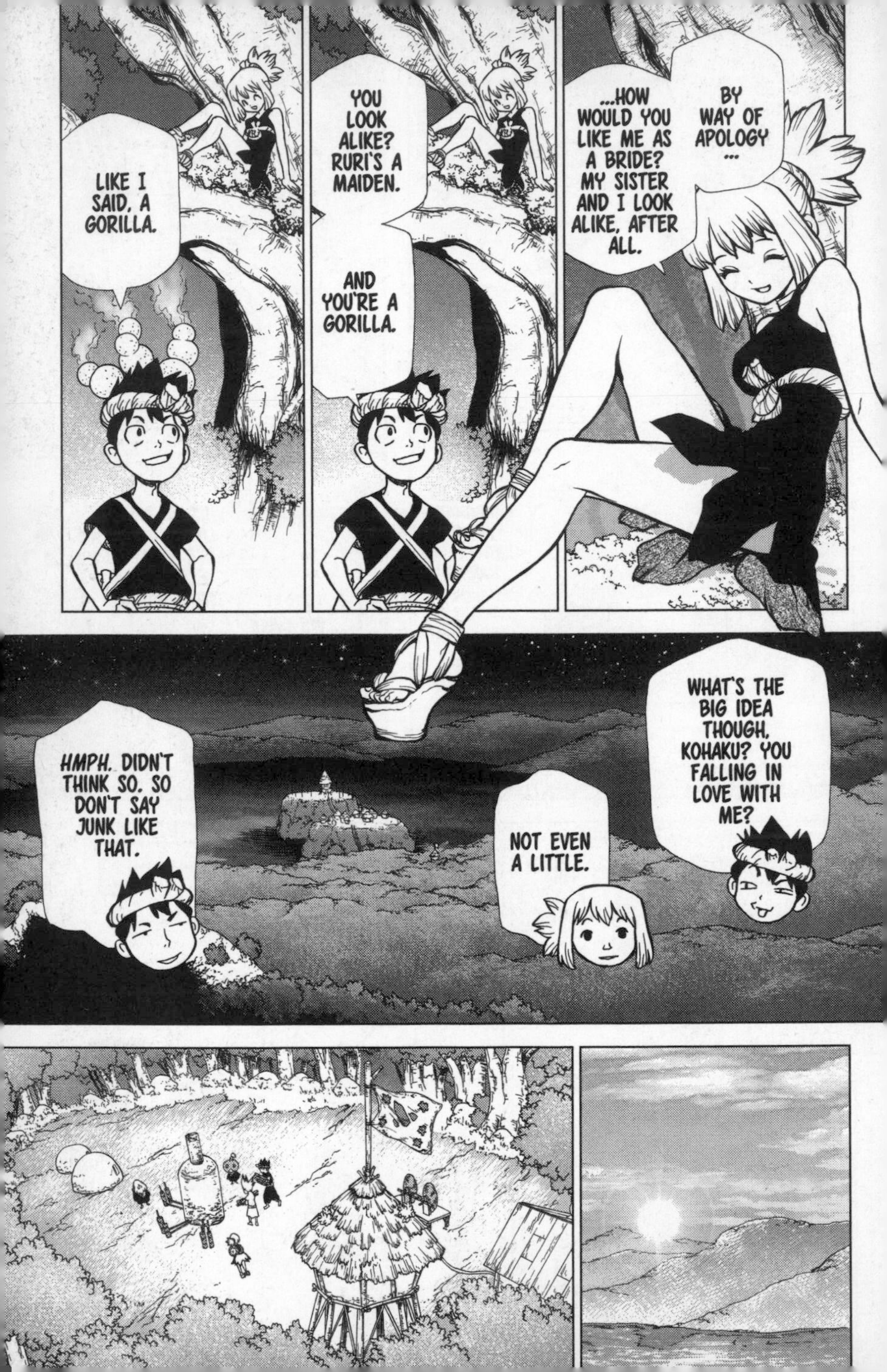
BY WAY OF APOLOGY...
...HOW WOULD YOU LIKE ME AS A BRIDE? MY SISTER AND I LOOK ALIKE, AFTER ALL.
YOU LOOK ALIKE? RURI'S A MAIDEN.
AND YOU'RE A GORILLA.
LIKE I SAID, A GORILLA.
WHAT'S THE BIG IDEA THOUGH, KOHAKU? YOU FALLING IN LOVE WITH ME?
NOT EVEN A LITTLE.
HMPH. DIDN'T THINK SO. SO DON'T SAY JUNK LIKE THAT.

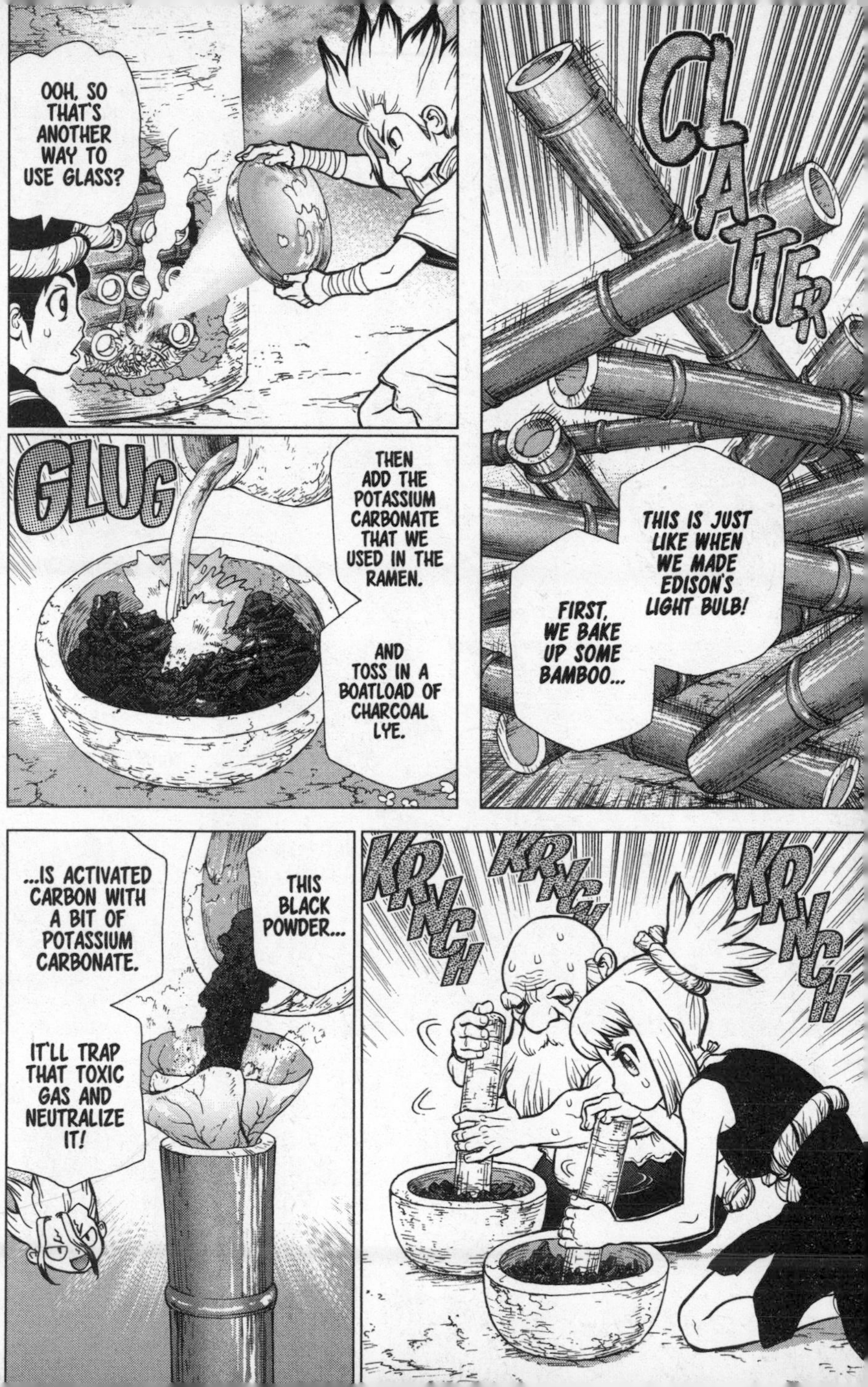
CLATTER
THIS IS JUST LIKE WHEN WE MADE EDISON'S LIGHT BULB!
FIRST, WE BAKE UP SOME BAMBOO...
OOH, SO THAT'S ANOTHER WAY TO USE GLASS?
GLUG
THEN ADD THE POTASSIUM CARBONATE THAT WE USED IN THE RAMEN.
AND TOSS IN A BOATLOAD OF CHARCOAL LYE.
KRNCH
KRNCH
KRNCH
THIS BLACK POWDER...
...IS ACTIVATED CARBON WITH A BIT OF POTASSIUM CARBONATE.
IT'LL TRAP THAT TOXIC GAS AND NEUTRALIZE IT!

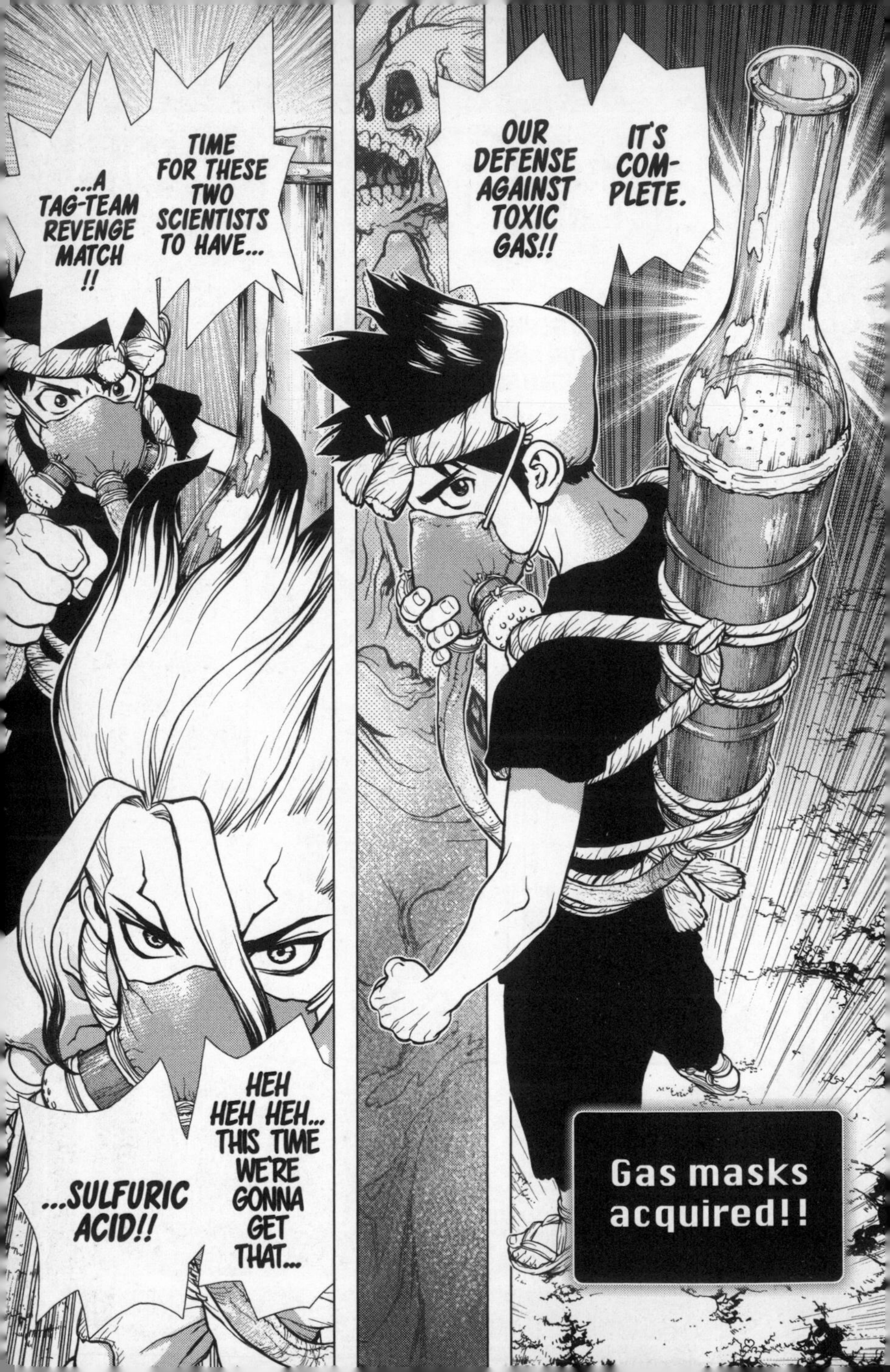
IT'S COM-PLETE.
OUR DEFENSE AGAINST TOXIC GAS!!
Gas masks acquired!!
TIME FOR THESE TWO SCIENTISTS TO HAVE...
...A TAG-TEAM REVENGE MATCH !!
HEH HEH HEH... THIS TIME WE'RE GONNA GET THAT...
...SULFURIC ACID!!

MECHA SENKU Q&A SEARCH

Question Corner

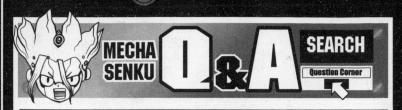

Chrome calls Kohaku a gorilla and all of a sudden his head's covered in lumps! Did Kohaku somehow get him back for that jab? How'd she do it?!

TS-san from Miyagi Prefecture

SEARCH

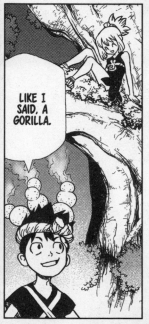

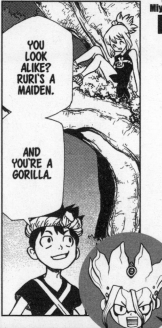

YOU LOOK ALIKE? RURI'S A MAIDEN.
AND YOU'RE A GORILLA.
LIKE I SAID, A GORILLA.

Kohaku rapidly pounded Chrome's head with her stone shoes, as if dribbling a basketball!

Z=32: Brains & Heart

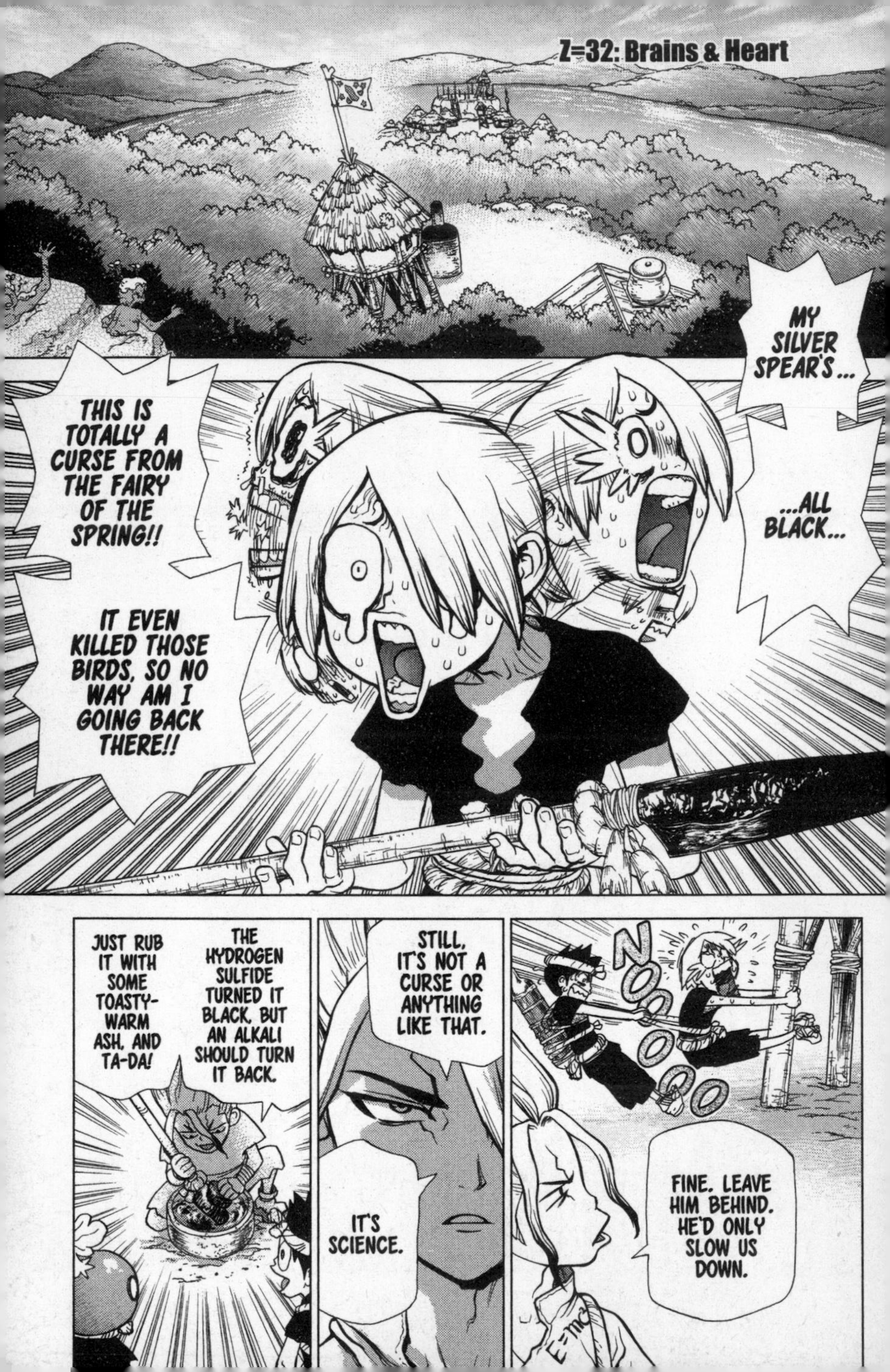

MY SILVER SPEAR'S...
...ALL BLACK...
THIS IS TOTALLY A CURSE FROM THE FAIRY OF THE SPRING!!
IT EVEN KILLED THOSE BIRDS, SO NO WAY AM I GOING BACK THERE!!
NOOOOOO
FINE. LEAVE HIM BEHIND. HE'D ONLY SLOW US DOWN.
STILL, IT'S NOT A CURSE OR ANYTHING LIKE THAT.
IT'S SCIENCE.
THE HYDROGEN SULFIDE TURNED IT BLACK, BUT AN ALKALI SHOULD TURN IT BACK.
JUST RUB IT WITH SOME TOASTY-WARM ASH, AND TA-DA!

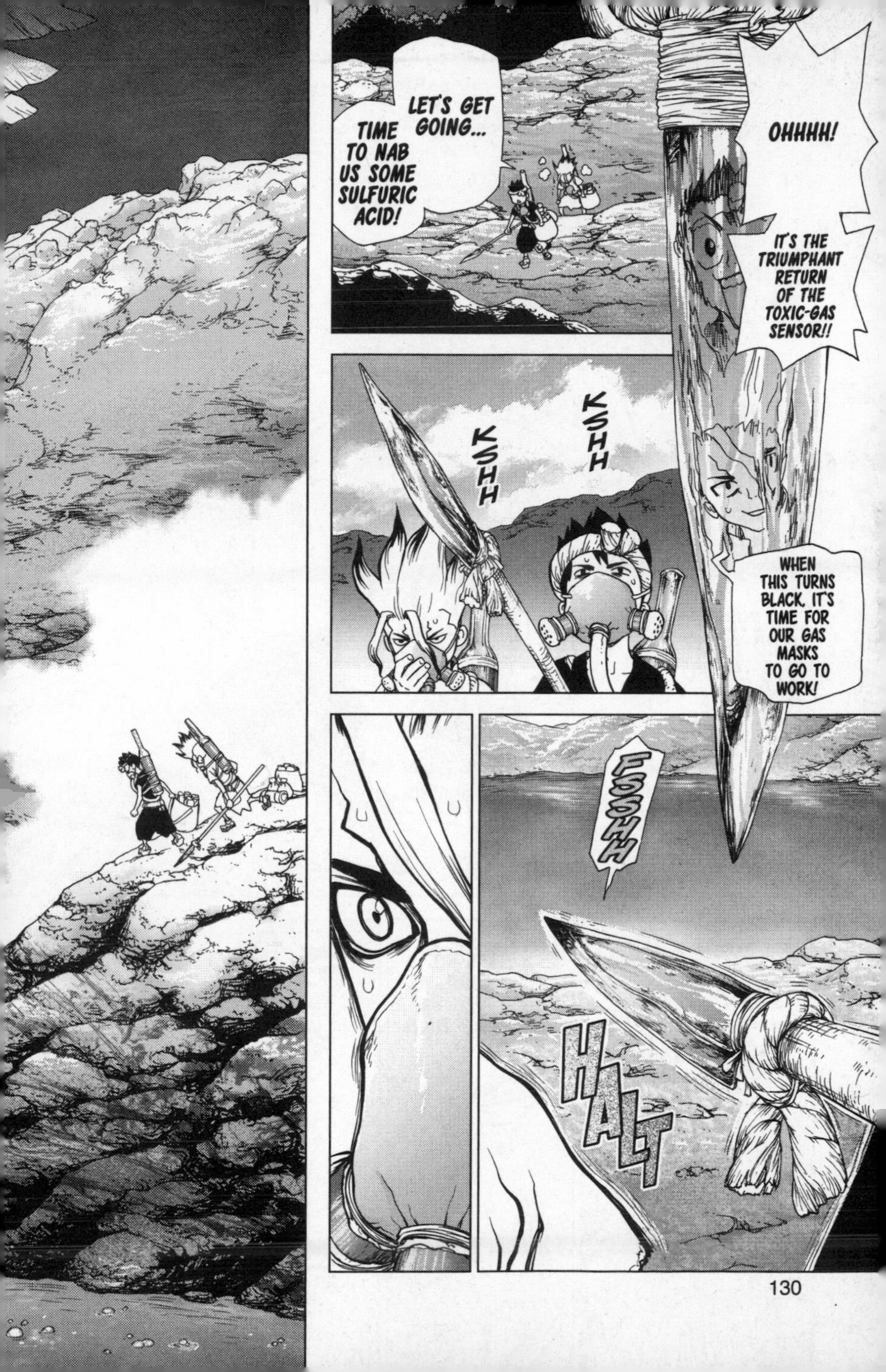
OHHHH!
IT'S THE TRIUMPHANT RETURN OF THE TOXIC-GAS SENSOR!!
WHEN THIS TURNS BLACK, IT'S TIME FOR OUR GAS MASKS TO GO TO WORK!
LET'S GET GOING...
TIME TO NAB US SOME SULFURIC ACID!
KSHH
KSHH
FSSHH
HALT

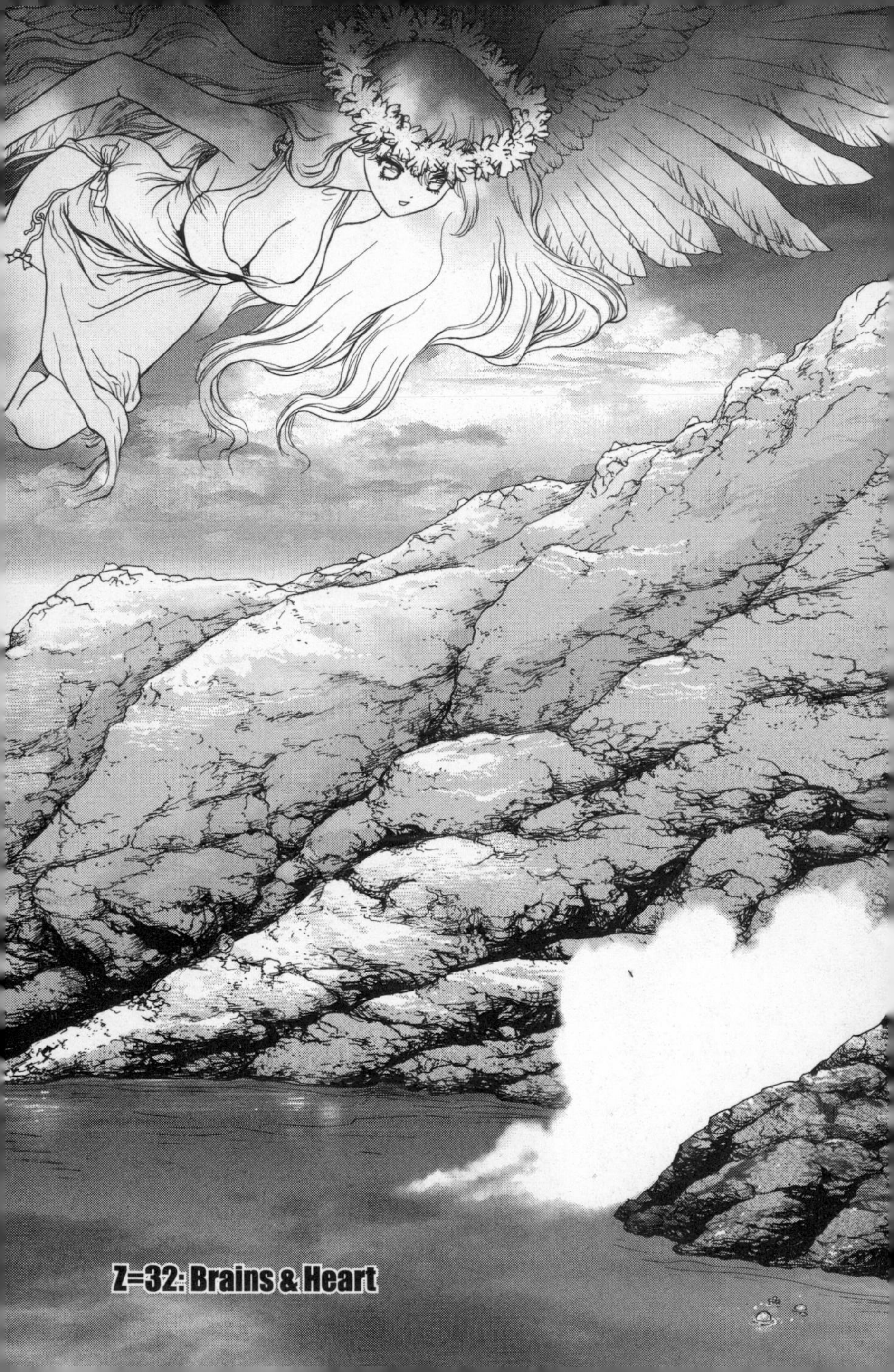
Z=32: Brains & Heart

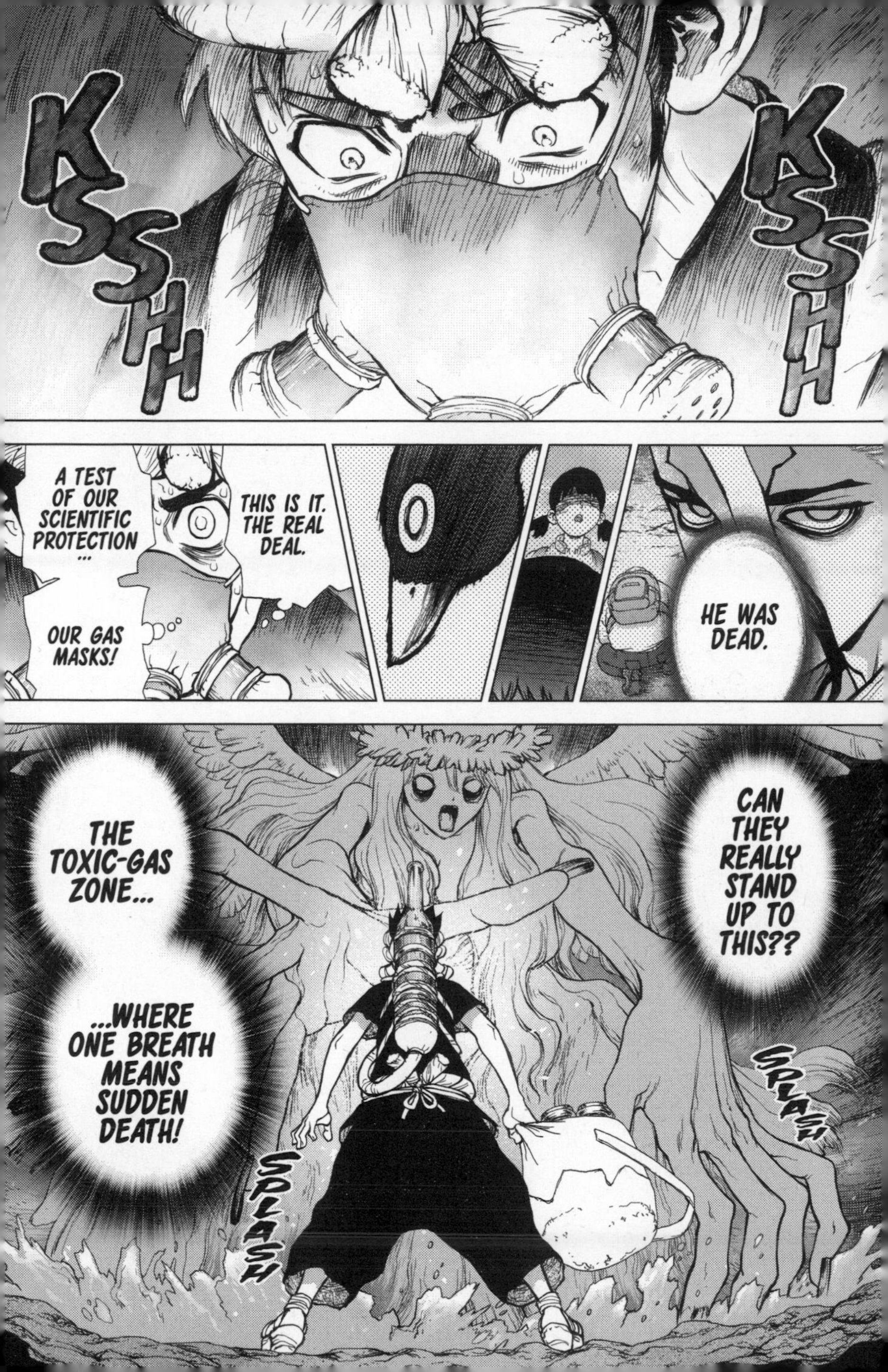
KSSHH
KSSHH
HE WAS DEAD.
THIS IS IT. THE REAL DEAL.
A TEST OF OUR SCIENTIFIC PROTECTION...
OUR GAS MASKS!
CAN THEY REALLY STAND UP TO THIS??
THE TOXIC-GAS ZONE...
...WHERE ONE BREATH MEANS SUDDEN DEATH!
SPLASH
SPLASH

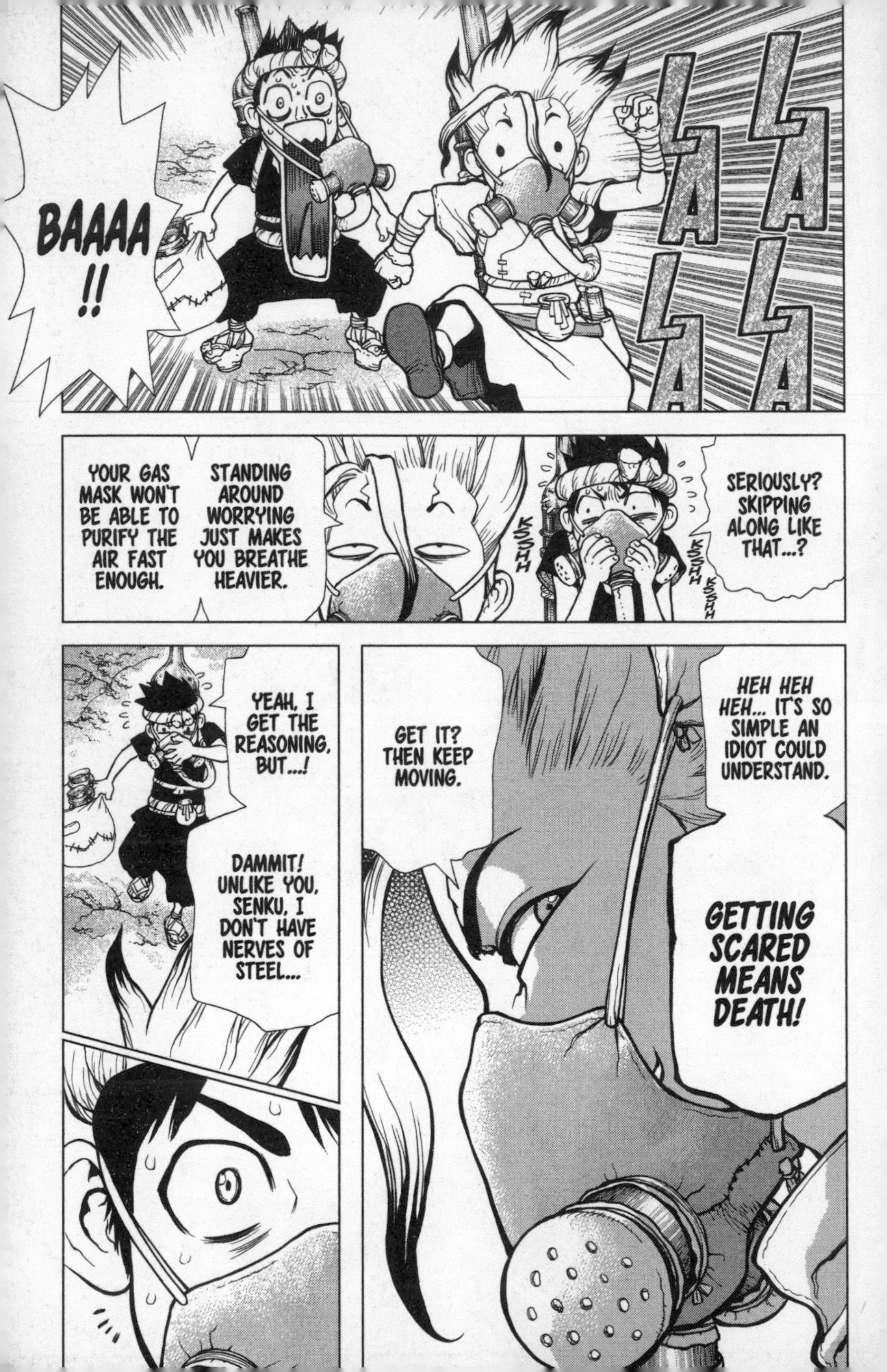
LALA
LALA
BAAAA!!
SERIOUSLY? SKIPPING ALONG LIKE THAT...?
STANDING AROUND WORRYING JUST MAKES YOU BREATHE HEAVIER.
YOUR GAS MASK WON'T BE ABLE TO PURIFY THE AIR FAST ENOUGH.
HEH HEH HEH... IT'S SO SIMPLE AN IDIOT COULD UNDERSTAND.
GET IT? THEN KEEP MOVING.
GETTING SCARED MEANS DEATH!
YEAH, I GET THE REASONING, BUT...!
DAMMIT! UNLIKE YOU, SENKU, I DON'T HAVE NERVES OF STEEL...

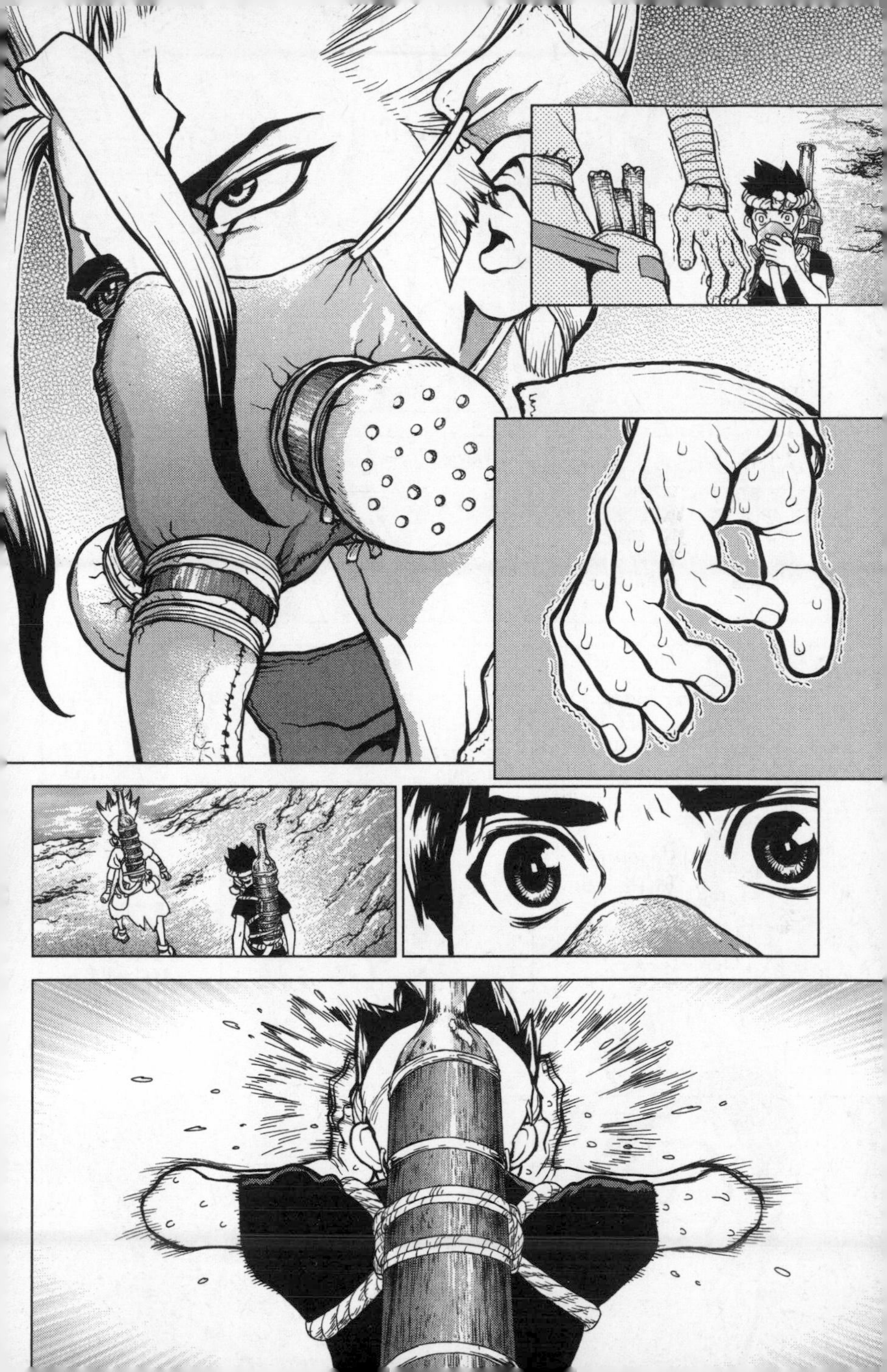

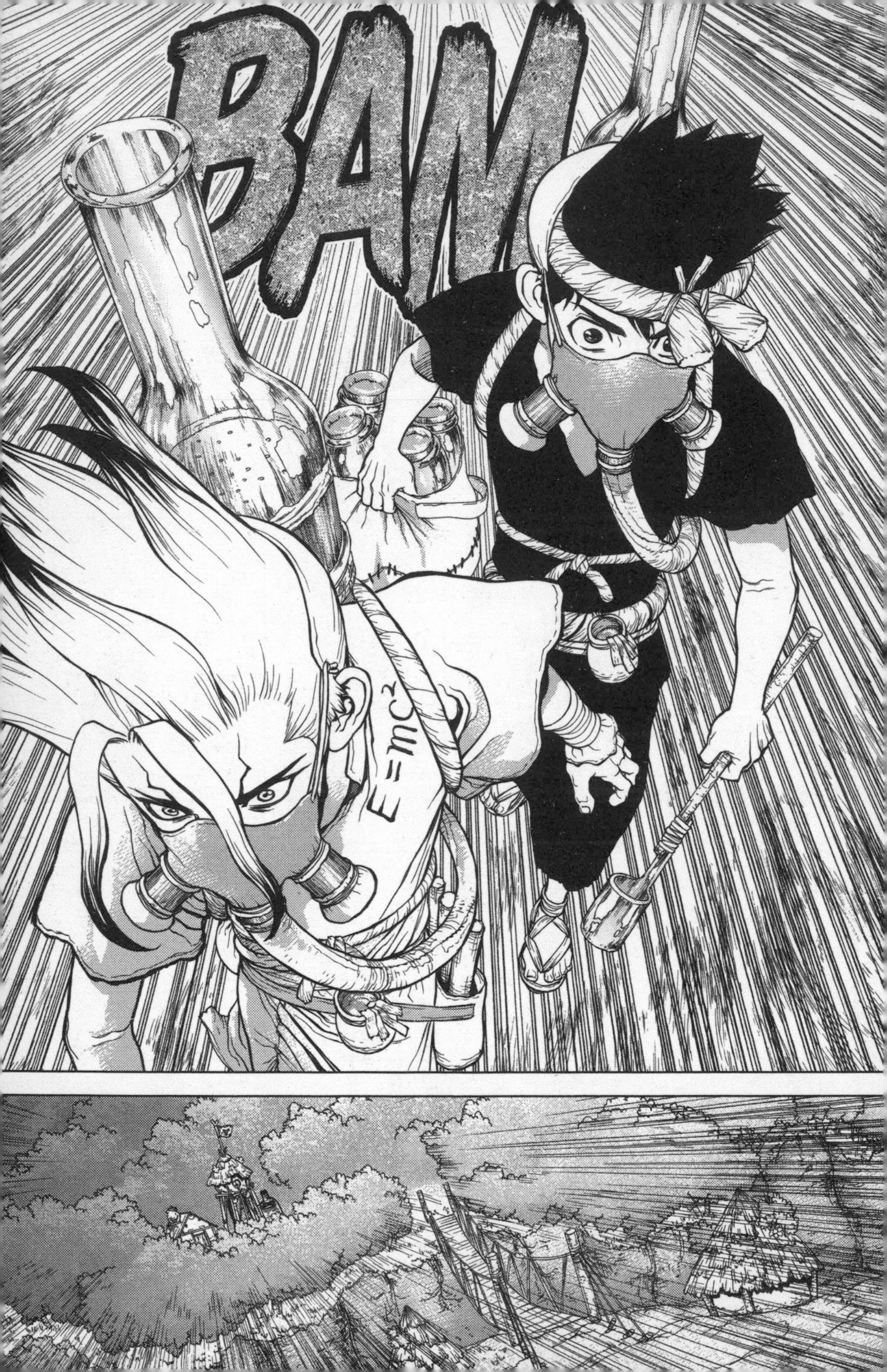
BAM
$E=mc^2$

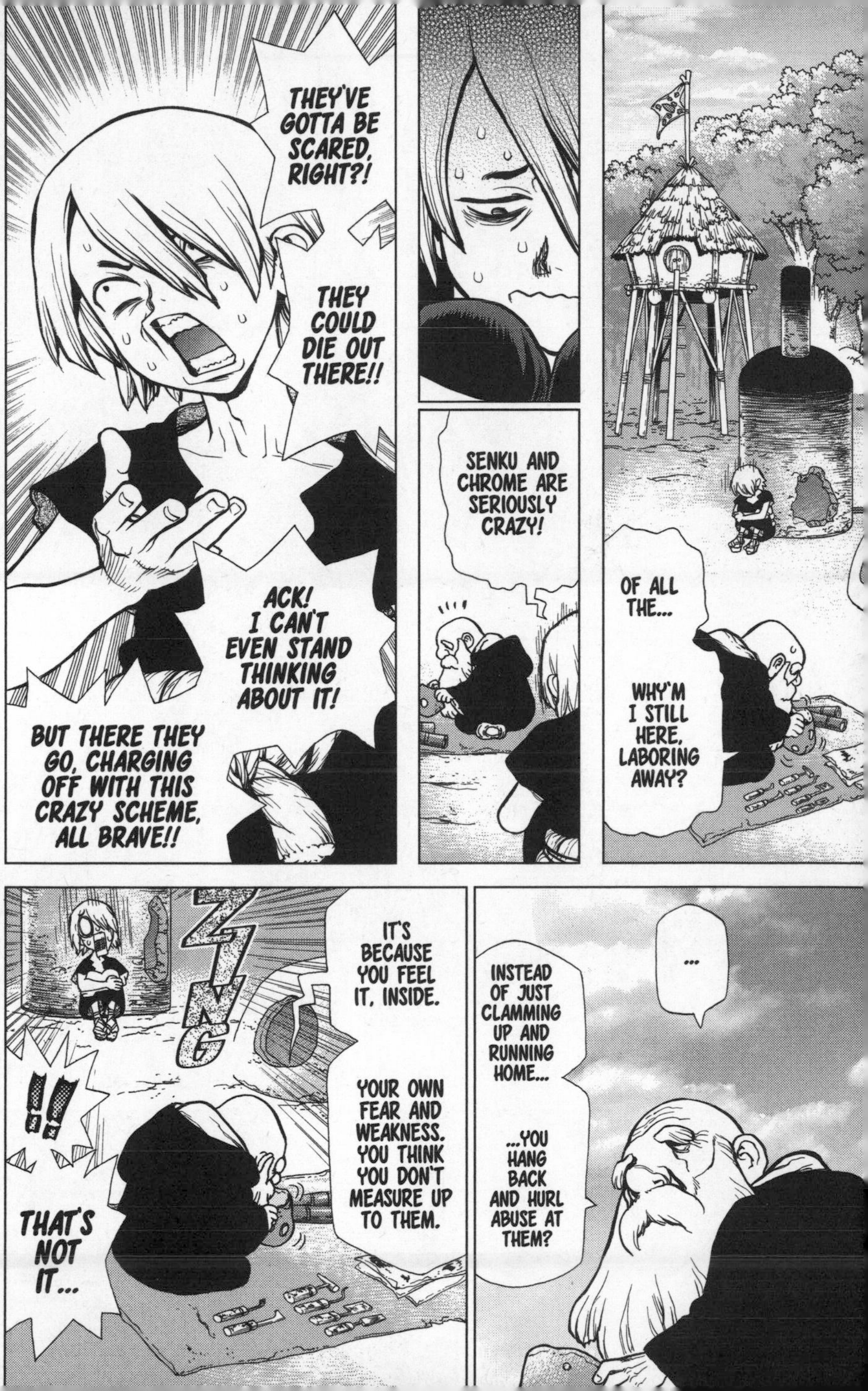
OF ALL THE...
WHY'M I STILL HERE, LABORING AWAY?
SENKU AND CHROME ARE SERIOUSLY CRAZY!
THEY'VE GOTTA BE SCARED, RIGHT?!
THEY COULD DIE OUT THERE!!
ACK! I CAN'T EVEN STAND THINKING ABOUT IT!
BUT THERE THEY GO, CHARGING OFF WITH THIS CRAZY SCHEME, ALL BRAVE!!
...
INSTEAD OF JUST CLAMMING UP AND RUNNING HOME...
...YOU HANG BACK AND HURL ABUSE AT THEM?
IT'S BECAUSE YOU FEEL IT, INSIDE.
ZING
YOUR OWN FEAR AND WEAKNESS. YOU THINK YOU DON'T MEASURE UP TO THEM.
!!
THAT'S NOT IT...

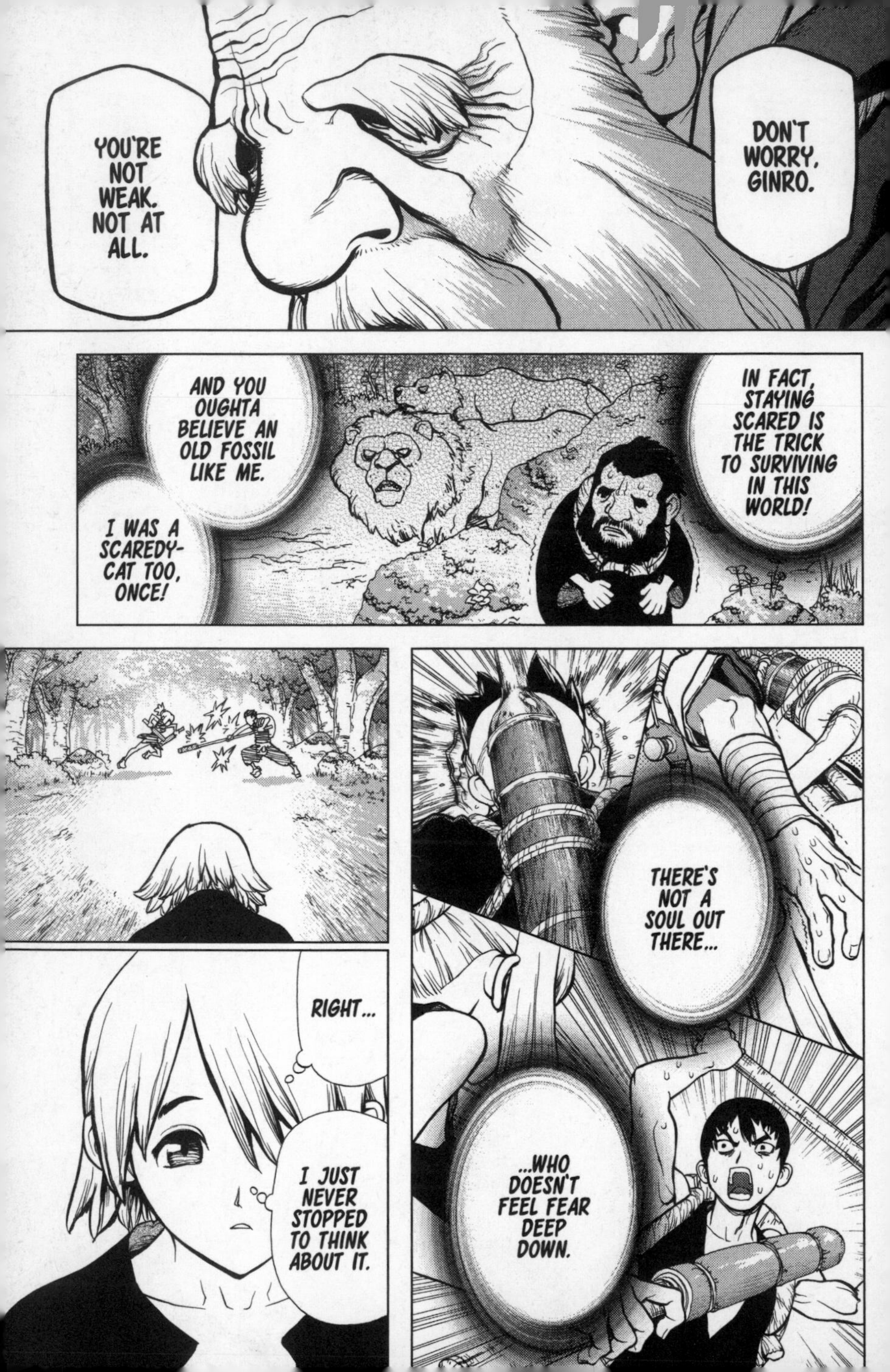
DON'T WORRY, GINRO.
YOU'RE NOT WEAK. NOT AT ALL.
IN FACT, STAYING SCARED IS THE TRICK TO SURVIVING IN THIS WORLD!
AND YOU OUGHTA BELIEVE AN OLD FOSSIL LIKE ME.
I WAS A SCAREDY-CAT TOO, ONCE!
THERE'S NOT A SOUL OUT THERE...
...WHO DOESN'T FEEL FEAR DEEP DOWN.
RIGHT...
I JUST NEVER STOPPED TO THINK ABOUT IT.

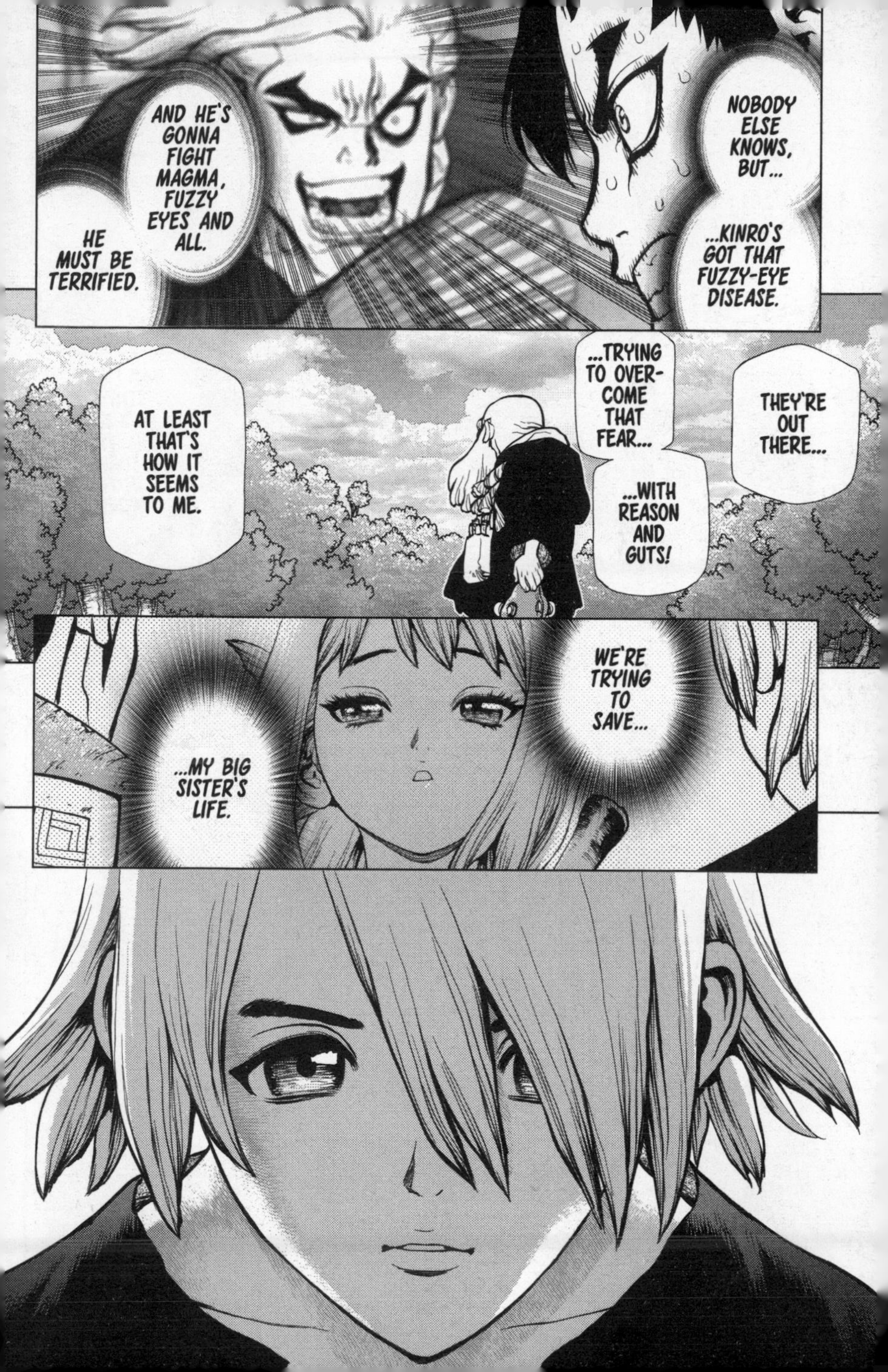
NOBODY ELSE KNOWS, BUT...
...KINRO'S GOT THAT FUZZY-EYE DISEASE.
AND HE'S GONNA FIGHT MAGMA, FUZZY EYES AND ALL.
HE MUST BE TERRIFIED.
THEY'RE OUT THERE...
...TRYING TO OVER-COME THAT FEAR...
...WITH REASON AND GUTS!
AT LEAST THAT'S HOW IT SEEMS TO ME.
WE'RE TRYING TO SAVE...
...MY BIG SISTER'S LIFE.

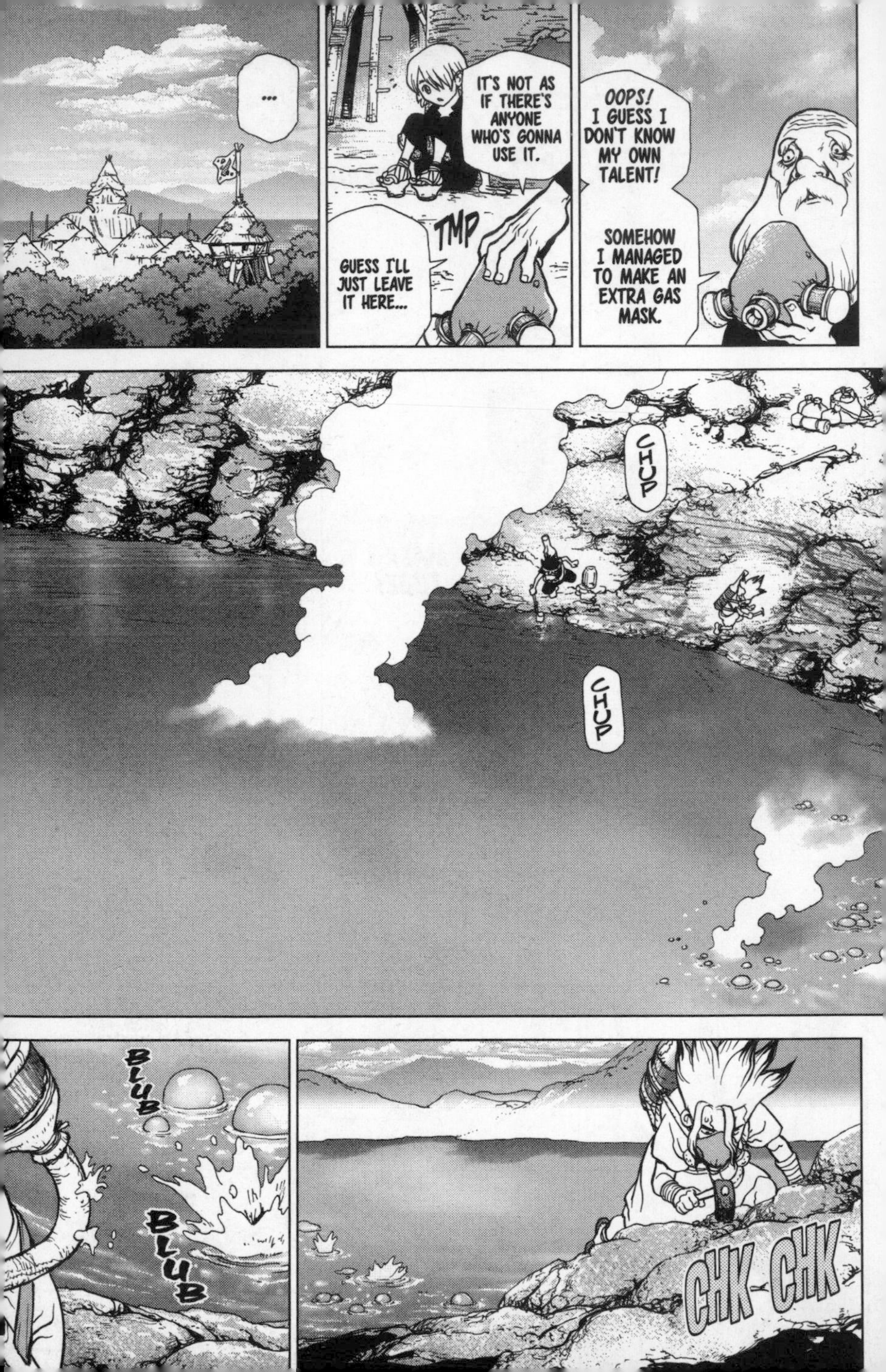
OOPS! I GUESS I DON'T KNOW MY OWN TALENT!
SOMEHOW I MANAGED TO MAKE AN EXTRA GAS MASK.
IT'S NOT AS IF THERE'S ANYONE WHO'S GONNA USE IT.
TMP
GUESS I'LL JUST LEAVE IT HERE...
...
CHUP
CHUP
CHK CHK
BLUB
BLUB

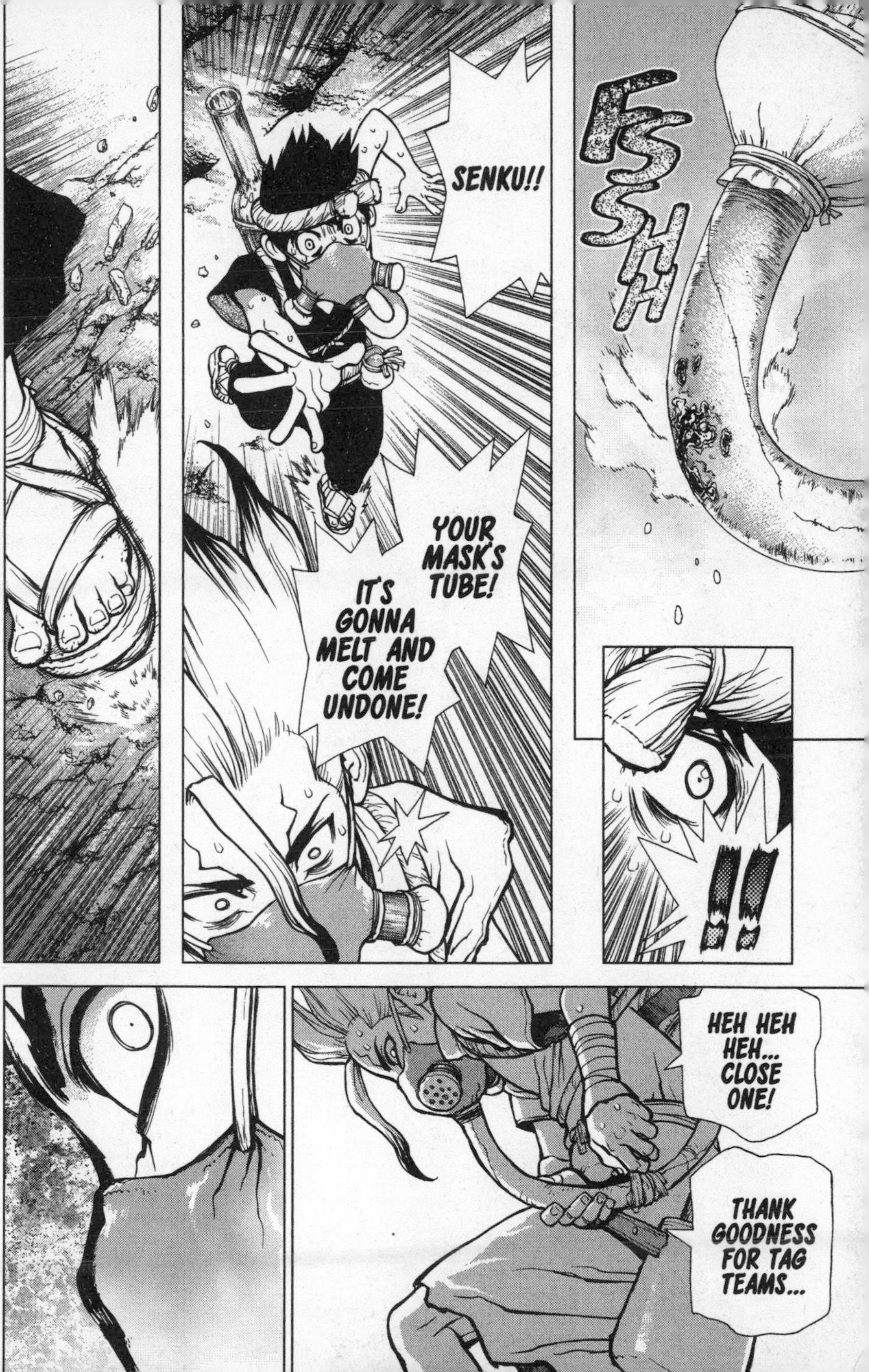
FSSHH
!!
SENKU!!
YOUR MASK'S TUBE!
IT'S GONNA MELT AND COME UNDONE!
HEH HEH HEH... CLOSE ONE!
THANK GOODNESS FOR TAG TEAMS...

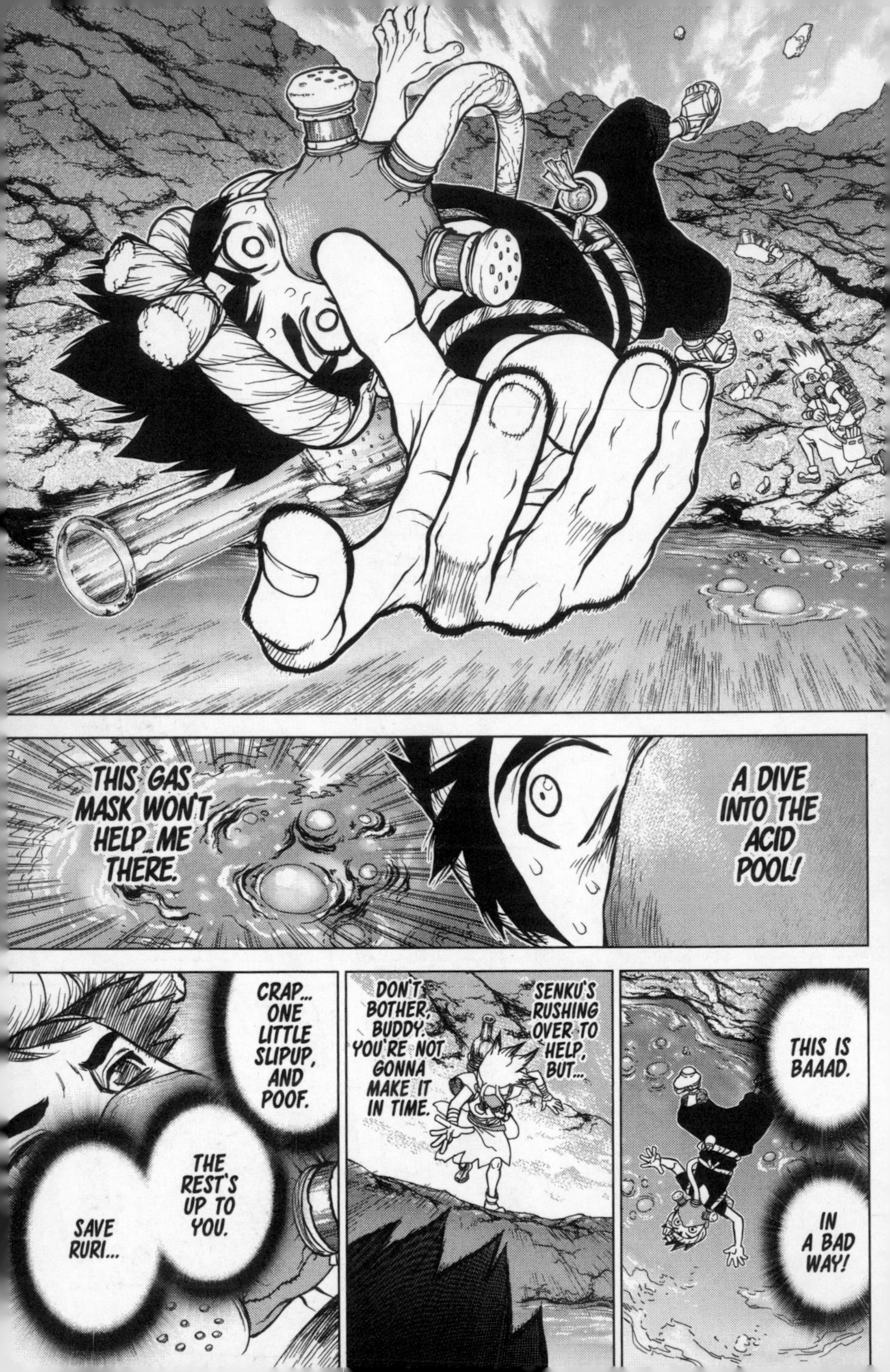
A DIVE INTO THE ACID POOL!
THIS GAS MASK WON'T HELP ME THERE.
THIS IS BAAAD.
IN A BAD WAY!
SENKU'S RUSHING OVER TO HELP, BUT...
DON'T BOTHER, BUDDY. YOU'RE NOT GONNA MAKE IT IN TIME.
CRAP... ONE LITTLE SLIPUP, AND POOF.
THE REST'S UP TO YOU.
SAVE RURI...

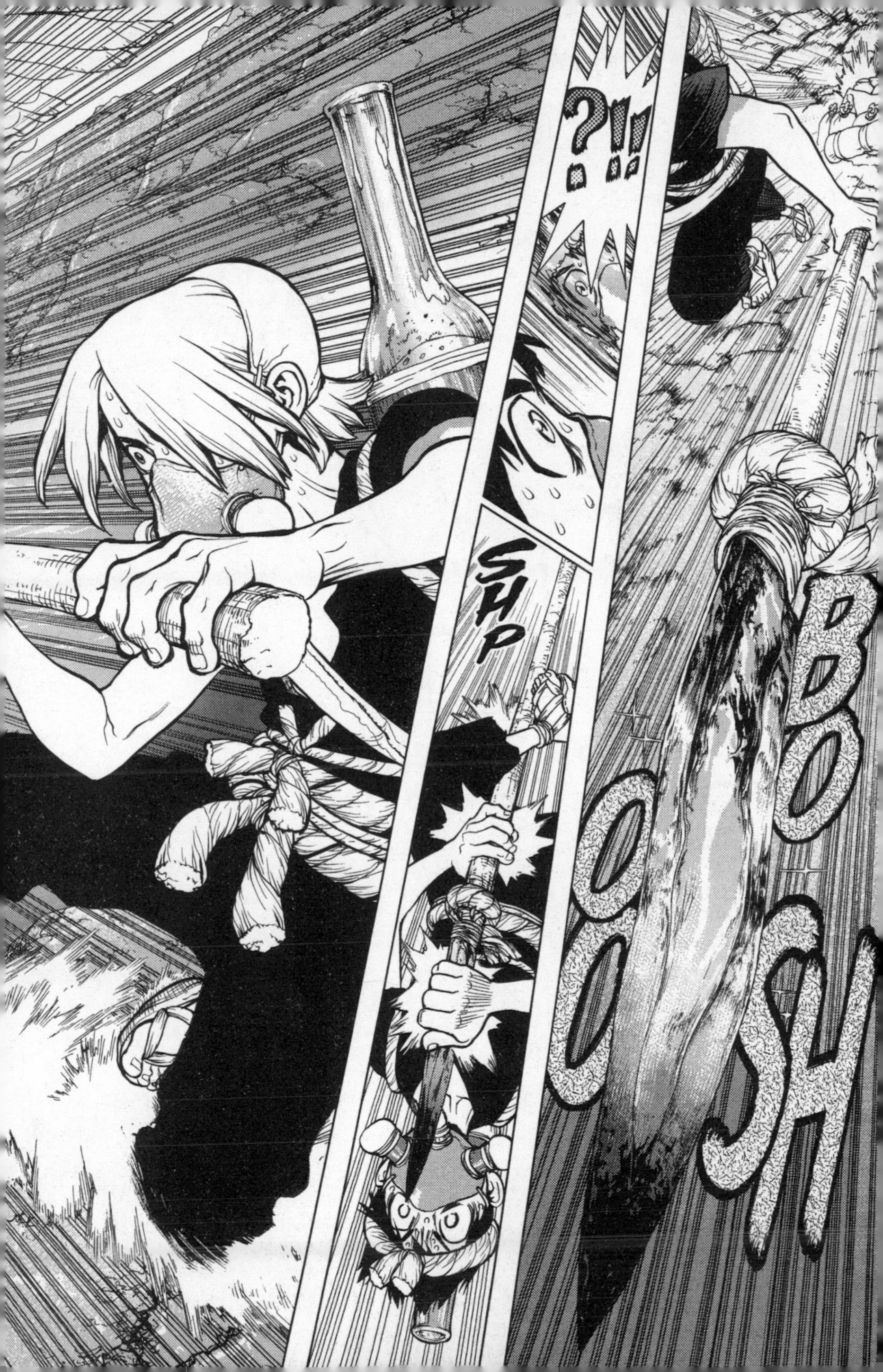
BOOOOSH
?!!
SHP

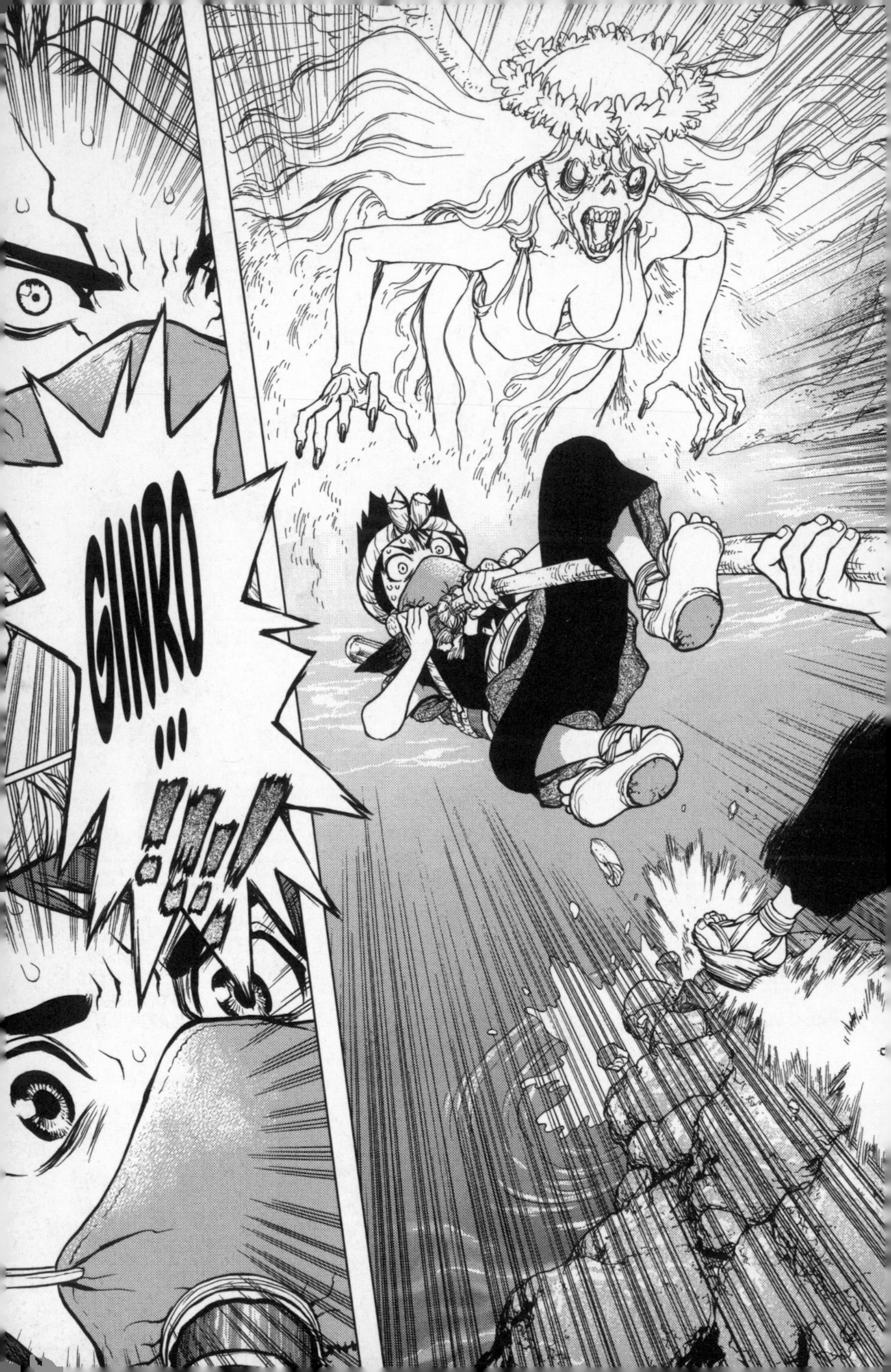
GINRO
...!!!!

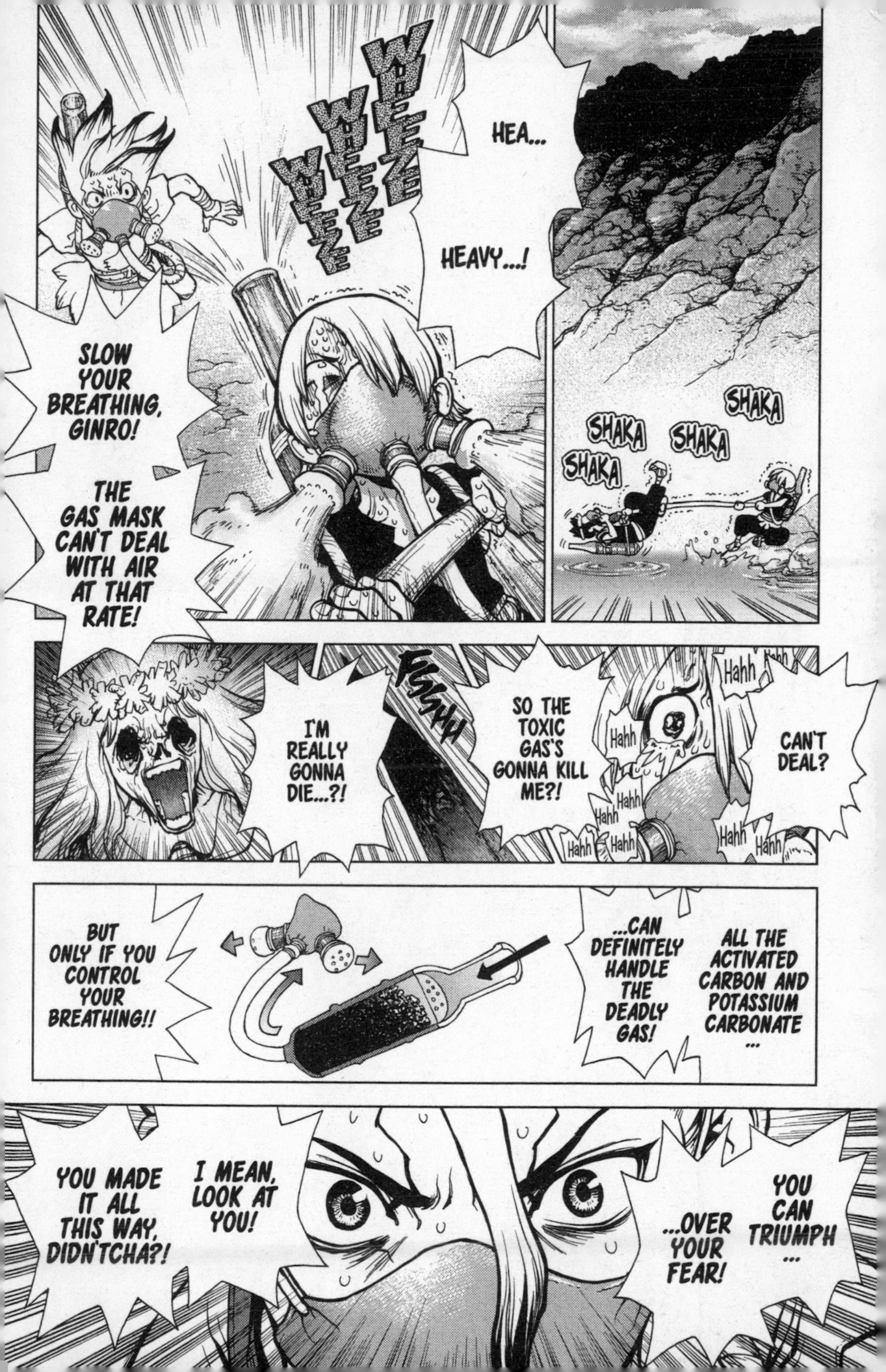
SHAKA
SHAKA
SHAKA
HEA...
HEAVY...!
WHEEZE
WHEEZE
WHEEZE
SLOW YOUR BREATHING, GINRO!
THE GAS MASK CAN'T DEAL WITH AIR AT THAT RATE!
CAN'T DEAL?
Hahh
Hahh
Hahh
Hahh
Hahh
Hahh
Hahh
Hahh
SO THE TOXIC GAS'S GONNA KILL ME?!
I'M REALLY GONNA DIE...?!
ALL THE ACTIVATED CARBON AND POTASSIUM CARBONATE...
...CAN DEFINITELY HANDLE THE DEADLY GAS!
BUT ONLY IF YOU CONTROL YOUR BREATHING!!
YOU CAN TRIUMPH...
...OVER YOUR FEAR!
I MEAN, LOOK AT YOU!
YOU MADE IT ALL THIS WAY, DIDN'TCHA?!

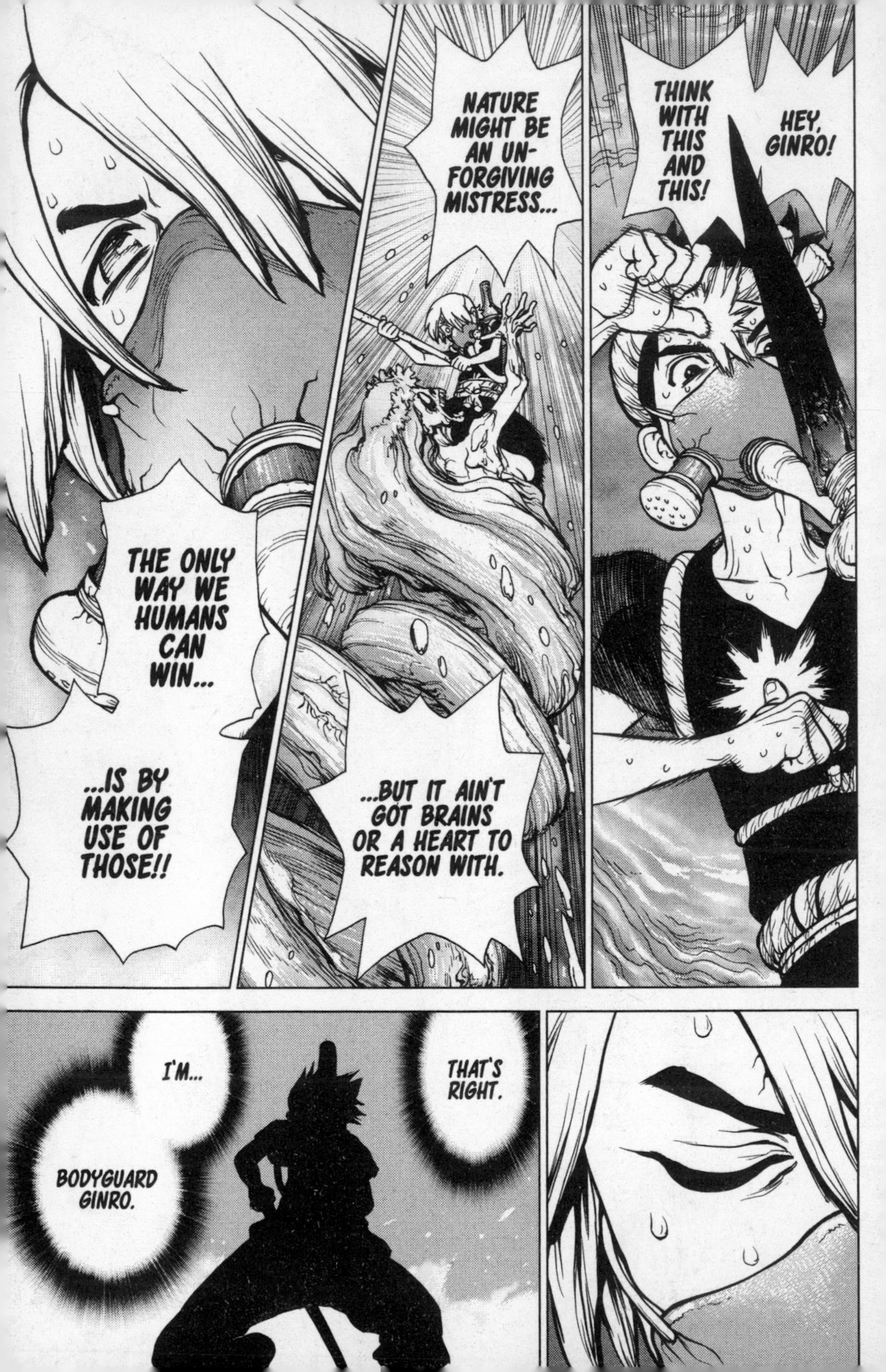
HEY, GINRO!
THINK WITH THIS AND THIS!
NATURE MIGHT BE AN UN-FORGIVING MISTRESS...
...BUT IT AIN'T GOT BRAINS OR A HEART TO REASON WITH.
THE ONLY WAY WE HUMANS CAN WIN...
...IS BY MAKING USE OF THOSE!!
THAT'S RIGHT.
I'M...
BODYGUARD GINRO.

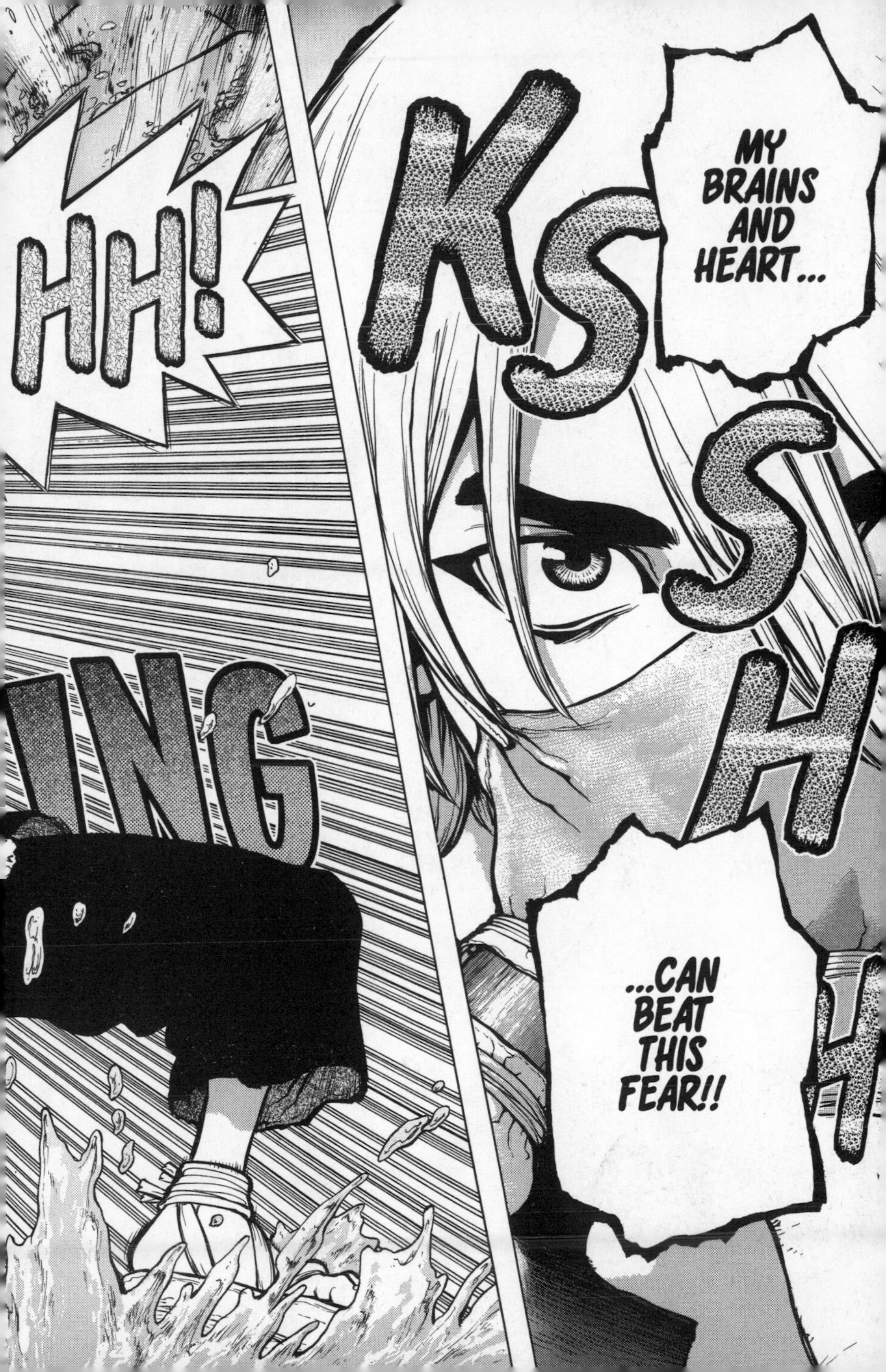
MY BRAINS AND HEART...
KSSHH
...CAN BEAT THIS FEAR!!
HH!
NG

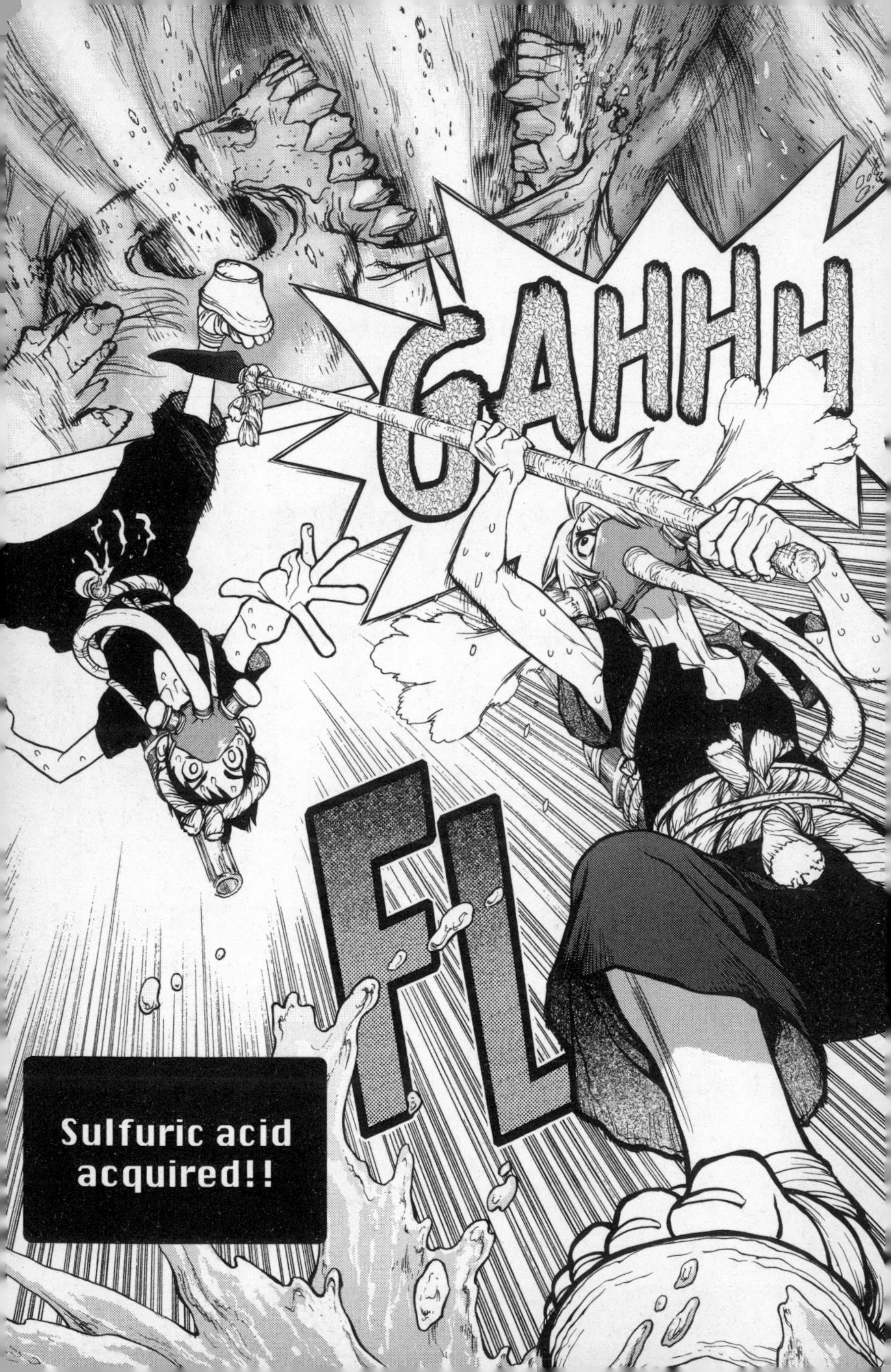
GAHHH
FL
Sulfuric acid acquired!!

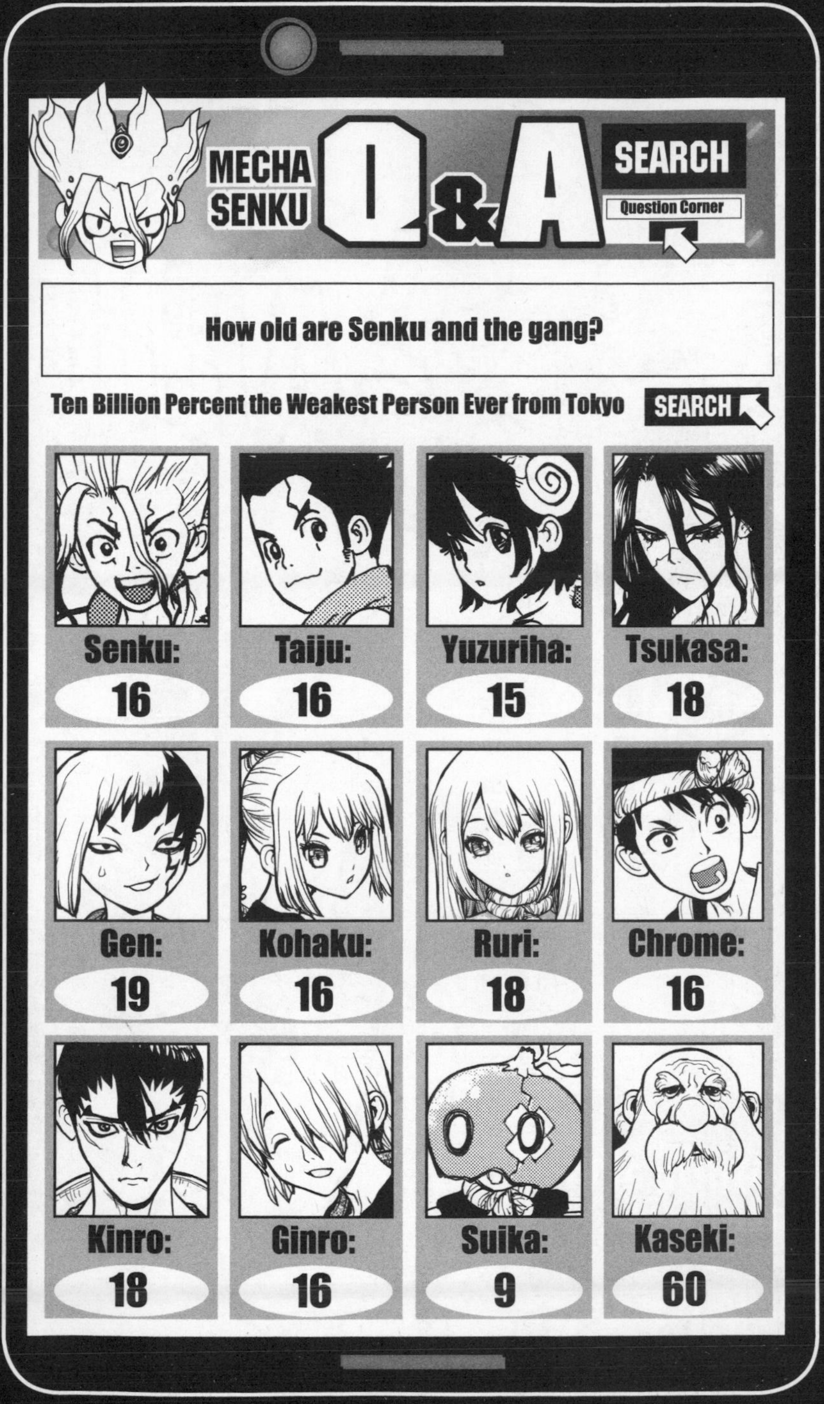

MECHA SENKU
Q&A
SEARCH
Question Corner
How old are Senku and the gang?
Ten Billion Percent the Weakest Person Ever from Tokyo
SEARCH
Senku: 16
Taiju: 16
Yuzuriha: 15
Tsukasa: 18
Gen: 19
Kohaku: 16
Ruri: 18
Chrome: 16
Kinro: 18
Ginro: 16
Suika: 9
Kaseki: 60

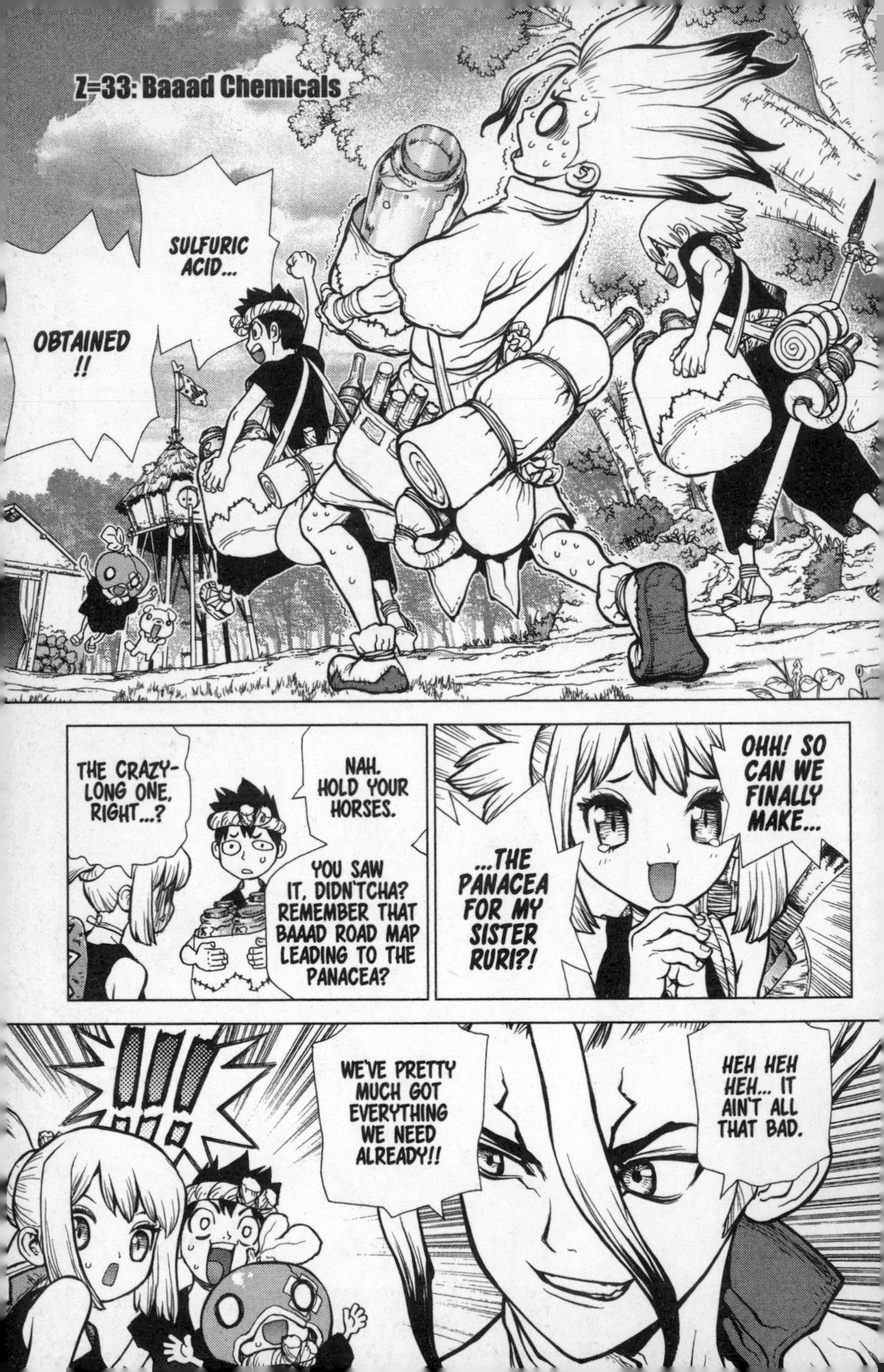
Z=33: Baaad Chemicals
SULFURIC ACID...
OBTAINED!!
OHH! SO CAN WE FINALLY MAKE...
...THE PANACEA FOR MY SISTER RURI?!
NAH. HOLD YOUR HORSES.
THE CRAZY-LONG ONE, RIGHT...?
YOU SAW IT, DIDN'TCHA? REMEMBER THAT BAAAD ROAD MAP LEADING TO THE PANACEA?
HEH HEH HEH... IT AIN'T ALL THAT BAD.
WE'VE PRETTY MUCH GOT EVERYTHING WE NEED ALREADY!!
!!!

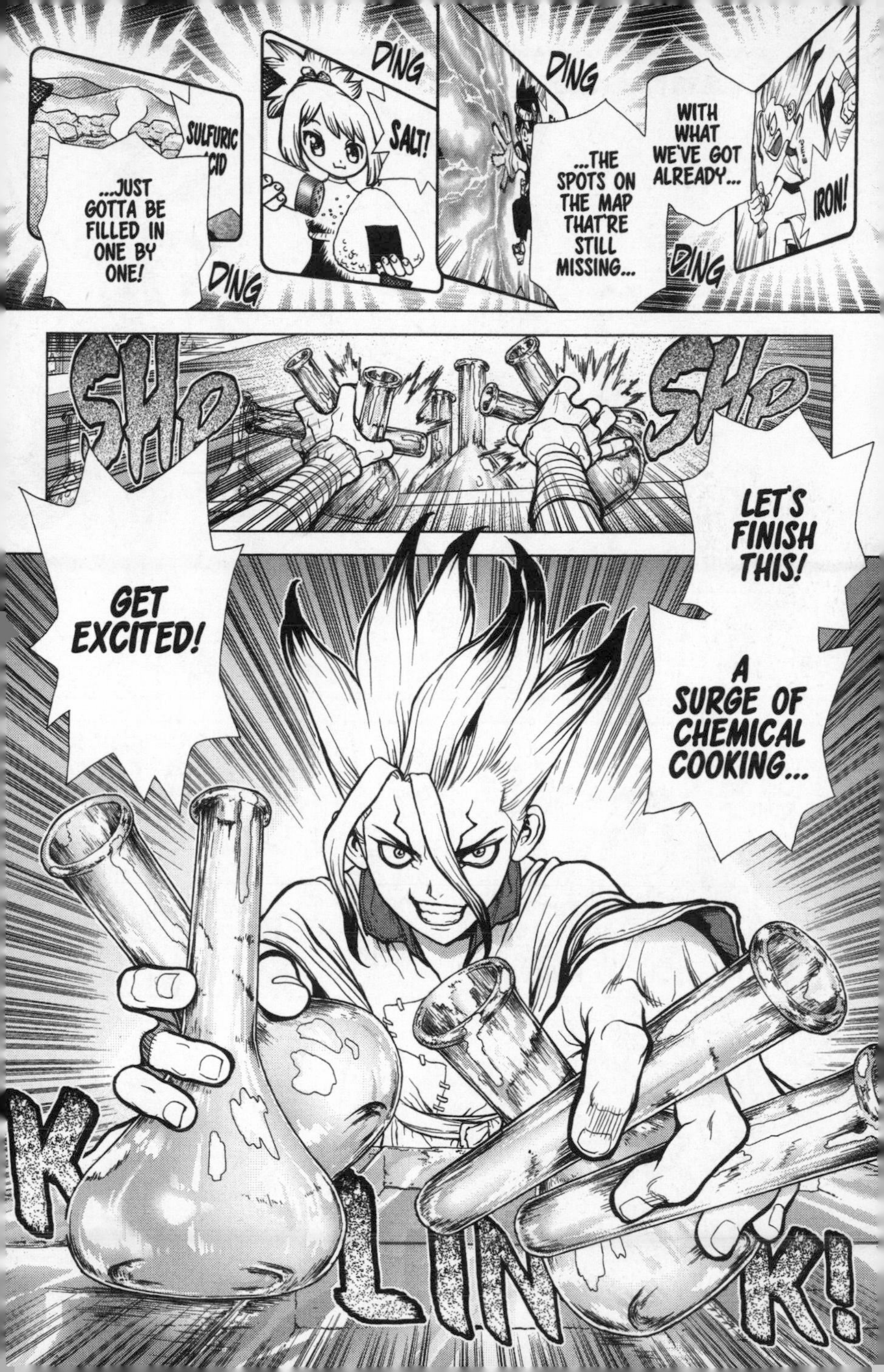
WITH WHAT WE'VE GOT ALREADY...
IRON!
DING
...THE SPOTS ON THE MAP THAT'RE STILL MISSING...
DING
DING
SALT!
SULFURIC
CID
...JUST GOTTA BE FILLED IN ONE BY ONE!
DING
SHP
SHP
LET'S FINISH THIS!
A SURGE OF CHEMICAL COOKING...
GET EXCITED!
KLINK!

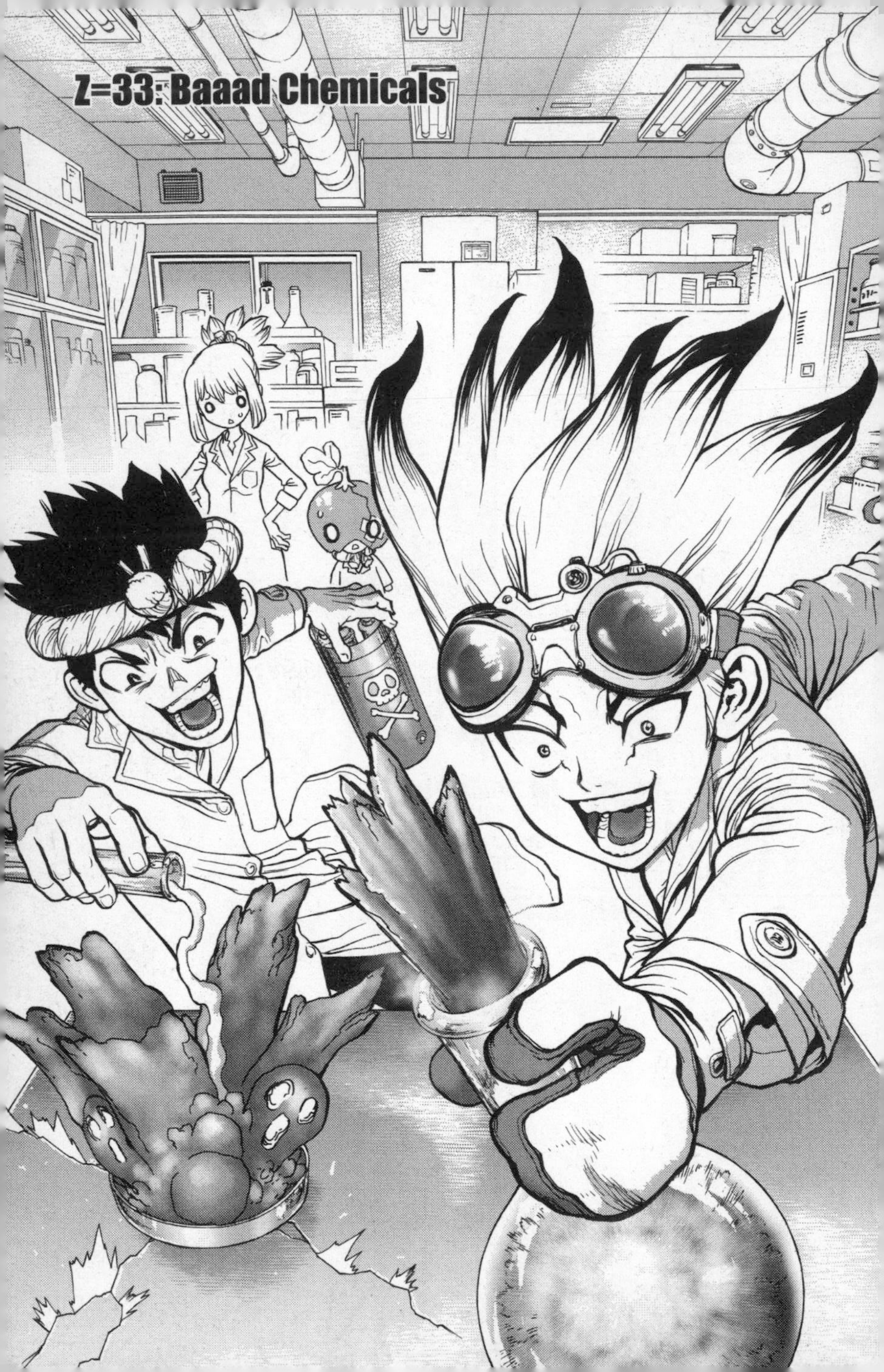
Z=33: Baaad Chemicals

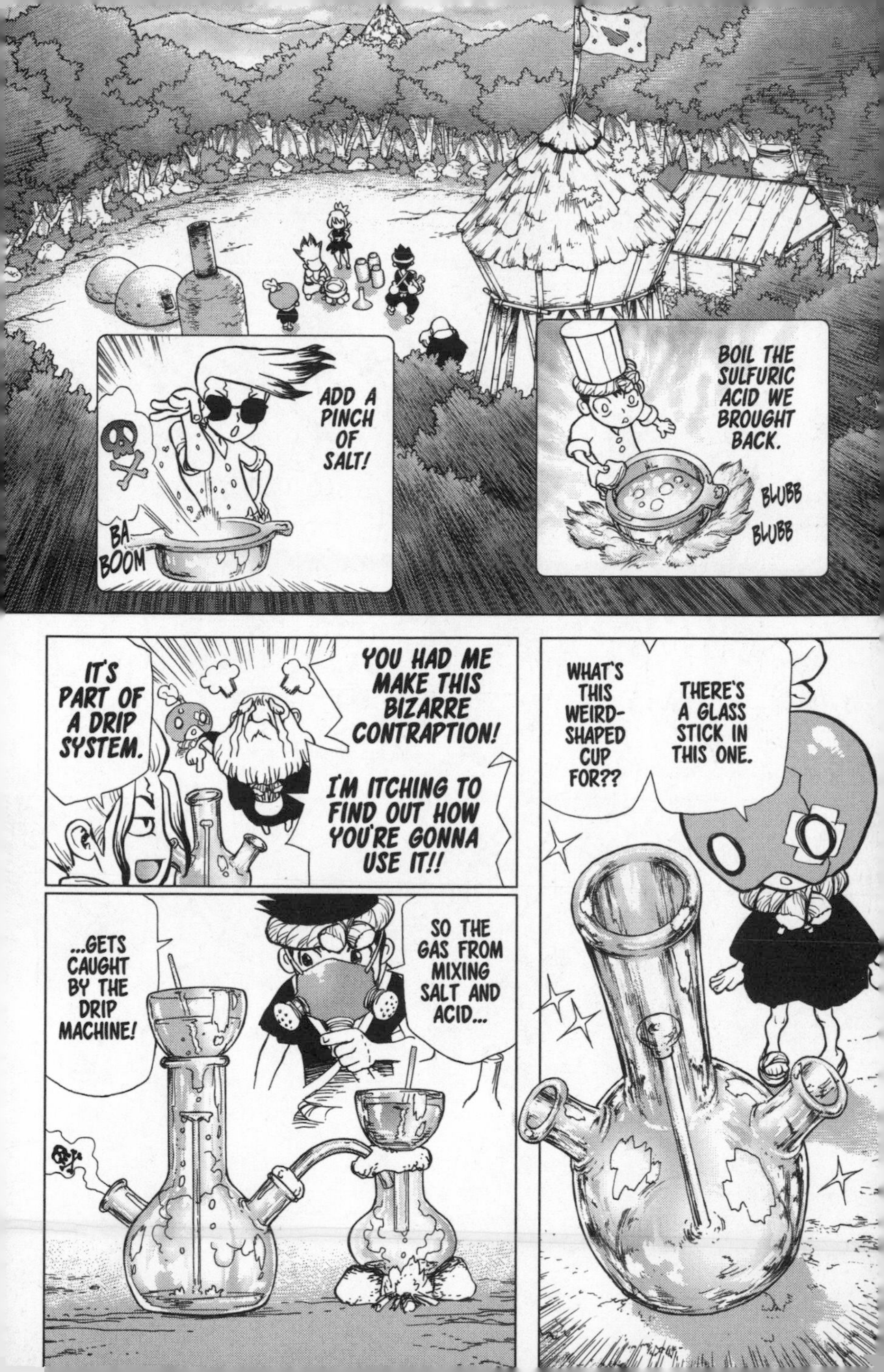
BOIL THE SULFURIC ACID WE BROUGHT BACK.
BLUBB
BLUBB
ADD A PINCH OF SALT!
BA BOOM
THERE'S A GLASS STICK IN THIS ONE.
WHAT'S THIS WEIRD-SHAPED CUP FOR??
YOU HAD ME MAKE THIS BIZARRE CONTRAPTION!
I'M ITCHING TO FIND OUT HOW YOU'RE GONNA USE IT!!
IT'S PART OF A DRIP SYSTEM.
SO THE GAS FROM MIXING SALT AND ACID...
...GETS CAUGHT BY THE DRIP MACHINE!

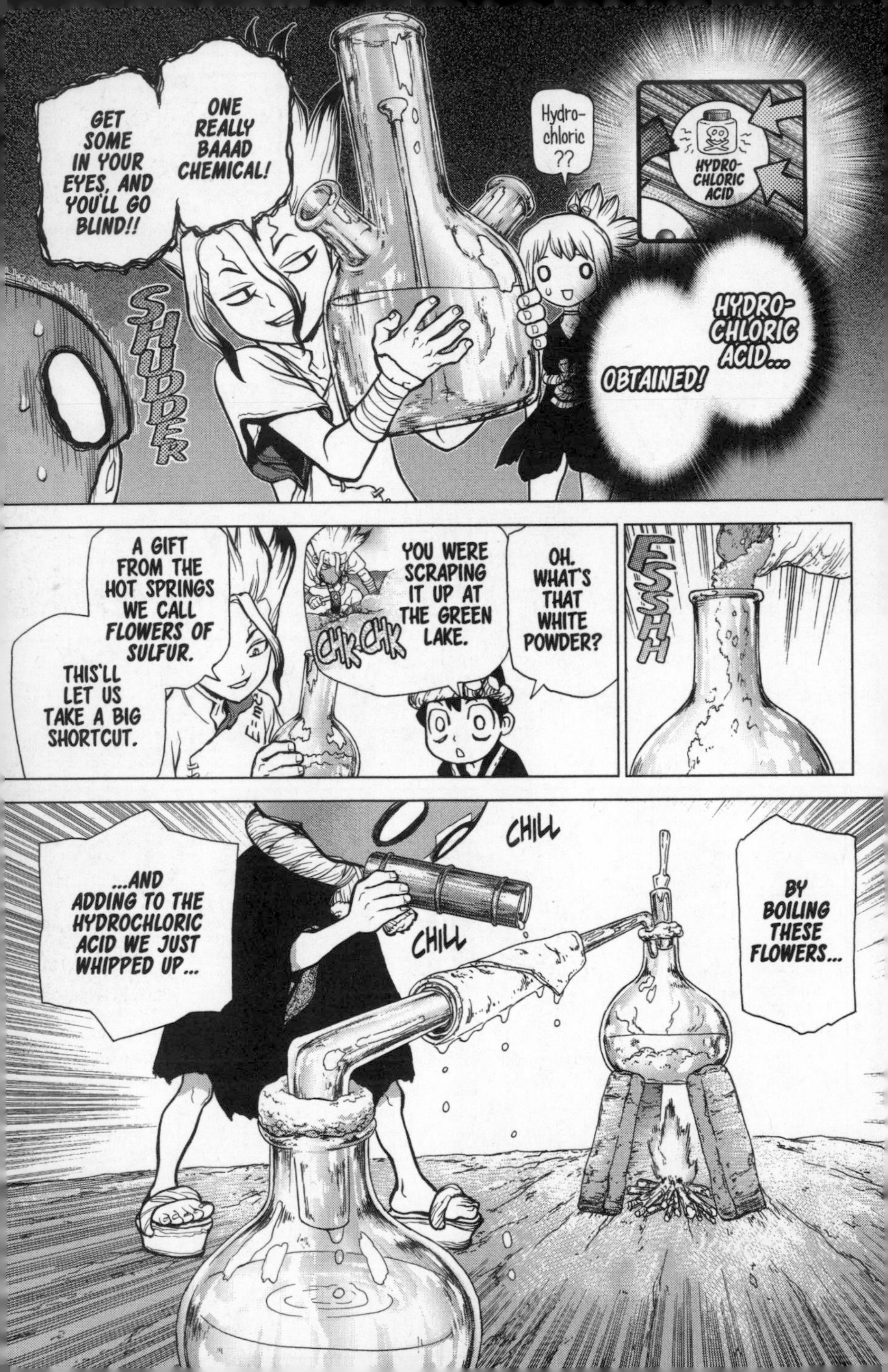
HYDRO-CHLORIC ACID
Hydro-chloric ??
ONE REALLY BAAAD CHEMICAL!
GET SOME IN YOUR EYES, AND YOU'LL GO BLIND!!
HYDRO-CHLORIC ACID...
OBTAINED!
SHUDDER
FSSHH
OH. WHAT'S THAT WHITE POWDER?
YOU WERE SCRAPING IT UP AT THE GREEN LAKE.
CHK CHK
A GIFT FROM THE HOT SPRINGS WE CALL FLOWERS OF SULFUR.
THIS'LL LET US TAKE A BIG SHORTCUT.
BY BOILING THESE FLOWERS...
CHILL
CHILL
...AND ADDING TO THE HYDROCHLORIC ACID WE JUST WHIPPED UP...

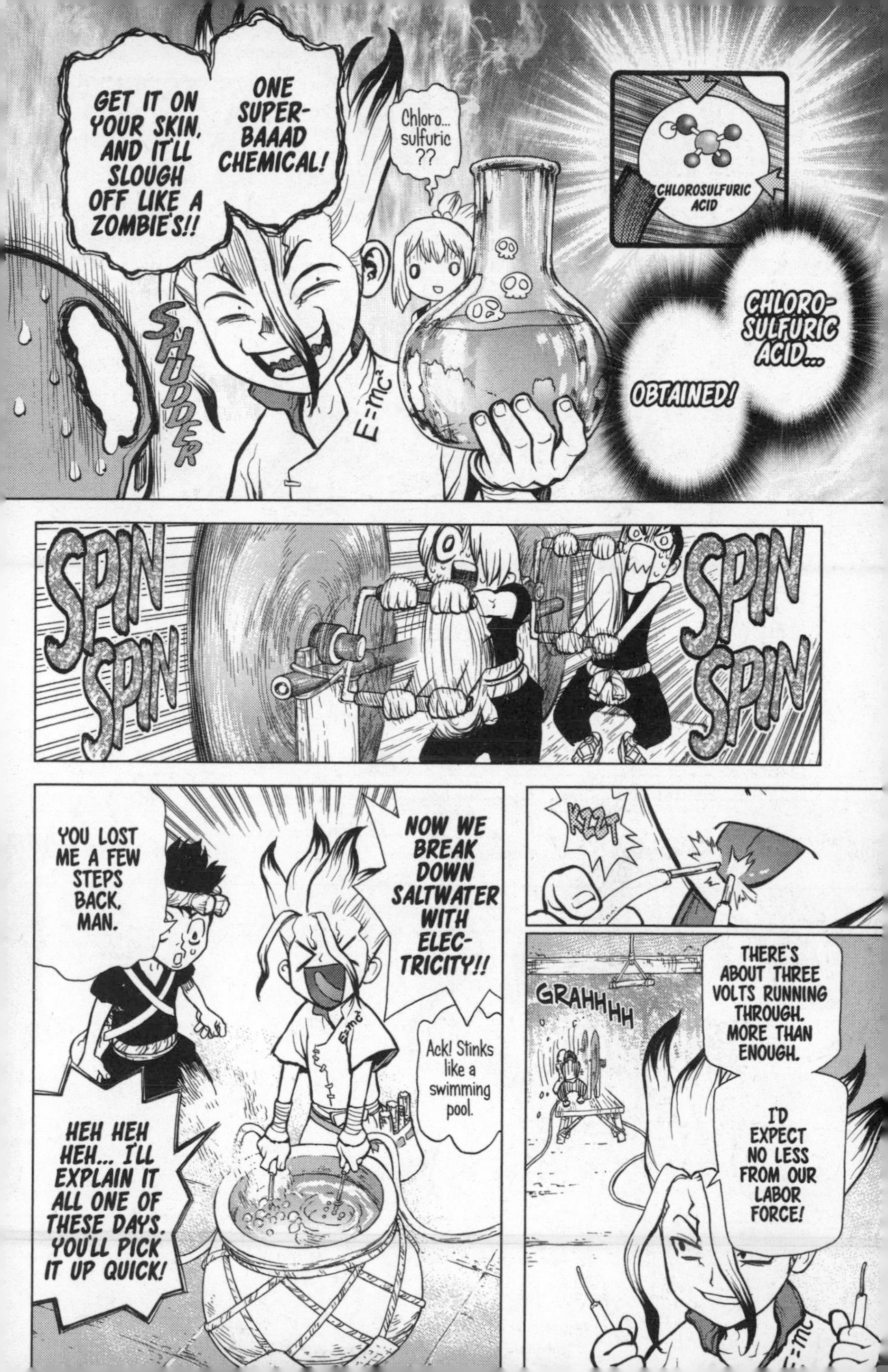
CHLOROSULFURIC ACID
CHLORO-SULFURIC ACID...
OBTAINED!
Chloro... sulfuric ??
ONE SUPER-BAAAD CHEMICAL!
GET IT ON YOUR SKIN, AND IT'LL SLOUGH OFF LIKE A ZOMBIE'S!!
SHUDDER
SPIN SPIN
SPIN SPIN
KZZT
THERE'S ABOUT THREE VOLTS RUNNING THROUGH. MORE THAN ENOUGH.
I'D EXPECT NO LESS FROM OUR LABOR FORCE!
GRAHHHH
NOW WE BREAK DOWN SALTWATER WITH ELEC-TRICITY!!
YOU LOST ME A FEW STEPS BACK, MAN.
Ack! Stinks like a swimming pool.
HEH HEH HEH... I'LL EXPLAIN IT ALL ONE OF THESE DAYS. YOU'LL PICK IT UP QUICK!

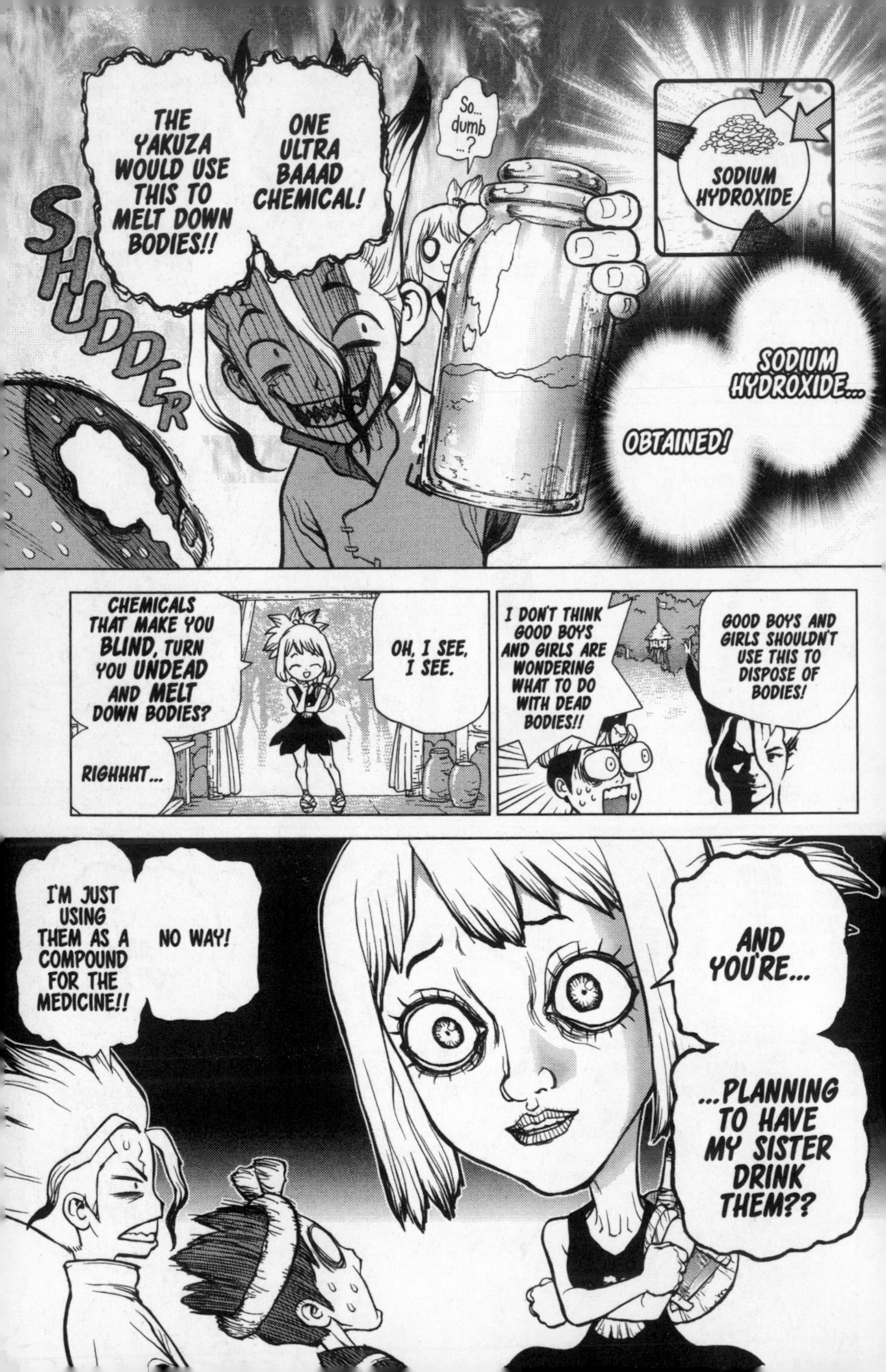
SODIUM HYDROXIDE
SODIUM HYDROXIDE...
OBTAINED!
So... dumb ...?
ONE ULTRA BAAAD CHEMICAL!
THE YAKUZA WOULD USE THIS TO MELT DOWN BODIES!!
SHUDDER
GOOD BOYS AND GIRLS SHOULDN'T USE THIS TO DISPOSE OF BODIES!
I DON'T THINK GOOD BOYS AND GIRLS ARE WONDERING WHAT TO DO WITH DEAD BODIES!!
OH, I SEE, I SEE.
CHEMICALS THAT MAKE YOU BLIND, TURN YOU UNDEAD AND MELT DOWN BODIES?
RIGHHHT...
AND YOU'RE...
...PLANNING TO HAVE MY SISTER DRINK THEM??
NO WAY!
I'M JUST USING THEM AS A COMPOUND FOR THE MEDICINE!!

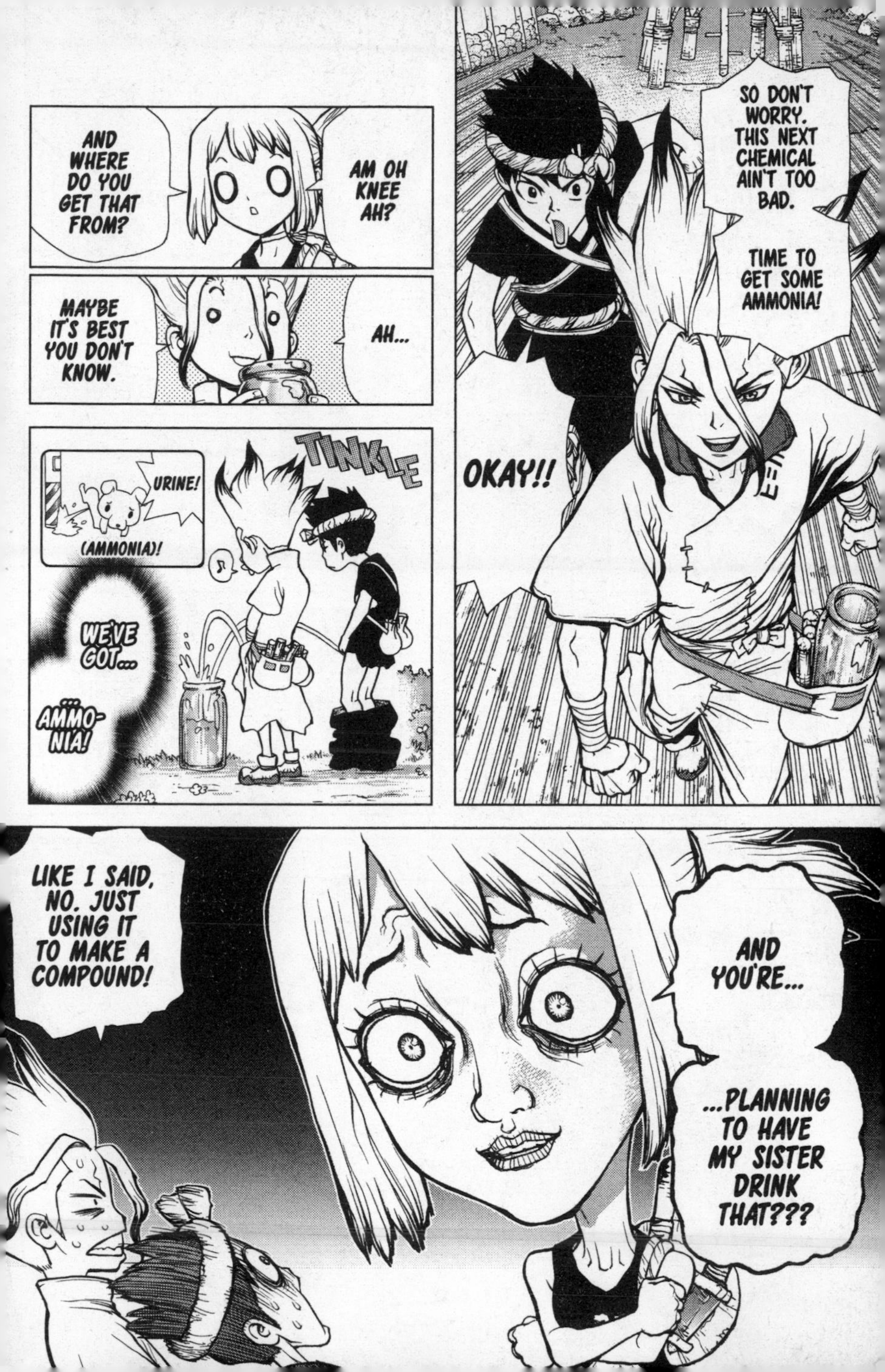
SO DON'T WORRY. THIS NEXT CHEMICAL AIN'T TOO BAD.
TIME TO GET SOME AMMONIA!
OKAY!!
AM OH KNEE AH?
AND WHERE DO YOU GET THAT FROM?
AH...
MAYBE IT'S BEST YOU DON'T KNOW.
TINKLE
URINE!
(AMMONIA)!
WE'VE GOT...
...AMMONIA!
AND YOU'RE...
...PLANNING TO HAVE MY SISTER DRINK THAT???
LIKE I SAID, NO. JUST USING IT TO MAKE A COMPOUND!

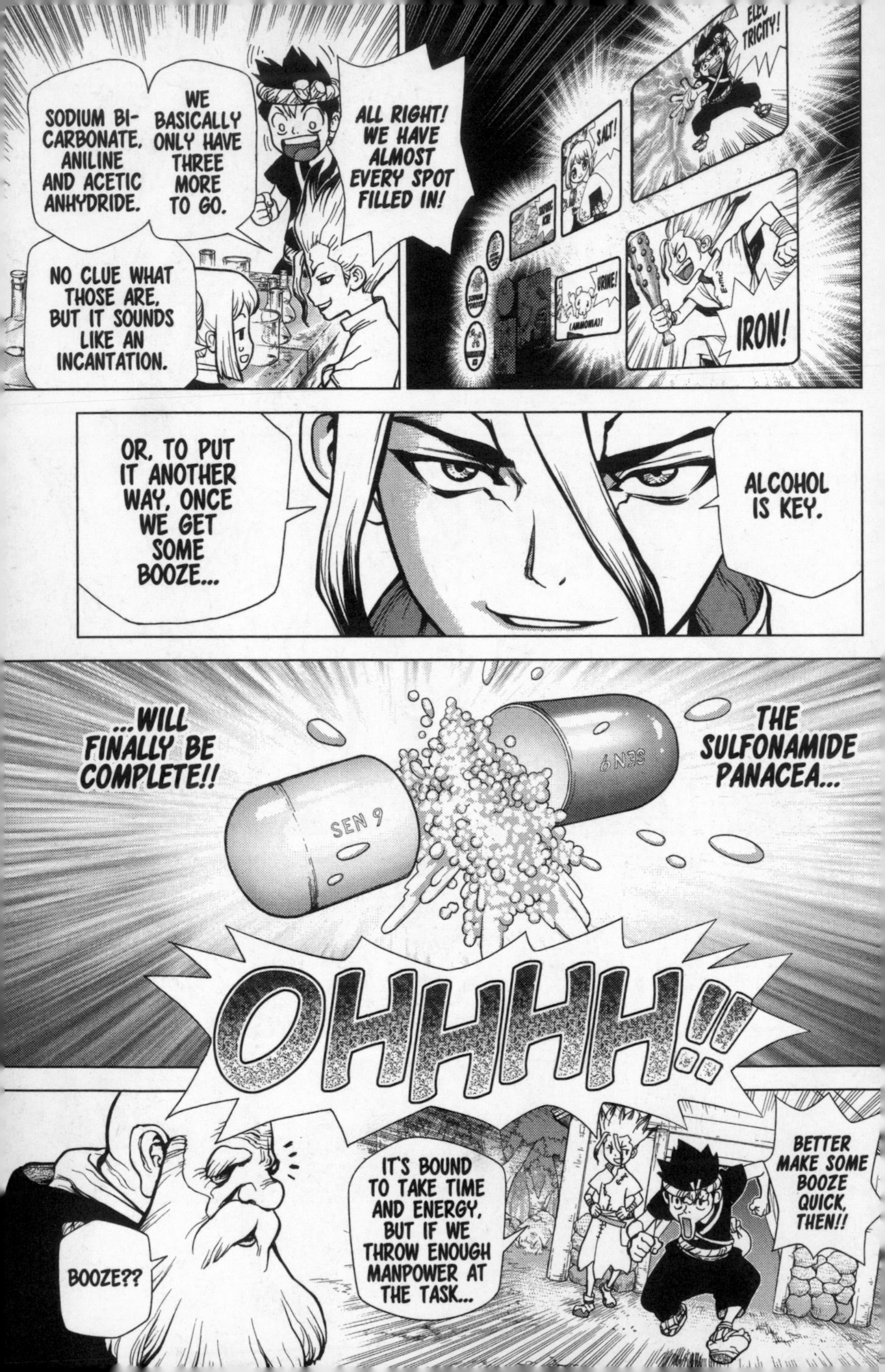
ELECTRICITY!
SALT!
IRON!
URINE!
(AMMONIA)!
ALL RIGHT! WE HAVE ALMOST EVERY SPOT FILLED IN!
WE BASICALLY ONLY HAVE THREE MORE TO GO.
SODIUM BI-CARBONATE, ANILINE AND ACETIC ANHYDRIDE.
NO CLUE WHAT THOSE ARE, BUT IT SOUNDS LIKE AN INCANTATION.
ALCOHOL IS KEY.
OR, TO PUT IT ANOTHER WAY, ONCE WE GET SOME BOOZE...
THE SULFONAMIDE PANACEA...
SEN 9
SEN 9
...WILL FINALLY BE COMPLETE!!
OHHHH!!
BETTER MAKE SOME BOOZE QUICK, THEN!!
IT'S BOUND TO TAKE TIME AND ENERGY, BUT IF WE THROW ENOUGH MANPOWER AT THE TASK...
BOOZE??

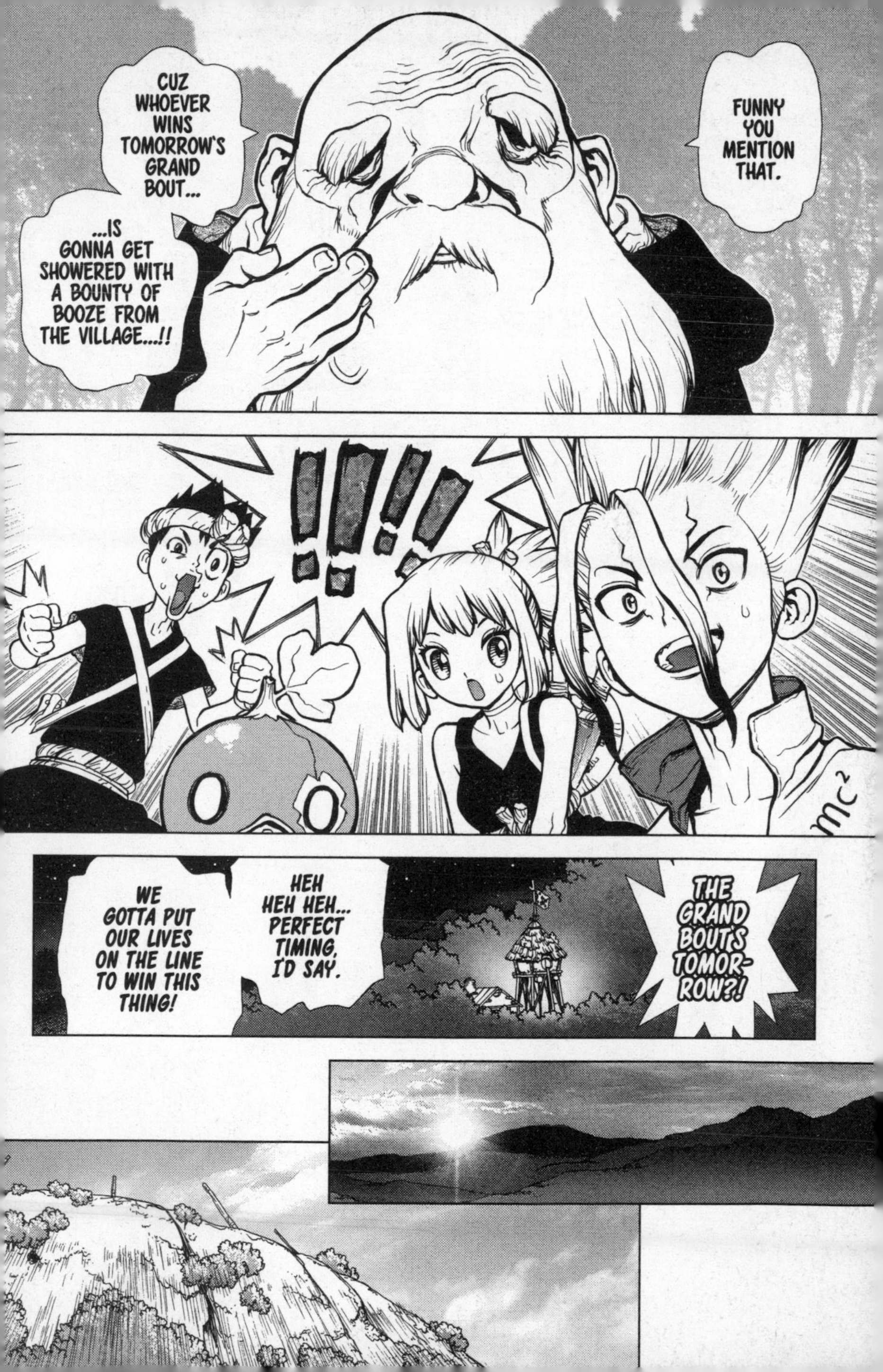
FUNNY YOU MENTION THAT.
CUZ WHOEVER WINS TOMORROW'S GRAND BOUT...
...IS GONNA GET SHOWERED WITH A BOUNTY OF BOOZE FROM THE VILLAGE...!!
THE GRAND BOUT'S TOMORROW?!
HEH HEH HEH... PERFECT TIMING, I'D SAY.
WE GOTTA PUT OUR LIVES ON THE LINE TO WIN THIS THING!

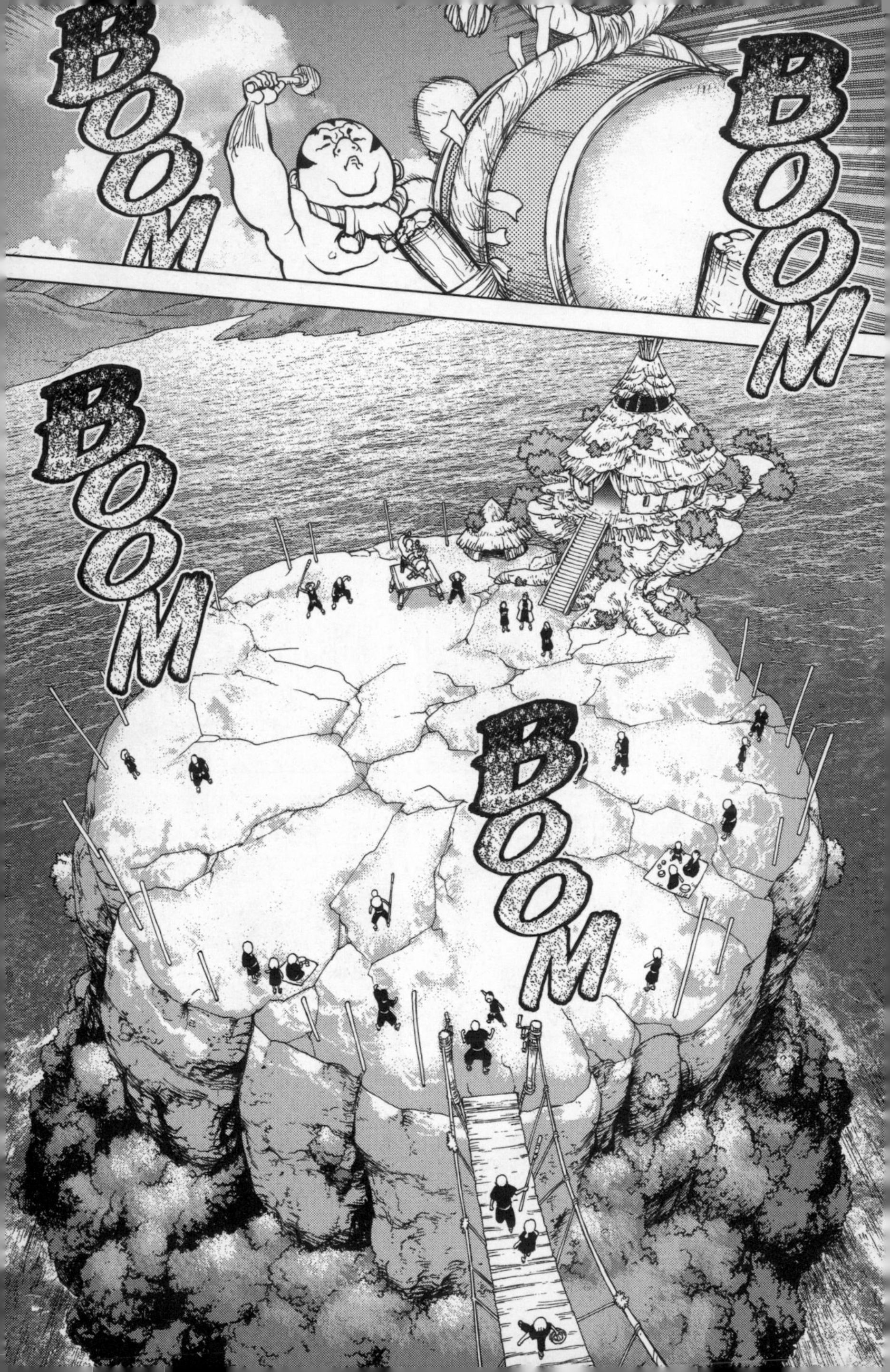
BOOM
BOOM
BOOM
BOOM

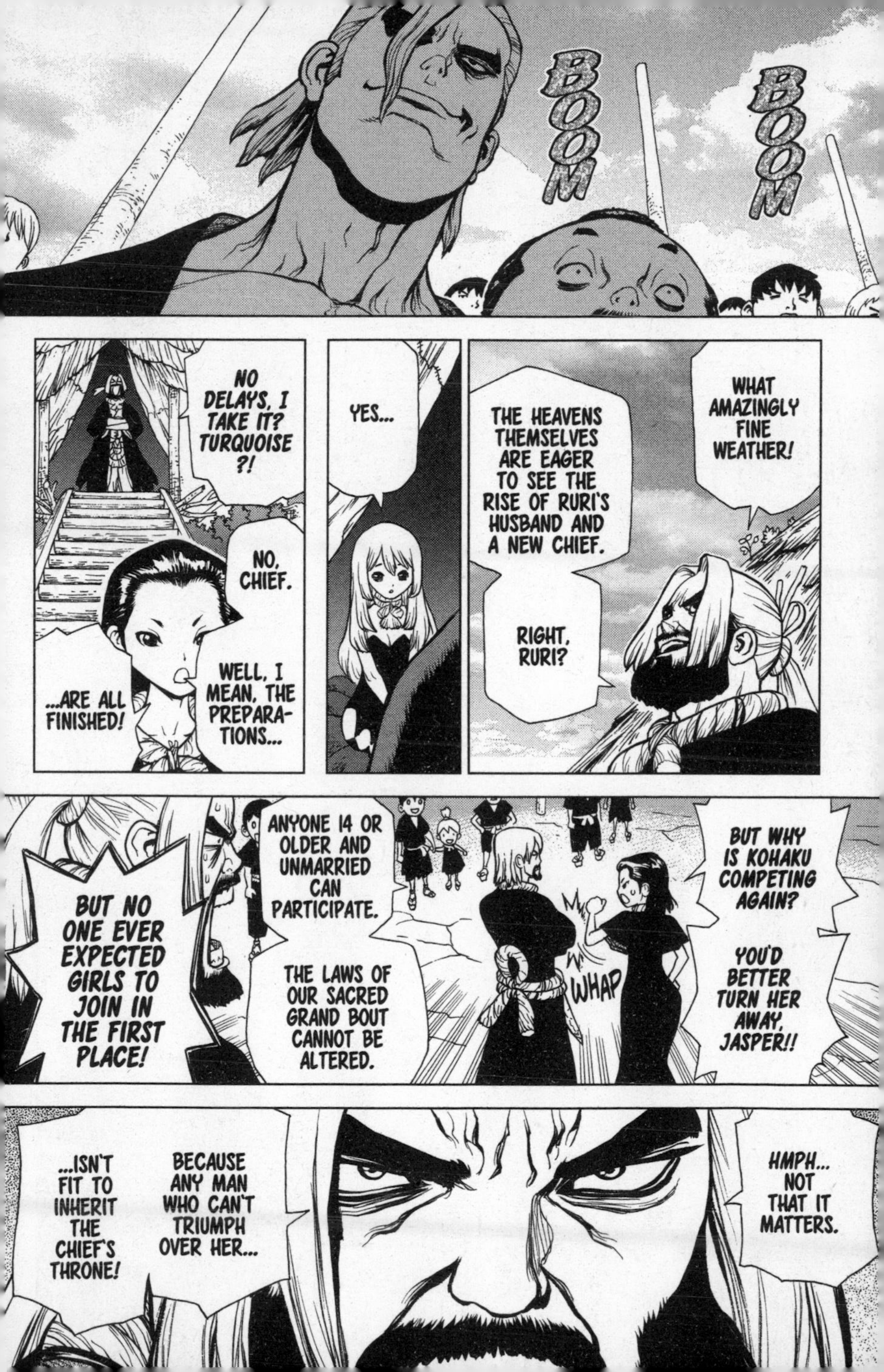
BOOM
BOOM
WHAT AMAZINGLY FINE WEATHER!
THE HEAVENS THEMSELVES ARE EAGER TO SEE THE RISE OF RURI'S HUSBAND AND A NEW CHIEF.
RIGHT, RURI?
YES...
NO DELAYS, I TAKE IT? TURQUOISE?!
NO, CHIEF.
WELL, I MEAN, THE PREPARATIONS...
...ARE ALL FINISHED!
BUT WHY IS KOHAKU COMPETING AGAIN?
YOU'D BETTER TURN HER AWAY, JASPER!!
WHAP
ANYONE 14 OR OLDER AND UNMARRIED CAN PARTICIPATE.
THE LAWS OF OUR SACRED GRAND BOUT CANNOT BE ALTERED.
BUT NO ONE EVER EXPECTED GIRLS TO JOIN IN THE FIRST PLACE!
HMPH... NOT THAT IT MATTERS.
BECAUSE ANY MAN WHO CAN'T TRIUMPH OVER HER...
...ISN'T FIT TO INHERIT THE CHIEF'S THRONE!

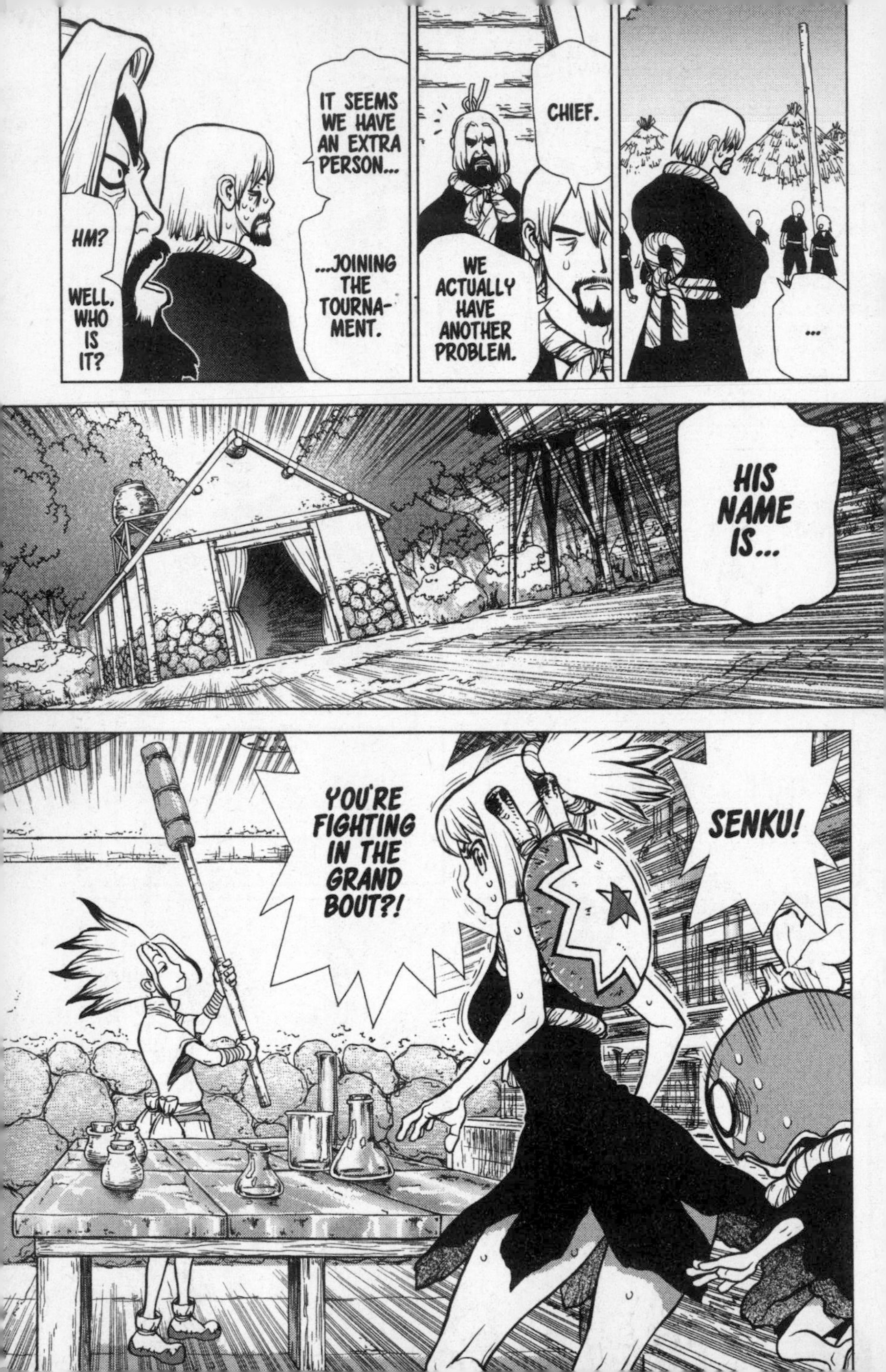
...
CHIEF.
WE ACTUALLY HAVE ANOTHER PROBLEM.
IT SEEMS WE HAVE AN EXTRA PERSON...
...JOINING THE TOURNA-MENT.
HM?
WELL, WHO IS IT?
HIS NAME IS...
SENKU!
YOU'RE FIGHTING IN THE GRAND BOUT?!

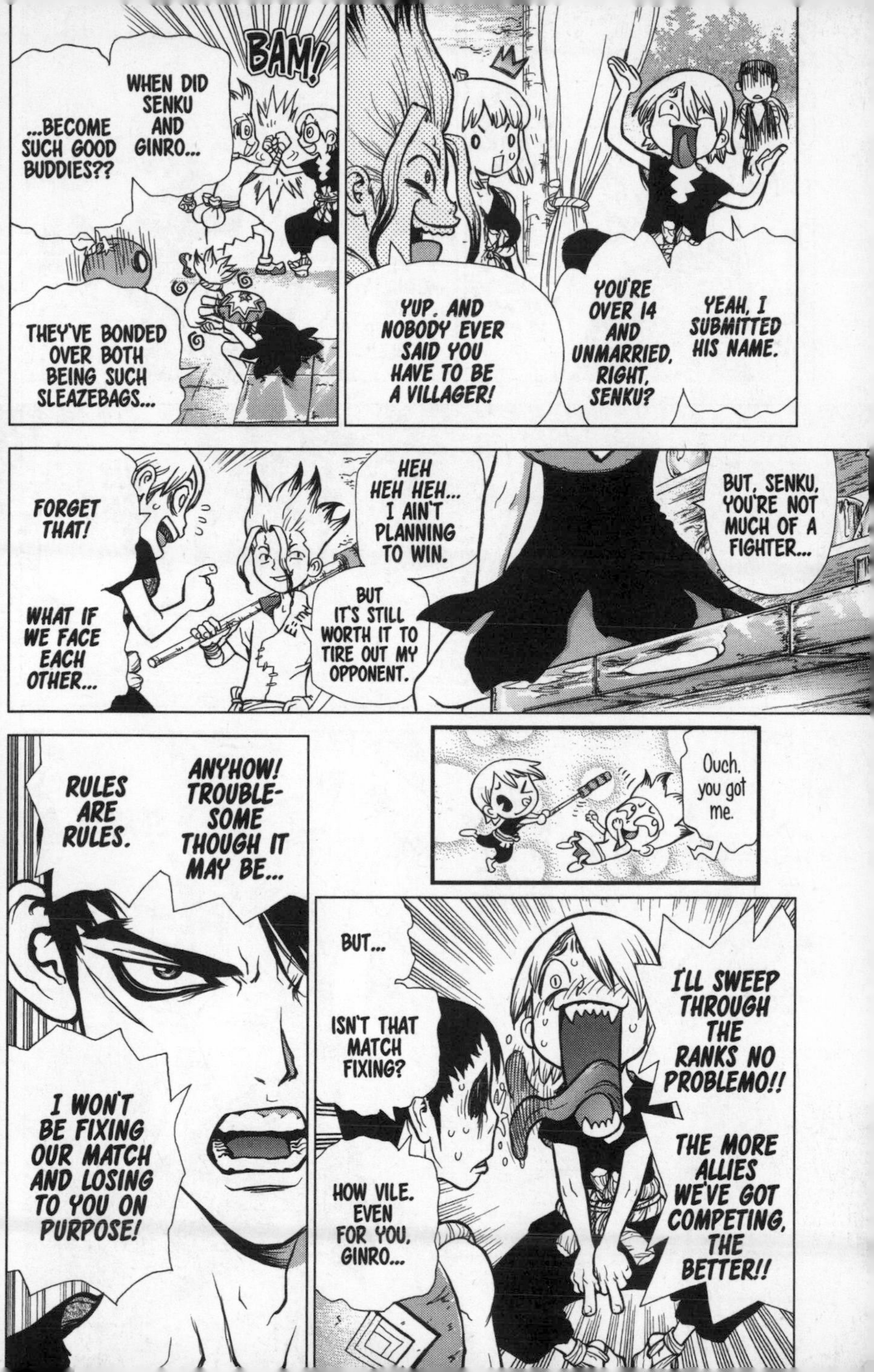
YEAH, I SUBMITTED HIS NAME.
YOU'RE OVER 14 AND UNMARRIED, RIGHT, SENKU?
YUP. AND NOBODY EVER SAID YOU HAVE TO BE A VILLAGER!
BAM!
WHEN DID SENKU AND GINRO...
...BECOME SUCH GOOD BUDDIES??
THEY'VE BONDED OVER BOTH BEING SUCH SLEAZEBAGS...
BUT, SENKU, YOU'RE NOT MUCH OF A FIGHTER...
HEH HEH HEH... I AIN'T PLANNING TO WIN.
BUT IT'S STILL WORTH IT TO TIRE OUT MY OPPONENT.
FORGET THAT!
WHAT IF WE FACE EACH OTHER...
Ouch, you got me.
I'LL SWEEP THROUGH THE RANKS NO PROBLEMO!!
THE MORE ALLIES WE'VE GOT COMPETING, THE BETTER!!
BUT...
ISN'T THAT MATCH FIXING?
HOW VILE. EVEN FOR YOU, GINRO...
ANYHOW! TROUBLE-SOME THOUGH IT MAY BE...
RULES ARE RULES.
I WON'T BE FIXING OUR MATCH AND LOSING TO YOU ON PURPOSE!

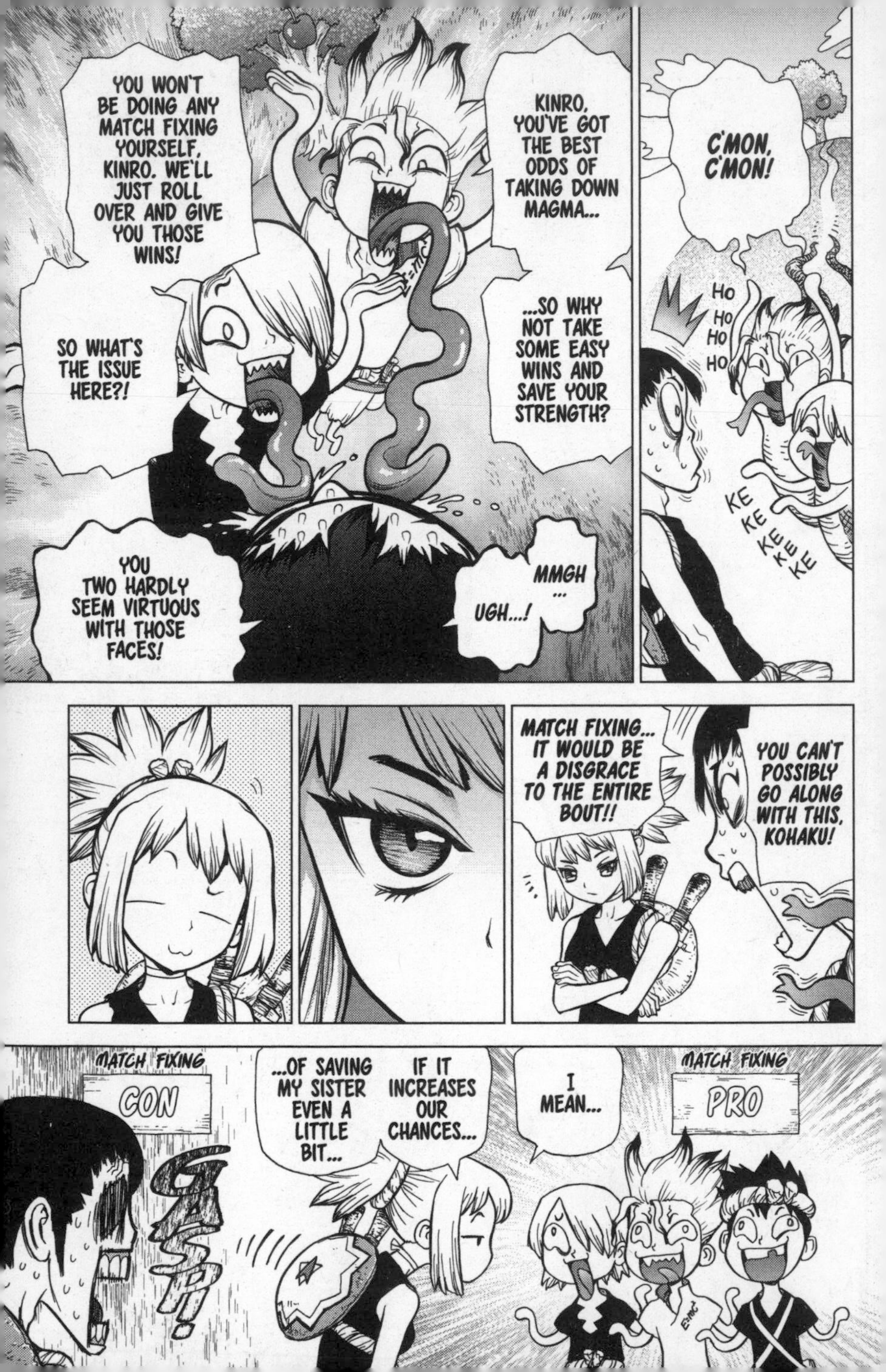
C'MON, C'MON!
Ho Ho Ho Ho
KE KE KE KE KE
KINRO, YOU'VE GOT THE BEST ODDS OF TAKING DOWN MAGMA...
YOU WON'T BE DOING ANY MATCH FIXING YOURSELF, KINRO. WE'LL JUST ROLL OVER AND GIVE YOU THOSE WINS!
...SO WHY NOT TAKE SOME EASY WINS AND SAVE YOUR STRENGTH?
SO WHAT'S THE ISSUE HERE?!
MMGH ...
UGH...!
YOU TWO HARDLY SEEM VIRTUOUS WITH THOSE FACES!
YOU CAN'T POSSIBLY GO ALONG WITH THIS, KOHAKU!
MATCH FIXING... IT WOULD BE A DISGRACE TO THE ENTIRE BOUT!!
MATCH FIXING
PRO
I MEAN...
IF IT INCREASES OUR CHANCES...
...OF SAVING MY SISTER EVEN A LITTLE BIT...
MATCH FIXING
CON

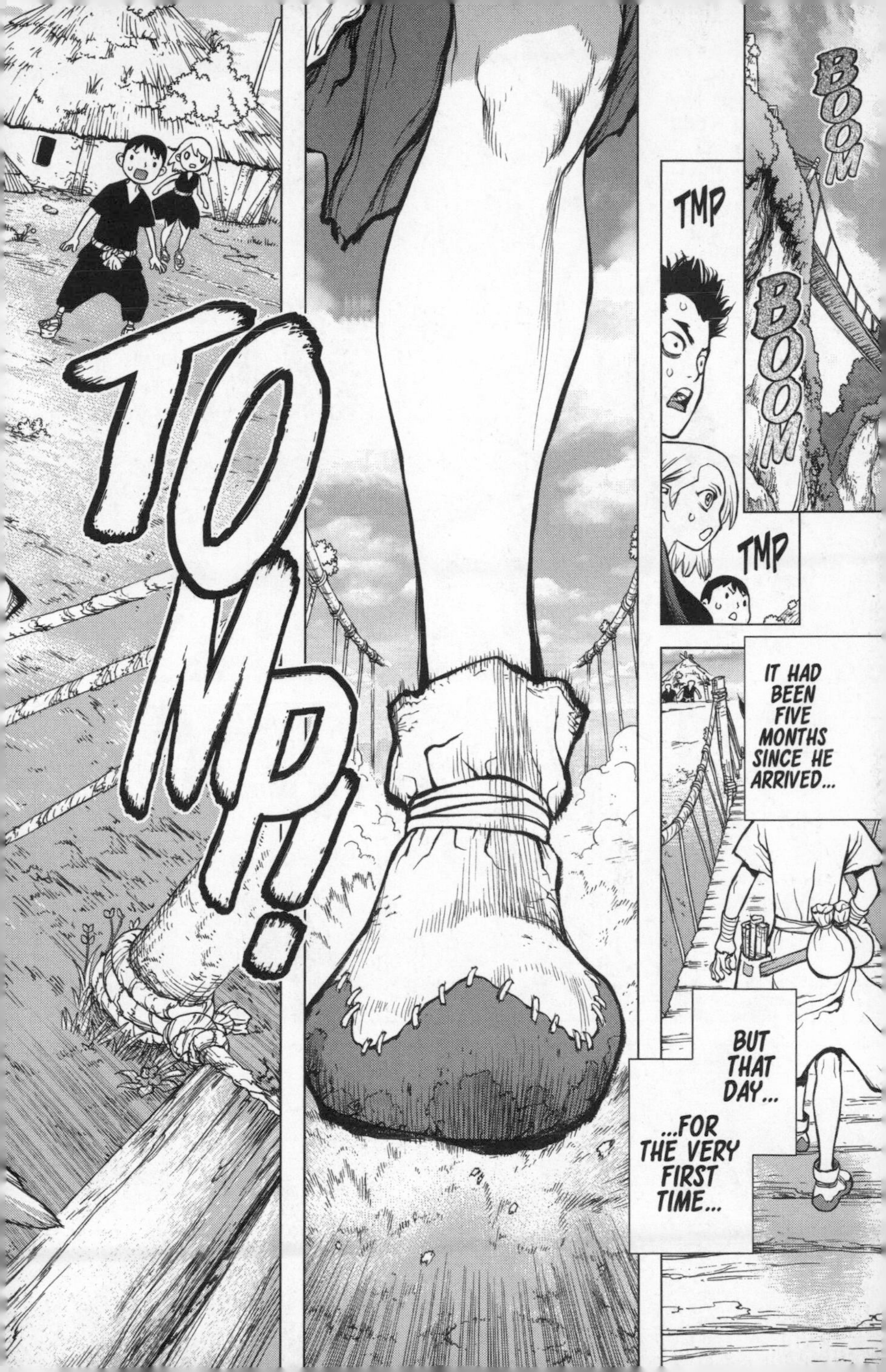
BOOM
BOOM
TMP
TMP
IT HAD BEEN FIVE MONTHS SINCE HE ARRIVED...
BUT THAT DAY...
...FOR THE VERY FIRST TIME...
TOMP!

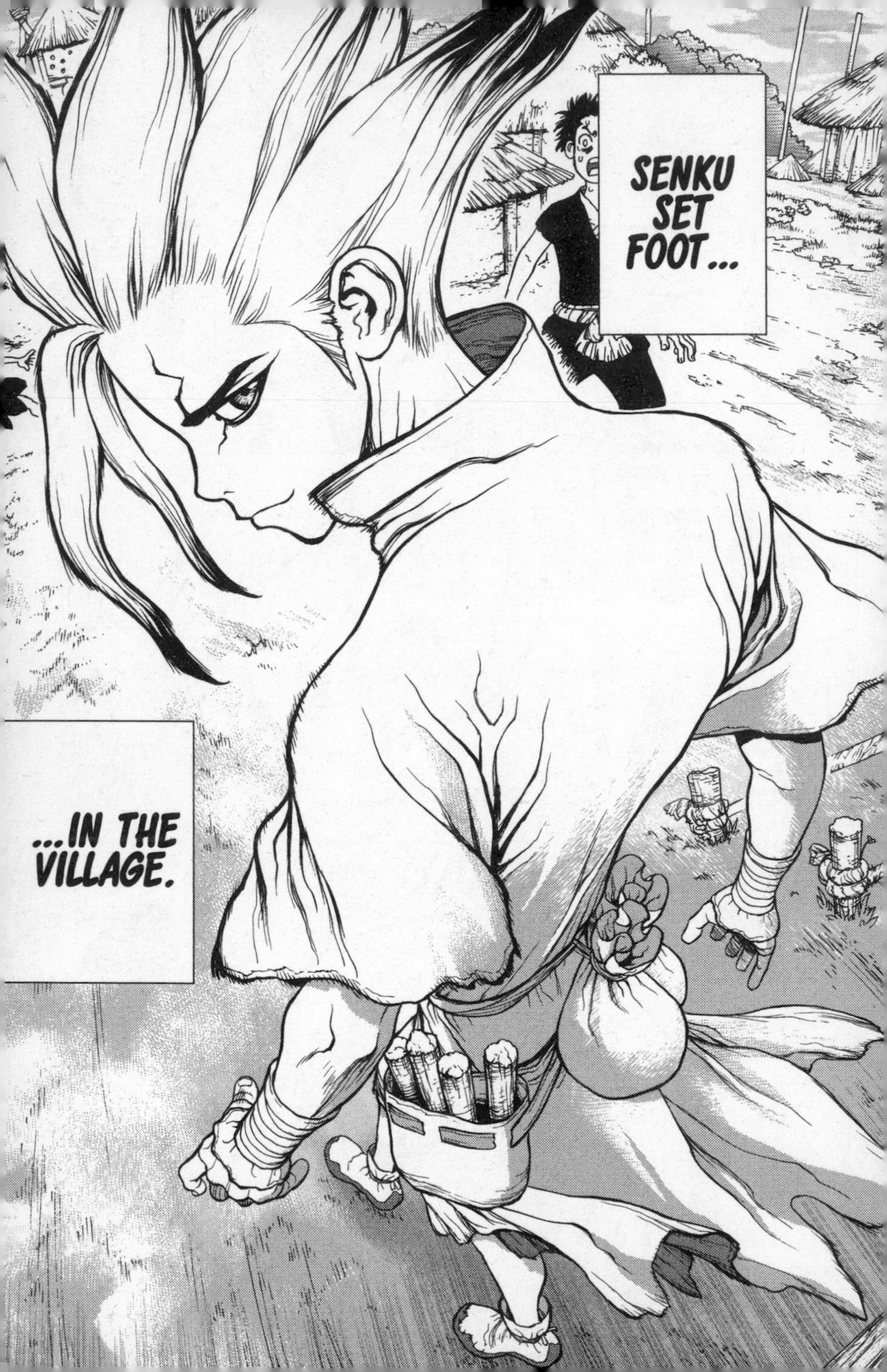
SENKU SET FOOT...
...IN THE VILLAGE.

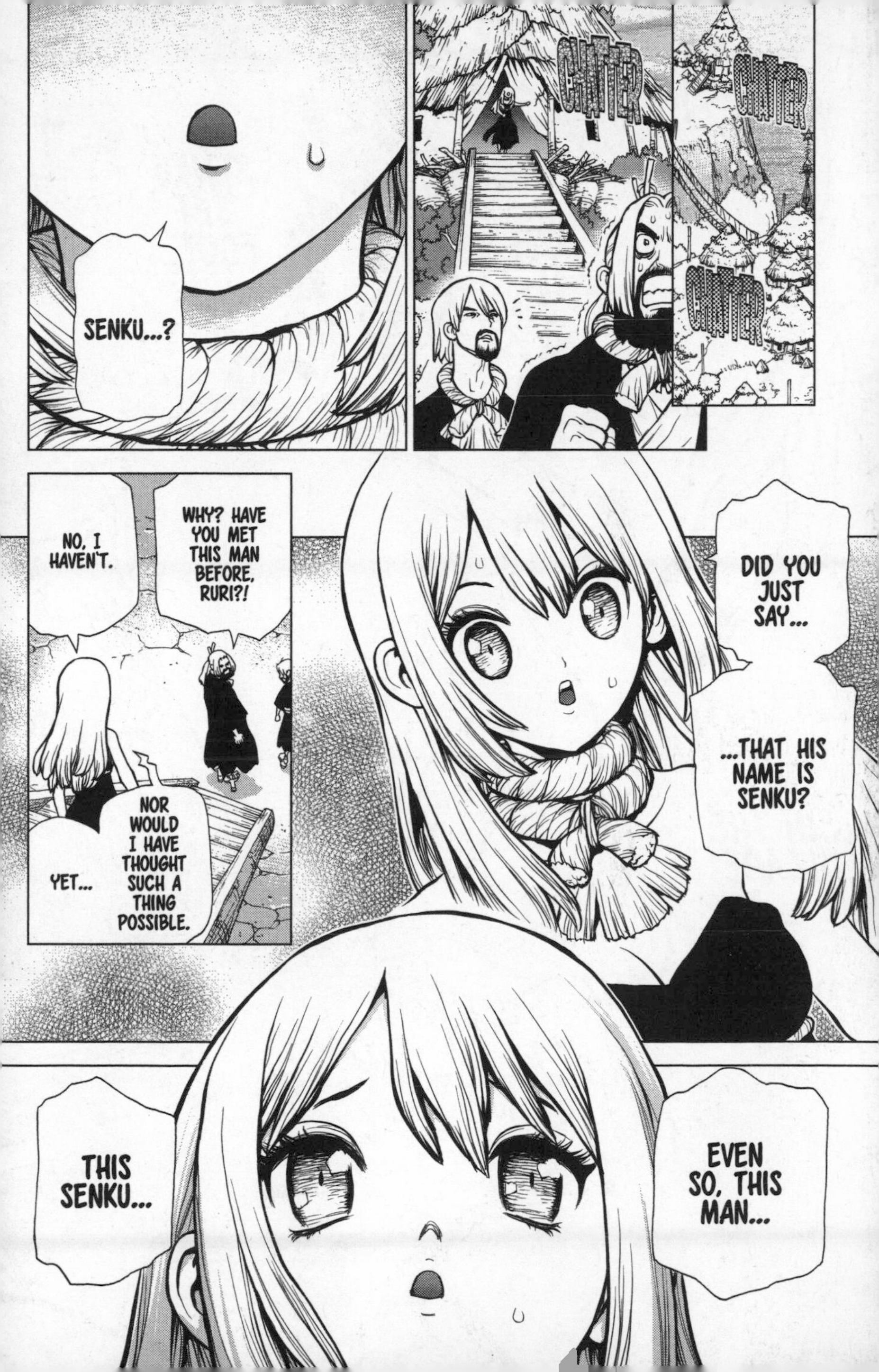
CHATTER
CHATTER
CHATTER
SENKU...?
DID YOU JUST SAY...
...THAT HIS NAME IS SENKU?
WHY? HAVE YOU MET THIS MAN BEFORE, RURI?!
NO, I HAVEN'T.
NOR WOULD I HAVE THOUGHT SUCH A THING POSSIBLE.
YET...
EVEN SO, THIS MAN...
THIS SENKU...

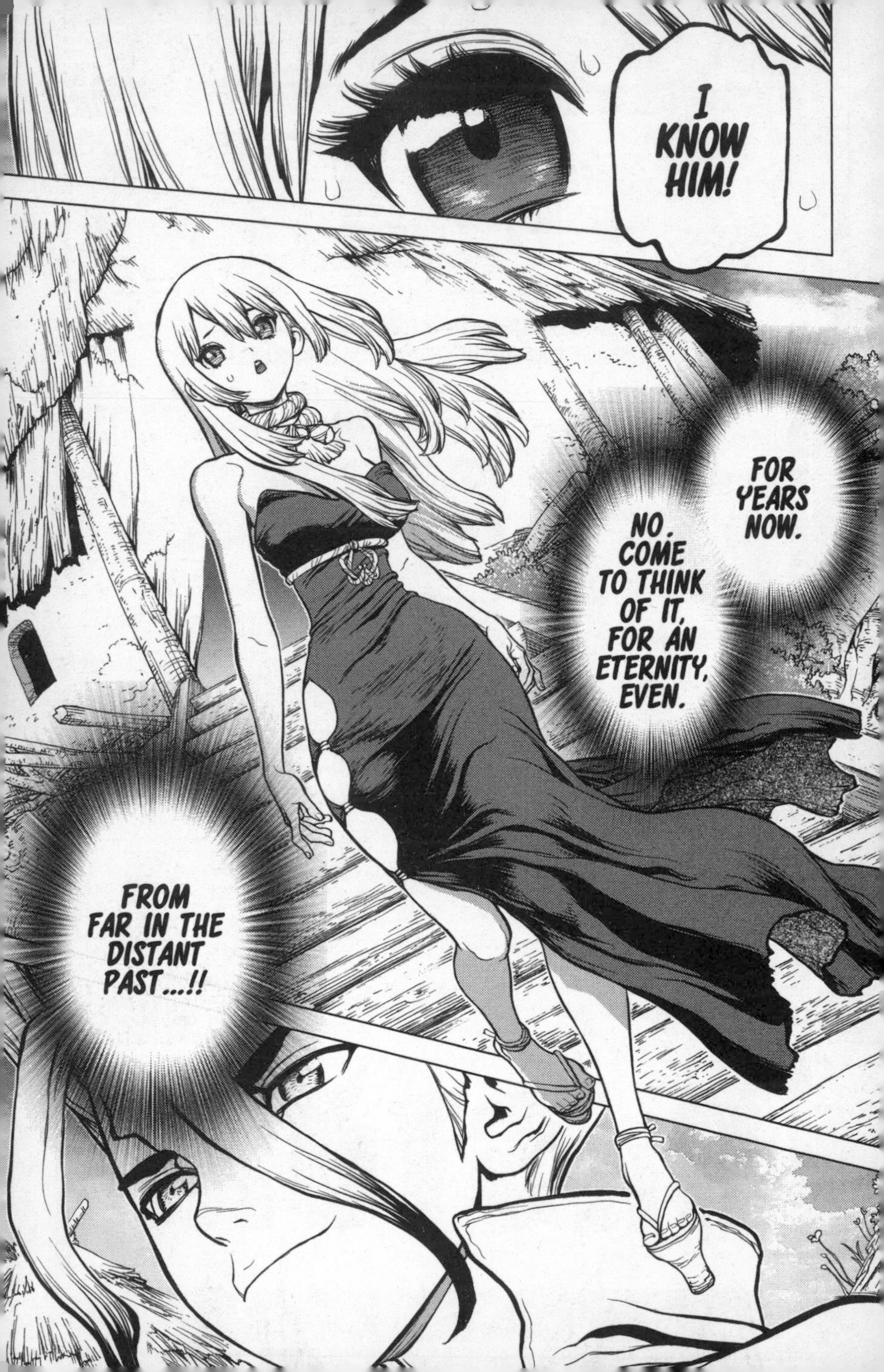
I KNOW HIM!
FOR YEARS NOW.
NO. COME TO THINK OF IT, FOR AN ETERNITY, EVEN.
FROM FAR IN THE DISTANT PAST...!!

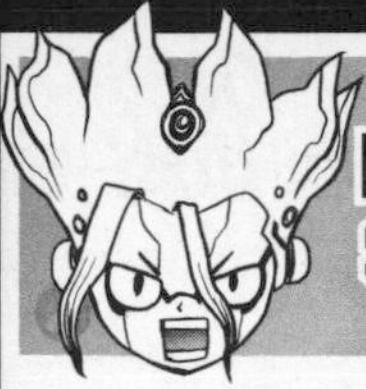

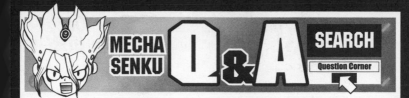

MECHA SENKU Q&A

SEARCH

Question Corner

I want to have hair like Senku's, so please tell me what products to use!!

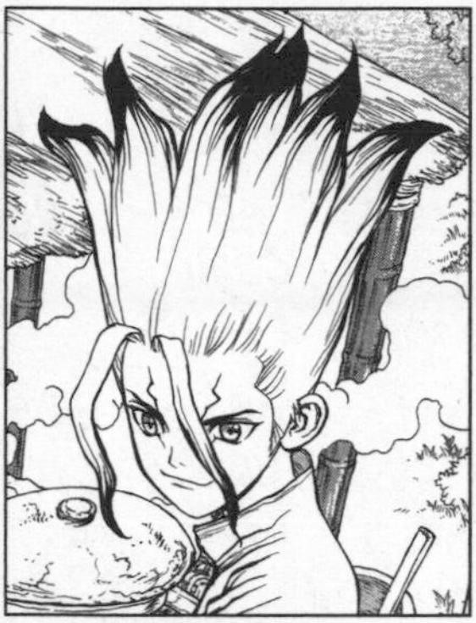

ST-san from Nara Prefecture (and others) SEARCH

No products. Those are simply cowlicks! His particularly unruly hair automatically takes that form!

When one engages in as much thinking as Senku does, the brain waves travel into one's hair like electric shocks... That is one theory, in any case!

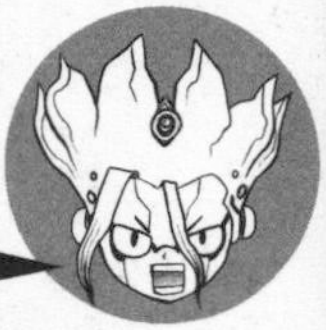

Science Questions	How does one make gasoline out of plastic bottle caps?
Character Questions	If Taiju and Tsukasa really fought, who would win?
Questions That Aren't Really Questions	I wanna get petrified and challenge myself to count the seconds...

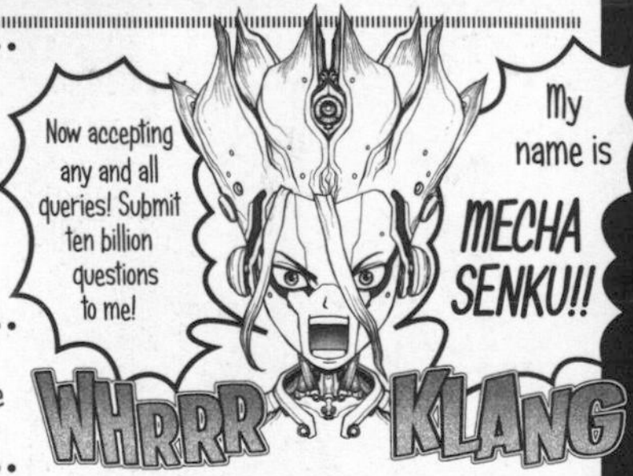
Now accepting any and all queries! Submit ten billion questions to me!
My name is MECHA SENKU!!
WHRRR
KLANG

Dr.STONE

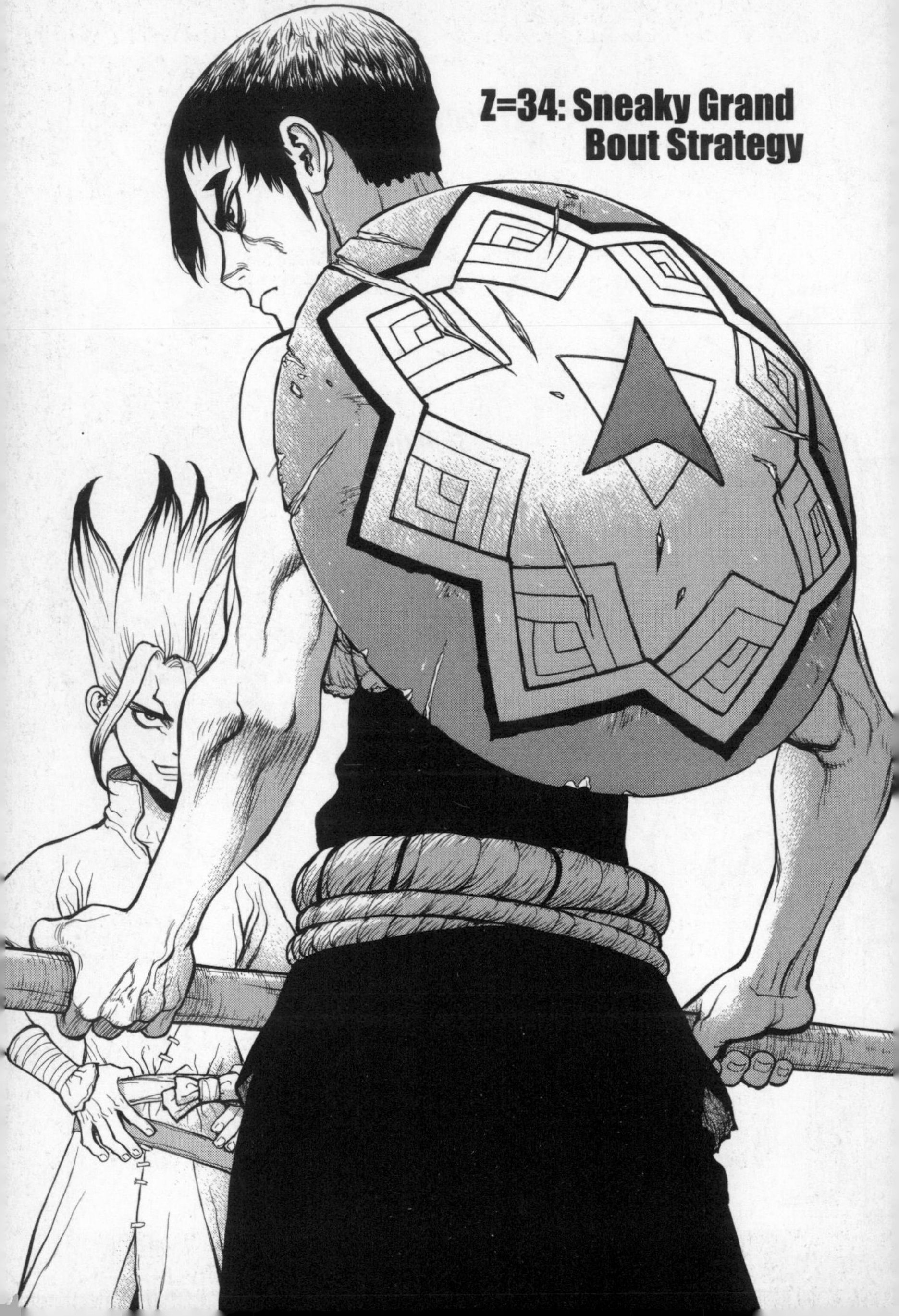
Z=34: Sneaky Grand Bout Strategy

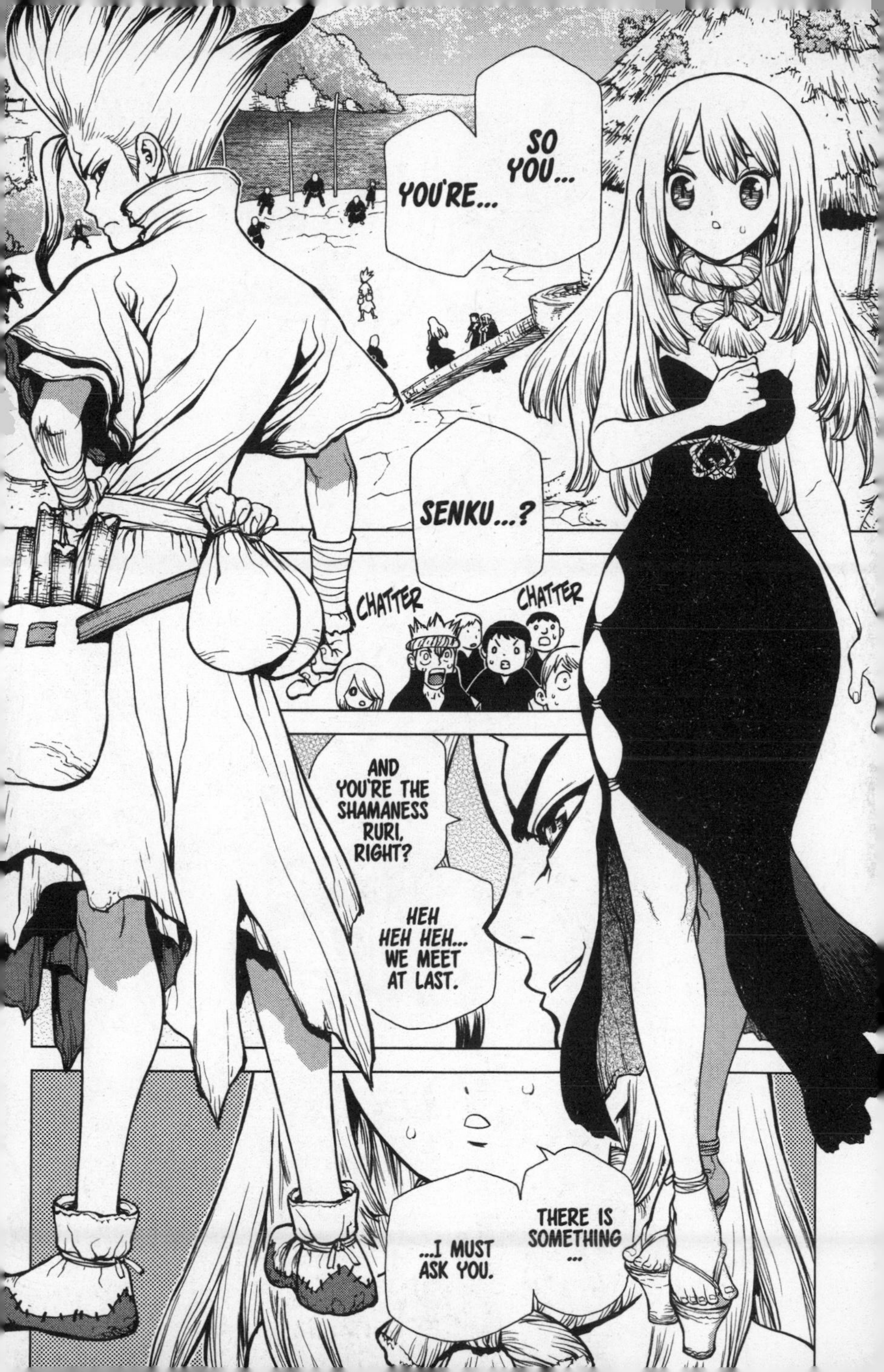
SO YOU... YOU'RE...
SENKU...?
CHATTER
CHATTER
AND YOU'RE THE SHAMANESS RURI, RIGHT?
HEH HEH HEH... WE MEET AT LAST.
THERE IS SOMETHING...
...I MUST ASK YOU.

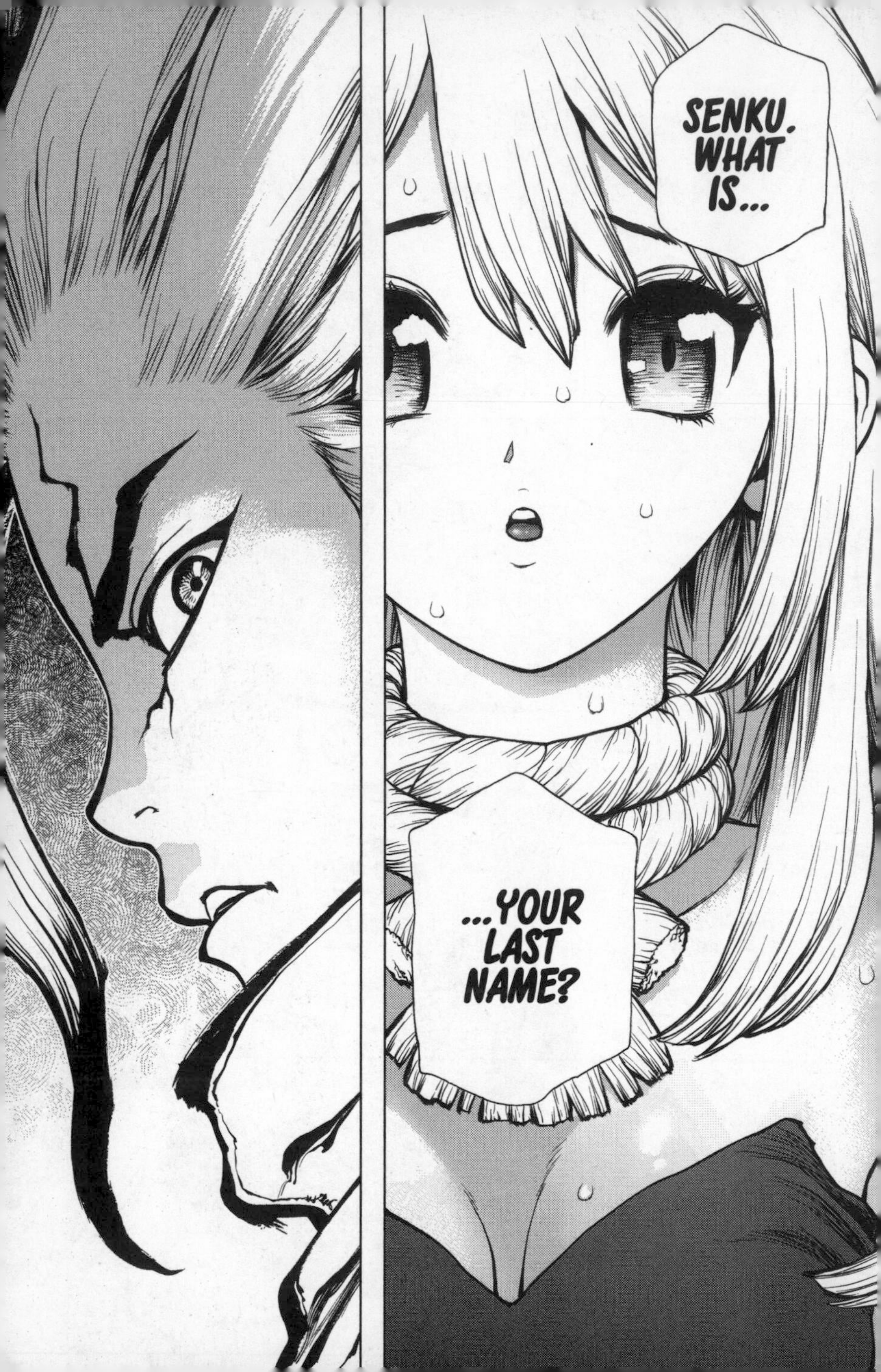
SENKU. WHAT IS...
...YOUR LAST NAME?

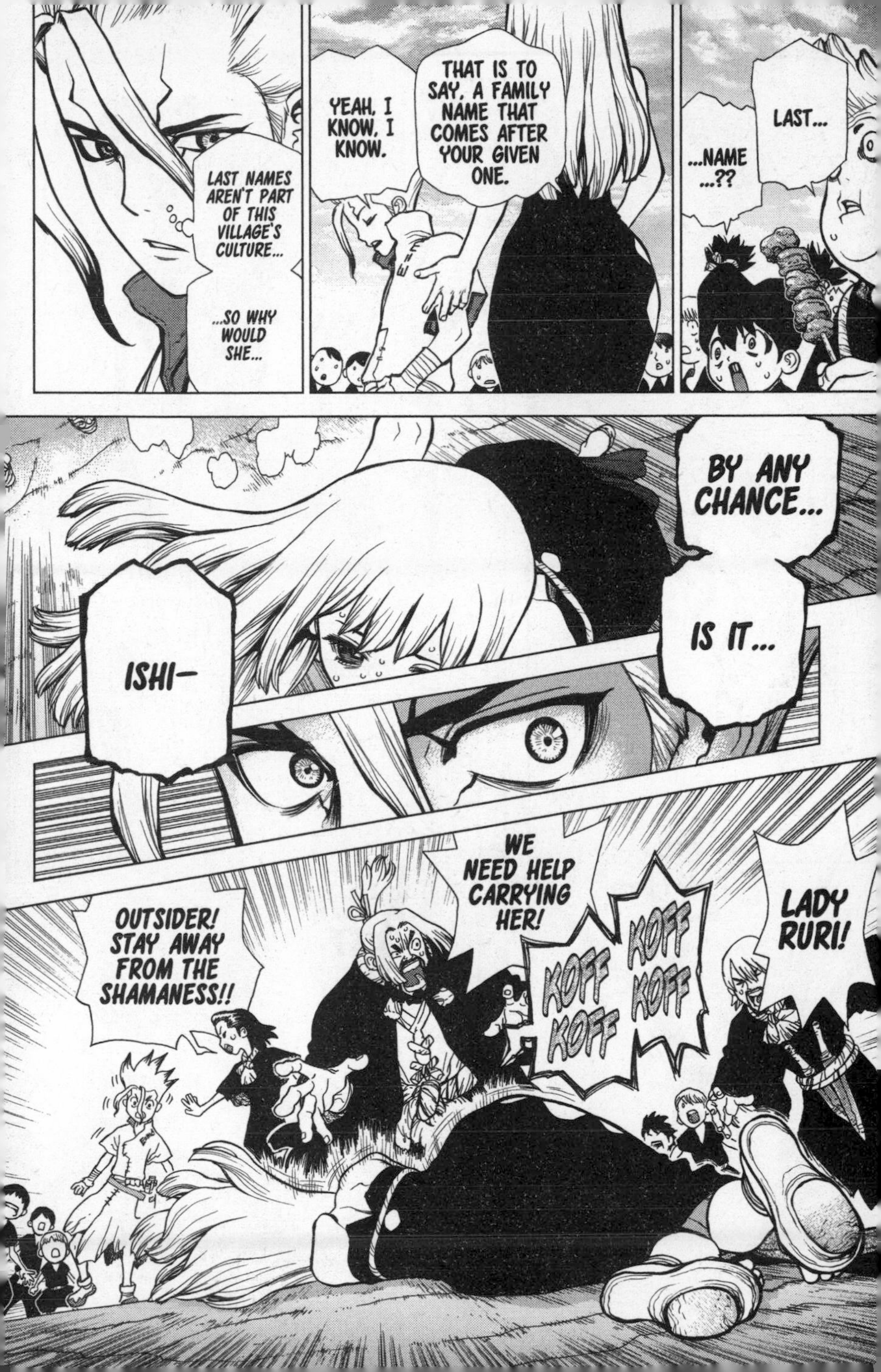
LAST...
...NAME ...??
THAT IS TO SAY, A FAMILY NAME THAT COMES AFTER YOUR GIVEN ONE.
YEAH, I KNOW, I KNOW.
LAST NAMES AREN'T PART OF THIS VILLAGE'S CULTURE...
...SO WHY WOULD SHE...
BY ANY CHANCE...
IS IT...
ISHI-
LADY RURI!
KOFF KOFF
KOFF KOFF
WE NEED HELP CARRYING HER!
OUTSIDER! STAY AWAY FROM THE SHAMANESS!!

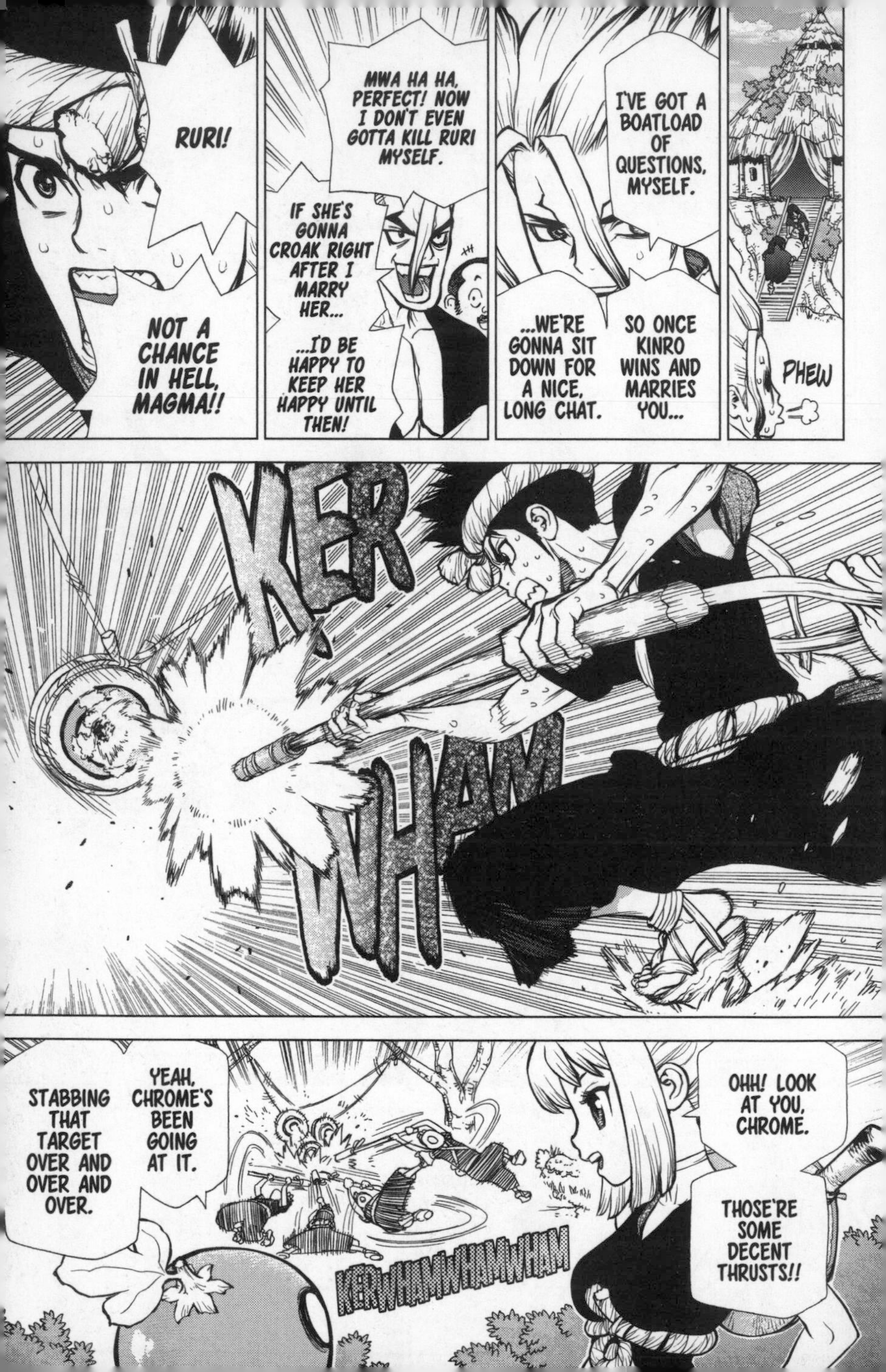
PHEW
I'VE GOT A BOATLOAD OF QUESTIONS, MYSELF.
SO ONCE KINRO WINS AND MARRIES YOU...
...WE'RE GONNA SIT DOWN FOR A NICE, LONG CHAT.
MWA HA HA, PERFECT! NOW I DON'T EVEN GOTTA KILL RURI MYSELF.
IF SHE'S GONNA CROAK RIGHT AFTER I MARRY HER...
...I'D BE HAPPY TO KEEP HER HAPPY UNTIL THEN!
RURI!
NOT A CHANCE IN HELL, MAGMA!!
KER
WHAM
OHH! LOOK AT YOU, CHROME.
THOSE'RE SOME DECENT THRUSTS!!
KERWHAMWHAMWHAM
YEAH, CHROME'S BEEN GOING AT IT.
STABBING THAT TARGET OVER AND OVER AND OVER.

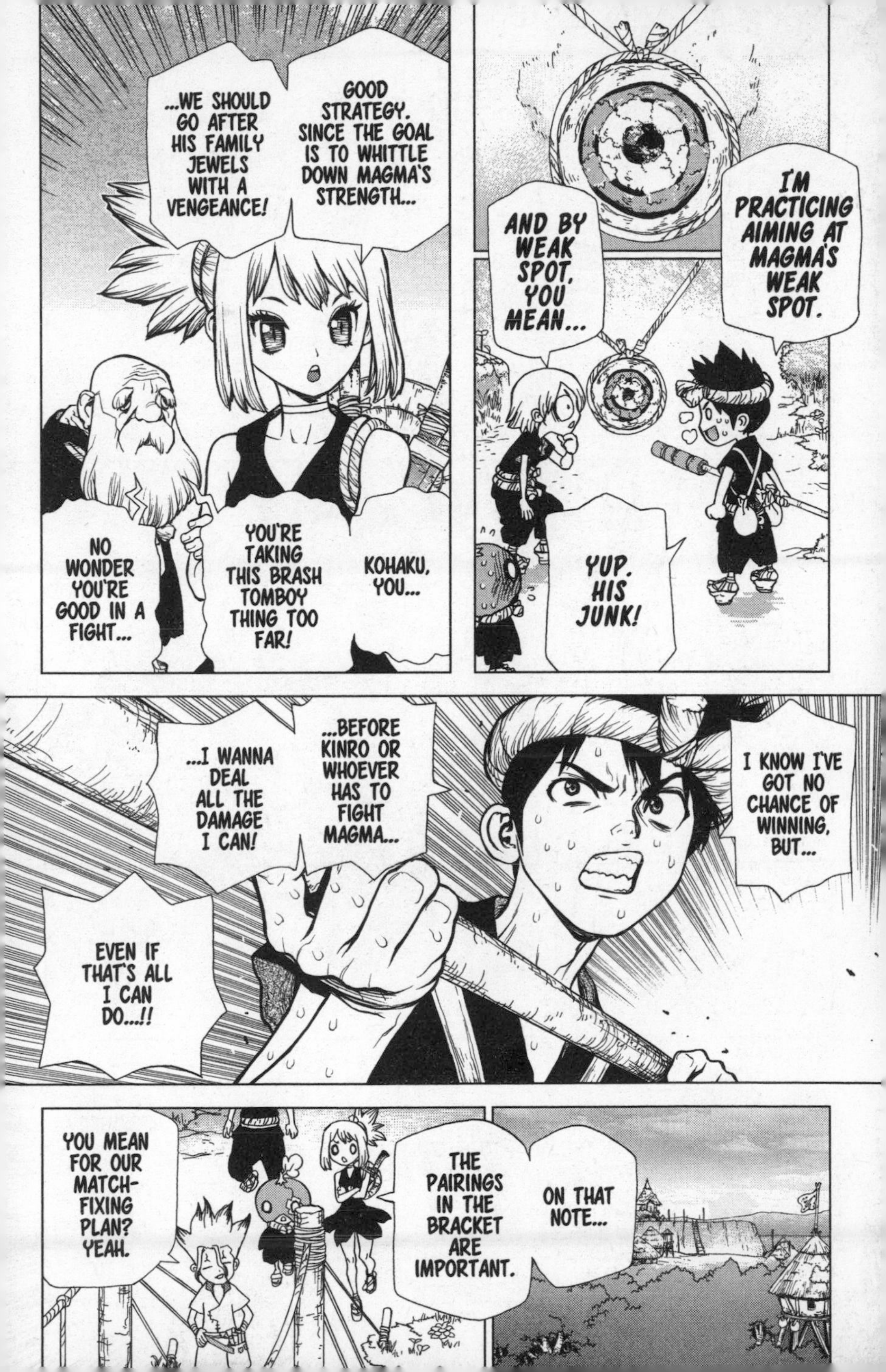
I'M PRACTICING AIMING AT MAGMA'S WEAK SPOT.
AND BY WEAK SPOT, YOU MEAN...
YUP. HIS JUNK!
GOOD STRATEGY. SINCE THE GOAL IS TO WHITTLE DOWN MAGMA'S STRENGTH...
...WE SHOULD GO AFTER HIS FAMILY JEWELS WITH A VENGEANCE!
KOHAKU, YOU...
YOU'RE TAKING THIS BRASH TOMBOY THING TOO FAR!
NO WONDER YOU'RE GOOD IN A FIGHT...
I KNOW I'VE GOT NO CHANCE OF WINNING, BUT...
...BEFORE KINRO OR WHOEVER HAS TO FIGHT MAGMA...
...I WANNA DEAL ALL THE DAMAGE I CAN!
EVEN IF THAT'S ALL I CAN DO...!!
ON THAT NOTE...
THE PAIRINGS IN THE BRACKET ARE IMPORTANT.
YOU MEAN FOR OUR MATCH-FIXING PLAN? YEAH.

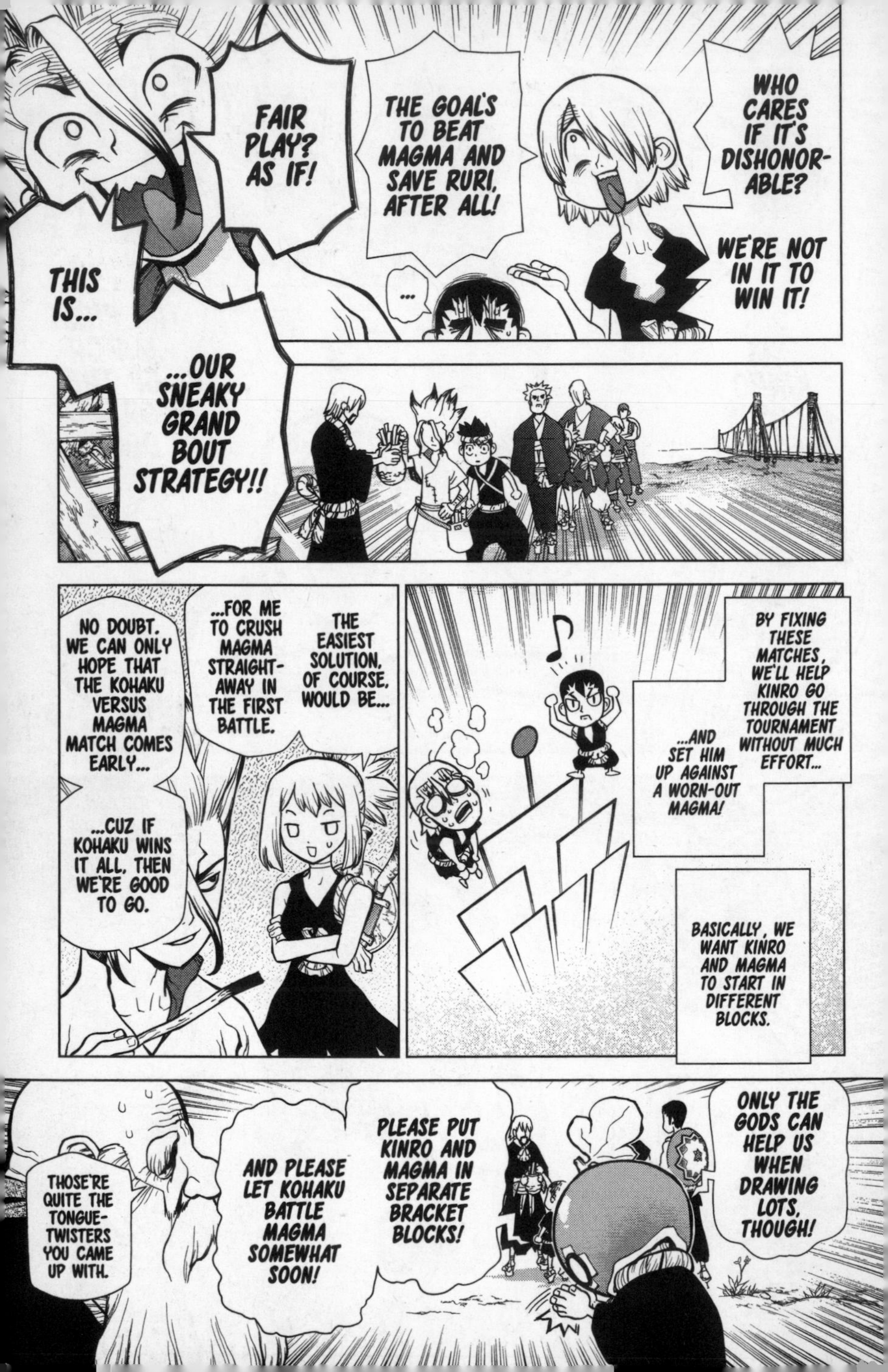
WHO CARES IF IT'S DISHONORABLE?
WE'RE NOT IN IT TO WIN IT!
THE GOAL'S TO BEAT MAGMA AND SAVE RURI, AFTER ALL!
...
FAIR PLAY? AS IF!
THIS IS...
...OUR SNEAKY GRAND BOUT STRATEGY!!
BY FIXING THESE MATCHES, WE'LL HELP KINRO GO THROUGH THE TOURNAMENT WITHOUT MUCH EFFORT...
...AND SET HIM UP AGAINST A WORN-OUT MAGMA!
BASICALLY, WE WANT KINRO AND MAGMA TO START IN DIFFERENT BLOCKS.
THE EASIEST SOLUTION, OF COURSE, WOULD BE...
...FOR ME TO CRUSH MAGMA STRAIGHTAWAY IN THE FIRST BATTLE.
NO DOUBT. WE CAN ONLY HOPE THAT THE KOHAKU VERSUS MAGMA MATCH COMES EARLY...
...CUZ IF KOHAKU WINS IT ALL, THEN WE'RE GOOD TO GO.
ONLY THE GODS CAN HELP US WHEN DRAWING LOTS, THOUGH!
PLEASE PUT KINRO AND MAGMA IN SEPARATE BRACKET BLOCKS!
AND PLEASE LET KOHAKU BATTLE MAGMA SOMEWHAT SOON!
THOSE'RE QUITE THE TONGUE-TWISTERS YOU CAME UP WITH.

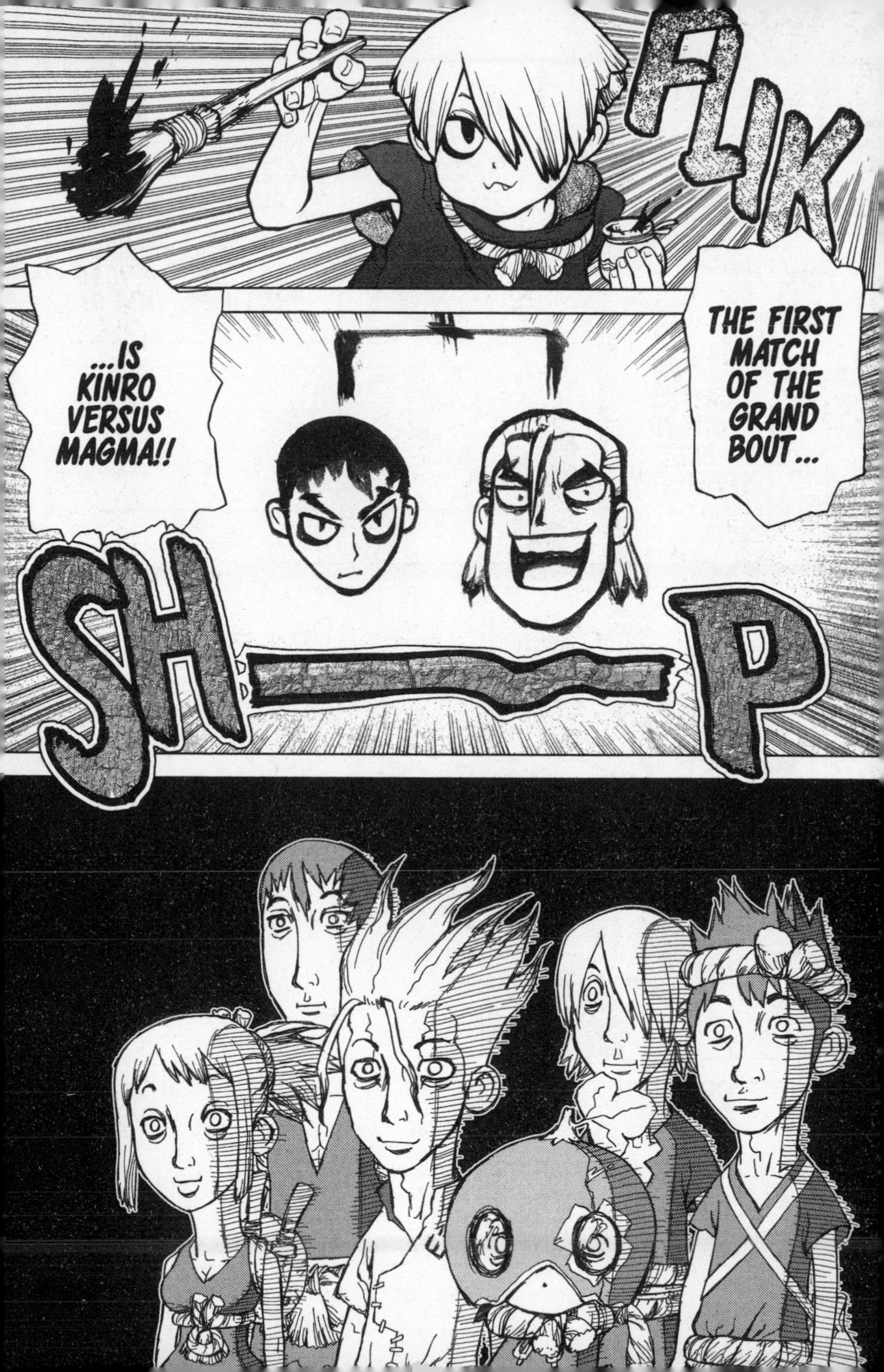
FLIK
THE FIRST MATCH OF THE GRAND BOUT...
...IS KINRO VERSUS MAGMA!!
SH—P

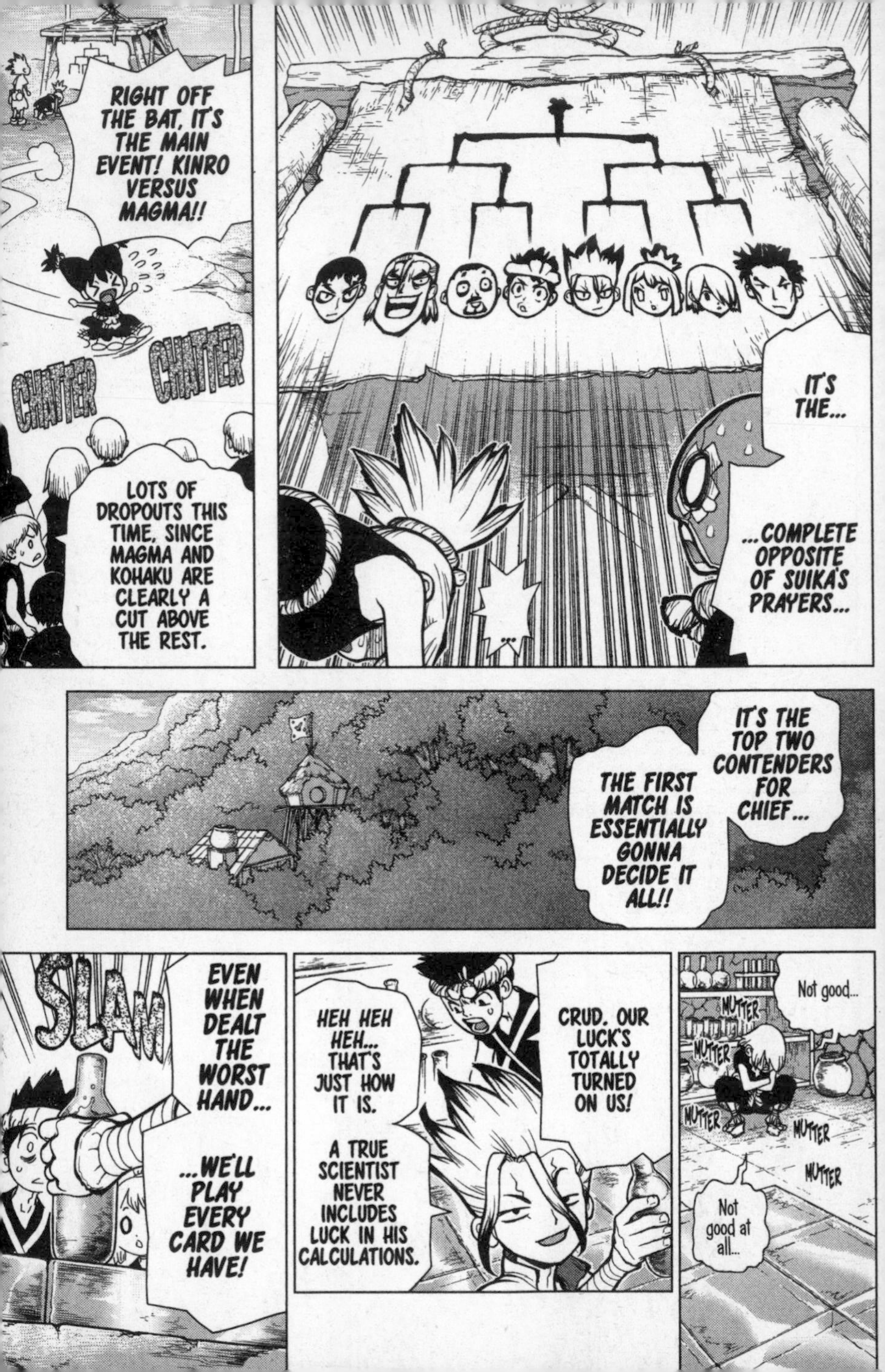
IT'S THE...
...COMPLETE OPPOSITE OF SUIKA'S PRAYERS...
...
RIGHT OFF THE BAT, IT'S THE MAIN EVENT! KINRO VERSUS MAGMA!!
CHATTER
CHATTER
LOTS OF DROPOUTS THIS TIME, SINCE MAGMA AND KOHAKU ARE CLEARLY A CUT ABOVE THE REST.
IT'S THE TOP TWO CONTENDERS FOR CHIEF...
THE FIRST MATCH IS ESSENTIALLY GONNA DECIDE IT ALL!!
Not good...
MUTTER
MUTTER
MUTTER
MUTTER
MUTTER
Not good at all...
CRUD. OUR LUCK'S TOTALLY TURNED ON US!
HEH HEH HEH... THAT'S JUST HOW IT IS.
A TRUE SCIENTIST NEVER INCLUDES LUCK IN HIS CALCULATIONS.
SLAM
EVEN WHEN DEALT THE WORST HAND...
...WE'LL PLAY EVERY CARD WE HAVE!

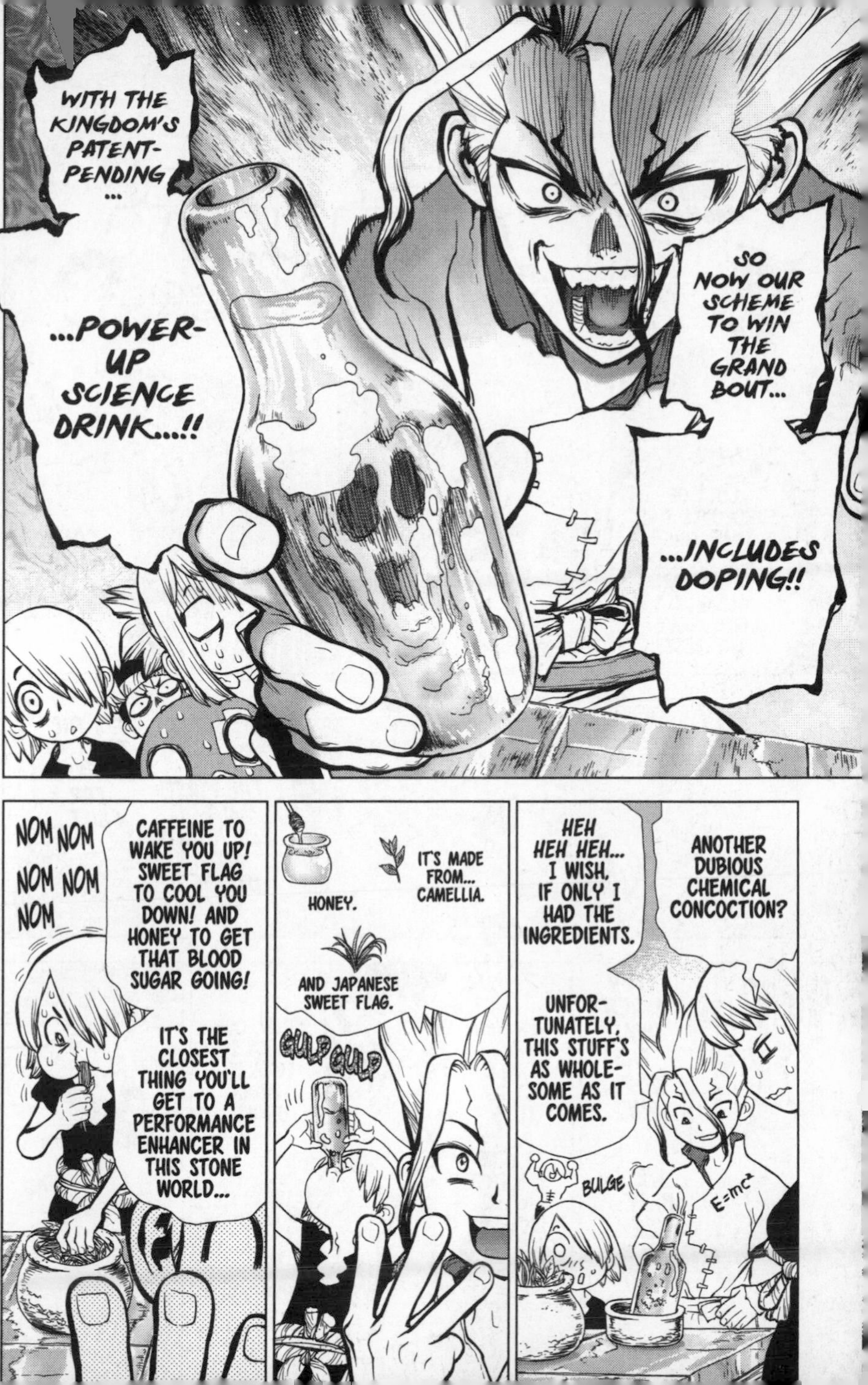
SO NOW OUR SCHEME TO WIN THE GRAND BOUT...
...INCLUDES DOPING!!
WITH THE KINGDOM'S PATENT-PENDING...
...POWER-UP SCIENCE DRINK...!!
ANOTHER DUBIOUS CHEMICAL CONCOCTION?
HEH HEH HEH... I WISH, IF ONLY I HAD THE INGREDIENTS.
UNFORTUNATELY, THIS STUFF'S AS WHOLESOME AS IT COMES.
BULGE
E=mc²
IT'S MADE FROM... CAMELLIA.
HONEY.
AND JAPANESE SWEET FLAG.
GULP GULP
CAFFEINE TO WAKE YOU UP! SWEET FLAG TO COOL YOU DOWN! AND HONEY TO GET THAT BLOOD SUGAR GOING!
NOM NOM NOM NOM NOM
IT'S THE CLOSEST THING YOU'LL GET TO A PERFORMANCE ENHANCER IN THIS STONE WORLD...

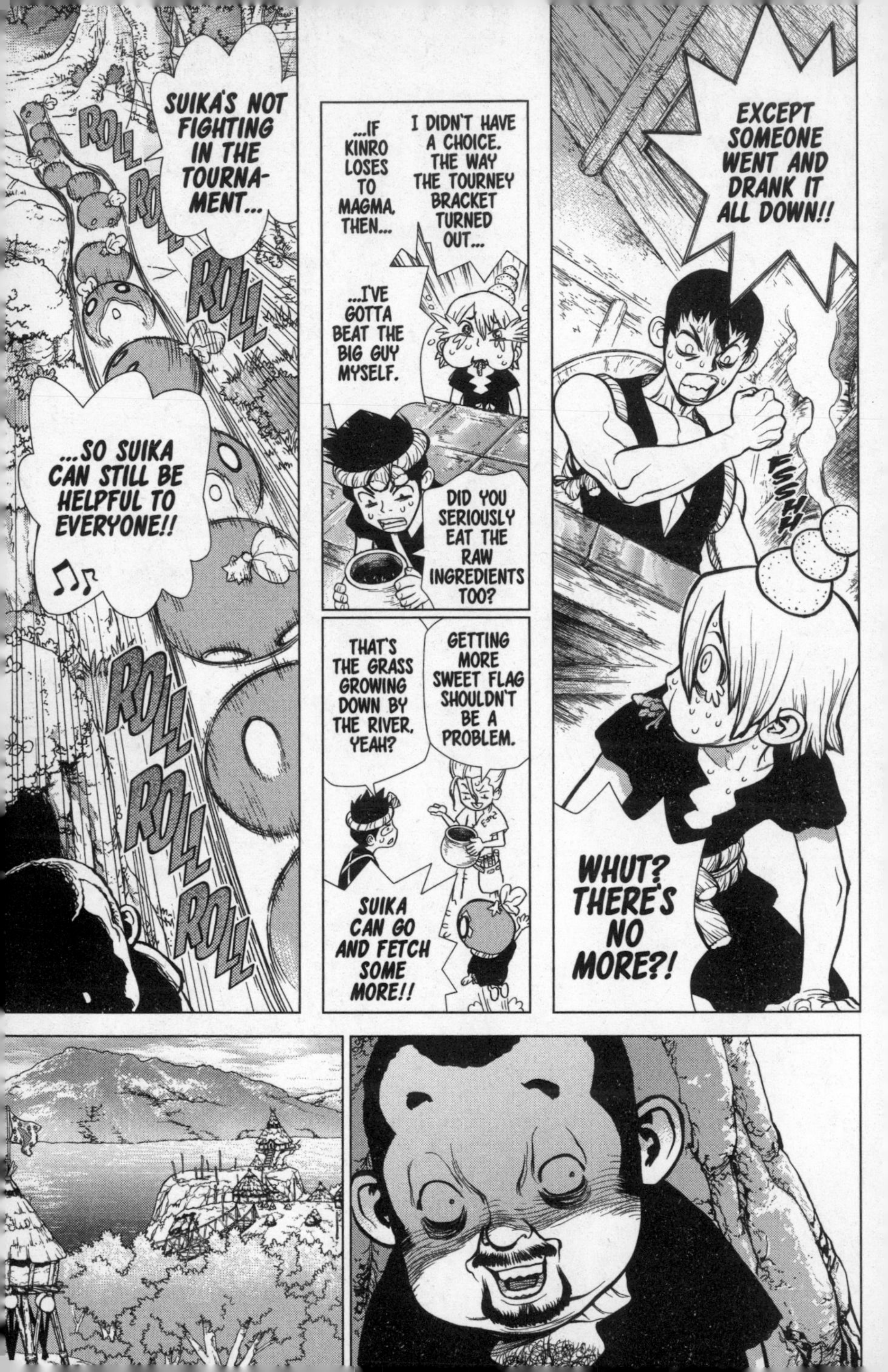
EXCEPT SOMEONE WENT AND DRANK IT ALL DOWN!!
FSSHH
WHUT? THERE'S NO MORE?!
I DIDN'T HAVE A CHOICE. THE WAY THE TOURNEY BRACKET TURNED OUT...
...IF KINRO LOSES TO MAGMA, THEN...
...I'VE GOTTA BEAT THE BIG GUY MYSELF.
DID YOU SERIOUSLY EAT THE RAW INGREDIENTS TOO?
GETTING MORE SWEET FLAG SHOULDN'T BE A PROBLEM.
THAT'S THE GRASS GROWING DOWN BY THE RIVER, YEAH?
SUIKA CAN GO AND FETCH SOME MORE!!
SUIKA'S NOT FIGHTING IN THE TOURNAMENT...
ROLL ROLL ROLL
ROLL
...SO SUIKA CAN STILL BE HELPFUL TO EVERYONE!! ♫♪
ROLL ROLL ROLL

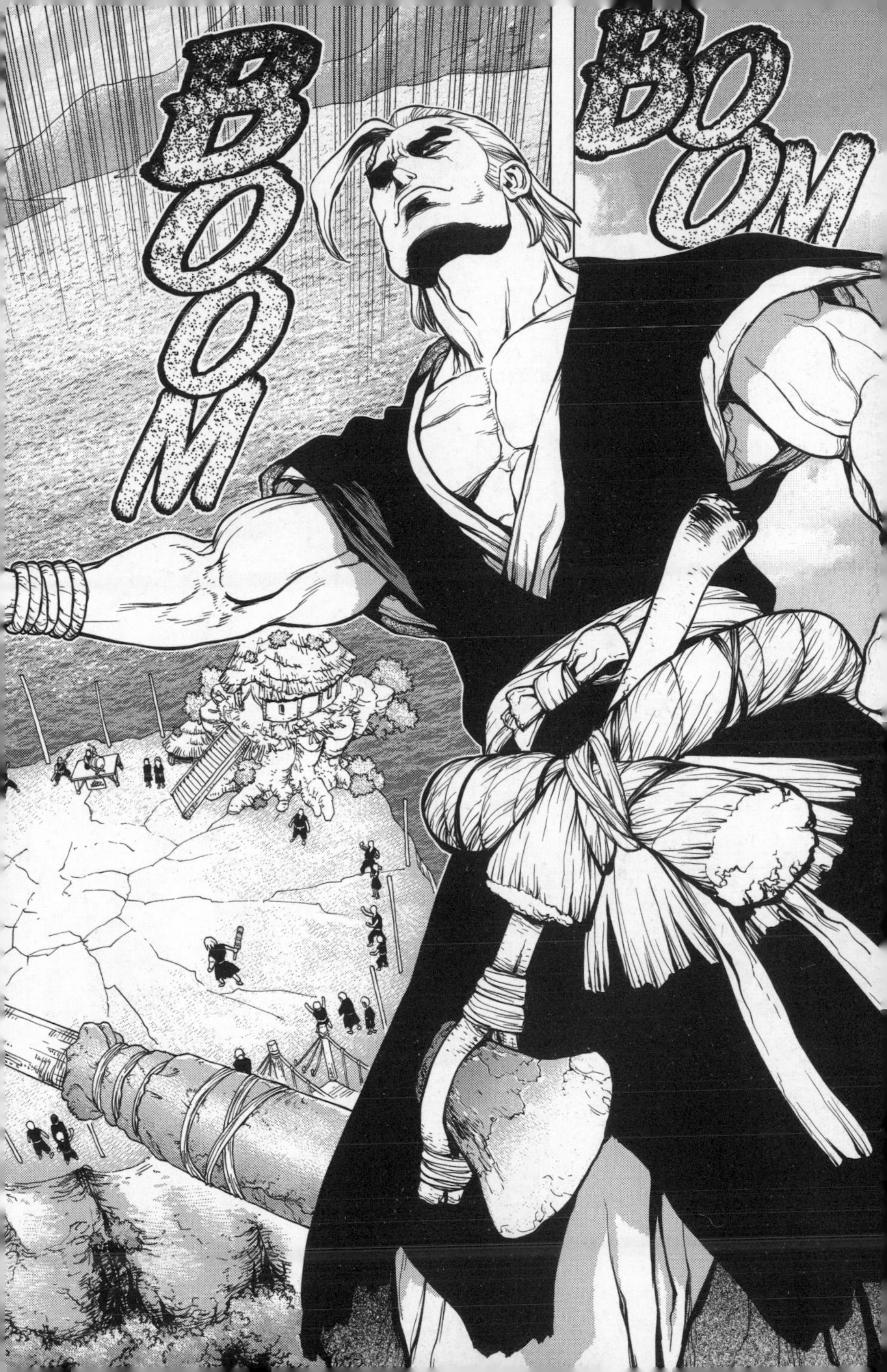
BOOM
BOOOOM

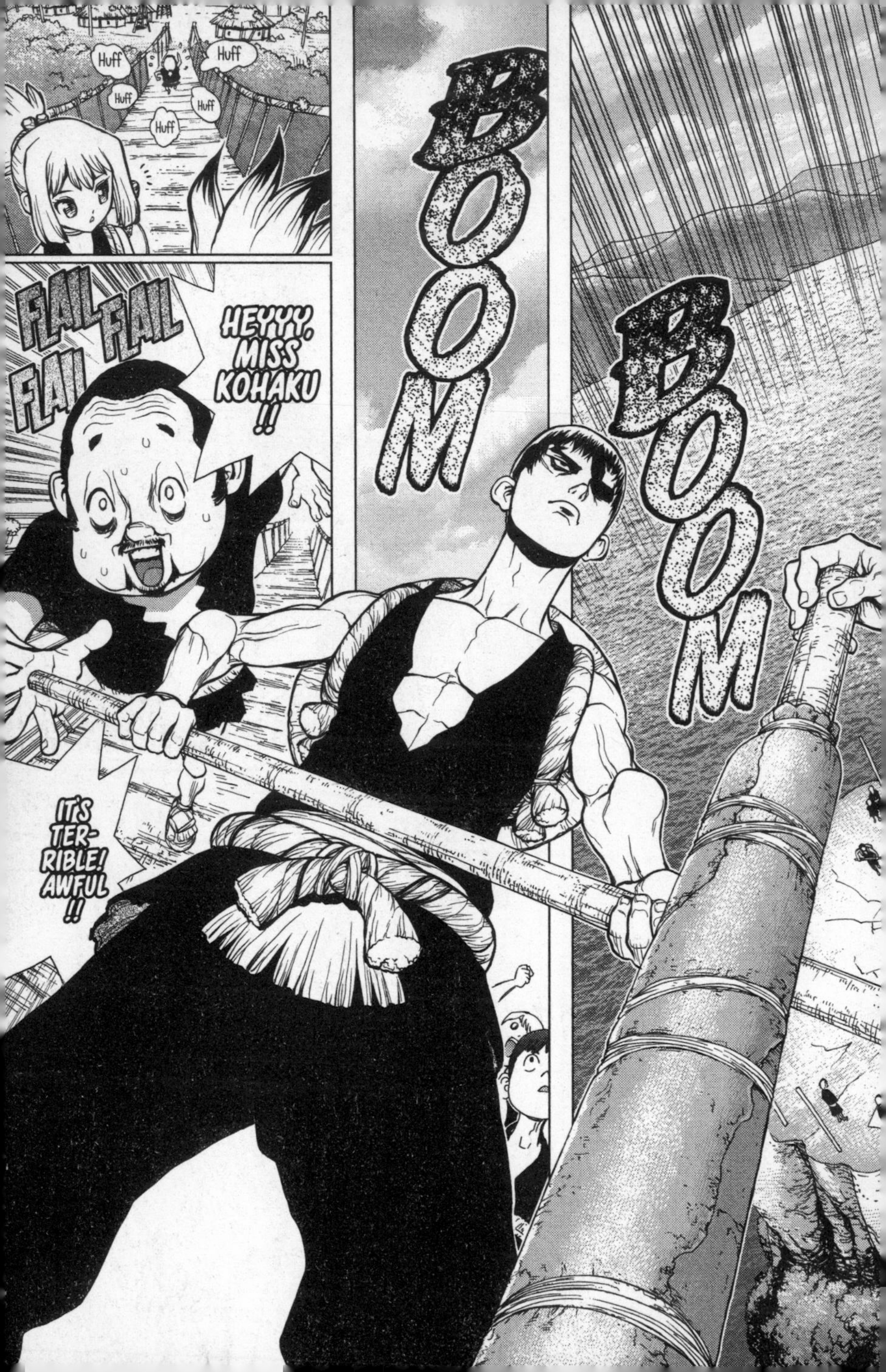
BOOOM
BOOM
Huff
Huff
Huff
Huff
Huff
FLAIL FLAIL FLAIL
HEYYY, MISS KOHAKU!!
IT'S TER-RIBLE! AWFUL!!

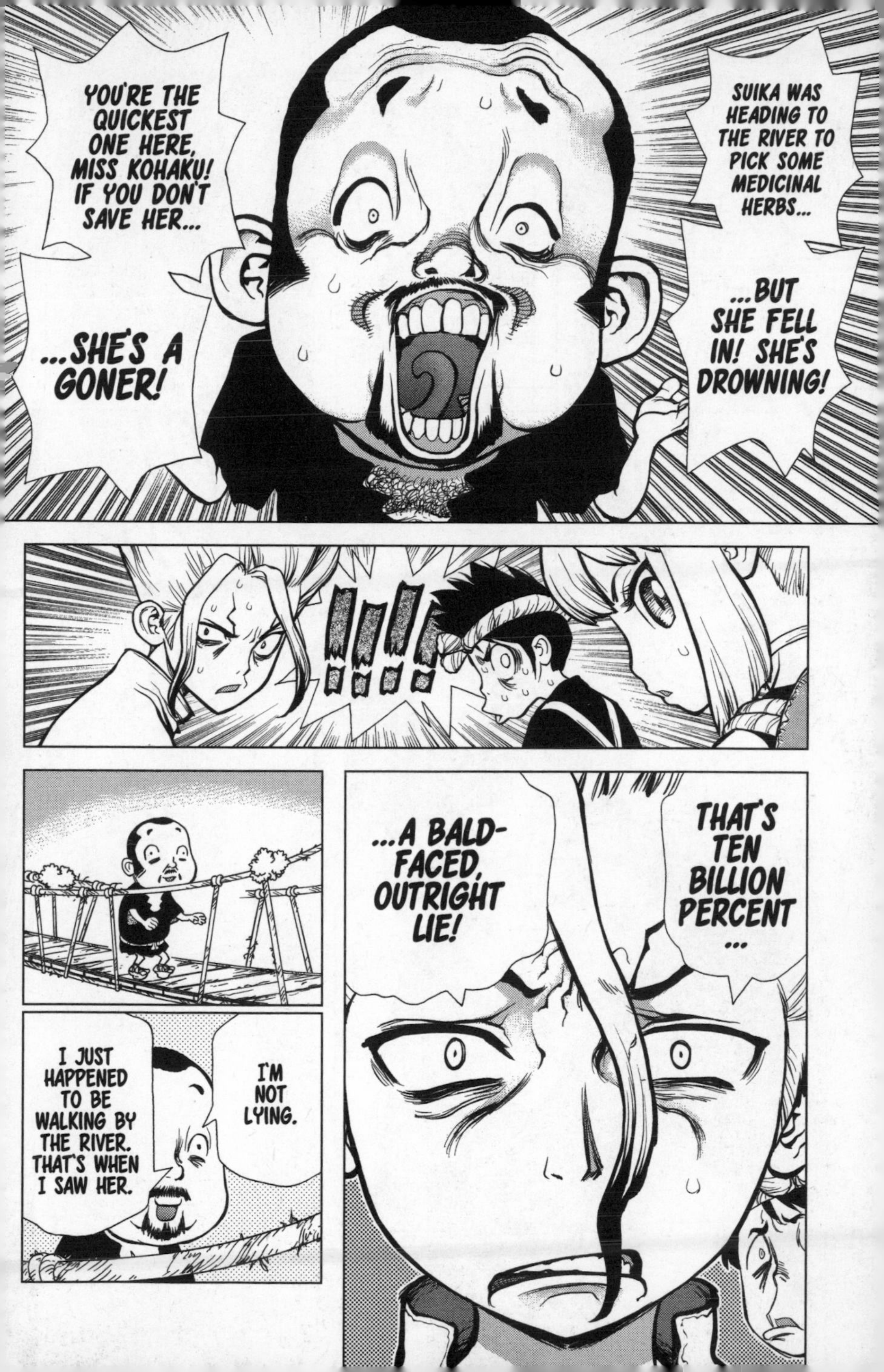
SUIKA WAS HEADING TO THE RIVER TO PICK SOME MEDICINAL HERBS...
...BUT SHE FELL IN! SHE'S DROWNING!
YOU'RE THE QUICKEST ONE HERE, MISS KOHAKU! IF YOU DON'T SAVE HER...
...SHE'S A GONER!
!!!!
THAT'S TEN BILLION PERCENT ...
...A BALD-FACED, OUTRIGHT LIE!
I'M NOT LYING.
I JUST HAPPENED TO BE WALKING BY THE RIVER. THAT'S WHEN I SAW HER.

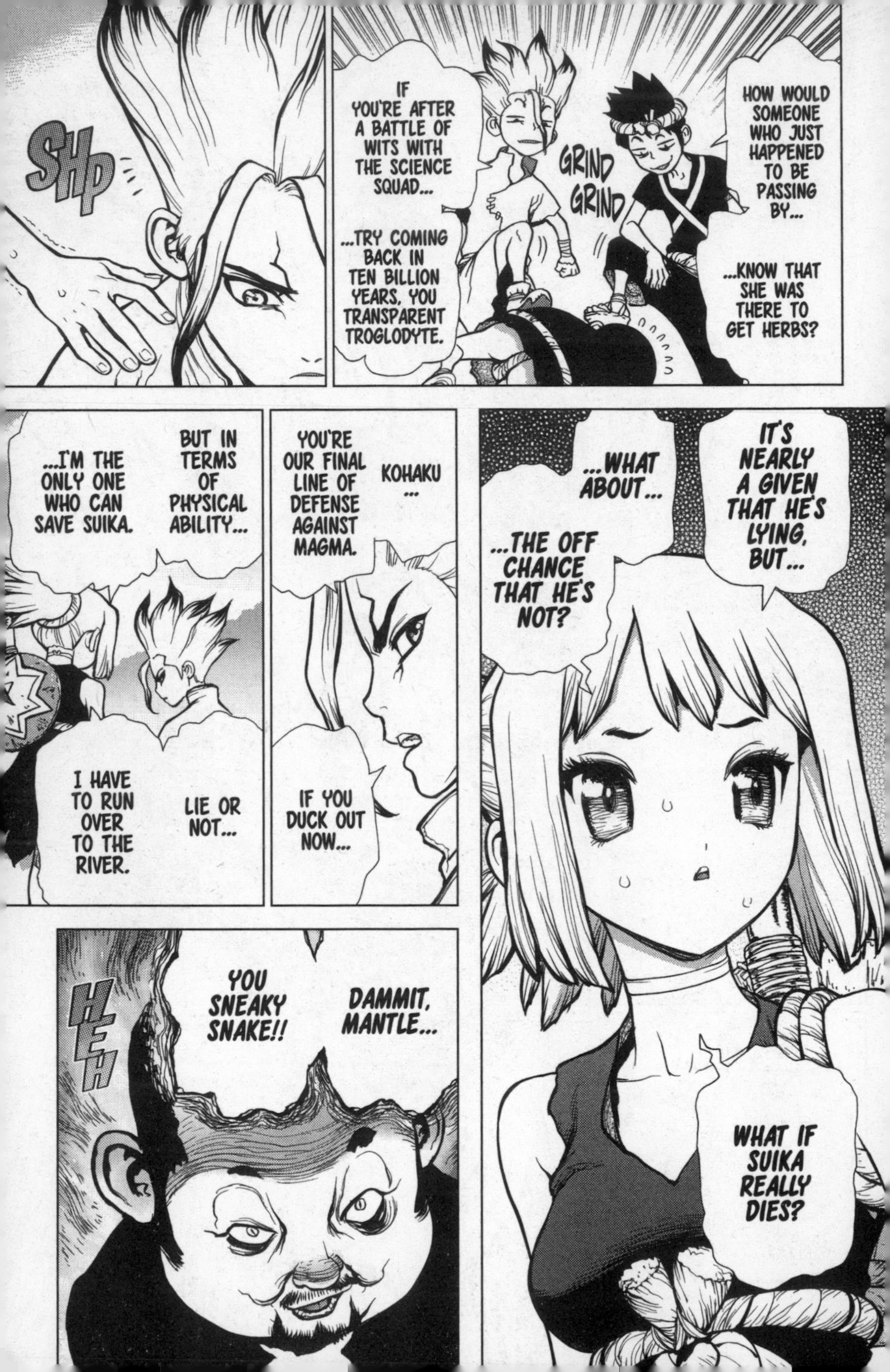
HOW WOULD SOMEONE WHO JUST HAPPENED TO BE PASSING BY...
...KNOW THAT SHE WAS THERE TO GET HERBS?
GRIND GRIND
IF YOU'RE AFTER A BATTLE OF WITS WITH THE SCIENCE SQUAD...
...TRY COMING BACK IN TEN BILLION YEARS, YOU TRANSPARENT TROGLODYTE.
SHP
IT'S NEARLY A GIVEN THAT HE'S LYING, BUT...
...WHAT ABOUT...
...THE OFF CHANCE THAT HE'S NOT?
WHAT IF SUIKA REALLY DIES?
KOHAKU...
YOU'RE OUR FINAL LINE OF DEFENSE AGAINST MAGMA.
IF YOU DUCK OUT NOW...
BUT IN TERMS OF PHYSICAL ABILITY...
...I'M THE ONLY ONE WHO CAN SAVE SUIKA.
LIE OR NOT...
I HAVE TO RUN OVER TO THE RIVER.
DAMMIT, MANTLE...
YOU SNEAKY SNAKE!!
HEH

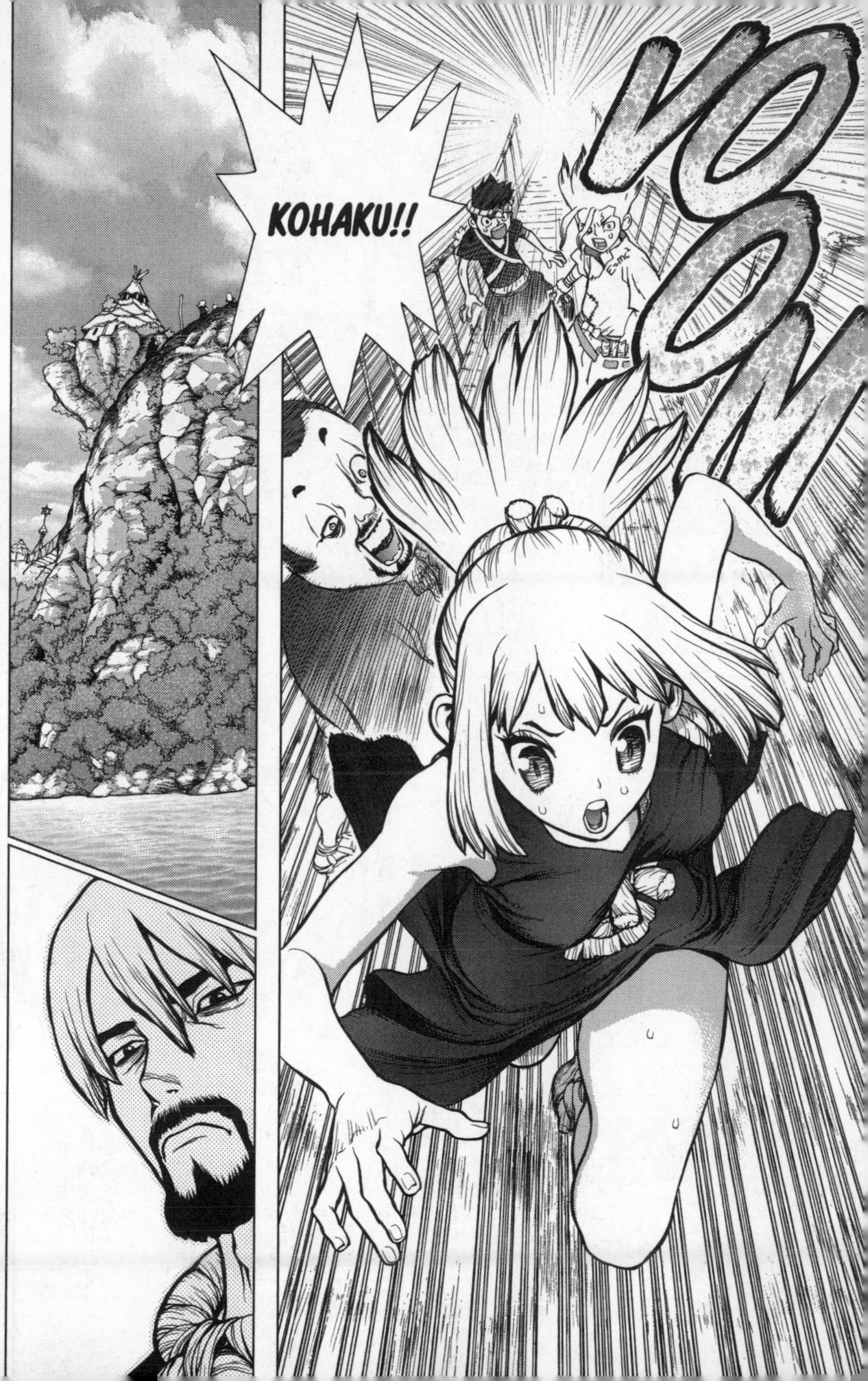
KOHAKU!!
VOOM

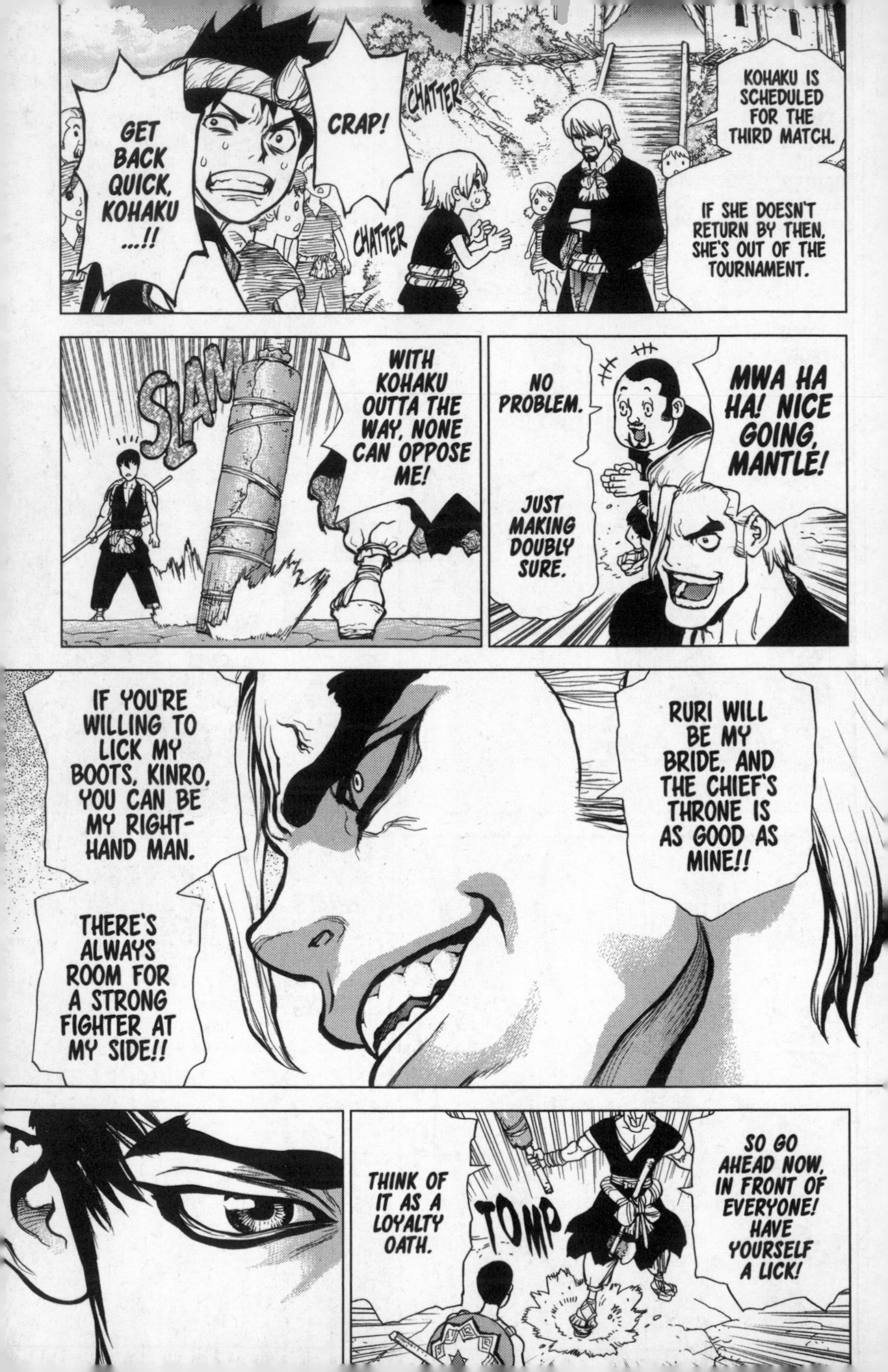
KOHAKU IS SCHEDULED FOR THE THIRD MATCH.
IF SHE DOESN'T RETURN BY THEN, SHE'S OUT OF THE TOURNAMENT.
CHATTER
CRAP!
CHATTER
GET BACK QUICK, KOHAKU ...!!
MWA HA HA! NICE GOING, MANTLE!
NO PROBLEM.
JUST MAKING DOUBLY SURE.
WITH KOHAKU OUTTA THE WAY, NONE CAN OPPOSE ME!
SLAM
RURI WILL BE MY BRIDE, AND THE CHIEF'S THRONE IS AS GOOD AS MINE!!
IF YOU'RE WILLING TO LICK MY BOOTS, KINRO, YOU CAN BE MY RIGHT-HAND MAN.
THERE'S ALWAYS ROOM FOR A STRONG FIGHTER AT MY SIDE!!
SO GO AHEAD NOW, IN FRONT OF EVERYONE! HAVE YOURSELF A LICK!
TOMP
THINK OF IT AS A LOYALTY OATH.

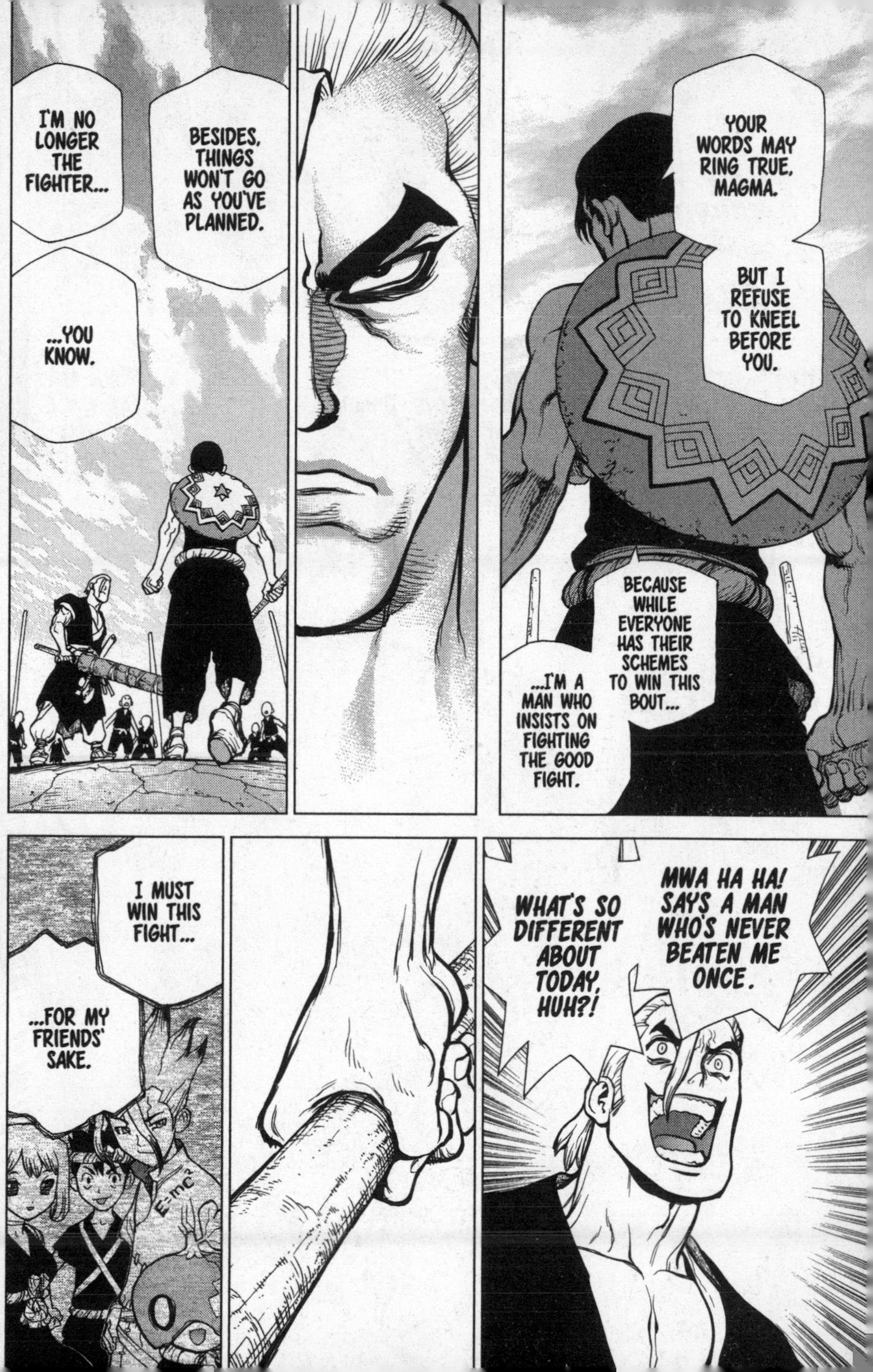
YOUR WORDS MAY RING TRUE, MAGMA.
BUT I REFUSE TO KNEEL BEFORE YOU.
BECAUSE WHILE EVERYONE HAS THEIR SCHEMES TO WIN THIS BOUT...
...I'M A MAN WHO INSISTS ON FIGHTING THE GOOD FIGHT.
BESIDES, THINGS WON'T GO AS YOU'VE PLANNED.
I'M NO LONGER THE FIGHTER...
...YOU KNOW.
MWA HA HA! SAYS A MAN WHO'S NEVER BEATEN ME ONCE.
WHAT'S SO DIFFERENT ABOUT TODAY, HUH?!
I MUST WIN THIS FIGHT...
...FOR MY FRIENDS' SAKE.

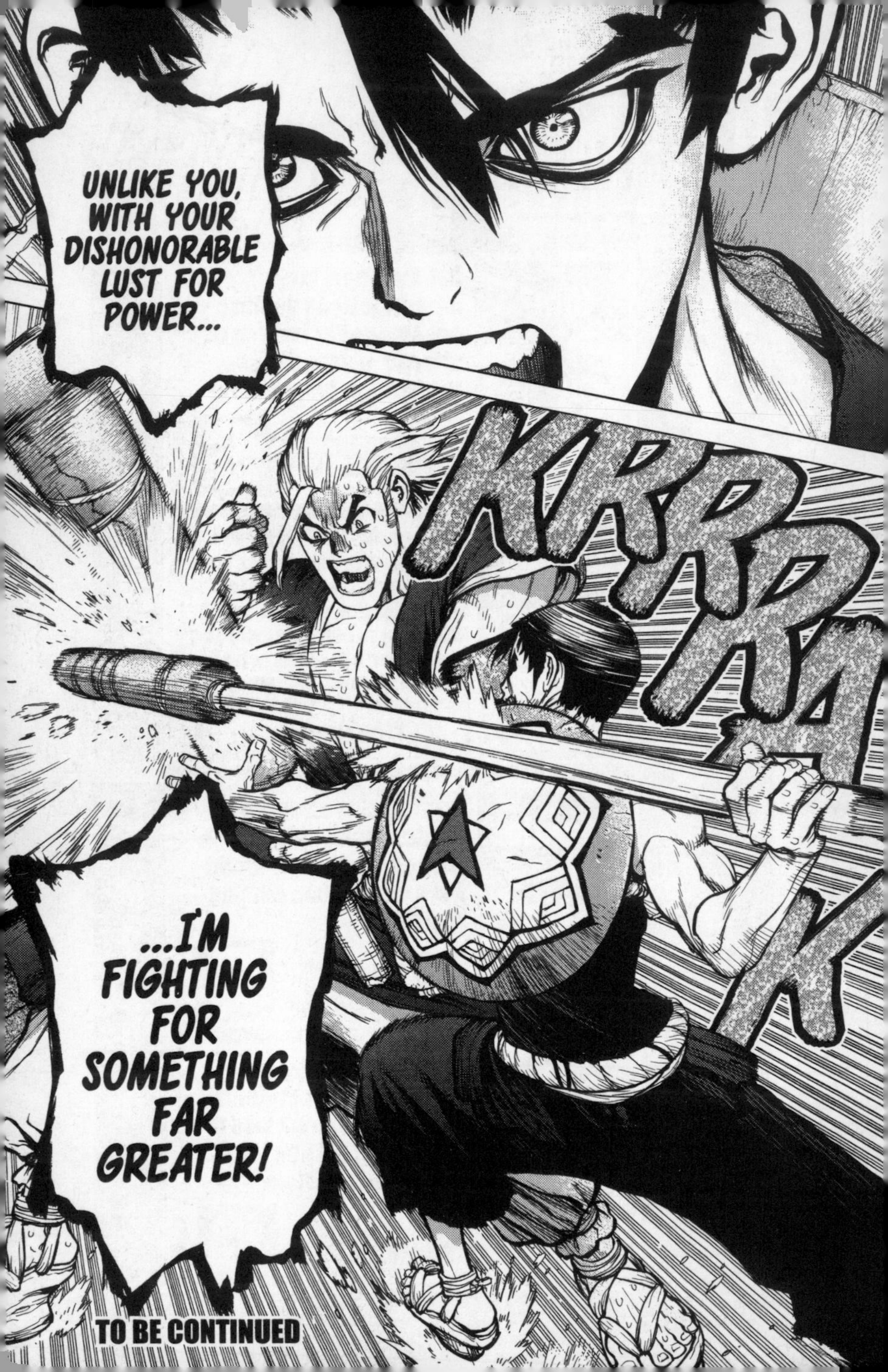
UNLIKE YOU, WITH YOUR DISHONORABLE LUST FOR POWER...
KRRRAK
...I'M FIGHTING FOR SOMETHING FAR GREATER!
TO BE CONTINUED

COMBATANTS IN-DEPTH ANALYSIS!!

Matchup 1

Kinro

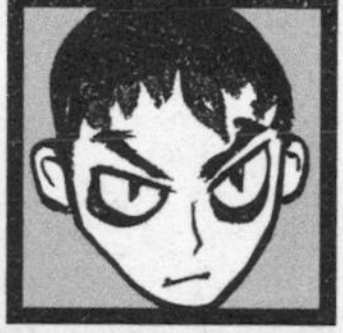

Astoundingly high potential. Good defense, but somewhat lacking on offense. It's time to see the fruits of his training!

Balanced Type **S**

Magma

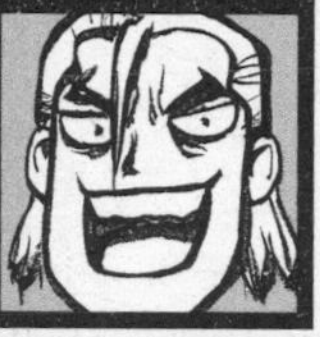

Even I couldn't beat this guy in a contest of pure power. His overconfidence will lead to sloppy fighting early on, so it's important to beat him before he cools down and starts actually using his head.

Power Type **SS**

Matchup 2

Mantle

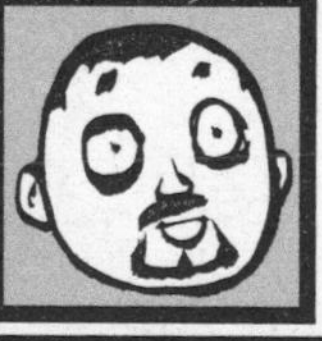

No offensive strength at all. He's reasonably quick, though, so Chrome might have a hard time pinning him down.

Speed Type **C**

Chrome

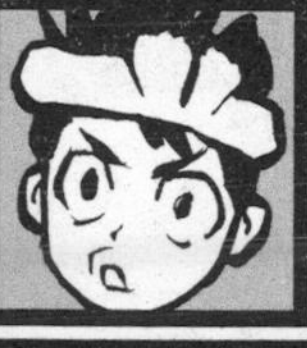

Years of exploring have granted him exceptional fortitude. He won't lose to Mantle, but pulling off the win could take time.

Strategic Type **C**

Kohaku's

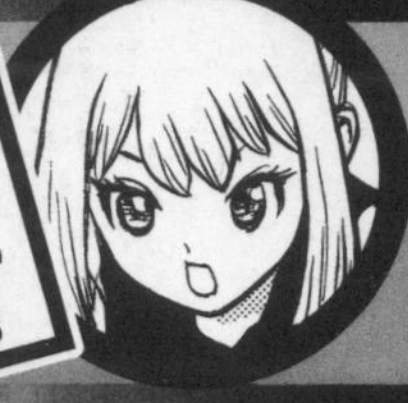

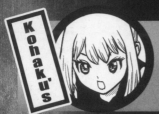

GRAND BOUT

Matchup 3

Senku

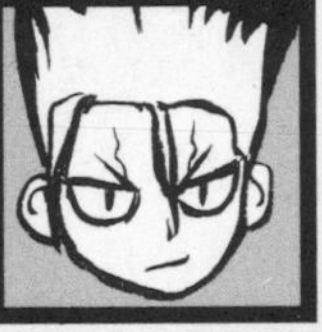

Strong? Weak? Doesn't matter, since he has virtually no fighting experience. But he might use his incredible intelligence to outmaneuver his opponent...

D Strategic Type

Kohaku

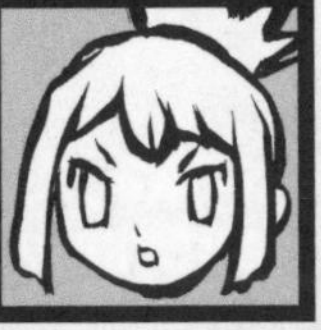

I won't lose to anyone in speed. If I end up facing Magma, I believe I can win, if only by a narrow margin.

SS Speed Type

Matchup 4

Ginro

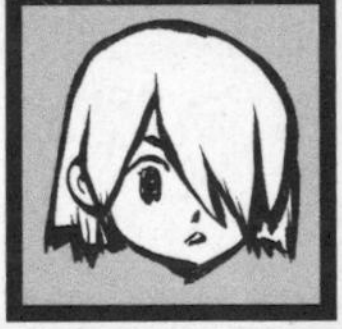

The fastest fighter here, besides me. Not too powerful, though. He'll turn tail and run as soon as he realizes he's at a disadvantage, which is a real problem.

B Speed Type

Argo

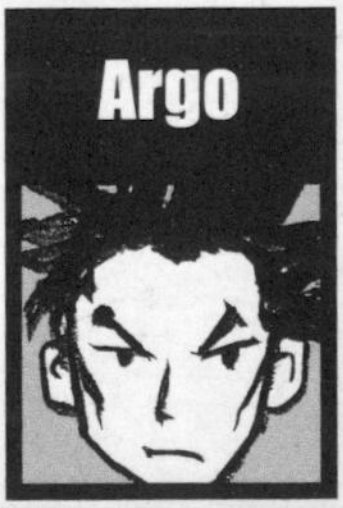

A mighty warrior on par with Kinro. I've only given him an "A" ranking because Ginro would chicken out if he thought Argo was an "S"!

A Power Type

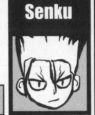

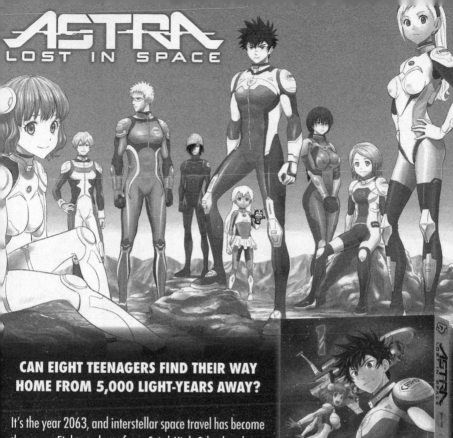

ASTRA LOST IN SPACE

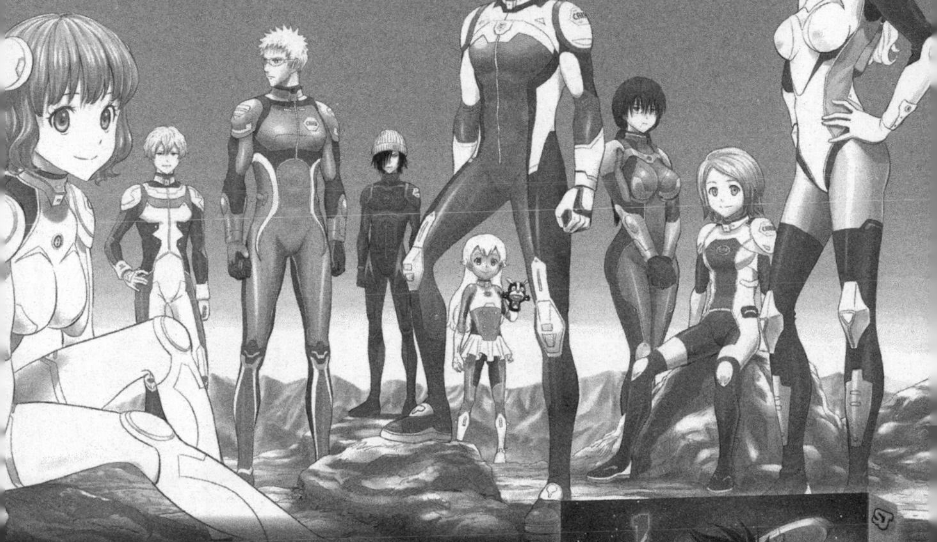

CAN EIGHT TEENAGERS FIND THEIR WAY HOME FROM 5,000 LIGHT-YEARS AWAY?

It's the year 2063, and interstellar space travel has become the norm. Eight students from Caird High School and one child set out on a routine planet camp excursion. While there, the students are mysteriously transported 5,000 light-years away to the middle of nowhere! Will they ever make it back home?!

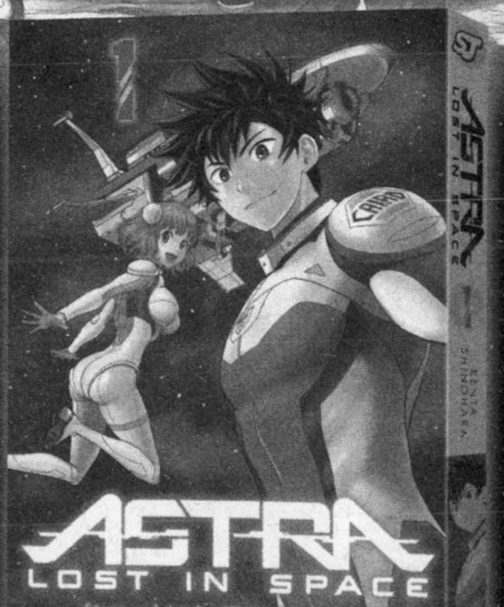
ASTRA
LOST IN SPACE
Story and Art by KENTA SHINOHARA
VIZ

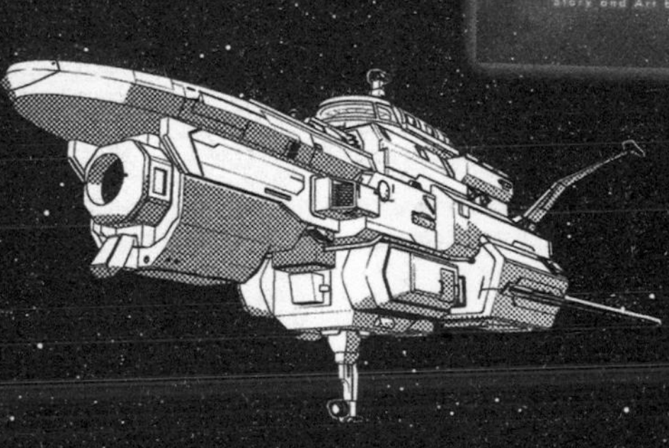

VIZ
viz.com

RATED T TEEN

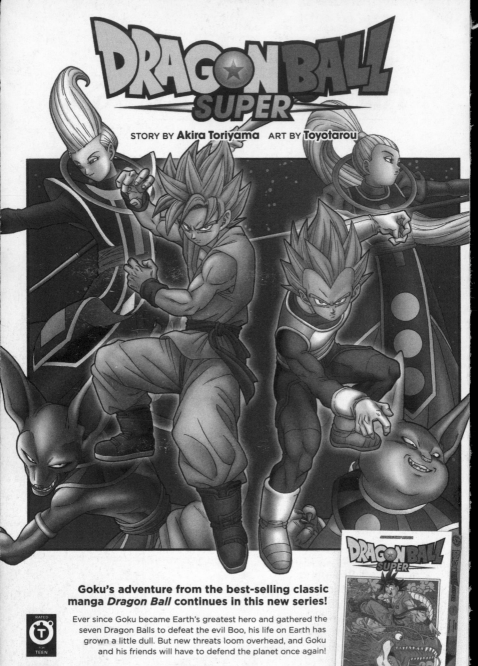

DRAGON BALL SUPER

STORY BY **Akira Toriyama**   ART BY **Toyotarou**

Goku's adventure from the best-selling classic manga *Dragon Ball* continues in this new series!

Ever since Goku became Earth's greatest hero and gathered the seven Dragon Balls to defeat the evil Boo, his life on Earth has grown a little dull. But new threats loom overhead, and Goku and his friends will have to defend the planet once again!

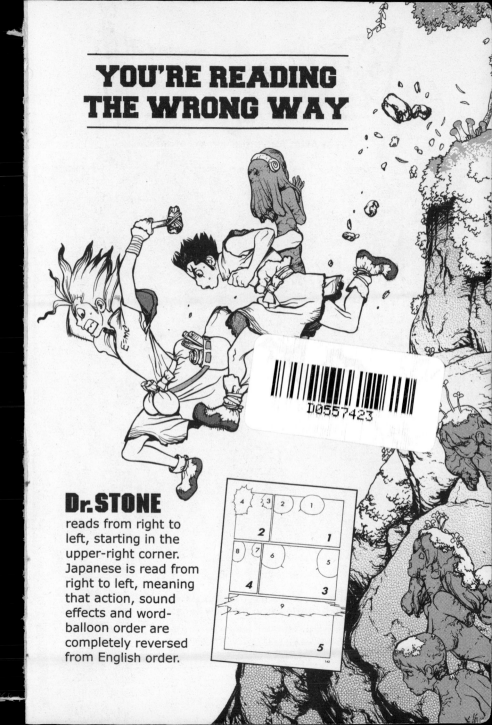

YOU'RE READING THE WRONG WAY

Dr. STONE

reads from right to left, starting in the upper-right corner. Japanese is read from right to left, meaning that action, sound effects and word-balloon order are completely reversed from English order.